INTERSECTIONS
WITH
ATTACHMENT

INTERSECTIONS
WITH
ATTACHMENT

Edited by
Jacob L. Gewirtz
William M. Kurtines
Florida International University

BF
575
.A86
I56
1991

LEA LAWRENCE ERLBAUM ASSOCIATES, PUBLISHERS
1991   Hillsdale, New Jersey   Hove and London

Lawrence Erlbaum Associates, Inc., Publishers
365 Broadway
Hillsdale, New Jersey 07642

Library of Congress Cataloging-in-Publication Data

Intersections with attachment / edited by Jacob L. Gewirtz, William M.
  Kurtines.
    p. cm.
  Includes bibliographical references and indexes.
  ISBN 0-8058-0176-6
  1. Attachment behavior. 2. Attachment behavior in children.
3. Imprinting (Psychology) 4. Psychology, Comparative.
I. Gewirtz, Jacob L. II. Kurtines, William M.
BF575.A86I56 1991
155.9′2—dc20   90-20026
                                                CIP

Printed in the United States of America
10 9 8 7 6 5 4 3 2 1

6/16/92

Contents

This Volume is dedicated to

Eckhard H. Hess
Psychologist/Ethologist
Late of the University of Chicago

and to

Lawrence Kohlberg
Developmental Psychologist/Philosopher
Late of Harvard University

The untimely passing of these extraordinary psychologists was a great loss to the field and to us all. Their collaborative chapters in this volume are among their last works.

Preface

Attachment has emerged as a key area (for some, the most salient area) of social development. Theory and research on attachment, as process and as outcome, has flourished in recent years. No longer does research concentrate only on one-year-old humans with their mothers in one setting. Work on attachment processes has proliferated with a variety of species and with humans in diverse cultures and at various points in the life cycle, including the later years. Further, the attachment concept that was initially applied to the bond of infants/children to their mothers and significant others has come to be applied increasingly also to the bond of mothers (and others) to the infants/children in their care. Indeed in some recent approaches, the conception of *bonding* has been applied to the process whereby infants and mothers concurrently attach to one another. In this frame, increasing attention has been devoted to the meaning and implications of the attachment concept, possible indices of attachment, the role of learning, whether or not attachment is best treated as continuous or discontinuous (emergent), and whether or not attachment should be viewed as a trait across environmental settings or as a process with functions that operate differently in different settings.

Finally, important concepts, methods, and theoretical orientations have, in their different ways, increasingly come to relate to or touch on—to *intersect* with—attachment and in that way to push out in many directions the implications of the attachment conception. At the same time, such intersecting concepts as communication, identification, relationships, love, stress/distress, pathology, economic demands, imprinting and ethology, and such intersecting methods as interspecies, intergroup, interage, and normal–abnormal comparisons are themselves being impacted by being examined in relation to attachment, at various levels of analysis.

The chapters of this volume constitute a collection of original works that results from and contributes to the rapidly changing research and theoretical literature on the attachment process, as detailed in the preceding sections. In particular, these chapters detail relations to other important psychological-process concepts, such as imprinting, relationships, and identification, and important dimensions, such as interlife-cycle segments, cultures, and species in terms of which the attachment process can be better understood.

Despite the emergence of a substantial empirical and theoretical literature on the attachment process as a key theme of development, and separately on the conceptions of theory and method that intersect with attachment, there exists no single source of information on recent developments in this conceptual sector. The present volume seeks at least partially to fill this gap by bringing together in one source a representative set of writings of prominent scholars from diverse areas of psychology and psychiatry who are active researchers on attachment in development. The individual chapters can provide the reader with an introduction to the diversity of conceptual and research issues, and methods in the rapidly growing and evolving attachment literature. At the same time, they can illustrate diverse perspectives on attachment and its intersections as well as on recent innovative developments associated with this central theme of development. Thus, active workers in the field provide not only an introduction to recent developments, but they also make unique, substantive contributions to the research and conceptual literature. Equally important, because the contributors are active researchers and theorists, the volume may also serve to set trends and determine directions to shape the literature for years to come. The 14 individual chapters organized into seven sections illustrate diverse perspectives on attachment and its intersections as well as recent innovative developments in the field.

This volume would not have been possible without the cooperation and assistance of a number of people and institutions. Invaluable support was received at various stages in its preparation from the College of Arts and Sciences and the Department of Psychology at Florida International University, as well as by the Bi-University Child Development Institute of the University of Miami and Florida International University.

Jacob L. Gewirtz
William M. Kurtines

Contributors' Biographies

Jean Bernholtz is a graduate student in clinical psychology in the Department of Psychology of the University of Miami, Coral Gables, FL 33124. She is continuing her research on child memory in poor and good readers.

Michael L. Commons is Lecturer and Research Associate in the Department of Psychiatry, Harvard University Medical School, Boston, MA 02115-6196. He received his doctorate in general psychology from Columbia University. His interests have involved advancing operant-learning conceptions as well as the application of such conceptions to stage approaches to cognitive development.

Richard J. Davidson is Professor of Psychology at the University of Wisconsin-Madison, Madison, WI 53706. He received his doctorate in personality, psychopathological, and psychophysiological psychology from Harvard University. His research program has focused on hemispheric asymmetry and emotion.

Rhett Diessner is Assistant Professor of Psychology and Education at Lewis-Clark State College, Lewiston, Idaho 83501. He received his doctorate in education from Harvard University. His research has focused on moral development and education.

Candice Feiring is Associate Professor of Pediatrics in the Institute for the Study of Child Development of the University of Medicine and Dentistry of New Jersey, New Brunswick, NJ 08903. She received her doctorate in social psychology from the University of Pittsburgh. Her research has concentrated on family systems and social networks.

Seymour Feshbach is Professor of Psychology in the University of California at Los Angeles, Los Angeles, CA 90024. He received his doctorate in clinical psychology from Yale University. He has written extensively and reported research in the areas of clinical psychology and personality processes.

Tiffany M. Field is Professor of Pediatrics, Psychiatry, and Psychology in the Mailman Center for Child Development at the University of Miami Medical School, Miami, FL 33101. She received her doctorate in developmental psychology from the University of Massachusetts. Her research program has focused on topics in diverse areas, including infant cognitive and affective development, anomalous development, physical enrichment, separation, stress, and attachment.

Nathan Fox is Associate Professor of Human Development in the Institute of Child Study at the University of Maryland, College Park, MD 20742. He received his doctorate in developmental psychology from Harvard University. His research interest has been on attachment and its physiological levels.

Jacob L. Gewirtz is Professor of Psychology at Florida International University, Miami, FL 33199, and Clinical Professor of Pediatrics at the University of Miami Medical School. He received his doctorate in developmental and experimental psychology from the University of Iowa. His theoretical and research foci have been on the topics of social learning and development including attachment acquisition and loss, departure and separation protests, imitation/identification, parent-child interaction and directions of influence, and the behavioral effects of shifts in maintaining environments.

Eckhard H. Hess is late Distinguished Professor of Psychology in the Department of Behavioral Sciences of the University of Chicago. He received his doctorate in comparative psychology from the Johns Hopkins University. He has published extensively reporting his research on imprinting, on conceptualizing the imprinting process, and on other ethological topics.

Lawrence Kohlberg is late Professor of Education and Social Psychology and Director of the Center for Moral Education and Development in the Graduate School of Education of Harvard University, Cambridge, MA 02138. He obtained his doctorate in psychology from the University of Chicago, where he embarked upon his lifelong work on the development of morality and moral reasoning. He has also detailed a cognitive-developmental approach to social development with particular emphasis on sex typing and the identification process.

William M. Kurtines is Professor of Psychology at Florida International University, Miami, FL 33199. He received his doctorate from the Johns Hopkins University. Dr. Kurtines' current areas of interest include social, personality, and moral development.

Mary Levitt is Associate Professor of Psychology at Florida International University, North Miami Campus, Miami, FL 33181. She received her doctorate in life-span psychology from Syracuse University. Her research program is focused on attachments/relationships across the life span.

Michael Lewis is Professor of Pediatrics and Psychiatry and Director of the Institute for the Study of Child Development in the University of Medicine and Dentistry of New Jersey, New Brunswick, NJ 08903. He received his doctorate in developmental psychology from the University of Pennsylvania. His program of research has concentrated on diverse topics in early human social, affective, and cognitive development, including self acquisition and recognition, fear, intelligence, attachment, and anomalous infant development.

Gilda A. Morelli is Assistant Professor of Psychology at Boston College, Boston, MA 02167. She received her doctorate in developmental psychology from the University of Massachusetts. Her interest has focused on the application of cross-cultural methods to issues of human emotional development.

Hanuš Papoušek received his doctorate in medicine from the Purkinje University, Brno, and a doctorate in sciences from Charles University, Prague, Czechoslovakia. He recently retired from the position of Head of Projects in Developmental Psychobiology in the Max-Planck Institute for Research in Psychiatry in Munich, Germany, and became a Special Professor in Developmental Psychology at the Free University of Amsterdam, The Netherlands, Departments of Developmental Psychology and Human Movement Sciences. His basic research programs in pediatrics and psychobiology have focused on the early development of learning, cognition and social communication.

Mechthild Papoušek received her doctorate in medicine from the University of Tuebingen, Germany. Her early work as a research neurologist and psychiatrist covered the chronobiological aspects of psychiatric disorders. Later on she joined the Research Project on Developmental Psychobiology in the Max-Planck Institute for Research in Psychiatry in Munich and focused on the preverbal development of communication. At present she is Head of Projects in Developmental Psychobiology at Munich University, Department of Social Pediatrics.

Gayle S. Paully is a Research Associate in the Primate Research Laboratory in the Department of Psychiatry, SUNY Health Science Center, Brooklyn, NY 11203. She received her doctorate in comparative psychology from The State University of New York Health Science Center at Brooklyn. Her research has been on primate parent-child behavior.

Martha Peláez-Nogueras is a doctoral student in the Department of Psychology at Florida International University, Miami, FL 33199, and research supervisor of the Child Development Research Laboratory. Her interests include experimental analysis of behavior, direction of influence in mother-infant interactions, contextual determinants in learning, and rule-governed behavior.

Slobodan B. Petrovich is Associate Professor of Psychology and Director of the Interdisciplinary Program at the University of Maryland Baltimore County,

Catonsville, MD 21228. He received his doctorate in biological psychology from the University of Chicago. His research program includes work on the imprinting process, behavior-genetic issues, and the conceptualization of attachment in diverse species.

Charles Rahn is Research Psychologist in the Laboratory of Comparative Ethology, National Institute of Child Health and Human Development, NIH, Bethesda, MD 20892. He did graduate work in psychology at the University of Virginia. He has been involved in research on concepts of intuitive parenting with infants.

Leonard A. Rosenblum is Professor of Psychology and Director of the Primate Behavior Laboratory in the Department of Psychiatry, SUNY Health Science Center, Brooklyn, NY 11203. He received his doctorate in comparative psychology from the University of Wisconsin. His research has been on social, sexual, and parent-child behavior in nonhuman primates.

Donald K. Routh is Professor of Psychology and Pediatrics and Director of Clinical Training in the Department of Psychology at the University of Miami, Coral Gables, FL 33124. He received his doctorate in clinical psychology from the University of Pittsburgh. His program of research is on mother-presence effects on children's reactions to stress.

Stephen Suomi is Chief of the Laboratory of Comparative Ethology, National Institute of Child Health and Human Development, NIH, Bethesda, Maryland 20892. He received his doctorate in comparative psychology from the University of Wisconsin. Dr. Suomi's research program with nonhuman primates has focused on early affective and social development, the effects of separation and stress, and parenting.

Edward Z. Tronick is Chief of the Child Development Unit, Children's Hospital, Boston, MA 02115 and Associate Professor of Pediatrics and Education at Harvard University. He received his doctorate in developmental psychology from the University of Wisconsin. His research has been on neonatal development, the communication patterns between infant and parent in early infancy, and the application of cross-cultural procedures to the study of infant social development.

THE ENVIRONMENT AND ATTACHMENT

1 Attachment as Personal Characteristic or a Measure of the Environment

Michael Lewis
Candice Feiring

ABSTRACT

In trying to understand the etiology of human development, three basic models have been utilized: a trait model, an environmental model, and an interactional model. These three models, prototypes of various views of development, make clear how certain assumptions are used to understand the etiology of human behavior. The attachment model is the most accepted and utilized theory on the development of social relationships and has as its central thesis the assumption that one set of social experiences is directly connected to the next. Most studies on the outcome of early attachment behavior have not considered the nature of the child's environment at the time the outcome status of the child is measured. The failure to do so is evidence of a paradigm which holds attachment to operate as a trait. Longitudinal data are examined to understand how attachment and early and subsequent environment predict behavior problems. The results suggest that attachment in fact may be a measure of environment as much as it is a measure of a child's characteristic.

In the study of social development, certain beliefs are accepted as facts, because they fit the current zeitgeist or paradigm (Kuhn, 1962). The paradigm under which most of social development operates is one that states that the child's earliest social experiences impact on its later life and that these early social experiences are for the most part caused by particular parenting, specifically the mother–child interaction and relationship. Currently, beliefs exist that support this general paradigm. These beliefs are spoken of as facts, although there is considerable reason to doubt the validity of each one.

The first of these facts has to do with childrens' responsivity to the social environment as an attribute of their humanness. This responsivity supposedly occurs immediately and is demonstrated by children's preferences for human faces and face-like stimuli to all other visual stimuli. This finding is attributable to a result first reported by Fantz (1965), which was subsequently repudiated by him when the correct analyses were performed on the data. However, this unreplicated result has found its way into texts on development. Fantz' early work did not control for stimulus complexity, and when controlled by presenting scrambled faces instead of a real face, no preference in the very young organism is found for human faces. Nevertheless, this fact, that children are from the moment of birth socially oriented toward conspecifics, remains a strong belief in spite of the evidence that this is not the case.

The second fact centers on the mother–child relationship and the issue of responsivity. By the late 1960s, the notion of responsive maternal behavior as a cause of appropriate social development had become well fixed (Lewis & Goldberg, 1969). Of concern to some scientists was the idea that responsivity was more appropriately defined as reinforcement. Reinforcement of specific behaviors, such as cry, should lead to more cry behavior. In contrast, the responsivity notion asserted that a responsive mother, rather than reinforcing crying and perpetuating the crying response, should satisfy the child's basic need that the crying response reflects. Thus, it should not lead to more crying. In a study by Bell and Ainsworth (1972), maternal responsivity toward infant crying in the first three months of life was compared to infants cry behavior during months 10–12. The authors concluded that a mother's responsivity to her infant's cry did not lead to more crying behavior but led to more communicative behavior. The importance of this study is considerable, because it confirmed the belief that maternal responsivity, especially to infant cry, leads to positive consequences, not more crying. Although this study is widely referenced, Gewirtz and Boyd's (1977) critique is not. Gewirtz and Boyd (1977) were able to show that the design and analysis of the study does not allow us to conclude what Bell and Ainsworth (1972) asserted. Nevertheless, the results of this study remain as facts, because they fit the common beliefs that responsive mothering produces socially healthy infants.

Harlow and his now classical work on motherless monkeys stands as the best demonstration of the effect of the lack of mothering experience on children's subsequent peer and psychosexual development. Recall that Harlow (1958) demonstrated that children raised without their mothers showed severe problems as adults: difficulty engaging in sexual reproductive acts, and once the females had become pregnant, inadequate mothering. Many of these motherless monkeys were abusive and even killed their children. Harlows' work (Harlow & Harlow, 1965; Harlow, 1969) stands as the best demonstration of the effect of the lack of mothers in one generation on the mothering behavior of the children in the next. More recently, this work has come under question from several sources. To begin with, the motherless monkeys were deprived of all social experiences. They were raised in social isolation. It would be difficult to conclude, therefore, that the effects observed in adulthood were due to the lack of the mother rather than the lack of any social contact. Even more critical, however, is the fact that these motherless monkeys behaved quite differently to their second child than to their first child (Suomi & Harlow, 1978; Suomi, 1978). If the poor mothering experience, or in this case the lack of mothering experience, led to poor mothering behavior in the next generation as a result of a trait, one would have anticipated that this characteristic of the monkeys should have extended to all children they raised. The evidence suggests that their mothering behavior was not fixed by their early lack of mothering experience. Thus, even if the major effect of being raised in isolation was the lack of mothering experience, it can not be said that these motherless monkeys were inherently abusive or bad mothers, because their maternal behavior changed significantly from first to second born infants.

In discussing child abuse, two issues emerge that are difficult to explain in terms of the consequences of the mother–child experience on the child's subsequent social development. The first is the often repeated finding that human children who are abused by their mothers will become abusing mothers themselves. Unfortunately, as far as can be determined, all the studies that report such findings are retrospective in nature; that is, abused children are observed in clinics and data gathered on their parent who are found themselves to have been abused in their childhood. This retrospective finding creates a logically incorrect notion that abuse in one generation will lead to abuse in the next. Although this may be the case, there is no proper evidence to support this assertion, because a retrospective analysis of this kind does not allow for the observation of those children who are not abused but who have parents who were abused as children. Without prospective study and analyses, it is not possible to determine the effect of abuse in one generation upon abuse in the next.

Finally, some recent work on child abuse that suggests that the supposed link between early negative mothering and subsequent child disturbance is not a causal one. Cicchetti and Braunwald (1984), reported that there are significant numbers of abused and neglected children who are securely attached. This finding and ones like it raise serious questions about attachment as a measure of the parent–child relationship, but even more importantly, on the nature of the parent–child interaction and how it impacts on the child's attachment status or mental health. If these securely attached children are truly secure and are also abused or neglected, then there would be strong evidence to suggest that unresponsive maternal behavior does not necessarily constitute the only variable that produces different types of attachment. In other words, poor mothering (e.g., abuse and neglect) does not necessarily lead to poor adjustment (e.g., insecure attachment).

These five fallacies of early childhood social behavior raise the serious question about the nature of early social experience as it impacts on subsequent development. The attachment paradigm as delineated by Bowlby (1969) and subsequently by Ainsworth, Blehar, Waters, and Wall (1978) represents the most extensively researched model of the belief that early experience impacts on later adjustment and as such will serve as our focus for the general broader model it represents.

The attachment model is the most accepted and utilized theory on the development of social relationships and has as its central thesis the assumption that one set of social experiences is directly connected to the next. More specifically, the model argues for a linear relationship such that the child adapts to one relationship, and from this one relationship, all subsequent ones follow. This model is characterized by three features: (a) sequence, (b) determinism, and (c) trait or structural quality. This last feature, the trait or structural quality of attachment, will be the focus of this chapter.

THE ISSUE OF TRAIT

The issue and controversy surrounding the notion of a trait or enduring aspect of personality has dominated much contemporary thinking (Pervin, 1983). The issue is raised again when considering the effect of one relationship on another and speaks to one of the differences between the epigenetic attachment model and the social network model (see Lewis, 1987). One example of a difference between the epigenetic and social network systems model can be observed by considering the issue of multiple attachment. That an individual child can have multiple attachments and that some of them may be secure whereas others are not suggests that attachment refers to relationships not to the quality or trait of a particular baby. Thus, by considering multiple attachments, we are forced to move from a consideration of a trait notion, a quality located in the child, to a systems notion in which the various relationships vis-a-vis a system influence the child. Simple attachment relationships give rise to endogenous qualities within the child as explanations for behavior, thus, an epigenetic cause, whereas multiple relationships give rise to exogenous forces such as the nature of the social network. In the attachment view, the mother–child attachment relationship endows the infant with a trait or characteristic-like structure that is located within the organism, thus the expression an "A" baby or a "B" baby. This trait or its absence then determines subsequent relationships. The nature of the trait has not been clarified, however. Sroufe (1979) and Block and Block (1979) for example, have associated it with ego skills. Although such a notion is reasonable, the trait could be self-esteem or self-efficacy or some combination of the two. Whatever its nature, it is the presence or absence of the trait-like structure that influences other relationships. An often-used metaphor is that the child is like an empty vessel that needs filling. Once filled, the child can move on to new relationships. If the child is not filled, movement will be inhibited, or the new relationships will differ in their nature or degree from those of the filled child. Thus, the task of the earliest attachment relationship is to fill the vessel, or as is sometimes thought, to give the child those skills necessary to develop normally. In these explanations, the force for the establishment of subsequent relationships rests with an adaptability coping mechanism that resides within the organism.

The notion of a trait provides a mechanism for the deterministic nature found in the attachment model. One relationship can affect another through the creation of a trait within the child. The child then brings this trait to bear in its next relationship. Moreover, this trait or its absence based on the outcome of the first relationship may not easily be affected by experience. Thus, for example, a securely attached infant is competent at a later age due to the possession of that competence attribute or is incompetent due to its lack. The use of the term attribute does not imply a static or unchanging characteristic but merely implies that some aspect of the child is affecting his or her behavior. Such an explanation is less than adequate when applied to attachment given that the attachment classification of an individual child appears stable only as long as the environment in which the child functions remains stable (see Thompson & Lamb, 1983a, 1983b; Thompson, Lamb, & Estes, 1982; Vaughn, Egland, Sroufe, & Waters, 1979; Vaughn, Gove, & Egland, 1980; Waters, 1979). Such findings suggest that environmental attributes must be considered and must play some role in developmental outcomes in psychopathology (Mischel, 1968). Alternatively, one might view children's social development in terms of environmental attributes. Here the early behavior of the child is dependent on the environment, and, thus, the attachment classification can be seen as a manifestation of the environment rather than the child. Changes in the environment will be reflected in changes in the child's behavior or attachment classification. The competence of the child at a later point in time reflects a concomitant positive environment. The relationship between the child's earlier and later behavior is not mediated by the attributes of the child but by the fact that the environments at both earlier and later points in time (i.e., when the original attachment classification was observed, and when the child's behavior is subsequently observed) are related. Unlike a static trait, the behavior of the child exists only so long as the environment supports or maintains that behavior. The strong environmental or situational view is that the secure attachment and later social competence are no more than measures of a positive environment at two points in time. As we shall see, it is interesting that this model is rarely if ever tested in spite of the fact that there are data to do so. A third model, one in which one looks at both the nature of a social environment as well as the attribute of the child may be necessary to explain children's subsequent social behavior and adjustment. In such a model, stability and change need to be seen as a function of both factors, the characteristic of the child as well as the environment in which the child lives. An infant, for example, who is securely attached as a function of a positive environment in the first year will show competence at a later age as a function of both the early secure attachment as well as the nature of the environment at a later age. Not addressed is whether the attribute exists as an independent factor and interacts with the current environment to produce a new set of behaviors or whether the attribute itself is transformed by the current environment thereby producing a new set of behaviors. The former view would be favored by an interactional approach (see Lewis, 1972), whereas the latter would be favored by a transactional view (see Sameroff & Chandler, 1975). For example, does a securely attached child at time t_1 show negative behavior at t_2 because: (a) secure attachment at t_1 has interacted with a negative environment at t_2 to produce negative behavior (positive attachment x negative environment leads to negative behavior), or (b) the secure attachment at t_1 has interacted with a negative environment at t_2 to produce an insecure attachment at t_2, and it is this insecure attachment that produces negative behavior? The model here would look like positive attachment x negative environment leads to a negative attachment that leads to negative behavior. Whatever the explanation, the study of how the infant–mother relationship may be related to the development of subsequent social behavior or psychopathology in childhood needs to be explored.

To explore this problem, behavior from a longitudinal study of children seen from birth through their sixth year of life will be examined. Some of these data have been presented previously, but the models necessary to address the question of attachment as a trait or as a measure of the environment requires that this data be reviewed.

MODELS OF ATTACHMENT

Attachment as a Characteristic of the Individual

Figure 1.1 presents the traditional model of attachment as a trait that impacts on subsequent behavior. Notice that the child's characteristics at t_1 is predictive of the child's characteristic at t_2. The child's characteristic at t_1 is related to the mothers behavior at t_1. Thus, in the traditional model, the mother–child relationship either at t_1 or at t_{n-1} affects the child's attachment relationship at t_1. In this model, the child's attachment relationship subsequently affects the child outcome measure at t_2. This outcome measure can be the child's peer relationship, ego strength, dependency, or psychopathology. Nevertheless, the model holds that the relationship between child at t_1 and child at t_2 is a function of the characteristic of the child as seen at t_1 and is caused by the earlier mother–child relationship.

Attachment as a Function of the Environment

Figure 1.2 presents the model of attachment as a function of the social environment that is an alternative to the notion of attachment as a trait. Notice that the relationship between Ct_1 and Ct_2 also exists (the dotted line in the figure indi-

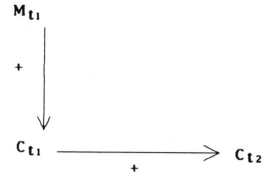

Relationship of Ct_1 to Ct_2 is a function of the

child's characteristic at Ct_1

FIG. 1.1. Attachment as Trait.

cates the existence of a relationship over these two points in time). However, the cause of this association can be found in other relationships; the mother (or environment) acts on the child at t_1, and the (mother or environment) also acts on the child at t_2. As long as over time the environment remains constant, there will be a relationship between Ct_1 and Ct_2. However, the relationship is not determined by a trait or characteristic of the child but by the consistency or inconsis-

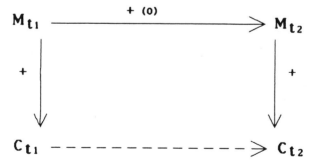

Relationship of Ct_1 to Ct_2 is a function of
consistency/inconsistency of environment

FIG. 1.2. Attachment as Environment.

tency of the environment. It should be noted that the environment can refer to many things, for example: the family system including interactions and relationships of parents and siblings; the social network or relatives, peers, non related adults; and the physical environment. In the discussion to follow, we focus on the maternal environment, as it is the central environmental feature of the attachment model. However, the arguments we present apply in general to other environmental operators as well.

Although the attachment-as-environment model appears reasonable, few if any studies using the attachment paradigm have considered either the Mt_1-Mt_2 relationship or the relationship at t_2 of the child and mother (or environment). In general, only the trait aspect of the attachment paradigm is tested, for example, the mother at t_1 (Mt_1) leads to a child characteristic of security/insecurity (Ct_2), and the child characteristic then leads to an outcome at t_2. As FIG. 1.2 suggests, it is possible that the Ct_1-Ct_2 relationship can be a function of the consistency of the environment. Tests of this alternative model are hard to find in the attachment literature, perhaps because confirmation rather than refutation has been emphasized in the social sciences (Popper, 1972). If studies of attachment are designed without measures of the environment at two points in time, the alternative model can not be tested. Those few studies that have examined consistency of maternal or environmental factors and also looked at the consistency of the child's attachment between 12 and 18–20 months have found that overall stability of attachment classification ranged from 96% to 48% in 10 studies (see Lamb, Thompson, Gardner, & Charnov, 1985). The findings suggest that such a model of strong environmental influence is not only feasible but potentially a likely source in accounting for the consistency (or inconsistency) of the child's social behavior over two points in time.

Attachment as a Trait x Environmental Model: The Invulnerable Child

There are several models that attempt to look at attachment as a function of both trait and environment. The first is the notion of the invulnerable child. The invulnerable child is defined as the child who becomes relatively impervious to environmental influence due to some genetic or early environmental factors. From an attachment point of view, the early experience of the child creates an invulnerability to subsequent environmental perturbations. This type of explanation is actually a form of the trait model. The child possesses something that is determined earlier by experience but that eventually does not continue to interact with the environment. Consider the model shown in FIG. 1.3. First, the positive mothering (Mt_1) impacts on the child at Ct_1. The positive mothering remains consistent (Mt_2) and impacts on the child at Ct_2. For example, this is the case where the mother affects the child at three months and at one year resulting in a secure attachment. Next, suppose as in the top line of FIG. 1.3 a perturbation

"INVULNERABLE CHILD"

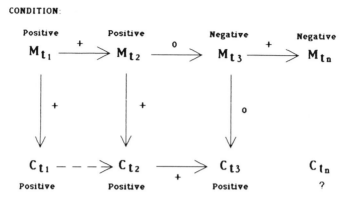

FIG. 1.3.   Attachment as Trait x Environment.

occurs such that maternal behavior at Mt_3 becomes negative. From an environment model point of view, this should exert a negative effect on the child at Ct_3. On the other hand, the invulnerability model predicts that the child's behavior at Ct_3 would remain positive despite the negative environment because of the invulnerability trait or characteristic of the child (FIG. 1.3 also demonstrates that Ct_3 remains positive). It also is of interest to consider the consequences, if the environment remains negative from t_3 on. What will the effect be on the child's behavior at t_n, if the environment remains negative? Such a change will not affect the child's status, if invulnerability operates as an absolute trait. However, if invulnerability is considered as a threshold model, then the environment may have some impact. From a threshold model, the negative environment will have an effect, but the effect will be either less severe, because it is moderated by an invulnerability (protective) factor, or the effect will take longer to produce (i.e., require larger amounts of negative experience).

Attachment as a Trait x Environmental Model: Vulnerable Child

Figure 1.4 presents attachment as a trait–environment interaction using the concept of the vulnerable child. The vulnerable child is one who is readily affected by negative environmental influences due to some genetic or early environmental factors. From an attachment point of view, the early experience of the child creates a risk factor that will be expressed, if and when the environment becomes negative (i.e., stressful). Again, mothering, in this case negative at Mt_1 and Mt_2, produces an insecure child at Ct_2. If the environment is positive, such as at Mt_3, the child shows no problem at t_3, although the child is insecurely attached. It is

'VULNERABLE CHILD' (b)

CONDITION:

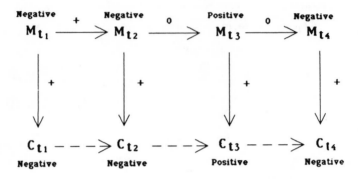

FIG. 1.4.   Attachment as Trait x Environment.

only when the environment becomes negative, as in Mt_4, that the child shows problems (Ct_4). Unlike the model of the invulnerable child, where the major effects are located within the child, the major effects in the vulnerable child are located in the environment. The child's behavior reflects the nature of the environment.

The models discussed use as their example children's attachment relationships. Currently, most research has provided data on the first model as presented in FIG. 1.1. Using data from a longitudinal study may aid in determining which of these models best describes children's social relationships as a function of early experience. In doing so, it may be possible to address the broad question of whether attachment or personal characteristics should be considered as a trait or individual characteristic, a measure of the environment, or a personal characteristic that is malleable.

Experimental Design

In order to explore this problem, data from a longitudinal study were analyzed to examine the outcome of psychopathology at six years, both as a function of children's attachment classification at a year as well as to the family environment at six years. Figure 1.5 presents the experimental design. Mt_1 was measured by the maternal–infant interaction at 3 months. Mt_2 was measured by the maternal playroom behavior at 12 months. Mt_3 represents the mothers report of the family's level of cohesiveness and conflict at six years. This measure was used to represent the family environment rather than using a maternal characteristic. The child measures include the child's attachment classification at one year (Ct_2) and the child's level of behavior problems at six years (Ct_3) as measured by the Child Behavior Profile (Achenbach & Edelbrock, 1981). Exploration of the model is in FIG. 1.5 as measured by data from the longitudinal study should provide information on a variety of issues. This discussion will focus on psychopathology as a function of the attachment quality at one year or as a function of the family cohesion/conflict level at six years. The intention of our analysis is not so much to argue that one set of information is better than another but rather to point out that our traditional model of attachment as a trait has tended to neglect environmental factors. In order to fully understand children's social development and any perturbations in that development, the full model including environmental factors as well as children's specific behavior needs to be considered.

One hundred and thirteen children (57 females, 56 males) and their mothers were seen when the children were one and six years of age. The subjects were participants in a longitudinal study that examined children and their development from three months through six years. The socioeconomic status of the subjects was white middle-class. The fathers and mothers had an average of 15.32 and 13.86 years of formal education, respectively.

Observation of Mother–Infant Interaction at Age 3 Months: Home Observation.   Each mother–infant pair was observed in the home for a two-hour period while the infant was awake. Infant behaviors coded at 3 months were: (a) eyes closed, (b) vocalization, (c) extra movement, (d) fret/cry, (e) feed-bottle, (f)

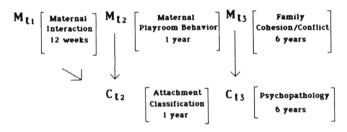

12 week maternal interaction: maternal responsivity, initiation, proximal and toy play behavior.

1 year maternal playroom behavior: approval, smile, vocalize and responsivity.

1 year child attachment: A/C insecure; B secure.

6 year family environment: Moos Scales of cohesion and conflict.

6 year child psychopathology: Achenbach & Edelbrock Child Behavior Profile above 90th percentile.

FIG. 1.5.   Experimental Design.

feed-spoon, (g) play-object, (h) play-person, (i) play-self, (j) smile/laugh, (k) burp, sneeze, cough, (l) looking at mother, and (m) sucking-nonfeed. Mother behaviors coded at 3 months were (a) touch, (b) hold, (c) vocalization, (d) vocalization to other, (e) look, (f) smile/laugh, (g) play with child, (h) change diaper/bath, (i) feed, (j) rock child, (k) read/TV, (l) kiss, and (m) give toy/pacifier. From the frequency of infant and mother behaviors, a summary measure of maternal initiation and responding to infant activity were obtained.

Interactions at 12 Months: Playroom Observation. At age 12 months, mother–infant dyads were observed and videotaped in a playroom at the laboratory. The observation consisted of a fifteen-minute free play period in an unstructured situation in which mother and infant had the opportunity to interact with each other and toys.

Infant behaviors coded at 12 months were: (a) vocalization, (b) looking, (c) smile, (d) touch, (e) fret/cry, (f) seek approval, (g) seek help, (h) gesture, (i) seek proximity, (j) toy/nontoy play, (k) move/door, (l) lap, and (m) hold/hug. Maternal behaviors coded at 12 months were: (a) vocalization, (b) looking, (c) smile, (d) touch, (e) kiss, (f) hold, (g) give directions, (h) read, (i) seek proximity, (j) toy/nontoy, (k) show toy, (l) manipulate toy, and (m) demonstrate toy. Also obtained was a measure of maternal responsivity.

Attachment Classification at 1 Year. Following the unstructured, free-play situation, mothers left the playroom, and infants remained alone in the playroom for three minutes, or until they became distressed. The mother reentered the playroom, and the free-play episode continued an additional five minutes. The infant's behavior was coded during the last three minutes of the initial free-play period, during the entire separation episode, and during the first three minutes of reunion according to procedures delineated by Ainsworth et al. (1978). On the basis of this procedure, infants were assigned to one of three attachment categories: (a) avoidant, characterized primarily by avoidant behavior during reunion; (b) secure, characterized by proximity and contact-seeking behaviors during reunion; and (c) ambivalent, characterized generally by maladaptive behavior, particularly by anger or passivity throughout the entire situation. This assessment procedure constitutes a modification of the Ainsworth and Wittig (1969) Strange Situation insofar as it involves only one separation and no stranger. This modified version has also been used by Waters, Wippman, and Sroufe (1979) and has been judged to be a valid system for assessing the quality of the child's attachment relationship. Interobserver reliability was .93 for the assignment of 30 subjects to attachment groups A, B, and C.

Environment Assessment at 6 Years. The Family Environment Scale (FES) is a questionnaire designed to tap different aspects of the family environment including family relationships, personal growth, and system maintenance (Moos & Moos, 1976). The questionnaire consists of 100 true/false items from which the following 10 scales (10 items per scale) are obtained: cohesion, expressiveness, conflict, independence, achievement orientation, intellectual-cultural orientation, moral-religious emphasis, organization, and control. Based on a sample of 1067 families, the internal consistency and item-subscale correlations are adequate. Two month test–retest reliability ranges from .68–.86 for the subscales and 12 months subscale stability ranges from .52 to .89. When the children in our sample were six years of age, their mothers completed the FES. For each family, we obtained 10 subscale scores that were converted to standardized scores using the metric provided by Moos & Moos (1976).

Competence Assessment at 6 Years. When their children were 6 years of age, mothers were asked to complete the Child Behavior Profile (CBP) (Achenbach, 1978), which was one of many measures taken at this age. The CPB is primarily a scale of measuring behavioral problems, although there are several sets of questions designed to assess the child's competence in school, peer behavior, and social activities. The normalization procedures applied to the CBP (Achenbach & Edelbrock, 1981) enable children with emotional problems to be differentiated from those without problems. In addition, CBP generates a continuum of emotional functioning on the basis of the total CBP score.

PREDICTING PSYCHOPATHOLOGY
FROM ATTACHMENT

The attachment data as reported in Lewis, Feiring, McGuffog, and Jaskir (1984) explored the relationship between attachment quality and subsequent psychopathology. A relationship between attachment classification at one year and subsequent psychopathology was found for male but not female subjects. Examination of the male subjects' data revealed an interesting relationship between attachment and subsequent psychopathology. Only 5% of securely attached male subjects showed subsequent psychopathology compared to 40% of the insecurely attached males. These results support the belief that attachment has some relationships to latter psychopathology. At least two questions are raised by these results; (a) what is the role of the intervening environment between one and six years, and (b) why do only 40% of insecure subjects show subsequent psychopathology? In order to explore these issues, the intervening variables of stress and family background were observed. Lewis et al. (1984) reported that insecurely attached males who were subject to high stress showed psychopathology at six years whereas insecurely attached males who did not experience high stress were unlikely to show any psychopathology. Such findings supports the model that when the environment is unfavorable, children are likely to show developmental psychopathology, if they were insecurely attached.

Looking at the stress factors for the securely attached males, Lewis et al. (1984) found that stress had little effect on subsequent psychopathology. The finding that for securely attached males there is no interaction between attachment, stress, and subsequent psychopathology supports the model of the invulnerable child. In this study, it appeared as if male children who were securely attached were not affected by environmental perturbations and did not end up with psychopathology. The vulnerable child did show an interaction between attachment, stress, and psychopathology. For the insecure-vulnerable child, psychopathology was dependent on environmental factors. If these environmental factors were positive, there was no pathology. However, if they were negative, psychopathology was more likely to occur. These data, at least for males, lead to the conclusion that attachment quality and environmental factors in early childhood may be related, at least for some children, and both are important in determining whether or not a child will show psychopathology.

PREDICTING PSYCHOPATHOLOGY
FROM THE ENVIRONMENT

Children's characteristics at one year are somewhat useful in predicting psychopathology, especially for males, and predictability is enhanced, if environmental factors are considered. An environmental model, as presented in FIG. 1.6, asserts that the environment both at one and six years affects the child's status. In the same manner in which the maternal environment at one (or before) affects the child's attachment, the environment at six should affect the child's psychopathology. In order to explore the relationship of the child's psychopathology and environment at six years, two scales on the Moos FES measure were selected: cohesion and conflict. The scores on these two scales were combined, and a distribution of the top 25% of the families (called conflictual) and the bottom 25% (called harmonious) were empirically determined. Examination of the sample revealed that of the conflictual families, 25% of their children showed psychopathology scores compared to only 3% of the children from harmonious families. For male children, 50% of conflictual families have children classified with psychopathology compared to 0% for the children in harmonious families. Observation of the data for females once again indicates the inability to predict female psychopathology. The analysis for females indicates that none of the conflicted families have children with psychopathology, whereas 7% of the children in the harmonious families have psychopathology. Thus, there is no relationship for female children between family harmony/conflict at six years and child psychopathology.

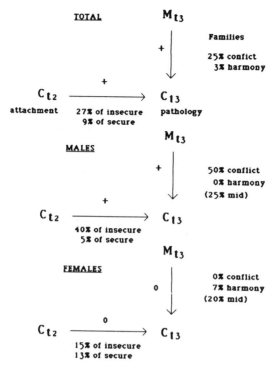

FIG. 1.6. Family environment and attachment as related to psycho-pathology.

PREDICTING PSYCHOPATHOLOGY
FROM ATTACHMENT AND ENVIRONMENT

Figure 1.6 presents the data on psychopathology including the relationship between attachment at one year, the family environment at six years, and psychopathology at six years. Notice that for the total sample, 27% of the insecurely attached children compared to 8% for securely attached children show subsequent psychopathology. On the other hand, 25% of the conflictual families compared to 3% of the harmonious families have children who show psychopathology. For male subjects, 40% of the insecure and 5% of securely attached males at one year show psychopathology, whereas 50% of the conflictual families compared to none of the harmonious families have children with psychopathology. For females, neither attachment classification at a year nor conflictual family environment at six are related to psychopathology at six years.

CONCLUSIONS

These data reveal several points. First, the environment at both one year (maternal environment) and at six years (family conflict/cohesion) are related to the child's status as measured by first attachment quality and later by psychopathology. In the case of attachment at one year, maternal behavior both at three months and at one year are related to children's attachment classification at one year (see Lewis & Feiring, 1989). In the case of children's psychopathology at six, environmental stress (family conflict vs. harmony) is related to psychopathology. Thus, there is reason to suppose that the child's status in infancy and childhood is related to the environment at each of these points. Moreover, when the data from the longitudinal study of maternal behavior at three and 12 months are compared to the family environment scale at six years, a moderate and positive correlation is found (r = .21, p < .05). These results indicate that there exists some stability within the environment of the child from infancy into the early school years. Some caution is necessary: The two measures of the environment at one and six years are not comparable enough to assess stability across age with confidence, because maternal behaviors were measured at one and family variables at six years (see FIG. 1.5). These results suggest that the model proposed in FIG. 1.2 may be a better way to conceptualize the developmental paths, especially if included in the model is the cross-lag relations.

Figure 1.7 presents this complete model of influences. Analysis of the cross-lag correlations are difficult to produce in part because of the type of statistic used to study the phenomena. Rather than focusing on amount of psychopathology, numbers of individual children with or without psychopathology have been studied. Using this type of number of person analyses, it is not possible to obtain

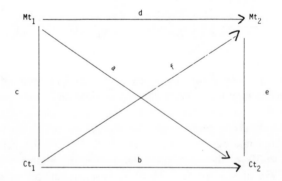

Mt_1 = Mother factors time 1
Ct_1 = Child factors time 1
Mt_2 = Mother factors time 2
Ct_2 = Child factors time 2

FIG. 1.7.   Model of mother and child influences across time.

the cross-lag correlations. Nevertheless, there is reason to believe that child and environment factors are mutually influencing relationships. Thus, the maternal environment at 12 months should be related to children's subsequent psycho-pathology in the same way that children's attachment at 12 months should be related to family conflict/harmony at six years. The point here is not to exclude the myriad of factors that influence children's subsequent psychopathology but to emphasize the limitations of the attachment construct when considered solely as a trait. Recall that when this trait model is used as in FIG. 1.1, it is argued that it is the child's status at Ct_1 that is related to the child's outcome at Ct_2. The model as proposed in FIG. 1.2 and FIG. 1.7 suggests that the analysis is incomplete unless the environment of the child as well as the child's status is measured. When this is done, as in the present investigation, it is found that environmental influences act on the child at each point in time. Thus, the notion of attachment as "filling the vessel of the child" and as a consequence "being filled" the child has or does not have, subsequent psychopathology is an insufficient model of development. Rather it is necessary to look to a more complicated model, as proposed in FIG. 1.7. In this model, all possible paths to subsequent child outcome are considered. Early infant characteristics lead to later child outcome (a); early environment influences early infant characteristics, which influence later outcome (c + b); early environment influences later environment, which influences later child outcome (d + e); early environment is related to early infant characteristics, which influence later environment, which is related to later outcome (c + f + e). When the notion of attachment as a trait is held, it is not possible to explore the multiple paths of outcomes that can occur. It is quite remarkable that most studies on the outcome of early attachment behavior have not considered the nature of the child's environment at the time they measure the outcome status of the child. The failure to do so is evidence of a paradigm that holds attachment to operate as a trait. The data presented here point to the need to include environmental factors in our understanding of attachment and its consequences. Attachment in fact may be a measure of environment as much as it is a measure of a child's characteristic.

ACKNOWLEDGMENTS

Support for this research and paper comes from the William T. Grant Foundation.

REFERENCES

Achenbach, T. M. (1978). The child behavior profile: I. Boys aged 6–11. *Journal of Consulting and Clinical Psychology, 46,* 478–488.

Achenbach, T. M., & Edelbrock, C. S. (1981). Behavioral problems and competencies reported by parents of normal and disturbed children aged 4 through 16. *Monographs of the Society for Research in Child Development, 46.*

Ainsworth, M. D. S., Blehar, M. C., Waters, E., & Wall, S. (1978). *Patterns of attachment.* Hillsdale, NJ: Lawrence Erlbaum Associates.

Ainsworth, M. D. S., & Wittig, B. A. (1969). Attachment and exploratory behavior of one-year-olds in a strange situation. In B. M. Foss (Ed.), *Determinants of Infant Behavior* (*Vol. 4,* pp. 111–136).

Bell. S. M., & Ainsworth, M. D. S. (1972). Infant crying and maternal responsiveness. *Child Development, 43,* 1171–1190.

Block, J., & Block, J. H. (1979). The role of ego control and ego resiliency in the organization of behavior. In W. A. Collins (Ed.), *Minnesota Symposia on Child Psychology,* Vol. *13.*

Bowlby, J. (1969). *Attachment and loss (Vol. 1): Attachment.* New York: Basic Books.

Cicchetti, D., & Braunwald, K. G. (1984). An organizational approach to the study of emotional development in maltreated infants. *Infant Mental Health Journal, 15,* 172–183.

Fantz, R. L. (1965). Visual perception from birth as shown by pattern selectivity. *Annals of the New York Academy of Sciences, 118,* 793–814.

Gewirtz, J. L., & Boyd, E. F. (1977). Does maternal responsivity imply reduced infant crying. A critique of the 1972 Bell & Ainsworth report. *Child Development, 48,* 1200–1207.

Harlow, H. F. (1958). The nature of love. *American Psychologist. 13,* 673–685.

Harlow, H. F. (1969). Age-mate or peer affectional system. In D. S. Lehrman, R. A. Hinde, & E. Shaw (Eds.), *Advances in the study of behavior* (Vol. 2, pp. 333–383). New York: Academic Press.

Harlow, H. F., & Harlow, M. D. (1965). The affectionate systems. In A. M. Schrier, H. F. Harlow, & F. Stollnitz (Eds.), *Behavior of nonhuman primates* (Vol. 2, pp. 287–334). New York: Academic Press.

Kuhn, T. S. (1962). *The structure of scientific revolutions.* Chicago: University of Chicago Press.

Lamb, M. E., Thompson, R. A., Gardner, W., & Charnov, E. L. (1985). *Infant-mother attachment: The origins and developmental significances in strange situation behavior.* Hillsdale, NJ: Lawrence Erlbaum Associates.

Lewis, M. (1972). State as an infant–environment interaction: An analysis of mother–infant interaction as a function of sex. *Merrill-Palmer Quarterly, 18,* 95–121.

Lewis, M. (1987). Social development in infancy and early childhood. In J. Osofsky (Ed.), *Handbook of infancy* (Second edition, 419–493). New York: Wiley.

Lewis, M., & Feiring, C. (1989). Infant, mother, and mother–infant interaction behavior and subsequent attachment. *Child Development, 60,* 831–837.

Lewis, M., & Goldberg, S. (1969). Perceptual-cognitive development in infancy: A generalized expectancy model as a function of the mother–infant interaction. *Merrill-Palmer Quarterly, 15,* 81–100.

Mischel, W. (1968). *Personality and assessment.* New York: Wiley.

Moos, R., & Moos, B. (1976). A typology of family social environments. *Family Process. 15,* 357–372.

Pervin, L. (1983). Theoretical approaches to the analysis of individual–environment interaction. In L. A. Pervin & M. Lewis (Eds.), *Perspectives in interactional psychology* (pp. 67–86). New York: Plenum.

Popper, K. R. (1972). *Conjectures and refutations: The growth of scientific knowledge.* U.K.: Butler & Tanner.

Sameroff, A. J., & Chandler, M. J. (1975). Reproduction risk and the continuum of caretaking casualty. In F. P. Horowitz (Ed.), *Review of child development research* (Vol. 4, pp. 187–244). Chicago: University of Chicago Press.

Sroufe, L. A. (1979). The coherence of individual development. *American Psychologist, 34,* 834–841.

Suomi, S. J. (1978). Maternal behavior by socially incompetent monkeys: Neglect and abuse of offspring. *Journal of Pediatric Psychology. 3*, 28–34.

Suomi, S. J., & Harlow, H. F. (1978). Early experience and social development in rhesus monkeys. In M. E. Lamb (Ed.), *Social and personality development* (pp. 252–271). New York: Holt, Rinehart & Winston.

Thompson, R. A., & Lamb, M. E. (1983a). Individual differences in dimensions of socioemotional development in infancy. In R. Plutchik & H. Kellerman (Eds.), *Emotion: Theory research, and experience Vol. 2. Emotions in early development* (pp. 87–114). New York: Academic Press.

Thompson, R. A., & Lamb, M. E. (1983b). Security of attachment and stranger sociability in infancy. *Developmental Psychology, 19*, 184–191.

Thompson, R. A., Lamb, M. E., & Estes, D. (1982). Stability of infant–mother attachment and its relationship to changing life circumstances in an unselected middle class sample. *Child Development, 53* 144–148.

Vaughn, B., Egeland, B., Sroufe, L. A., & Waters, E. (1979). Individual differences in infant–mother attachment at twelve and eighteen months: Stability and change in families under stress. *Child Development. 50*, 971–975.

Vaughn, B., Gove, F., & Egeland, B. (1980). The relationships between out-of-home care and the quality of infant–mother attachment in an economically disadvantage sample. *Child Development. 51*, 1203–1214.

Waters, E., Wippman, J., & Sroufe, L. A. (1979). Attachment, positive affect, and competence in the peer group: Two studies in construct validation. *Child Development. 50*, 821–829.

2 Evolutionary and Environmental Factors Influencing Attachment Patterns in Nonhuman Primates

Leonard A. Rosenblum
Gayle S. Paully

ABSTRACT

The prolonged and intense attachment of infant nonhuman primates and their mothers can be understood as part of a matrix of comparative, evolutionary relationships between the human and nonhuman primates. These relationships relate in part to the comparable reproductive strategies within the primate order, the evolutionary trends towards neoteny in primates, and the allometric relationships to body size that primates hold in common. Our research indicates that within this framework, nonhuman primate mothers and their infants alter their attachment towards one another in relation to varying demands of their physical environment and in particular to the relative stability of their feeding ecology and the work requirements imposed on the mothers. Effects of these alterations are seen both in the acute reactions of the partners and in terms of the security of the infants in the presence of the mother and their reactions to maternal loss.

Human and nonhuman primates share many features in common, not the least of which is the uniquely intense and enduring attachment that emerges between mother and infant in the neonatal period and can remain a pivotal element throughout life. The close affinity between man and the other primates has been recognized at least since the time of Galen, nearly 2000 years ago. However, it is not merely the phylogentic closeness of man to the nonhuman primates that permits their use in explicating the incredible diversity of factors shaping human development. Relatively close common ancestry does not in itself specify the communality of ontogentic demands exerted during development. Rather it is in the nature of the problems confronted during development and the physical and psychological properties held in common with the other primates that make the primate data of importance to those involved in human research and clinical treatment.

REPRODUCTIVE STRATEGIES

Across the broad sweep of animal forms, reproductive patterns can be characterised somewhat grossly as falling within so-called "r and K strategies" (Martin, 1975). Species that show rapid fluctuations in population, paralleling environmental abundance or adversity, employ the r strategy; mothers produce as many offspring as possible at each parturition, with few of the members of each birth group surviving past infancy. In some species employing this strategy, little or no parental care is involved after initial fertilization of eggs. In those species in which care does exist, resource availability may markedly influence the degree of maternal investment. When food is scarce, for example, r strategists may not regularly feed their young. Lion mothers, for example, may allow cubs to starve when food supplies are severely limited (Schaller, 1972). Although the r strategist's maternal investment in an infant's survival is not zero, her presumptive commitment to her own "inclusive fitness," including the production of other broods, means that the essence of this strategy involves a relatively minimal and quite labile investment in the nurturance and survival of any individual offspring.

In contrast to these r strategists, the reproductive patterns of the primates emphasizes "quality rather than quantity." Individual offspring are quite altricial, or helpless at birth, are born at rather long intervals, and each receives considerable and generally prolonged parental investment both before and after birth (K strategy). Moreover, the size of primate infants at birth follows a negative allometric function, with the smallest species having relatively larger infants in comparison to maternal body weight, than is true of the larger forms (Leutenegger, 1973). Only the very smallest species, such as the marmoset, caught at the limits of the allometry of infant to maternal size deliver two or more relatively smaller infants rather than one quite large in relative size.

However, there is a precondition, an environmental characteristic, that must be present for this "quality" maternal strategy to evolve and function. If investment in the fine tuning of individual offspring is to emerge, the reproductive environment must be relatively stable and predictable. To invest in the development of a single offspring only to find that it is unsuited to the world into which it finally emerges is clearly an evolutionary dead end. As Martin (1975) pointed out:

> Primates as a group are not adapted for rapid colonization or recolonization, and the larger-bodied species are necessarily the most threatened because of their lower reproductive rates. Environmental stability was probably a key factor in primate evolution; the loss of such stability could be a key factor in primate extinction. (p. 57)

On both theoretical (Crook & Gartlan, 1966; Clutton-Brock, 1977) and empirical grounds (Altmann, 1974; Spuhler & Jorche, 1975), it is reasonable to
overgeneralize somewhat by saying that for primates the nature of the environmental stability required for successful reproduction and development consists of
the presence of a familiar social group and a relatively stable source of nutrition.

THE IMPORTANCE OF THE SOCIAL GROUP

Considering the maternal side of the dyadic attachment pattern, it is clear from an
extensive body of data that when the setting for reproduction and development
lacks the appropriate social elements, the entire process often goes awry. Although a number of examples in monkeys might be cited (e.g., Harlow, Harlow,
Dodsworth, & Arling, 1966), Nadler (1984) provided an excellent comparative
example of the role of species-relevant social contexts for maternal behavior in
the great apes. Both orangutans and chimpanzees have been quite successful in
rearing their infants following the latter's birth in captivity. Gorilla mothers on
the other hand had been notoriously less successful under these conditions. After
a review of the world's literature on gorilla births, Nadler noted that of eight
mothers that successfully reared their young, seven were living in social settings,
whereas of nine that were socially isolated during the postnatal period, eight
abused or neglected their offspring. Nadler's review of the field literature indicated that orangutans in fact are one of the few primate species that rear their
young and generally live in social isolation. Moreover, although chimpanzees do
live in social groups, mothers maintain no permanent associations with other
unrelated adult members of the community, and the dyad is involved in little
social interaction with others during the early postnatal period.

Gorillas, on the other hand, live in relatively stable harem groups, and they
rear their infants in the presence of a group of close associates with whom they
frequently interact. These data led Nadler (1984) to conclude "that congenial
companionship facilitates the maternal behavior of captive gorillas, whereas
social isolation contributes to neglect and abuse of the offspring (p. 117)."
Nadler's subsequent experience at the Yerkes Primate Center has borne out this
conclusion. It is worth noting that data of this type have led primatologists
(including Nadler, 1984; Plimpton & Rosenblum, 1983) to suggest that disruption of species-characteristic social settings in humans may also impede or distort
maternal patterns, particularly in vulnerable individuals.

Human observers of course have also directed increasing attention to the role
of social context in human parental response (Lewis, 1984). Particularly under
conditions of developmental disturbance but also when more normal circumstances prevail, investigators are noting the important role of the larger social
network including grandparents, other adults, friends, and the larger social com-

munity in influencing the total parenting milieu of the human infant. Considering the problem of loss, Feinman and Lewis (1984) noted that, for example:

> Infants who are extensively socially connected appear to be less vulnerable when one primary caregiver is absent. . . . Children who have multiple caregivers may, indeed, be less dependent on any one particular person for their physical and emotional needs. (p. 27)

Similarly, regarding more immediate distortions of nurturent parental behavior, (Garbarino & Crouter, 1978) wrote: "The likelihood of child maltreatment varies in direct relation to the availability, adequacy and use made of a family's supportive resources in the community (p. 604).

NEOTENY

The altricial characteristics held in common by primate neonates also presupposes a crucial impact of the postnatal environment in shaping development. We cannot discount of course the often strong and direct role of genetic and prenatal factors affecting the ontogenty of the primates (e.g., Reinisch, 1983), reflected most clearly for example in early species and sex differences (Rosenblum, 1961, 1971a, 1971b; Maccoby & Jacklin, 1974; Reinisch, Rosenblum, Rubin, & Schulsinger, 1986). However, the entire path of the evolution of the modern primates has been characterized by a prominent psychological (and physiological) trend that is of pivotal developmental significance. That trend is known as neoteny. This term generally refers to a slowing down of various features of physical development (for example, the lengthening of the duration of gestation, the attainment of nutritional independence, attainment of puberty). As a result, characteristics that are lost relatively quickly during development in more ancestral species are retained for longer and longer periods in later evolving forms. The relatively "child-like" shape of the human skull is a classic example of this trend. A large, rounded cranium is characteristic of the infant and juvenile macaque for example but is rapidly lost during the progress to maturity. The prolongation of the jaw that produces the muzzle of the mature monkey appears later and to a far less degree in humans with the result that humans have a relatively inflated cranium throughout life.

In more behavioral terms, this neotenous trend means that patterns that mature rather rapidly in monkeys take longer in the apes and are particularly protracted at the human level. The positive payoff of this evolutionary shift is increased flexibility and lability of behavioral development with more responsivity to the experiences encountered along the way.

The relative neoteny of apes and humans is the product of both the basic trends of primate evolution and of the larger physical size of the more advanced primates. Throughout the animal kingdom, it is generally the case that larger forms live longer than smaller ones. It is important to note, however, that recent analyses of lifespan in primates (Economos, 1980) indicate that they follow the general allometric rates for biological phenomena involving time; that is, for primates, a logarithmic regression of lifespan to body size falls on a slop of 0.25. This means that larger primates live longer than smaller ones, but this increase in lifespan is not linearly related to size; instead, the increase follows the quarter-power of mass. This is the typical slope of time-related functions.

However, when one considers weaning time, i.e. the approximate point at which nutritional independence from the mother appears ("total psychological independence" may never emerge in some species), one obtains another, somewhat steeper slope, suggesting a developmentally neotenous departure from the slope predicted from most allometric perspectives. Although precise times at weaning are not always readily discernible in the literature, analysis of data from 23 primate taxa allowed Schwartz and Rosenblum (1983) to conclude that weaning in primates, scales not to the quarter power of mass, as one would expect, but to its half. Thus, with the smaller primates as the basis of comparison, the larger, more advanced primates, including man, wean their young at a much later point than would be predicted from the wealth of allometric data gathered on endotherms in general (Lindstedt & Calder, 1981). With brain growth in the early postnatal period proceeding at virtually prenatal rates and the relationship with the primary caregiving figure prolonged, the influence of the physical and social environment on primate parenting and infant development can be expected to be considerable.

Not only are the attachment behaviors of the mother primate potentially disturbed by the absence of a species appropriate social setting in which to raise her young, but as a reflection of its slow development, the infant's behavior is also affected to a marked degree by the nature of the social setting in which it is raised. Although it is well known that infant primates of some species (but not all; see Sackett, Holm & Rupenthal, 1976) suffer considerable behavioral disruption when reared in the absence of a primary caregiver, even the infant raised by its mother but in isolation from a group suffers negative developmental consequences as well (Rosenblum & Alpert, 1977).

As is the case with any attempt to characterize a complex realm of data in these schematic terms, important details of species, group, and individual variations around these themes is inevitably lost. This caveat notwithstanding, we can describe the early period of the life of most primates as spent in nearly continuous contact with the ventral or dorsal surface of the mother's body. A significant portion of this contact time the infant retains the nipple in its mouth, sucking intermittantly. The infant may, even in its first hours of life, be explored, sniffed, touched, and even (in a few species) carried by someone other than the mother; in other species, the neonate will be zealously guarded by the mother, and for this and other reasons some neonates may have no close contact with any other member of the species than the mother for some time.

The infant gradually moves towards nutritional, physical, and psychological independence, feeding more and more on its own, spending less and less time in contact with the mother, and ultimately depending less and less on her for emotional and physical security. It is important, however, to make a distinction between general patterns of the diminution of the physically nurturient aspects of the relationship and the continuing psychosocial aspects of the mother–offspring attachment patterns. Although as discussed earlier, weaning may proceed at a regularly predictable allometric pace, under average conditions, dissolution of other aspects of attachment to the primary (and often other) caretaker and even weaning itself, may be subject to conditions that result in considerable variability in these developmental milestones.

It is clear that contextual factors (i.e., the social and environmental conditions in which the infant is reared) may influence even the earliest aspects of the attachment relationship. As we saw above, in gorillas, even the initiation of supportive maternal care may be inhibited in the absence of social partners. In monkeys, we have also determined that even when maternal patterns are "in place," the social environment still affects the developmental pattern. Experimental data on bonnet macaques, for example, has shown that these animals, which normally live in quite gregarious social groups, show marked effects of rearing in the absence of conspecifics, in terms of the infant's earliest responses to the mother. Contrary to the intuitive possibility that the presence of other mothers of the species in close contact might retard infant specificity of attachment responses to the mother, our data suggest just the opposite. When bonnet infants are raised in social groups containing many mother–infant or other adult members with whom they interact, discrimination of the mother from another female conspecific emerges at about 12 weeks. Females tend to make this discrimination more clearly and several weeks earlier than males. However, when infants are reared by their mothers alone (i.e., in the absence of any other members of their species), discrimination is generally delayed by several months, and some of the single-dyad reared infants were not making significant discriminations at one year of age (Rosenblum & Alpert, 1977). Subsequent research (Alpert, 1978) indicated that infants first learn to make specific individual discriminations between mother and only later, presumeably following the opportunity to make a number of such discriminations, does the infant discriminate "mother" from the class, "nonmother." Thus, from the earliest days of life onward, not only does the presence of the "normal" social group provide the basis for the infant's extra-dyadic socialization, but the presence of the group affects the pattern of relations within the dyad itself.

There is a considerable amount of other evidence of social influences on the expression of attachment in the dyad. Maternal dominance status within the group, for example, may permit a more or less restraining pattern of maternal behavior to emerge (Stynes, Rosenblum, & Kaufman, 1968) with consequently more independent infant behavior. Similarly the presence of a matrilineal kinship group (Rosenblum, 1971b) or a frequent alternate caretaker ("aunt"; Rosenblum, 1968) may permit more freedom of activity away from the mother. These and a number of far more complex social forces that may be observed under wild conditions (e.g., Cheney, 1977) have been increasingly cited in the primate developmental literature. However, what I wish to focus on for the remainder of this chapter are the less well explicated aspects of the physical environment as these act to shape the course of infant attachment.

The marked attachment of the single primate infant to its mother, which characterizes the primate order in general, is potentially influenced in both its initial emergence and in the course of its subsequent duration and intensity by a number of environmental elements. As we have come to recognize at the human level, the attachment relationship is affected by the reactions of both members and cannot be understood simply in terms of factors shaping maternal patterns. The infant is highly sensitive to any alterations in maternal response that may be triggered by various social and physical environmental features, but the infant must be seen to respond to those features directly as well. That is, both the infant and mother, in response to the milieu within which the dyad functions, alter their patterns with regard to each other.

SEX DIFFERENCES IN INFANT RESPONSE
TO COMPLEX ENVIRONMENTS

Even when we are unable to specify specific ingredients of the environment that are influencing the attachment patterns we observe, the capacity of the members of the dyad to respond to differing conditions are readily apparent. As demonstrated in an early study on the patterns of infant attachment/independence and as will be reflected in other data to be presented below, even gross environmental instability may alter the course of infant reliance on the mother, and these alterations may be influenced by characteristics of the infant, including its sex.

When squirrel monkeys are reared in stable social groups containing a number of mother–infant dyads and within an unchanging physical environment, there are few differences in the patterns of attachment in males and females during the first six months of life. However, when the physical environment and the social group within which they live are repeatedly shifted, a striking difference in the early development of the independence of males and females emerges. As we can anticipate from the allometric data, the considerable initial investment of the mother in the prolonged gestation of the primates results in the fact that the first several weeks of life are relatively inviolate regarding the continued maternal support of their offspring, regardless of sex of infant, social status of the mother, or the nature of the physical environment. This was clearly reflected in the squirrel monkey maternal behavior observed in our unstable environment.

During the first 10 weeks of life, males and females did not differ from one another, nor did either sex differ from dyads living in more stable settings. However, by the end of the third month of life, female infants in the unstable setting showed marked increases in the intensity of their attachment behavior to the mother, breaking contact with her significantly less than females in more stable conditions. Male infants on the other hand began leaving their mothers at an increasing rate in comparison to their stable environment counterparts. What is of importance here is the fact that these sex differences in the development of independent functioning took place in spite of rather than because of differences in maternal patterns. In fact, the squirrel monkey mothers in the unstable condition in comparison to those in the stable environment showed little change in their response to females and were attempting to restrain their male infants more and were rejecting them less often (Rosenblum, 1974). Thus, both the infant and the mother each may reflect in their dyadic behavior various aspects of the environment as it impinges upon them directly.

THE ROLE OF FORAGING DEMANDS

As we examine more closely the role of specific factors in the physical environment that may impact upon the course of attachment processes in the primates, we return again and again to the incredible diversity of factors with which the mother and infant must contend in their common goal of producing a viable, reproductively active offspring. Of the diverse environmental dimensions that may influence primate patterns, one factor has received the most attention in the evolutionary and comparative literature—the role of the foraging ecology (i.e., the relative abundance and distribution of food within the environment and the relative effort that must be expended in obtaining the nutrient resources necessary for life, reproduction, and growth) (Rosenblum & Sunderland, 1981).

As a consequence, in our efforts to understand the complex matrix of demands that undoubtedly influences primate attachment patterns, we have begun a program of systematic manipulation of the difficulty and stability of foraging demands made on our social groups and the mothers and infants within them. It should be noted here that our goal is not the study of food deprivation nor the capacity of our subjects to develop specific foraging skills. Rather, we seek to understand the effects of varied work requirements necessary for the extraction of necessary food (which is in fact always available) from the environment, whereas other factors are as much as possible kept relatively constant. In keeping with these goals, we have found that the specific nature of the foraging task is not of central importance—having used a wide variety of methods for manipulation of the foraging task from operant devices to digging into sawdust, we have generally concluded that the time and work involved is the crucial factor regardless of the specific manipulations the animals must perform (Paully, 1984).

It is clear that primate mothers will respond to changes in the foraging demands placed upon them in these various ways by adjusting their response to their infants as well as to the foraging environment itself. Whatever the energetic costs of acquiring food may be in a given situation, the burden of carrying a growing infant adds considerably to those costs. This is not to say of course that the mother can afford to sacrifice the ultimate well-being of her offspring to her foraging needs—some balance of these competing fitness demands must be maintained (Andrews & Rosenblum, 1988). Nonetheless, even under relatively acute conditions of increased foraging demand, maternal rejections and reductions in contact will be observed.

MATERNAL RESPONSES TO ACUTE INCREASES IN FORAGING DEMAND

In a recently completed study in our laboratory, we observed two groups of squirrel monkey mother–infant dyads under one of two conditions. Each day subjects were moved into a pen whose floor was covered with 6–10 inches of wood-chip bedding material for a one hour period. Contained within the bedding were food crackers that could be obtained by digging through the dry, light-weight material. Counterbalanced across days, subjects were either pre-fed or not prior to their transfer to the foraging pen.

The results were clearcut. Although the infants were all less than four-months-old (and still nursing), on days in which prefeeding had not occurred, mothers spent considerable time foraging in the bedding material. In initiating their foraging, mothers showed dramatic increases in rejection and removal of their infants, leaving them behind on the high shelves of the pen as they moved to the floor in search for food. This rise in rejection resulted in marked decreases in mother–infant contact time and heightened levels of infant affective distress. On the days of prefeeding, neither foraging nor rejection occurred, and infants were more relaxed and playful.

SUSTAINED EFFECTS OF VARIATIONS IN MATERNAL WORK LOAD

When dyads are subjected to more prolonged alterations in their foraging environment, more sustained and enduring effects are observed. In our initial work of this type (Rosenblum & Paully, 1984), three groups of five mother–infant bonnet macaque dyads were studied across a 14-week period during the first six months of life. Using foraging devises within which we could vary the costs of foraging, one group was maintained on a constant low foraging demand (LFD), one on a constant high demand (HFD), and in the third group the demand alternated between low and high every two weeks (variable demand-VFD). The results of this study speak directly to our concern regarding the role of environmental factors in influencing the course of infant attachment in these animals. At the start of the study, the groups were quite comparable in the ages of infants as well as in the pattern of adult interaction. Typical of bonnet macaque groups, the adults of each group were initially quite gregarious, spending long periods in close physical contact with one another. Similarly, hierarchical behavior (i.e., behaviors relating to dominance and subordinance, aggression and displacement) were quite low. Infant attachment and maternal protection and responsivity to the infants were normally strong for infants of a relatively young age.

The LFD subjects followed the pattern that we have generally observed in bonnet groups in our laboratory over the last 25 years. The group remained peaceful and in frequent contact, and the infants, after their initial period of continued closeness and without any significant amount of maternal rejection, gradually moved towards increasing independence—spending longer and longer periods off their mothers, engaging in social play and environmental explorations. The HFD subjects responded to their more difficult environment in what now appears a characteristic pattern—the group showed an initial decrease in contact huddling amongst the adults and showed intermittant increases in hierarchical patterns as they attempted to adjust to their heightened foraging demands (Plimpton, Swartz, & Rosenblum, 1981). Maternal rejection patterns were somewhat increased as the mothers occupied themselves with relatively prolonged efforts at foraging. As a consequence, HFD infants in the first half of the study were off their mothers relatively more than their counterparts in LFD and appeared in several ways to be more independent. As we shall see below, however, this seeming diminution of attachment behaviors observed in the HFD infants was apparently induced by the abdyadic behavior of the mother rather than as a result of infant initiative, and these infants, regardless of their separations from the foraging mother, had by no means diminished their attachment nor dependence on her. Nonetheless, by the end of the 14 weeks of observations, the HFD group had settled down, and gregarious patterns were largely restored to levels comparable to those in LFD. Similarly their infants were, on the surface at least, at levels of attachment/independence quite comparable to the infants of LFD.

The VFD group on the other hand, despite their comparability at the start of the study, followed a different course. Adults became increasingly agitated, less and less gregarious, and more and more contentious of their social status. Indeed by the end of the study, the adults had became more aggressive towards one another than any bonnets we have ever observed. As FIG. 2.1 reflects, by the end of the study, the VFD group were showing more than four times as much hierarchical behavior as they had at the start of observations, unlike the LFD and HFD groups whose levels were essentially unchanged and quite low. The moth-

HIERARCHICAL BEHAVIOR

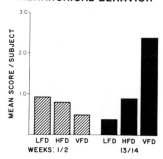

FIG. 2.1. Adult hierarchical behavior at the beginning and end of fourteen weeks of living under the three foraging demand conditions. LFD = Low Foraging Demand; HFD = High Foraging Demand; VFD = Variable Foraging Demand.

ers, experiencing difficulty with their inability to predict the nature of the demands that confronted them from week to week, not with their foraging tasks per se, became increasingly rejecting of their infants.

These heightened levels of maternal rejection, coupled perhaps with the increasingly agonistic quality of group behavior, had marked effects on the infants' emotionality. In clear distinction to developmental patterns observed under more reliable environmental conditions, as indicated in FIG. 2.2, the infants of VFD showed strikingly high and sustained levels of emotional disturbance when off the mother. As a correlate of this heightened disturbance, these infants made repeated attempts to return to mother after contact was broken. As we see in FIG. 2.3, when

DISTURBANCE IN INFANTS

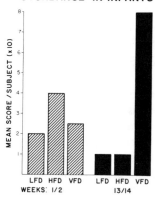

FIG. 2.2. Levels of infant emotional disturbance at the beginning and end of 14 weeks of rearing under the three foraging demand conditions (legend as in FIG. 2.1).

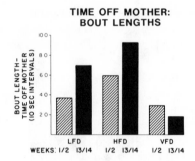

FIG. 2.3.   Bout lengths of infant excursions away from mother at the beginning and end of the study period in the three treatment groups (legend as in FIG. 2.1).

one examines the bout lengths of time off mother (i.e., the durations of excursions of independent activity), VFD infants were in fact spending shorter rather than longer periods out of contact as they grew older.

As a particularly dramatic manifestation of the disturbance of these VFD infants when their mothers engaged themselves in foraging was the fact that three of the five infants to varying degrees showed evidence of the type of behavioral depression that has been reported as the "despair" reaction to mother–infant separation. This separation-like depression occurred, even though their mothers were in visual contact but "unavailable" to them. This depression pattern, in which the infant sits immobile, hunched over in a collapsed posture, relatively unresponsive to their playmates or the rest of their environment, has rarely been recorded even in fully separated bonnets. To our knowledge, this pattern has never been reported in any nonhuman primate in the continued physical presence of the mother. (Rosenblum, 1984).

LATENT EFFECTS OF ENVIRONMENTALLY INDUCED ALTERATIONS IN ATTACHMENT PATTERNS

It is important to note, however, that some of the effects of the differing patterns of maternal response to various foraging demands are not always apparent under the conditions in which they are invoked but may be evidenced in subsequent infant response to particular challenges to their attachment relationship. In an effort to examine some of these latent effects of the early pattern of mother–infant relations, the subjects of the LFD and HFD groups described above were studied before and after a two-week period of mother removal. (Plimpton, 1981; Plimpton & Rosenblum, 1987)

Despite the fact that in the presence of their mothers the infants of the HFD group seemed to be relatively independent in comparison to those reared in the

LFD setting, their responses to separation indicated that in fact their attachment to mother was unusually strong. Despite comparable levels of affect during the preseparation period, during separation HFD infants showed significantly more depressed behavior and little evidence of recovery of complex environmental interactions and positive social patterns such as play during the two weeks of separation. The LFD infants on the other hand, although initially mildly disturbed immediately following separation (all subjects were over six months of age at separation) showed a decrease in disturbance and a sharp recovery of positive functioning by the second week of separation. Unfortunately, VFD subjects were unavailable for this separation research.

In a more recent, related study in our laboratory, M. Andrews has shown a similar latent effect on attachment of early rearing under different foraging conditions. Two groups of three bonnet dyads each were studied under either LFD or VFD conditions for a period of months during the first half year of life. The experimental conditions in this study were not imposed until subjects were two- to three-months-old, and few overt differences between the treatment groups were in evidence during the repeated observations in the home cage conditions. Nonetheless, when the dyads were shifted to a novel room (when infants were in the 6–8 month age range), marked differences between the groups emerged. LFD infants rapidly moved from their mothers and actively engaged the novel environment at levels at or above those observed in the home pen. In contrast to their home pen behavior, once placed in the novel pen, the VFD infants refused to leave their mothers, behaving in many respects in a way that resembled infants much younger in age.

SPECIES DIFFERENCES IN NORMATIVE ATTACHMENT PATTERNS

These experimental demonstrations of the more immediate, sustained, and latent, long-term effects of variations in the patterns of maternal response to environmental conditions fit nicely with some comparative observations made in our laboratory of the long-term patterns of attachment in pigtail and bonnet infants raised under generally LFD-type conditions. Under these conditions as described previously, bonnet adults are quite socially oriented, and mothers are quite permissive with their infants. Early in life, bonnets do little to restrain the excursions of their infants, permitting them to come and go as they please in the relatively benign social atmosphere that characterizes bonnet groups under these "easy" conditions. Similarly even as the mothers approach rebreeding time towards the end of the first half year of their infant's life, bonnet mothers rarely engage in overt rejection or forceable weaning of their infants. In the pigtail, on the other hand, a very different picture has been described. Members of pigtial groups, even under benign environmental conditions, are rather hostile towards one another, maintaining relatively large individual distances. Like their bonnet counterparts, pigtail dyads are initially mutually focused on one another, maintaining long periods of contact and nursing. But unlike the bonnets, pigtail mothers do not allow others to contact their young infants, and as the infants attempt their initial excursions from them, the pigtail mothers actively restrain and protect them closely. Within a few months, however, the pigtail mothers, as they move towards returning estrus, begin active and vigorous rejection, removal, and weaning of their four-to-eight-month-olds. (Rosenblum, 1971a).

LONG-TERM DIFFERENCES IN ATTACHMENT PATTERNS: RESPONSE TO SEPARATION AND KINSHIP INTERACTION

Of relevance to the diverse and often delayed effects of these differences in the pattern of the early attachment relationship are two salient outcomes of these normative species differences. Despite the fact or perhaps because of the fact that pigtail mothers actively reject their infants repeatedly over a period of months, pigtail infants, in marked contrast to similar aged bonnets, show dramatic negative responses, including mild depression following the birth of a sibling, and frequently show marked and often sustained depression in response to maternal separation (Rosenblum & Kaufman, 1968). Moreover, when observed over long periods of the life cycle, pigtails show continued high levels of attachment to their mothers and their siblings, whereas bonnets show little selectivity for contact or interaction with members of their consanguinal family units, including the mother (Rosenblum, 1971b). Thus, rejection by the mother, in spite of the increases in time apart that may initially ensue, nonetheless appears to result in increased rather than diminished dependence on and attachment to the maternal and other associated figures.

CONCLUSIONS

What then are the possible mechanisms through which these diverse patterns of early interaction impact upon the infant's developing changes in the intensity and exclusivity of attachment to the mother? I suggest that this body of data may be understood, at least in part, in terms of the way in which the infant's movements into the nondyadic world are orchestrated. In keeping with classic concepts of arousal and learning (cf. "The Yerkes-Dodson Law"), when infants are forced or otherwise coerced into breaking contact with the mother, their capacity to learn the distinguishing features of their environment and the responses appropriate to them is diminished as a consequence of the relatively high level of fear or anxiety that these young animals experience during these forced periods of noncontact.

Thus, they may be "off-mother" a great deal of the time when mother is rejecting, but their ability to cope with their extra-dyadic environment is not enhanced at all. The appearance of independence or reduced attachment is illusory. The infant who, on the other hand, is permitted to modulate its behavior in terms of its own affective state, moving away when relaxed or comfortable, returning at will to the reassuring contact of the "available" and "contingently responsive" mother (cf. Lewis & Goldberg, 1968), is likely to be in a state better suited to learning the complexities of coping with its social and physical world. Hence, it is the more permissive but responsive mother who facilitates the ultimate reduction of attachment that is necessary for her offspring to cope effectively with its social and physical world even in her absence.

ACKNOWLEDGMENT

The research reported in this paper was supported in part by USPHS Grant #MH15970, funds from the H. F. Guggenheim Foundation, and the State University of New York.

REFERENCES

Alpert, Stephanie. (1978). *The response of infant monkeys to mothers, familiars, strangers and peers: Development during the first 8 months of life.* Unpublished doctoral dissertation, SUNY Downstate Medical Center.

Altmann, S. A. (1974). Baboons, space, time, and energy. *American Zoologist, 14,*221–248.

Andrews, M. W., & Rosenblum, L. A. (1988) Relationship Between Foraging and Affiliative Social Referencing in Primates. In J. E. Fa & C. H. Southwick (Eds.), *The ecology and behavior of food-enhanced primate groups* (pp. 247–268). New York: Alan Liss.

Cheney, D. L. (1977). The acquisition of rank and the development of reciprocal alliances in freeranging immature baboons. *Behavioral Ecology Sociobiology, 2,*303–317.

Clutton-Brock, T. H. (Ed.). (1977). *Primate ecology: Studies of feeding and ranging behavior in lemurs, monkeys and apes.* London: Academic Press.

Crook, J. H., & Gartlan, J. S. (1966). Evolution of primate societies. *Nature, 210,*1200–1204.

Economos, A. C. (1980). Taxonomic differences in the mammalian life-span body weight relationship and the problem of brain weight. *Gerontology, 26,*90–98.

Feinman, S., & Lewis, M. (1984). Is there social life beyond the dyad? A social-psychological view of social connections in infancy. In M. Lewis (Ed.), *Beyond the dyad* (pp. 13–42). New York: Plenum.

Garbarino, J., & Crouter, A. (1978). Defining the community context for parent–child relations: The correlates of child maltreatment. *Child Development, 49,*604–616.

Harlow, H. F., Harlow, M. K., Dodsworth, R. O., & Arling, G. L. (1966). Maternal behavior of rhesus monkeys deprived of mothering and peer associations in infancy. *Proceedings American Philosophical Society, 110,* 58–66.

Leutenegger, W. (1973). Maternal-fetal weight relationships in primates. *Folia Primatologica, 20,*280–293.

Lewis, M. (1984). Social influences on development: An overview. In M. Lewis (Ed.), *Beyond the dyad* (pp. 1–12). New York: Plenum.

Lewis, M., & Goldberg, S. (1969). Perceptual-cognitive development in infancy: A generalized expectancy model as a function of mother–infant interaction. *Merill-Palmer Quarterly, 15,*81–100.

Lindstedt, S. L., & Calder, W. A. (1981). Body size, physiological time and longevity of homeothermic animals. *Quartarly Review Biology, 56,*1–16.

Martin, R. (1975). Strategies of reproduction. *Natural History,* November, 128 48–57.

Maccoby, E. E., & Jacklin, C. N. (1974). *The psychology of sex differences.* Stanford, CA: Stanford University Press.

Nadler, R. D. (1984). Biological contributions to the maternal behavior of great apes. In M. Lewis (Ed.), *Beyond the dyad* (pp. 109–128). New York: Plenum.

Paully, G. S. (1984). Feeding strategies in individual and group living bonnet Macaques. Unpublished doctoral dissertation, SUNY Downstate Medical Center.

Plimpton, E. H. (1981). Environmental variables and the response to maternal loss. Unpublished doctoral dissertation, SUNY Downstate Medical Center.

Plimpton, E., & Rosenblum, L. A. (1983). The ecological context of infant maltreatment in primates. In M. Reite (Ed.), *Child abuse: The nonhuman primate data* (pp. 103–117). New York: Alan Liss.

Plimpton, E. H., & Rosenblum, L. A. (1987). The ecological challenge of separation and loss: A review of the non-human primate literature. In S. Bloom Feshbach & J. Feshbach (Eds.), *The psychology of separation through the life-span* (pp. 63–86). New York: Jossey-Bass.

Plimpton, E. H., Swartz, K. B., & Rosenblum, L. A. (1981). The effects of foraging demand on social interactions in a laboratory group of bonnet Macaques. *International Journal of Primatology, 2,*175–185.

Reinisch, J. M. (1983). Influence of early exposure to steroid hormones on behavioral development. In W. Everaerd, C. B. Hindley, A. Bot, & J. J. van der Werff ten Bosch (Eds.), *Development in adolescence* (pp. 63–113). Boston: Martinus Nijhoff.

Reinisch, J. M., Rosenblum, L. A., Rubin, D., & Schulsinger, F. (1986). *Sex differences in behavioral milestones in the first year of life.* Manuscript submitted for publication.

Rosenblum, L. A. (1961). *The development of social behavior in the rhesus monkey.* Unpublished doctoral dissertation, University of Wisconsin.

Rosenblum, L. A. (1968). Mother–infant relations and early behavioral development in the Squirrel Monkey. In L. A. Rosenblum & R. W. Cooper (Eds.), *The Squirrel Monkey* (pp. 207–234). New York: Academic Press.

Rosenblum, L. A. (1971a). The ontogeny of mother–infant relations in Macaques. In H. Moltz (Ed.), *The ontogeny of vertebrate behavior.* (pp. 315–367). New York: Academic Press.

Rosenblum, L. A. (1971b). Kinship interaction patterns in pigtail and bonnet Macaques. In J. Biegert (Ed.), *Proceedings of the Third International Congress of Primatology* (pp. 79–84). Basel: Karger.

Rosenblum, L. A. (1974). Sex differences, environmental complexity and mother–infant relations. *Archives of Sexual Behaviour, 11,* 117–128.

Rosenblum, L. A. (1984). Monkeys' response to separation and loss. In M. Osterweis, F. Solomon, & M. Green (Eds.), *Bereavement: Reactions, consequences and care* (pp. 179–198). Washington, DC: National Academy Press.

Rosenblum, L. A., & Alpert, S. (1977). Response to mother and stranger: A first step in socialization. In S. Chevalier-Skolnikoff & F. E. Poirier (Eds.), *Primate bio-social development* (pp. 463–478). New York: Garland.

Rosenblum, L. A., & Kaufman, I. C. (1968). Variations in infant development and response to maternal loss in monkeys. *American Journal of Orthopsychiatry, 38,* 418–426.

Rosenblum, L. A., & Paully, G. S. (1984). The effects of varying environmental demands on maternal and infant behavior. *Child Development, 55,* 305–314.

Rosenblum, L. A., & Sunderland, G. (1981). Feeding ecology and mother–infant relations. In L. W. Hoffman, R. Gandelman, & H. R. Schiffman (Eds.), *Parenting: Its causes and consequences* (pp. 75–110). NJ: Lawrence Erlbaum Associates.

Sackett, G. P., Holm, R. A., & Rupenthal, G. C. (1976). Social isolation rearing: Species differences in behavior of macaque monkeys. *Developmental Psychology, 12,* 283–288.

Schaller, G. *The Serengeti Lion.* (1972). Chicago: University of Chicago Press.

Schwartz, G. G., & Rosenblum, L. A. (1983). Allometric influences on primate mothers and infants. In L. A. Rosenblum & H. Moltz (Eds.), *Symbiosis in parent–offspring interaction* (pp. 215–248). New York: Plenum.

Spuhler, J. N., & Jorche, L. B. (1975). Primate phylogeny, ecology, and social behavior. *Journal of Anthropological Research, 31,* 376–405.

Stynes, A. J., Rosenblum, L. A., & Kaufman, I. C. (1968). The dominant male and behavior in heterospecific monkey groups. *Folia Primatologica, 9,*123–134.

3 Efe Multiple Caretaking and Attachment

Gilda A. Morelli
Edward Z. Tronick

ABSTRACT

A model for understanding the process of attachment formation during the infant's first year of life is developed using as way of illustration the early caregiving pattern of a group of forest gatherers and hunters, the Efe. The Efe engage in a system of extensive multiple caregiving beginning at birth and continuing for at least the first 4 months of the infant's life. It appears, however, that in the context of multiple care, one-year-olds form special relationships with their mothers. The model proposed to account for this process takes into consideration the strategies used by caregiver and infant to guide the allocation of material and psychological resources. Caregiver investment strategies are shaped by sociocultural and historical factors; infant resource acquisition strategies are initially under strong genetic control, but soon take more culturally appropriate forms. Both sets of strategies allow individuals to better deal with situational factors. The strategic model is compared to theory of attachment advanced by Bowlby, Ainsworth and others.

We conceptualize normal development as occurring through an interaction of mutually regulatory behavioral strategies flexibly deployed by children and caregivers in the service of achieving short- and long-term goals. For children, these strategies are referred to as child resource acquisition strategies and for caregivers as caregiver investment strategies. The resources acquired and invested are both material and psychological. Their form and content are guided by cultural values and beliefs, characteristics of the sociocultural environment, past experience, and evolved capacities and motivations (see also Lamb, Thompson, Gardner, & Charnov, 1985; Chisolm, 1983).

   Caregiver–child strategies are aimed at accomplishing three universal goals: infant survival and eventual reproduction, economic self-sufficiency, and enculturation (LeVine, 1977), but the strategies used to achieve them are different for caregiver and infant. Caregivers draw on knowledge that is culturally based to guide their investment of material and psychological resources in their children. Material resources include food, shelter, heat; psychological resources include attention, emotions, and instruction. Their strategies are prefitted to relatively stable sociocultural and environmental conditions. These caregiver investment strategies are extremely valuable. They dramatically reduce the cost and effort required to (re)create appropriate caretaking patterns that protect the infant from major environmental hazards and result in appropriate development in each generation.

Infants share these goals, and they have acquisition strategies in the form of signaling and other manipulative behaviors as well as underlying capacities for accumulating the necessary energetic, affectional and informational resources from conspecifics to realize these goals (Tronick, Winn, & Morelli, 1985). Infants' initial strategies are under strong genetic control, but as they develop, their strategies are modified by the caretaking they receive in such a way as to increasingly conform to culturally prescribed strategies. Note that neither conscious decision making nor awareness are required by this view, although some of each is certainly possible.

Caregiver investment and infant acquisition strategies, therefore, are aimed at the goals outlined by LeVine and vary according to various sociocultural systems. They are flexibly deployed depending on individual needs and environmental conditions. This position assumes that there is no best prototypical caretaking strategy or pattern of development, although there are certainly underlying universal constraints that all caregiver–child strategies must fulfill (Hinde, 1982). Thus, there are strategies that allow individuals to better deal with circumstances or situational factors that affect the achievement of their respective goals. For example, Caudill and Weinstein (1969) demonstrated that Japanese mothers engage in a pattern of care that is quite different from the American pattern of care and that Japanese infants' pattern of development differs from that of American infants'. However, both of these patterns fulfill goals of initial survival and conform to cultural values.

The position that most contrasts with the caregiver–child strategies model is attachment theory (Bowlby, 1969; Ainsworth, Bleher, Waters, & Wall, 1978; Sroufe & Waters, 1977). Attachment as a *psychological* construct originally referred to the type of relationship that existed exclusively between infants and their mothers. The propensity to form an attachment to a single caregiver, the mother, was assumed to be an infant characteristic under strong genetic control. This position was later modified, and infants were considered capable of forming secondary attachments to significant others (Bowlby, 1982). However, the status awarded to their first and primary attachment relationship, which emerged during the second half-year of life, remained unchanged.

The security of the attachment that developed from the interactive experiences infants had with their mothers was of cardinal importance in influencing infants' psychological development (Ainsworth et al., 1978; Bowlby, 1969, 1982; Bretherton, 1980, 1985; Vaughn, Deane, & Waters, 1985). Predictable, sensitive, responsive, and playful exchanges were considered to foster secure attachments (Bretherton, 1980), whereas insensitive and noncontingent exchanges fostered one of two types of insecure attachments (Ainsworth et al., 1978). Assessment of the quality of a child's attachment was made using the Strange Situation procedure. This procedure mildly stresses the infant so that the child's ability to utilize his or her parent as a secure base can be evaluated.

Interpretation of the patterns of behavior observed in the Strange Situation followed from Bowlby's ethological model, which is based on evolutionary theory. Bowlby (1969) argued that the attachment behavioral system is a strongly canalized, species-wide characteristic. It evolved in response to predator pressures and functioned to promote infant survival by keeping infants in proximity to their mothers or mothering figures (Bowlby, 1969). This was referred to as a monotropic tendency in the infant. Secure attachments were considered more adaptive than insecure attachments because infants were more likely to survive if the organization of proximity seeking and exploratory behaviors around attachment figures were contingent on environmental exigencies.

Findings based on the Strange Situation have affected our thinking on the evolutionary significance of attachment and parental behaviors. Securely attached, B-group infants were considered as having a selective advantage over insecurely attached, A- and C-group infants. "Advantage" implied reproductive advantage, although this was never directly discussed and has never been assessed. Furthermore, complementary to the argument advanced for the B-type attachment, it was argued that environmental forces had operated to produce a pattern of parental behavior that was also adaptive (i.e., most likely to produce B-type infants). This behavior pattern included sensitive, responsive, and playful interactions by a single caregiver. Deviations from this normative, species-typical pattern of behavior were thought to jeopardize infant survival and to compromise their psychological development.

The contrast between attachment theory and the caregiver–child strategic development model is striking. Attachment theory implies that there is a universal *optimum* for development and a universal process for achieving it: This developmental outcome is tightly constrained by evolved capacities that tend to be obligatory. It downplays the role of other factors as influencing this process and considers caretaker (mother) and infant in a predominantly cooperative relationship. In addition, it has a specific procedure for assessing the outcome of the developmental process. By comparison, the strategic model argues that although there are constraints that must be fulfilled, there is no prototypical form for meeting these constraints only strategies that are better fitted to circumstances and the interplay of a multiplicity of factors, none of which is dominant. Furthermore, the strategic model argues that some conflict between caregiver and infant is inherent in their mutual regulation of one another and that no specific procedure is universally applicable for the assessment of social-emotional development or attachment.

Until recently, much of what was known about early social-emotional development and attachment in particular, was based on research using the Strange Situation with middle-class American infants raised in intact, nuclear families. The studies showed that approximately 65% of the one-year-olds observed were B-group infants, 20% A-group, and 15% C-group infants. Furthermore, mothers of securely attached infants were more likely to be described as sensitive and responsive caregivers than were mothers of insecurely attached infants. These results were consistent with the prevailing theories on attachment and encouraged the continued use of the Strange Situation.

Crosscultural research on attachment theory raised doubts concerning the validity of the Strange Situation and supported, although not explicitly, the strategic approach (see Chisholm, 1983). Differences in the proportion of infants classified as A-, B-, and C-types in non US communities were probably the most important findings that prompted researchers to reevaluate their position on attachment and its study. Compared to American infants, more Japanese (Miyake, Chen, & Campus, 1985; Takahashi, 1986) and kibbutz-raised Israeli infants (Sagi, Lamb, Lewkowicz, Shoham, Duir, & Estes, 1985) were classified as C-types, and more West German infants were classified as A-types (Grossman and Grossman, 1985; Grossman, Spangler, Suess, & Unzner, 1985) when tested with their mothers in the Strange Situation. These findings led researchers to examine more closely the antecedents of attachment security. As a result of this work, factors other than maternal sensitivity and responsivity were identified as influencing infant behavior in the Strange Situation. Culturally based childrearing practices, cultural valuation of independence and self-reliance, and experience with strangers were among factors found to be of particular importance in shaping infants' attachment and interactive style.

Crosscultural research also raised doubts concerning the basic tenets of attachment theory. The assumption that infants form a single, primary attachment to their mother or mothering figure and that this attachment develops from the infant's near exclusive interactions with this figure was questioned by research on kibbutz-raised Israeli children (Fox, 1977) and to a lesser extent by studies on daycare children (Clark-Stewart & Fein, 1983). Furthermore, crosscultural research showed there was no reason to assume that a single pattern of attachment behavior, especially as assessed in the Strange Situation, was equally adaptive for infants of different cultures, and there were many reasons to argue against this assumption (Chisholm, 1983; Grossman & Grossman, 1985; Grossman, et al., 1985; Hinde, 1982; Lamb et al., 1985; Miyake et al., 1985; Sagi et al., 1985).

From the perspective of the strategic model, attachment can be seen as related to caregiver and infant goals. As a proximity maintenance system enacted by caregiver retrieval behaviors and infant proximity seeking behaviors, it partially fulfills the goal of survival by keeping the infant with adults who protect the infant from predators and prevent the infant from suffering exposure. As a further consequence of the maintenance of proximity, the infant is exposed to and begins to learn culturally appropriate social and subsistence behaviors through modeling and other processes, an observation made by Konner (1976) for the !Kung. This point is also emphasized by Caudill and Weinstein (1969), LeVine (1980), and the Whitings (1975).

Attachment theory's assumption of a monotropic tendency in the infant is compatible with the strategic model. However, acceptance of this assumption does *not* dictate that the infant be cared for by one person in a particular fashion. Rather from the strategic perspective, the caretaking strategy employed would be the result of attempts to meet this monotropic constraint as well as cultural, socioecological, and other constraints. For example, Gusii mothers are the sole and primary caregivers of their infants in the early months of life, but they see this care as readying the infant for care by an older sibling in the second half-year of life (Dixon, Tronick, Keefer, & Brazelton, 1981).

Crosscultural work is limited, and this limits our modeling of the developmental process. With a few notable exceptions—the work of Ainsworth et al. (1978) on the Baganda of Uganda and Konner (1972) on the !Kung of Botswana—most research involves the study of technologically advanced societies. In the majority of societies studied, caregiving is primarily the mother's responsibility. As a result, variation in behavioral patterns and the source of this variation remain unexplored. Without these data, statements about attachment, its development and function, are necessarily restricted.

The purpose of the proposed work is to provide a systematic and comprehensive study of the social-emotional development and attachment processes in 4- to 12-month-old children of a technologically simple people—the Efe (Pygmies) of the Ituri forest of Northeastern Zaire. The Efe are of particular importance in evaluating the strategic and attachment models because of their way of life as hunters and gatherers, a way of life argued to strongly resemble the niche of human adaptedness. This research project developed from and elaborates on previous work (Tronick, Morelli, & Winn, 1983; Tronick, Winn, & Morelli, 1984; Morelli, Winn, Zwahlen, & Peacock, 1984; Tronick, Winn, & Morelli, 1985; Tronick, Morelli, & Winn, 1987; Winn, Morelli, & Tronick, 1989).

The Efe, one of four groups comprising the Mbuti of the Ituri forest, are a particularly interesting people to study because of their subsistence pattern, lifestyle, and child-rearing practices. The Efe are a short-statured people who acquire forest foods by gathering and hunting using mainly bows and metal-tipped arrows. Cultivated foods are also an important part of the Efe diet (Bailey & Peacock, 1988) and are obtained in exchange for forest food and other services from the Lese—a group of horticulturalists with whom they have a long-standing, reciprocal relationship.

The majority of Efe live in transient camps established in small forest areas cleared of vegetation. Their leaf huts are used mainly for sleeping, food storage, and protection from inclement weather, and they are typically arranged around the camp's perimeter creating a large visually open communal living space. Efe also share many of their out-of-camp experiences with other individuals, therefore, most of an individual's daytime activities such as childcare, food preparation, interpersonal relations, and the like are common knowledge and open to observation.

The Efe are a seminomadic people, moving camp every four to six weeks to exploit seasonally available foods and for health or personal reasons. Camp location as well as hunting usually occur within a home range that is associated with a given Efe band over generations. Camps are often situated at or near old sites and rarely exceed a day's walk from a Lese village. Camp membership ranges from 6 to 50 people and is made up of one or several extended families. Each family consists of brothers and their wives, children, unmarried sisters, and parents. Familial ties influence the distribution of resources among camp members and the spatial arrangement of huts within the camp, but the extended family is not the basic social unit. The basic social unit is the nuclear family. When changes in camp composition occur, the nuclear family but not necessarily the extended family remains intact.

Efe culture requires individuals to: (a) be socially skilled in avoiding interpersonal conflicts, (b) be cooperative and sharing, (c) be loyal to their relatives, and (d) contribute to the group's successful functioning. At the same time, Efe must be able to cope with the frequent loss of relatives resulting from group fissioning, emmigration, and death. Emmigration is generally true for children who are adopted by relatives and for young women who are exchanged in marriage.

Efe values and beliefs are reflected in their pattern of child care, which prepares children to meet sociocultural demands as well as satisfy their biological and psychological needs (Tronick, Winn, & Morelli, 1985). The following description of Efe caregiving practices and the beliefs guiding their expression is based on the study of Efe children 0–4 and 12–39 months of age. Data were collected over a two-year continuous period using three complementary procedures: structured interviews, participant observations, and systematic naturalistic observations. Statements concerning the behavior of 4- to 12-month-olds is based solely on preliminary, nonstructured observations. Our data show that the Efe employ a system of multiple caregiving that begins at birth and continues in modified form through the first few years of life.

Efe women do not give birth on their own (cf. Konner, 1976 on the !Kung). Rather most female camp members attend the birth, and one or several women act as midwife. Immediately following delivery, the newborn is passed among the women present and is likely to be suckled by them whether or not they are lactating. Mothers are prohibited from being the first person to hold their infants during the initial postpartum period, because it is believed that to do so would bring harm to the newborn. As a result, a mother's first contact with her infant usually occurs several hours after birth (cf. Lozoff, 1983, on early birthing practices in technologically simple but predominately agricultural societies).

The newborn is nursed two to three times a day by another lactating woman until the mother's milk comes in. The importance of this practice is indicated by the fact that if a lactating woman does not reside in camp, then another lactating woman, Efe or Lese, is recruited to suckle the newborn. The mother also nurses her infant during this time, although the Efe believe that colostrum lacks nutritional value (Morelli, Winn, Zwahlen, & Peacock, 1984).

When a mother's normal work routine is resumed, three to five days postpartum, the infant may accompany her on out-of-camp trips. If this occurs, infant care is generally shared by individuals at the work site. Alternatively, a mother may leave her infant in the care of an individual who has chosen to remain in camp. Whether a mother decides to travel with her infant depends on a number of factors including the amount of time she plans to be away and where she intends to go.

Caregiving by individuals other than mother also occurs while the mother is in camp and is often unrelated to the mother's ongoing activities and availability. Our in-camp observations show that the percentage of time infants are cared for by individuals other than their mothers increases from 39% at 3 weeks to 60% at 18 weeks. The number of different individuals caring for an infant in the first 18 weeks of life averaged 14.2. An important aspect of this care includes being nursed by women other than the mother. Overall, 8 of the 10 infants observed experienced this culturally sanctioned practice (Tronick, et al., 1987).

Efe infants are not stressed by this multiple pattern of care. Most interactions with infants appear positive and playful. When infants show signs of distress, they are responded to immediately. Data on latency of response to fussing in 7- to 18-week-olds show that in over 75% of our observations, individuals, including the mother, attempted to comfort an infant within 10 seconds of a fuss (Winn, et al., 1989).

During the first 18 weeks of the infants' lives, individuals (especially girls and women) are willing and often want to engage in caregiving. Infants readily accept this care, but during the second half-year of life, it appears to us from our preliminary observations that infants' relationships with mothers and other caregivers change. This is suggested by the behavior of one-year-olds.

On the basis of nonstructured observations, toddlers seem to prefer the care of their mothers. Individuals whose caregiving and comforting attempts were once readily accepted are often refused by the one-year-old. Even offers of the breast from caregivers other than the mother are rejected. One-year-olds are also more likely to become upset when left by their mothers, and at times the distress is so acute that mothers return and collect them. In fact, it appears that older infants are more likely to accompany their mothers on out-of-camp trips than are younger infants. Toddlers who are left by their mothers often appear disconsolate for a period of time following their mothers' departure.

Mothers appear to be primarily responsible for the care of their one-year-olds. This is not to imply, however, that individuals other than mother abstain from caring for or interacting with toddlers. Rather it is probably more accurate to view the role that mother and other caregivers play in the life of the toddler as undergoing change. As caregiving responsibilities of other-than-mother caregivers decrease, other forms of social interactions (such as play) may increase. Therefore, camp members may be as involved in the lives of toddlers as they were in the lives of infants, but the nature of this involvement is different.

It appears that cultural beliefs support the change observed in the infant's relationship to mother and other caregivers. The Efe consider the second half-year of an infant's life to be a time of budding social awareness. They believe that by one year of age infants know the breast and face of their mothers and, therefore, prefer them to other caregivers. The ability "to know" begins, according to the Efe, around the fourth month of life. At this time, infants learn about the people who care for them, their mothers and other "mothers"—a term generally applied to women related to the mother. Mothers consciously teach their infants to recognize them by lightly tapping their breasts to the infants' mouth.

Infants' nighttime experiences provide another way for infants to differentiate mothers from other caregivers. It is our impression (from sleeping in camps and talking with mothers) that infants are cared for solely by their mothers during the night and that sleep is punctuated with periods of social interaction. According to one informant, an infant "begins to laugh and say things at night. At sunset he begins to talk, talk, talk, until sunrise."

However, there are other factors that also differentiate mother from other caregivers. Six- through 12-month-olds are notorious for interrupting the work routine of their caregiver, therefore, others are disinclined to care for an infant when engaged in tasks. This is probably exacerbated by the infant's reluctance to be left by mother or to be comforted by other individuals. Consequently, mothers become increasingly responsible for the care of their infants.

Thus, it seems to us that between the ages of 4–12 months, there are a number of factors that increase mother–infant contact, change the nature of their interactions, and possibly create a more focused relationship between them. These factors include a blend of cultural practices and beliefs concerning infants and their abilities, infant characteristics and constraints imposed by women's work responsibilities. However, because of the very preliminary nature of our observations of Efe caregiving practices, rather than drawing firm conclusions, we advance the following hypotheses to be evaluated in future work:

Efe infants develop primary attachments to their mothers by 12 months of age in the context of experiencing sensitive multiple caregiving during the first year of life. It is hypothesized that this attachment is supported by and grows out of the interplay of factors that are infant-, mother-, and culture-based.

1. *Infant-based factors*. Efe infants' resource acquisition strategy changes from one that is nonselective as to who provides material and psychological resources to one that is highly selective, such that infants increasingly solicit and accept resources from their mothers and increasingly reject resources from others over the first year of life.

This hypothesis, if substantiated, would lend support to Bowlby's formulation of a phylogenetically based monotropic tendency in infants.

2. *Mother-based factors*. The Efe mother is differentiated from other caregivers and becomes available as an attachment figure, because her caretaking investment strategy is characterized by mutual sleeping with and nursing of her infant, a pattern of care differing from that observed in other caregivers, and by an increasing willingness on her part to assume caretaking responsibilities.

Results consistent with this hypothesis would support DeVore and Konner's (1974) suggestion that secondary drives contribute to infants' attachment to appropriately nuturant figures and would question the primacy assigned to sensitive and playful interactions carried out by a single individual as the basis of attachment formation. Furthermore, such results would support the position advanced by the Whitings and others (Whiting & Whiting, 1975; Whiting, 1980; Edwards and Whiting, 1980; Harkness and Super, 1983, 1985 Whiting & Edwards, 1988) that the interactive experiences characteristic of certain dyad types shape infants' socialization and enculturation.

3. *Culture-based factors*. Infant care and enculturation come to be viewed as best accomplished in the mother–child relationship. This is because the culture sees infant social awareness of and need for his or her mother emerging during this period of time, and with these changes the cultural belief develops that the mother can best fulfill this need.

Support for this hypothesis would emphasize the importance of culture in shaping development by influencing the nature of and the meaning assigned to infants activities and social experiences.

Overall, support for these hypotheses would help substantiate the child–parent strategies model with its emphasis on a multiplicity of factors that affect the child's social-emotional development and parental practices. However, even if these particular hypotheses are not confirmed, the Efe caretaking system, which we believe to be one of the most extensive, naturally occurring multiple caretaking systems yet described, already serves to broaden our perspectives on allowable patterns of parental investment and infant resource aquisition strategies.

REFERENCES

Ainsworth, M. D. S., Blehar, M. L., Waters, E., & Wall, S. (1978). *Patterns of attachment.* New York: Wiley.

Bailey, R. C., & Peacock, N. R. (1988). Efe Pygmies of Northeast Zaire: Subsistence strategies in the Ituri Forest. In I. de Garine & G. A. Harrison (Eds.), *Uncertainty in food supply* (pp. 88–117). London: Oxford Press.

Bowlby, J. (1969). *Attachment Volume 1.* New York: Basic.

Bowlby, J. (1982). Attachment and loss: Retrospect and prospect. *American Journal Orthopsychiatry* 52(4), pg. 664–678.

Bretherton, I. (1980). Young children in stressful situations: The supporting role of attachment figures and unfamiliar caregivers. In G. V. Coelho & P. Ahmed (Eds.), *Uprooting and development* (pp. 179–210). New York: Plenum.

Bretherton, I. (1985). Attachment theory: Retrospect and prospect. In I. Bretherton & E. Waters (Eds.), *Growing points of attachment theory and research. Monographs of the Society for Research in Child Development.* 50(1–2, Serial No. 209), 3–35.

Caudill, W., & Weinstein, S. (1969). Maternal care and infant behavior in Japan and America. *Psychiatry, 32,* 12–43.

Chisholm, J. (1983). *Navajo infancy: An ethological study of child development.* New York: Aldine.

Clarke-Stewart, K. A., & Fein, G. G. (1983). Early childhood programs. In P. H. Mussen (Gen. Ed.), *Handbook of child psychology. Volume 2.* M. M. Haith & J. J. Campos (Vol. 2 Eds.), *Infancy and developmental psychobiology* (pp. 917–1000). New York: Wiley.

DeVore, I., & Konner, M. J. (1974). Infancy in Hunter-Gatherer Life: An Ethological Perspective. In N. F. White (Ed.), *Ethology and psychiatry* (pp. 113–141). From the Clarence M. Hincks Memorial Lectures, Held at McMaster University, 1970. Canada: University of Toronto Press.

Dixon, S., Tronick, E., Keefer, C., & Brazelton, T. B. (1981). Mother–infant interaction among the Gusii of Kenya. In T. Field (Ed.), *Culture and early interaction* (pp. 148–168).

Edwards, C. P., & Whiting, B. B. (1980). Differential socialization of girls and boys in light of cross-cultural research. *New Directions for Child Development, 8,* 45–57.

Fox, N. A. (1977). Attachment of Kibbutz infants to mother and metapelet. *Child Development, 48,* 1228–1239.

Grossmann, K. E., & Grossmann, K. (1985, July). *From attachment to dynamics of relationship patterns: A longitudinal approach.* Paper presented at 8th Biennial Meetings of the International Society for the Study of Behavioral Development, Tours, France.

Grossmann, K. E., Spangler, G., Suess, G., & Unzner, L. (1985). Maternal sensitivity and newborn's orientation responses as related to quality of attachment in northern Germany. In I. Bretherton & E. Waters (Eds.), *Growing points of attachment theory and research. Monographs of the Society for Research in Child Development,* 50(1–2, Serial No. 209), 3–35.

Harkness, S., & Super, C. M. (1983). The cultural construction of child-development. *Ethos, 11*(4), 221–231.

Harkness, S., & Super, C. M. (1985). The cultural context of gender segregation in children's peer groups. *Child Development. 56,* 219–224.

Hinde, R. A. (1982). Attachment: Some conceptual and biological issues. In J. Stevenson-Hinde & C. Murray Parkes (Eds.), *The place of attachment in human behavior* (pp. 60–76). New York: Basic.

Konner, M. J. (1972). Aspects of the developmental ethology of a foraging people. In N. Blurton Jones (Ed.), *Ethological Studies of Child Behaviour* (pp. 285–304). Cambridge: Cambridge University Press.

Konner, M. J. (1976). Maternal care, infant behavior, and development among the !Kung. In R. B. Lee & I. DeVore (Eds.), *Kalahari hunter gatherers* (pp. 218–245). Cambridge: Harvard University Press.

Lamb, M. E., Thompson, R. A., Gardner, W., & Charnov, E. (1985). *Infant–mother attachment: The origins and developmental significance of individual differences in Strange Situation behavior.* London: Lawrence Erlbaum Associates.

LeVine, R. A. (1977). Child rearing as cultural adaptation. In P. H. Leiderman, S. R. Tulkin, & A. Rosenfield (Eds.), *Culture and infancy: Variations in the human experience* (pp. 15–28). New York: Academic Press.

LeVine, R. A. (1980). A Cross-cultural perspective on parenting. In M. D. Fantini & R. Cardenas (Eds.), *Parenting in a multicultural society* (pp. 17–26). New York: Longman.

Lozoff, B. (1983). Birth and bonding in non-industrial societies. *Developmental Medicine and Child Neurology. 25,* 595–600.

Miyake, K., Chen, S., & Campos, J. J. (1985). Infant temperament, mode of interaction, and attachment in Japan: An interim report. In I. Bretherton & E. Waters (Eds.), *Growing points of attachment theory and research. Monographs of the Society for Research in Child Development. 50*(1–2, Serial No. 209), 276–297.

Morelli, G. A., Winn, S., Zwahlen, D., & Peacock, N. (1984). *Perinatal practices among the Efe.* Poster presented at The International Conference on Infancy Studies, New York.

Sagi, A., Lamb, M. E., Lewkowicz, K. S., Shoham, R., Duir, R., & Estes, D. (1985). Security of mother–infant, –father and metapelet attachments among Kibbutz–reared Israeli children. In I. Bretherton & E. Waters (Eds.), *Growing points of attachment theory and research. Monographs of the Society for Research in Child Development. 50*(1–2, Serial No. 209), 257–275.

Sroufe, L. A., & Waters, E. (1977). Attachment as an organizational construct. *Child Development. 48,* 1184–1199.

Takahashi, K. (1986). Examining the strange-situation procedure with Japanese mothers and 12-month-old infants. *Developmental Psychology* 22(2), pg. 265–270.

Tronick, E., Morelli, G., & Winn, S. (1983). *Multiple caretaking and personality formation in an environment of human adaptiveness.* Paper presented at the Boston Institute for the Development of Infants and Parents, Boston.

Tronick, E. Z., Morelli, G. A., & Winn, S. (1984). *Multiple caretaking in the niche of human evolution.* Paper presented at The International Conference of Infant Studies, New York.

Tronick, E. Z., Winn, S., & Morelli, G. A. (1985). Multiple caretaking in the context of human evolution. Why don't the Efe know the western prescription of child-care? In M. Reite & T. Field (Eds.), *Psychobiology of attachment* (pp. 293–322). New York: Academic Press.

Tronick, E. Z., Morelli, G. A., & Winn, S. (1987). Multiple caretaking of Efe (Pygmy) infants. *American Anthropologist, 89*(1), 96–106.

Vaughn, B. E., Deane, K. E., & Waters, E. (1985). The impact of out-of-home care on child–mother attachment quality: Another look at some enduring questions. In I. Bretherton & Waters, E. (Eds.), *Growing points of attachment theory and research. Monographs of the Society for Research in Child Development. 50*(1–2, Serial No. 209), 110–135.

Whiting, B. B. (1980). Culture and social behavior. *Ethos.8,* 95–116.

Whiting, B. B., & Whiting, J. (1975). *Children of six cultures: A psychocultural analysis.* Cambridge, MA: Harvard University Press.

Whiting, B. B., & Edwards, C. P. (1988). Children of different worlds: The formation of social behavior. Cambridge, MA: Harvard University Press.

Winn, S., Morelli, G. A., & Tronick, E. Z. (1989). The infant and the group: A look at Efe caretaking practices. In J. K. Nugent, B. M. Lester, & T. B. Brazelton (Eds.), *The cultural context of infancy.* Norwood, NJ: Ablex.

II | IMPRINTING AND ATTACHMENT

4 Ethology and Attachment: A Historical Perspective

Eckhard H. Hess
Slobodan B. Petrovich

ABSTRACT

An outline is presented of the assumptions underlying earlier and contemporary ethology. An example of ethological analysis is presented, with a focus on the ontogeny, mediating mechanisms of causation, function and evolution of cricket songs. In a historical frame, conceptual and methodological origins of modern ethology were sketched out and the significance of important trends explored. The conclusion of the analysis of this chapter is that researchers of human development studying attachment under the aegis of ethological theory have moved in a direction that diverges from the conceptualizations and research emphases of contemporary ethology.

This chapter describes elements of the ethological approach to attachment in an attempt to facilitate an interdisciplinary exchange among ethologists and developmental psychologists. Its purpose is to share a historical perspective and habits of thought, and to communicate theoretical and methodological developments and that have had an impact on the ethological study of behavior.

At the outset, our goal is to tell what ethology is about, in a historical context. As an example, the treatment considers the development, mediating mechanisms of causation, as well as the function and evolution of the cricket's song. Then we extrapolate some conceptual and methodological lessons of interest and of use to a wider audience. Our treatment proceeds with an appraisal of the contributions of ethology to the study of human attachment. Finally, we focus on some of the issues of relevance both to ethology and developmental psychology, and evaluate whether or not human-development theory and research on attachment in the frame of ethology have diverged from the emphases of contemporary ethology.

WHAT ETHOLOGY IS ABOUT: A HISTORICAL PERSPECTIVE ON SOME CONCEPTUAL AND METHODOLOGICAL EXTRAPOLATIONS

Ethology has been described as the biology of behavior (Eibl-Eibesfeldt, 1975; Hinde, 1982; Tinbergen, 1963). While ethology has a relatively long and interesting history (Burghardt, 1986; Jaynes, 1969), for its most recent recognition it owes much to the contributions of a small group of investigators, among whom Lorenz (1965, 1970, 1971, 1974), Von Frisch (1967), and Tinbergen (1951, 1972) have received widest recognition.

Currently, the ethological literature on various aspects of animal (including human) behavior is so voluminous and varied that it leaves one wondering what it is that ethologists do not study. Faced with similar concerns, Tinbergen (1963) suggested that, once behavior is adequately described and operationalized, ethologists study its ontogeny or development, its immediate causation or mechanisms, its adaptive significance or function, and its evolutionary origins. In the words of Hinde (1982),

> Suppose you were asked, 'Why does your thumb move in a different way from the other fingers?' You might give an answer in terms of the anatomy of the hand— the differences in skeletal structure and muscle attachments between the thumb and the other fingers: that would be an answer concerned with the immediate causation of thumb movement. You might give an answer in terms of the hand's embryology, describing how, as the finger rudiments developed, one came to have a different structure from the others. Or you might give a functional answer—an opposable thumb makes it easier for us to pick things up, climb trees, and so on. Or finally you might say that we are descended from monkey-like creatures, and monkeys have opposable thumbs, so of course we do too. This would be an answer in terms of evolutionary origin. All of these answers would be correct: no one would be complete.
>
> In the same way, ethologists are interested in questions of all four types of behavior. Indeed they believe that, although logically distinct and independent, questions concerning immediate causation, development, function and evolution are sometimes inter-fertile (p. 21).

As an example, we will briefly review the literature of cricket songs. The research involved is representative of ethological methodology. Our review includes the types of questions asked, the experimental subjects employed, the nature of the behavioral response studied and its measurement, comparative analyses within and across species, as well as how ecological and evolutionary factors were considered. This cricket-song example also can illustrate the process characteristic of ontogeny, causation, function, and evolution of species-typic isolation and of identification in simpler invertebrate systems. Invertebrates, and insects in particular, tell an interesting story (e.g., Wilson, 1975) and their message (even though unheard of in this volume) is important for an understanding of species-typic behavioral development.

Cricket-Song Study as an Example of Behavioral Analyses in Ethology

There are approximately 3,000 species of crickets, of which field crickets make up a special group of about 400. The field crickets are the most familiar. Relatively large, they are yellowish-brown insects known for their loud, musical chirping. Male crickets produce sounds by rubbing together stridulating areas located on the forewings and utilize a rapid fluttering motion to produce a typical vibrato chirp. The receiving auditory organs are tympana located within slits on the forelegs. Most cricket species chirp at night, some during the day, and others both day and night. In general, understanding of neurophysiological mechanisms involved in cricket bioacoustics has few parallels, if any, in the animal literature (Alexander, 1966; Bentley & Hoy, 1974; Ewing & Hoyle, 1964; Huber, 1962; Rose, 1986).

In a southeastern region of the United States during summer there are as many as 20 different species of tree crickets producing discrete sounds, mostly the male's calling song, the function of which is to attract the female for mating. How does a female distinguish the sounds of a conspecific? Studies have demonstrated that males of each species have a particular pulse rate in their song, and it is this pulse rate that provides a female with discriminative cues. It is also interesting to note that the metabolic and physiological processes in a cricket are functionally affected by outside temperatures, so that a pulse rate in the song changes with temperature, earning some species the appropriate label of "thermometer crickets." The refinement of the evolved system is remarkable when one considers that physiological mechanisms which determine females' responsiveness to a signal change at the same time in a fashion that parallels the males' pulse rate. The sound-producing repertoire of the male cricket serves a number of functions:

1. facilitating and establishing sexual contact (the calling song);
2. mediating sexual attraction at a relatively short distance (the courtship song);
3. signaling departure of a courted female (the courtship-interruption song);
4. repelling or dominating other males (the aggressive sound);
5. maintaining contact between a mated pair (the postcopulatory song);
6. a wide range of what appear to be recognition sounds (e.g., Alexander, 1966, 1968).

How does this brief commentary on cricket bioacoustics illustrate the importance of acoustic communication in cricket speciation and evolution? What are some of the factors that maintain the species-specific integrity of a gene pool of some 20 different species of tree crickets that are not geographically isolated? The species-specific characteristics of the male calling song and the recognition of that song by a conspecific female were identified as an important isolating mechanism (Alexander, 1966; Dixon & Cade, 1986; Walker, 1957; Wiedermann & Loher, 1984).

Viewed in the context of our understanding of evolutionary processes, crickets tell an interesting overt and covert story in evolutionary terms. Among the 3000 cricket species, many are isolated by their geography and habitat. When a number of species occupy the same habitat, then temporal, ethological, or mechanical isolating mechanisms maintain species integrity. Thus, one species will chirp at night and another during the day (temporal isolation). If more than one species occupy the same habitat and "sing" at the same time, then the differences in the pulse rate (ethological isolation) maintain species identity. Acoustic signals and communication serve in the prezygotic isolation of closely-related species.

The literature on the ontogeny of acoustic communication in crickets also deserves more attention from behavioral scientists than it has received to date. It should be kept in mind that many insects mature without hearing the signals of their own species, and that they sense many sounds that have absolutely no resemblance to signals that they as mature adults must eventually produce. As Alexander (1968) has pointed out, there must have been intensive selection pressure for resistance to irrelevant acoustic influences and toward fixed relationship between acoustic genotype and acoustic phenotype.

Experiments investigating the genetic correlates of communication signals in several species of crickets offer further support to this thesis (e.g., Alexander, 1966, 1968; Bentley & Hoy, 1974; Fulton, 1933). For example, as early as 1933, Fulton hybridized *Nemobius allardi* and *Nemobius tinnulus*. These two sibling species of ground crickets mature at the same time, overlap geographically and ecologically, but sing different songs. Fulton was able to develop F1 and F2 hybrids, carry out F1 backcrosses with parental species, and analyze the songs of various crosses. Fulton's results were generally clear cut and straightforward. Pulses in the song of F1 hybrids were delivered at a rate intermediate between those in the songs of the two parental generations. The songs of backcross progeny were more like the parent utilized in the backcross. Subsequent literature on other species has further elucidated the genetic determination of the song pattern of each cricket species. The songs are phenotypic expressions of different genotypes, thereby offering evidence that links together genetic information, developmental processes, structural and functional organization of the neuroendocrine system, and behavior (e.g., Bentley & Hoy, 1974; Schildberger, 1984).

In summary, crickets are sensitive to stimuli in other sensory channels: acoustic, chemical, visual, tactile, and thermal. This review has used one example to demonstrate how discrete acoustic signals function in species-typic isolation and identification, while it also offers overt and covert evidence for the proximate and the ultimate causation of such behaviors.

On the Relationship Between Ethological Theory and Research: Levels of Organization—Levels of Analysis

The development and the use of theory have been valued by researchers across disciplines and areas of inquiry. The characteristic thinking has been that theory generates research models and questions, thereby requiring that the empirical answers to those questions be referred back to evaluate merits of a particular model or, if need be, to modify or even discard an existing theory. Disciplined empiricism requires a theory, however informal or preliminary it may be or however difficult an investigator may find testing assumptions stemming from it.

The appreciation of what ethology is about is more meaningful if one is reminded of the early intellectual antecedents of present-day ethology. The clash involving an emphasis on laboratory-discovered facts as contrasted to naturalistic observation culminated in three famous debates at the French Academie des Sciences around the year 1830, in which the naturalistic evolutionary point of view suffered a profound defeat. Baron Cuvier had laboratory facts on his side, but as we have learned subsequently, by arguing for the immutability of the species, he was wrong in principle, whereas Geoffroy Saint-Hilaire was right in principle without the appropriate facts (Jaynes, 1969). The debates contributed to polarization between the two camps, with Cuvier's side insisting on the laboratory analysis and founding comparative psychology, while Geoffroy Saint-Hilaire's camp emphasized naturalistic observations and established ethology. Comparative neurophysiologist and protege of Cuvier, Pierre Flourens, the author of *Psychologie Comparee* (1864), is credited with developing a comparative psychology that synthesized the mechanistic neurophysiological approaches of Descartes' human psychology with Cuvier's animal psychology. It is worth noting, however, that during that same year and consistent with the intellectual bias of his school, Flourens (1876) published another book, leading French science's attack on Darwin's *Origin of Species* (1859). The comparative psychology that developed in North America around the turn of the century embraced the Darwinian view of the world, but it remained a laboratory science, and its failure to appreciate the importance of the ecological-naturalistic dimension of behavior contributed to its decline (e.g., Lockard, 1971).

By comparison, throughout the nineteenth century the naturalistic bias was advanced by other prominent biologists. Alfred Giard (1904) emphasized ethology and E. Haeckel (1898) pushed for "oecology" (presently ecology), then and now defined as the study of the relationships among organisms and environments. It is no accident that the more recent pioneers of ethology sought to avoid a dichotomy between field and laboratory research, and they succeeded in doing so under the conceptual framework of evolutionary theory (e.g., Eibl-Eibesfeldt, 1975; Hess, 1973; Jaynes, 1969; Lorenz, 1981; Schneirla, 1966; Thorpe, 1963; Tinbergen, 1951).

Levels of Organization—Levels of Analysis

Any behavioral problem can be conceived as varying along dimensions identified as levels of analysis. Each level can be defined in terms of its position on an information continuum. The major unifying and consensually valid theme in the ethological perspective is the synthetic theory of organic evolution.

When Darwin and Wallace in the 1850s proposed their theory of evolution by natural selection of the fittest and by specific examples demonstrated how these processes could account for the evolution of organisms, they planted the seeds of the powerful scientific and intellectual conceptualization that is still unfolding. From Malthus, Wallace and Darwin knew that organisms reproduced in far greater numbers than could be sustained by a particular environmental setting. Their observational evidence was that populations remain relatively constant. They therefore concluded that a large proportion of the offspring must fail to survive. Moreover, they knew that animals compete for the available resources of the environment and thereby participate in an active "struggle for existence" (Darwin, 1859/1869).

As Darwin (1859/1869) indicated:

> . . . owing to this struggle for life, any variation, however slight and from what-ever cause proceeding, if it be in any degree profitable to an individual of any species, in its infinitely complex relations to other organic beings and to external nature, will tend to the preservation of that individual and will generally be inher-ited by its offspring. The offspring, also, will thus have a better chance of surviv-ing, for, of the many individuals of any species which are periodically born, but a small number can survive. (p. 61)

Even though it was most important for the evolutionary theory that heritable variations be present in each generation, Darwin nevertheless freely conceded his ignorance of the mechanisms of inheritance. It was not until about 1900 that Mendel was rediscovered and that Hugo de Vries proposed his mutation theory by pointing out the likely possibility that the obvious morphological changes he observed in the evening primrose might provide the variations on which natural forces could exert selection pressure.

The major breakthrough and the beginnings of the modern synthesis surfaced in the 1930s, when R. A. Fisher (1930) published *The Genetical Theory of Natural Selection,* Dobzhansky (1937) produced *Genetics and the Origin of Species,* followed by Oparin's (1938) *The Origin of Life,* Mayr's (1942) *System-atics and the Origin of Species,* and Huxley's (1942) *Evolution: The Modern*

Synthesis. These works brought together diverse areas of human knowledge and inquiry. Organic evolution began to be viewed as a by-product of the chemical evolution of matter and biophysics, biochemistry and molecular biology surfaced as the new and exciting areas of inquiry. The new neo-Darwinian synthetic theory of organic evolution made sense out of taxonomy. It explained the fossil record as well as the fitness of adaptations between organisms and their habitats. The cell theory put forward convincingly in 1839 by German microscopists, Schleiden and Schwann, was given a new vision: The cell is a Mendelian unit carrying the genetic code of stored variability that is crucial to evolution and, at the same time, is a physiochemical entity obeying the laws of physics and chemistry. The bridge between particle physics and human evolution and ecology was formed. The door was left open for the new generation of Nobel laureates such as Watson and Crick (1953), who, by their elucidation of the double-helical, physiochemical structure of the DNA molecule and its role in heredity, provided one of the major empirical validations for the new synthesis.

Unfortunately, the behavioral sciences were largely left out of the modern synthesis (Dawkins, 1986; Hess, 1973; Lockard, 1971; Lorenz, 1965; Wilson, 1975). The reasons were many. The pursuit of the mysteries of life focused the concerns of the biological sciences on the molecular universe, thereby leaving the behavioral territory to psychology, sociology, anthropology, and psychiatry. In turn, many professionals in these disciplines found the nativist, materialist, determinist implications of the modern synthetic theory of organic evolution to be either irrelevant or difficult to accept and incorporate procedurally, professionally, politically, and personally. For example, until very recently the lack of emphasis on the role of hereditary factors in behavior has been one of the hallmarks of North American psychology and sociology. Thus, many behavioral scientists were surprised by the "unconventional" decision of the Nobel Foundation in 1973 to award the prize for physiology and medicine to three ethologists, Karl Von Frisch, Konrad Lorenz, and Nikko Tinbergen, thereby acknowledging the efforts of those individuals in bringing the study of behavior under the umbrella of the synthetic theory of organic evolution. With the subsequent advent of sociobiology (e.g., Wilson, 1975) and cultural materialism (Harris, 1966, 1979), the initial surprise gave way to exchanges characteristic of a paradigm clash (e.g., Cavalli-Sforza & Feldman, 1981; Gould, 1980; Rose, Lewontin, & Kamin, 1984; Lumsden & Wilson, 1981; Trivers, 1985).

Current ethology is occupied with four hierarchical biological questions and concerns: What are the ontogeny, causation, function, and evolution of behavior? Explanation and understanding require that attention be given to each of these questions and concerns and to the various levels of interrelationship among them. The magnitude of the hierarchical concerns requires a breadth of synthesis that transcends levels of analysis from genotype to behavior and ecology—a synthesis that transcends the extremes of levels of biological organization.

In general, the consensus among ethologists has been that: (a) organic evolution has been a by-product of the chemical evolution of matter, (b) animal species, including *Homo sapiens*, are the products of natural selection, and (c) genes are chemically code for phenotypic expressions. In terms of reproductive success, natural selection favors those animals whose genes, through their phenotypic expressions, successfully interact with the environment of the ecosystem. The above-listed considerations stem from the world view shared by ethologists (Dawkins, 1986). Even so, some considerations are often neglected. We now attempt to relate these considerations to levels of analysis in the behavioral sciences.

As can be seen in Fig. 4.1, the ethological model incorporates in a hierarchical fashion levels of organization from subatomic particles to ecosystems. No level of organization or analysis is conceived as more "important" or "adequate" than another, since a position on the information continuum is not in itself a criterion for importance or adequacy. The reduction of a behavioral problem to a neurophysiological one, or of a neurophysiological one to a biochemical one, does not in itself generate a more fundamental or a more important explanation of the original behavioral problem. Surely, we recognize that the water molecule has characteristics and properties independent of those of hydrogen and oxygen. At the same time, we must note that knowing the characteristics of hydrogen and oxygen does provide us with some important information about water. Thus, it

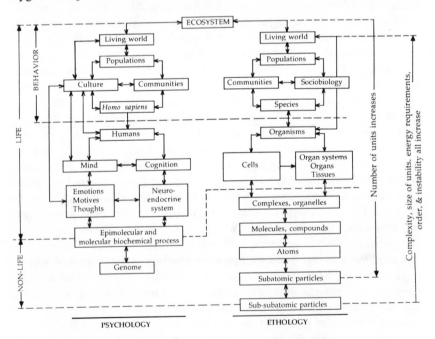

FIG. 4.1. Levels of analyses schematically illustrating ethological and psychological approaches to behavioral analyses.

follows that the usefulness and appropriateness of her particular level of analysis is circumscribed by theoretical orientation, parameters of the problem under investigation, and contextual circumstances, as well as by general purposes of the discipline or the investigator. Thus, as our introductory example indicates, a student in modern ethology investigating the behavioral biology of the cricket song would find it necessary to acquire at least some sophistication in language and the tools of genetics, neurophysiology and neuroanatomy, quantitative behavioral analysis, systematics, ecology, and evolution.

ETHOLOGY AND ATTACHMENT

The attachment behavior of young precocial fowl toward biologically-appropriate adults or surrogates including humans, was noted two thousand years ago (Hess & Petrovich, 1977). Konrad Lorenz's (1935) paper on companions as factors in the socialization of birds represents the first post-Darwinian experimental attempt to deal extensively with the phenomenon of "imprinting" (see Petrovich & Gewirtz, Chapter 5; for a review of the literature from a historical perspective, see Hess, 1973; Hess & Petrovich, 1977). The more recent interest in human attachment has been sparked by the elegant contributions of Bowlby (1958, 1969/1982, 1973, 1980) and by the derivative approach and refinements of Ainsworth (1969, 1982) and her associates (Ainsworth, Blehar, Waters, & Wall, 1978). Among students of human development, these contributions have come to be known as the *ethological approach to attachment.*

The attachment theory proposed by Bowlby (1969/1982) was developed in an attempt to extend and improve traditional psychoanalytic approaches. The three volumes of *Attachment and Loss* (1969, 1973, 1980) provide a modern synthesis that goes well beyond the modesty of Bowlby's original claims. Nevertheless, Ainsworth's (1969) observation that "In effect what Bowlby has attempted is to update psychoanalytic theory in the light of recent advances in biology" (p. 998) still rings true. Bowlby's (1969/1982) synthesis of psychoanalytic thought and ethological research was very compatible with the ethology of the 1950s and 1960s period. Patterns of infant-adult attachment were approached from a comparative cross-species perspective as evolved species-typical behavioral adaptations. Bowlby was careful to distinguish between "teleological assumptions" under which the purposes of behavior are assumed and "teleonomy" under which the contingencies facilitating the survival value of behavioral adaptations may be demonstrated. Bowlby attributed the evolutionary origins of attachment behavior to predatory selection pressures. This conceptualization of human attachment was articulated within the framework of biopsychosocial systems theory (Bowlby, 1969/1982; Bischof, 1975) that invites comparisons with levels of organization and analysis that we have identified as characteristic of the ethological approach.

If one reviews the methods and practices of present-day adherents of the ethological theory of attachment, there is found a mismatch between those conceptualizations and objectives of modern ethology (as we have elaborated them) (e.g., Ainsworth, Blehar, Waters, & Wall, 1978; Bretherton & Waters, 1985; Sroufe & Waters, 1977). In a striking contrast to the cricket song example, these contributions are characterized by the paucity of research on ontogeny, including mechanisms of causation, function, and evolution of attachment. Considerations of genetic, neurophysiological, neuroendocrine, functional analyses, the latter including such molar processes as perception, preverbal, nonverbal and verbal communication, and learning, and evolutionary processes of attachment are missing or are dealt with superficially.

In contemporary ethology, Darwinian formulations such as "adaptations for the good of the species" have given way to considerations of evolutionary strategies of ultimate causation and conditional probabilities in proximal development that are derived from theory and empirical evidence from both experimental and field ethology, population genetics, evolutionary biology, behavioral ecology, and developmental psychobiology. Among the researchers of human attachment, these developments have received but scant attention. We noted in an earlier section that Bowlby (1969/1982) was careful to distinguish between teleological and teleonomic assumptions. Admittedly, "adaptive" is a troublesome term incurring problems of teleology in its use, if ecologic-teleonomic contingencies of survival value are not specified. Moreover, given the biological history of *Homo sapiens,* various modes of adaptation may be outcomes of specific experiences rooted in learning and tradition as of genetically programmed processes. At some level of analysis, however, the modern view holds that conditional responses are an outcome from the coaction of these processes (probablistic epigenesis). Even so, analyses of these processes in a given ecological setting are required. Lack of sensitivity to these issues is noteworthy among human developmentalists investigating attachment under the aegis of ethology.

Contemporary ethology is neutral about the relative contributions of laboratory and field research. The consensual view holds that the problems of interest to researchers are to be found in nature. A laboratory is a tool that allows the investigator an opportunity to test specific hypotheses under controlled conditions and investigate experimentally puzzling aspects of behavioral development. In turn, laboratory solutions are evaluated in terms of their putative biological/ecological origins, thereby allowing researchers to explore the fitness of behavioral adaptations found in nature. By comparison, the application of the Strange-Situation laboratory procedure for assessing attachment has dominated the methodological landscape in the human-development approach to attachment under the conceptions of ethology. The relation of these laboratory assessments to the ecological dimensions of attachment have not been pursued systematically or with discipline (Lamb, Thompson, Gardner, Charnov, & Estes, 1984).

The treatment of functional aspects of behavior is limited. For example,

Waters' and Deane's (1985, p. 42) statement that "questions about what is learned during the attachment relationships, about the course of attachment after infancy, and about individual differences beyond security and anxiety have received little attention," is likely to be shared by any ethologists interested in molar and ecological dimensions of early socialization. The conceptualizations and research in modern ethology are characterized by testing hypotheses stemming from evolutionary processes of inclusive fitness, parental investment, and kin selection. Response to predation is just one measure of parental investment. Two decades ago, Bowlby (1969/1982) attributed the evolutionary origins of attachment to predatory selection pressure, a view that is still widely held by researchers of human development and by authors of texts of child development (e.g., Sroufe & Cooper, 1988). In contrast, from the perspective of contemporary ethology, the most plausible ultimate explanation of the origins of attachment is that behaviors denoting attachment increase the inclusive fitness of the individual whose mode of reproduction is characterized by intricate patterns of parental investment (Petrovich & Gewirtz, 1985; Petrovich, Gewirtz, & Hess, 1986).

REFERENCES

Ainsworth, M. D. S. (1969). Object relations, dependency and attachment: A theoretical review of the infant-mother relationship. *Child Development, 40,* 969–1025.

Ainsworth, M. D. S. (1982). Attachment: Retrospect and prospect. In C. M. Parkes & J. Stevenson-Hinde (Eds.), *The place of attachment in human behavior* (pp. 3–30). New York: Basic Books.

Ainsworth, M. D. S., Blehar, M. C., Waters, E., & Wall, S. (1978). *Patterns of attachment: A psychological study of the strange situation.* Hillsdale, NJ: Lawrence Erlbaum Associates.

Alexander, R. D. (1966). The evolution of cricket chirp. *Natural History, 75,* 26.31.

Alexander, R. D. (1968). "Arthropods." In T. A. Sebock (Ed.), *Animal communication.* Bloomington: Indiana University Press.

Bentley, D., & Hoy, R. R. (1974). The neurobiology of cricket song. *Scientific American, 231,* 34–44.

Bischoff, N. (1975). A systems approach toward the functional connections of attachment or fear. *Child Development, 46,* 801–817.

Bowlby, J. (1958). The nature of the child's tie to his mother. *International Journal of Psychoanalysis, 39,* 350–373.

Bowlby, J. (1969/1982). *Attachment and loss. Vol. 1. Attachment.* New York: Basic Books.

Bowlby, J. (1974). *Attachment and loss. Vol. 2. Separation anxiety and anger.* New York: Basic Books.

Bowlby, J. (1980). *Attachment and loss: Vol. 3. Loss, sadness, and depression.* New York: Basic Books.

Bretherton, I. (1985). Attachment theory: Retrospect and prospect. In I. Bretherton & E. Waters (Eds.), *Growing points of attachment theory and research: Monographs of the Society for Research in Child Development* (pp. 3–35), *50,* Nos. 1–2, Serial No. 209.

Burghardt, G. (1986). *Foundations of comparative ethology.* New York: Van Nostrand Reinhold.

Cavalli-Sforza, L. L., & Feldman, M. W. (1981). *Cultural transmission and evolution*. Princeton, NJ: Princeton University Press.

Darwin, C. (1869). *On the origin of species by means of natural selection, or the preservation of favored races in the struggle for life*. London: John Murray; New York: Appleton.

Dawkins, R. (1986). *The blind watchmaker*. New York: W. W. Norton.

Dixon, K. A., & Cade, W. (1986). Some factors influencing male-male aggression in the field cricket *Gryllus integer* (time of day, age, weight and sexual maturity. *Animal Behavior, 34*, 340–346.

Dobzhansky, T. (1937). *Genetics and the origin of species*. New York: Columbia University Press.

Eibl-Eibesfeldt, I. (1975). *Ethology: The biology of behavior*. New York: Holt, Rinehart & Winston.

Ewing, A., & Houle, G. (1965). Neuronal mechanism underlying control of sound production in a cricket: *Acheta domesticus*. *Journal of Experimental Biology, 43*, 139–153.

Fisher, R. A. (1930). *The genetical theory of natural selection*. Oxford: Clarendon.

Flourens, P. (1864). *Psychologie comparee*. Paris: Carnier Freres.

Frisch, K. von (1967). *The dance language and orientation of bees*. Cambridge, MA: Harvard University Press.

Fulton, B. B. (1933). Inheritance of song in hybrids of two subspecies of *Nemobius fasciatus* (Orthoptera). *Annals of the Entomological Society of America, 26*, 368–376.

Gewirtz, J., & Petrovich, S. B. (1982). Early social and attachment learning in the frame of organic and cultural evolution. In T. M. Field, A. Huston, H. C. Quay, L. Troll, & G. E. Finley (Eds.), *Review of human development* (pp. 3–19). New York: Wiley.

Giard, A. M. (1904). *Controverses transformistes*. Paris: C. Nand.

Gould, S. J. (1980). Is a new and general theory of evolution emerging? *Paleobiology, 6*, 119–130.

Haeckel, E. (1989). *Naturliche schopfungs-geschichte*. Berlin: Riemer.

Harlow, H. F. (1961). The development of affectional patterns in infant monkeys. In B. M. Foss (Ed.), *Determinants of infant behaviour*. London: Methuen.

Harris, M. (1966). The cultural ecology of India's sacred cattle. *Current Anthropology, 7*, 51–59.

Harris, M. (1979). *Cultural materialism: The struggle for a science of culture*. New York: Vintage Books.

Hess, E. H. (1973). *Imprinting: Early experience and the developmental psychobiology of attachment*. New York: Van Nostrand.

Hess, E. H., & Petrovich, S. B. (1973). The early development of parent-young interaction in nature. In J. R. Nesselroade & H. W. Reese (Eds.), *Life-span developmental psychology: Methodological issues* (pp. 25–42). New York: Academic Press.

Hess, E. H., & Petrovich, S. B. (Eds.) (1977). *Imprinting: Benchmark papers in animal behavior*. Stroudsburg, PA: Dawden, Hutchinson & Ross.

Hinde, R. A. (1974). *Biological bases of human behavior*. New York: McGraw-Hill.

Hinde, R. A. (1982). *Ethology*. New York: Oxford University Press.

Huber, F. (1962). Central nervous control of sound production in crickets and some speculations on its evolution. *Evolution, 16*, 429–442.

Huxley, J. S. (1942). *Evolution: The modern synthesis*. London: Allen and Unwin.

Jaynes, J. (1969). The historical origins of "ethology" and "comparative psychology." *Animal Behavior, 17*, 601–606.

Lamb, M. E., Thompson, R. A., Gardner, W., & Charnov, E. L. (1985). *Infant-mother attachment: The origins and developmental significance of individual differences in Strange Situation behavior*. Hillsdale, NJ: Lawrence Erlbaum Associates.

Lamb, M. E., Thompson, R. A., Garner, W. P., Charnov, E. L., & Estes, D. (1984). Security of infantile attachment as assessed in the "strange situation": Its study and biological interpretation. *The Behavioral and Brain Sciences, 7*, 127–171.

Lockard, R. B. (1971). Reflections on the fall of comparative psychology: Is there a message for us all? *American Psychologist, 26*, 168–179.

Lorenz, K. (1965). *Evolution and modification of behavior*. Chicago: University of Chicago Press.

Lorenz, K. (1970). *Studies in animal and human behavior, Vol. 1.* Cambridge, MA: Harvard University Press.

Lorenz, K. (1971). *Studies in animal and human behavior, Vol. 2.* Cambridge, MA: Harvard University Press.

Lorenz, K. Z. (1974). Analogy as a source of knowledge. *Science, 185,* 229–234.

Lorenz, K. Z. (1981). *The foundations of ethology*. New York: Springer-Verlag.

Lumsden, C. J., & Wilson, E. O. (1981). *Genes, mind and culture: The coevolutionary process.* Cambridge, MA: Harvard University Press.

Mayr, E. (1942). *Systematics and the origin of species*. New York: Columbia University Press.

Oparin, A. I. (1938). *The origin of life*. New York: Macmillan.

Petrovich, S. B., & Gewirtz, J. L. (1985). The attachment learning process and its relation to cultural and biological evolution: Proximate and ultimate considerations. In M. Reite & T. Field (Eds.), *The psychobiology of attachment and separation* (pp. 259–291). New York: Academic Press.

Petrovich, S. B., Gewirtz, J. L., & Hess, E. H. (1986). *Evolution and attachment*. Paper presented at the International Conference on Infant Studies, Los Angeles, California.

Rose, S., Lewontin, R. C., & Kamin, L. J. (1984). *Not in our genes*. Harmondsworth, Middlesex: Penguin.

Schneirla, T. C. (1966). Behavioral development and comparative psychology. *Quarterly Review of Biology, 41,* 283–302.

Sroufe, L. A., & Walters, E. (1977). Attachment as an organizational construct. *Child Development, 48,* 1184–1199.

Thorpe, W. H. (1966). *Learning and instinct in animals* (3rd ed.). Cambridge, MA: Harvard University Press.

Tinbergen, N. (1951). *The study of instinct*. Oxford: Clarendon.

Tinbergen, N. (1963). On aims and methods of ethology. *Zeitschrift fur psychologie, 20,* 410–433.

Tinbergen, N. (1972). *The animal and its world*. London: Allen and Unwin.

Trivers, R. (1985). *Social evolution*. Menlo Park, CA: Benjamin/Cummings.

Walker, T. J. (1957). Specificity in the response of female tree crickets to calling songs of the males. *Annals of the Entymological Society of America, 50,* 626–636.

Waters, E. (1981). Traits, behavioral systems, and relationships: Three models of infant-adult attachment. In K. Immelmann, G. W. Barlow, L. Petrinovich, & M. Main (Eds.), *Behavioral development: The Bielefeld Interdisciplinary Project* (pp. 621–650). Cambridge, England: Cambridge University Press.

Waters, E., & Deane, K. E. (1985). Defining and assessing individual differences in attachment relationships: Q-methodology and the organization of behavior in infancy and early childhood. In I. Bretherton & E. Waters (Eds.), *Growing points of attachment theory and research: Monographs of the Society for Research in Child Development* (pp. 41–65), *50,* Nos. 1–2, Serial No. 209.

Wiedenmann, G., & Loher, W. (1984). Circadian control of singing in crickets: Two different pacemakers for early evening and before dawn activity. *Journal of Insect Physiology, 30,* 145–151.

Wilson, E. O. (1975). *Sociobiology: The new synthesis*. Cambridge, MA: Belknap Harvard University Press.

5 Imprinting and Attachment: Proximate and Ultimate Considerations

Slobodan B. Petrovich
Jacob L. Gewirtz

ABSTRACT

Processes of imprinting and attachment are examined, and the attempt is made to cast the empirical record in a conceptual frame that views imprinting and attachment as a model of behavioral adaptation given the prevailing species-typical ecological contingencies affecting precocial and altricial-like species. The analysis explores issues in imprinting research and invites consideration of ways in which these may intersect with research on human attachment. The treatment compares processes of imprinting and attachment acquisition. In this, the heuristic emphasis is on the role of learning. As an example, the analysis focuses on the infant fear-of-strangers phenomenon. Moving toward synthesis, the analysis draws from the comparative literature and the concepts of inclusive fitness, kin selection, and parental investment, to speculate about the ultimate evolutionary-genetic origins of behaviors denoted by the terms imprinting and attachment. This synthesis proposes that attachment behaviors increase the inclusive fitness of individuals of species whose mode of reproduction is characterized by intricate patterns of parental investment. The kin-selection feature of the synthesis proposes that filial behaviors are likely to be found in interactions among organisms that share a significant proportion of their genes. Infanticide and serious infant abuse are thought likely to be observed under stressful conditions of intensified reproductive pressure, environmental-ecological depletion and/or where the mother's mate is not the infant's biological father. By focusing on the comparative life-span record, the treatment notes that, under ecologically-appropriate conditions, the processes of attachment acquisition and subsequent socialization are likely to result in the production of zygotes and offspring. In contrast, exposure to ecologically-inappropriate stimuli during early social development may place an organism at risk for isolation from a reproductive-generative population.

The imprinting phenomenon has had a relatively long and interesting history

(Hess, 1973; Hess & Petrovich, 1977; Spalding, 1873). The term *imprinting* represents the English translation of the German word *Pragung* (stamping in, coining), which Lorenz (1935) used to label a process by which the behavior of the newly hatched young of precocial avian species shows a pattern of close reliance on stimuli provided by a biologically-appropriate conspecific (e.g., parent) or, in its absence, by some other (surrogate) figure. Imprinting is typically denoted by the young animal's cued-response patterns to that parent. The term *attachment* ("tie," "bond") is a metaphor for the same type of outcome in altricial-like species. This chapter explores parallels between the behavior-pattern outcomes denoting *imprinting* in precocial species and those denoting *attachment* in altricial-like species. A comparative cross-species analyses focuses on the functionally-analogous features of the process, explores the role of learning in the proximal development of early social behavior, and relates the proximal mechanisms operating through the life span to the ultimate processes of evolutionary history.

From the 1950s on, imprinting research received a great deal of attention from students of early human social development. The striking features of the imprinting process have appealed to those who sought an animal model of attachment, bonding, and object fixation, even sexual channeling in the direction of biologically-inappropriate stimuli. In summarizing much of the comparative literature, Bowlby (1969, p. 223) concluded that the way in which human attachment behavior restricts orientation and preference to a focused discriminated figure is comparable to what has been observed in precocial mammalian and avian species and, thus, is qualified for consideration under the imprinting heading. However, this early enthusiasm for the imprinting paradigm appears to have dissipated. Current human-development textbooks seldom show those provocative photographs of Lorenz being followed by a line of goslings, or the earlier much-reprinted graph showing a critical period for imprinting in mallard ducklings. Hence, even the term "imprinting" may be an endangered term for the theorists of human development. This is regrettable, for numerous investigators have reiterated the similarities between the processes involved in imprinting in precocial species and those involved in early socialization and the formation of primary social bonds in such altricial-like species as the dog, the monkey, and the human (Hess, 1973; Hinde, 1974; Roy, 1980; Scott, 1960, 1968). Moreover, the identification of features of imprinting that are isomorphic with, parallel to, or diverge from the features of human attachment would make available to the developmentalist an expanded data base across species. Such an orientation has the potential for providing a more complete understanding of the proximal, life-span processes involved in behavioral development and, at the same time, potentially a better account of their evolutionary origins. Because in the past two decades theorists and researchers of human development have focused on the attachment phenomenon almost entirely, and on the imprinting phenomenon almost not at all, the focus of this chapter will emphasize in relatively greater detail features of the imprinting process.

This chapter outlines a frame for exploring the parallels between imprinting and attachment. It begins by examining imprinting phenomena and continues by identifying parallels between the infrahuman and human attachment cases. The chapter considers the functionally-analogous behavior patterns that are outcomes of the processes of imprinting and attachment. In this, the heuristic emphasis is on the proximal analysis and the role of learning. As an example, the analysis focuses on the infant fear-of-strangers phenomenon. In an evolutionary frame, the chapter concludes with a discussion of the role that filial behaviors (involved in both infrahuman imprinting and infrahuman and human attachment learning) play in fostering the inclusive fitness of individuals whose mode of reproduction is characterized by intricate patterns of parental investment.

IMPRINTING

In diverse avian and mammalian species, parent-offspring interactions may be initiated prior to hatching or birth to continue through an offspring's early development (e.g., Hess, 1973; Hinde, 1974; Roy, 1980). *Precocial* species are capable of complex perceptual-motor integration and locomotion soon after hatching/birth. They include the chicken, duck, goose, goat, and sheep. *Altricial*-like species are relatively underdeveloped for lengthy periods after hatching/birth. They include the pigeon, dove, cat, dog, monkey, and other primates as well as the human. When exposed to a moving object, the precocial-species hatchling-newborn is likely to follow that object then and, subsequently, while emitting biologically-prepared species-typical filial responses that denote imprinting. By comparison, newly hatched/newborn of altricial species possess a repertoire of nonlocomotor responses. In mammals the repertoire may include sucking, clinging, cooing, crying, and snuggling.

While attending to similarities between both precocial and altricial animal species and the human condition, there are also ecological and behavioral differences to be noted (Immelmann, 1975). Early students of imprinting used precocial, rapidly-maturing, avian species capable of complex perceptual-motor integration soon after hatching. It is highly adaptive for a mallard duckling to be able effectively to follow the hen and move in the water in the first 48 hours after hatching, because that behavioral repertoire mitigates against predation and provides access to food and shelter. The notions of preparedness and biological-ecological constraints are implicit in the imprinting conception. The ecological contingencies and species-specific maturation processes are surely different for the human infant, for whom there is a much better ecological and behavioral analog in altricial-species development (Hess, 1973; Klinghammer & Hess, 1964). Altricial young are relatively undeveloped at birth, and attachment and other social learning may require extensive periods of interaction with parents, siblings, and often also other members of a social unit (Cairns, 1966, 1972; Gewirtz, 1961, 1969; Hess, 1973; Hinde, 1974; Reite & Field, 1985; Roy,

1980). In this frame, Hess (1973) has argued that the imprinting process is characteristic of the ecology and socialization of precocial species and that its generalization to humans may be unwarranted and can deflect attention from the unique features of imprinting. In particular, the fact that critical periods in human behavioral development have yet to be shown conclusively led Hess to conclude that human "imprinting" was yet to be demonstrated.

Theoretical conceptualizations of imprinting have been numerous and varied (for overviews see Hess, 1973; Hess & Petrovich, 1977). Lorenz (1935) proposed that imprinting has several salient features: Imprinting takes place in a highly limited maturational period early in the life of the organism; imprinting may have lasting effects; resulting from natural selection, imprinting involves cues that are species typical; only specific response patterns of the young animal are involved in the imprinting to the social objects; and imprinting could affect later (e.g., sexual) behaviors not yet expressed by the young animal (p. 6).

Bateson's (1966) earliest conception of imprinting was that "The social preferences of many birds are restricted early in life to a specific class of objects by a learning process known as 'imprinting' " (p. 210). However, Bateson (1971) later even questioned the use of the term imprinting ". . . which refers to the learning process in the young, continues to be used even though the implication that the social preference develops as a result of a single brief experience is widely thought to be misleading" (p. 586).

Hess (1973) conceived imprinting to be "a type of process in which there is an extremely rapid attachment, during a specific critical period, of an innate behavior pattern to specific objects which thereafter become important elicitors of that behavior" (p. 65). Moreover, Hess viewed imprinting as:

". . . a particular type of learning process . . . which may be used by a species for the formation of a filial-maternal bond, pair formation, environment attachment, food preferences and perhaps other cases involving some sort of object-response relationship. It is, furthermore, a genetically programmed learning, with some species-specific constraints upon the kind of object that may be learned and upon the time of learning. In other words, imprinting is a genotype-dependent ontogenic process" (Hess, 1973, p. 351).

For Scott (1960), ". . . imprinting is a special example of the process of the formation of primary social relationships . . ." (p. 269). Scott conceived of imprinting in terms of a "primary social relationship," "primary bond," or "primary socialization" (1967, 1968). Sluckin (1965) defined imprinting as ". . . the formation by young precocial birds of relatively specific attachments" (p. 15).

Despite disagreements along some dimensions, all imprinting conceptualizations have assumed that learning is involved in the process, of which filial behaviors denoting social bonds/relationships are the outcome. Thus, Lorenz

(1935) and Hess (1959, 1973) have emphasized innate preparedness and biological constraints on the learning process, Sluckin (1962, 1965) and Salzen (1962, 1967) a perceptual-discrepancy learning basis for imprinting (that resurfaces subsequently in a modified form as the incongruity hypothesis underlying the fear-of-strangers phenomenon), Gewirtz (1961) an operant-learning conceptualization, and Hoffman and Ratner (1973a) a conceptualization in terms of several learning paradigms.

Methodological and Conceptual Issues

Scientists investigate a problem in a nonrandom way (Brush, 1974; Kuhn, 1962; Watson, 1968). In a conventional frame, theoretical orientations generate the models and hypotheses to be tested. The pursuit of the answer imposes its peculiar constraints on the experimental methodology embracing subjects, instrumentation, and data interpretation.

A critical assessment of the imprinting or attachment literatures is beyond the scope of this paper. Even so, some imprinting issues that contributed to disagreements about interpretations of research finding deserve special attention. For instance, subjects heterogeneous with respect to biological history and sensory capacity were obtained from diverse settings and sources. Subjects were maintained under diverse conditions and exposed to different experiences prenatally, postnatally, during imprinting exposure, as well as between imprinting and the subsequent imprinting assessment. Properties of imprinting stimuli and to what degree they involved movement differed. Procedures and instrumentation utilized to imprint subjects varied considerably from one laboratory to the next— some used straight runways, some circular ones, and others a circular apparatus without runways (Shapiro, 1970, 1980). Although there was no consensus about imprinting procedures and measures of the consequences of the imprinting experience (Guhl & Fisher, 1969; Hess, 1973; Sluckin 1972), the results were often interpreted as if imprinting were a unitary, cross-species, causal process independent of the operation of the above array of variables.

In the frame of imprinting research, the issue of continuity versus discontinuity of behavioral development can be collapsed down to the question of observations being made in terms of developmental versus post-hatch age in assessing the "sensitive period" for imprinting. Thus, nativistically-oriented discontinuity theorists found persuasive evidence for critical periods in terms of posthatch age (e.g., Hess, 1959, 1962, 1973). At the same time, it is not surprising that some theorists have accepted the utility of developmental age (e.g., Bateson, 1966, 1971; Hinde, 1970, 1974). Moreover, the parameters of the critical period for imprinting in birds have been modified by post-hatching experiences (e.g., Bateson, 1964, 1979; Gaioni, Hoffman, & DePaulo, 1978). These findings supported an interpretation of imprinting not constrained by considerations of critical periods in development based on age measures.

Compelling trends emerged from reports focusing on prenatal determinants of imprinting. A few days before hatching, ducklings and the brooding hen exchange signals in a vocal-auditory channel (Gottlieb, 1968). Ducklings are also capable of prenatal auditory discrimination, and natural maternal calls can acquire control over specific embryonic movements that are typically performed prior to hatching (Gottlieb, 1971; Heaton, 1972). Further, in nature some mallard hens appear biologically prepared to respond to vocal-auditory stimulation from their eggs as early as incubation-day 19, and the preference for specific features of the hen's call may develop in the duckling prior to hatching (Hess, 1972, 1973; Hess & Petrovich, 1973). These converging lines of evidence support the thesis that processes underlying imprinting manifest themselves prenatally, and that the demonstration of a critical period for imprinting based on posthatch age may require sampling the organism's behavior at the time it is biologically prepared to integrate sensory inputs across perceptual channels (Gottlieb, 1968, 1981; Hess, 1973). Subsequent research has revealed that for the development of the imprinting/attachment bond, species exploit a mix of sensory modalities, including the chemical, auditory, tactile, and thermal. When some of these ecological, contextual, or species-specific differences were filtered out, the emerging picture supported the thesis that many animals imprint/attach and that the development of such a process promotes the survival of the individual.

The Ecology of Learning Underlying Imprinting and Attachment

Different terms typically have been applied in precocial and altricial species to the process wherein, through systematic early exposure, offspring filial responses rapidly acquire a social-object focus, ordinarily the biological mother. It has been noted that the process has been termed "imprinting" in precocial species and "attachment" in altricial-like species. Given the prevailing ecological constraints, the ways responses denoting infant imprinting or attachment became focused on, and restricted to, a discriminated social object in precocial species and in such altricial-like mammals as infrahuman and human primates appear similar and functionally analogous.

On this planet, all animals have a common code of life. In addition, the lower the level of intraorganismic structure and function, the greater the phylogenetic similarity (e.g., comparative analyses of human and infrahuman tissues, cells, and hormones such as testosterone). The similarity of structure and function also increases across all levels of organization as the proximity to a common ancestor increases (see comparative analyses of human and other primate intraorganismic and organismic processes). Further, the study of the ecological adaptation of behavior—teleonomy—has provided presumptive evidence for the thesis that similar behaviors among unrelated, or distantly related, species as well as different behaviors among phylogenetically closely related species can result from differential survival values of behavioral adaptations to selection pressures characteristic of contingency demands of species-typical ecological niches (e.g., Eisenberg, 1982; Petrovich, 1978; Pittendrigh, 1958; Tinbergen, 1972). Thus, similar behavioral functions denoting imprinting and attachment across individuals of different species often have identical survival value and provide information on how similar selection pressures generate, through parallel or convergent evolution, analogous behavioral outcomes (Petrovich & Gewirtz, 1985).

In this frame, a comparison of similarities and differences among human and infrahuman species may be useful. Each species often reveals unique patterns of behavior. What is obscure, rudimentary, or nonexistent in one species may be displayed and exaggerated in another. By cataloging the behavioral patterns denoting attachment in different species, it may be possible to filter out the significance of specific features of the process. Thus, behavior patterns ranging from obscure to exaggerated stand better chances of being objectively described and understood from both phylogenetic and ontogenetic standpoints. Classificatory models derived from such data are capable of establishing interspecies comparisons of homologous behaviors (behavioral similarities due to common descent) and of functionally analogous behaviors (behavioral similarities based on consideration of commonality of function rather than on similarities in the genotype or in the structure).

The salient features of the comparative analogy rest on a comparison of the degree of similarity between behavior denoting human attachment and animal imprinting or attachment along four dimensions: (1) the contextual, situational-ecological, (2) the topographic and functional, (3) the development and/or acquisition of underlying mediating processes, and (4) the nature of the responding to systematic manipulation.

A comparison of the processes of imprinting-attachment may be made in genetic-biochemical terms, in which cases animal subjects may be valuable experimental tools. In other cases, development and manifestation of behavior may be mediated by neurophysiological factors (neurohormones, hormones, neural maturation), and laboratory rats, cats, and monkeys possess many functional characteristics that make them useful research subjects. Among behavioral mediating mechanisms are early experience, perception, learning, and socialization. In this case also a choice of the appropriate animal model depends on the behavioral mechanism of imprinting or attachment that is being investigated (e.g., Reite & Field, 1985; Roy, 1980). Thus, the terms imprinting and attachment are labels, heuristic tools, abstractions conceived to vary along a dimension of theoretical and analytical abstraction comprised of various levels of behavioral analysis, ranging from those on a microlevel (e.g., biochemical, physiological analyses) to those on a macrolevel (e.g., social, ecological analyses) (e.g., Hess, 1973; Reite & Field, 1985).

In a typical experimental demonstration of imprinting, a moving object is presented to a newly-hatched duckling (somewhere between 12 and 24 hours).

The subject responds filially by approaching, following, and snuggling up to the moving object, and by emitting calls denoting contentedness. If the object is withdrawn, the duckling emits calls denoting distress, coupled with irregular bursts of locomotor activity. When tested at some later point in time, the duckling again approaches and follows the original object to which it was imprinted. A few days after hatching and imprinting, the duckling also actively avoids unfamiliar objects.

It was noted that the early systematic investigators of imprinting in precocial species (Lorenz, 1935; Hess, 1959, 1964, 1973) interpreted this behavior-event pattern to mean that imprinting involved biologically-constrained early learning with some distinct, perhaps unique, features. However, since the pattern did not involve obvious reinforcers (food or water) for the filial response, the learning process was open to speculation. A suggestion was offered by Fabricius (1962) that the stimulation provided by the movement of the imprinting stimulus in the visual field appeared to be "innately reinforcing." Fabricius' assumption is problematic at the molar-analytic level, where only stimuli providing extrinsic reinforcers for features of behavior can be entertained in operant learning. Even so, the assumption of a "reinforcer" in imprinting received subsequent support from a mechanism uncovered in studies showing that representative vertebrate species (frog, rabbit, pigeon, cat, monkey) possess neural sites that respond innately only when a subject is exposed to stimulation stemming from the movement of an object across the visual field (Hubel, 1978; McIlwain, 1972). To be sure, for the operational reinforcer to be confirmed at the molar level, the stimulus change would have to be contingent on the filial behavior which, in turn, would have to increase in rate (or in some other attribute).

The relevance of Hubel's (1978, p. 47) findings to early social development becomes apparent when one considers that social privation may lead to abnormalities in the structural organization of the neural system mediating the expression of normal social behavior. In turn, these interpretations are consistent with imprinting-research evidence that it is the *moving* stimulus object that elicits filial behavior (James, 1959; Salzen, 1962). If stationary, the same object fails to elicit filial behavior (Hoffman, Eiserer, & Singer, 1972). Moreover, the static components of the imprinting stimulus (size, shape, color) apparently acquire the capacity to elicit innate filial reactions as a result of temporal and spatial association with the stimulation provided by movement of the duckling and the imprinting object. The research exploring signal processing in the duckling's auditory channel has produced similar interpretations. The recognition of a species-typical call and its efficacy as a vocal imprinting stimulus apparently depends on a summation of the outputs from a set of feature detectors, each sensitive to a particular acoustic feature of the call (Gottlieb, 1981; Gaioni & Evans, 1985). (For infant research parallels, see Papoušek, Papoušek, Soumi, & Rahn, Chapter 6.)

These findings of the innate efficacy of visual and auditory movement stimulation have enabled researchers on the imprinting process to conceptualize the importance of sensory stimuli that a mallard hen emits in the natural setting and the hypothetical neurophysiology of events that seem to mediate imprinting. Similar considerations led Hoffman and colleagues (Hoffman & DePaulo, 1977; Hoffman & Ratner, 1973a) to proposed a reinforcement model for learning processes that underlie the formation of imprinting and attachment. The Hoffman et al model is based on five premises that are consistent with previously present-ed empirical evidence: (1) precocial birds are innately prepared to respond filially to specific stimuli emitted by the moving, imprinting object; (2) stimuli that elicit innate filial responses function as reinforcers when contingent upon filial re-sponses; (3) the features of the object (e.g., size, shape, color) that were original-ly neutral with respect to filial behavior may elicit such behavior because over time they are associated-paired with the innately-potent stimuli; (4) ducklings show an increasing tendency over the first few days after hatching to respond fearfully to novel imprinting objects; and (5) the behavior of a naive duckling to a novel social object reflects a resolution of the competing tendencies that may be aroused by a particular stimulus to respond filially or fearfully.

The features of the Hoffman et al. analyses of imprinting and attachment are similar to those proposed earlier by Gewirtz (1961). He presented an account of the underlying process for both the imprinting and attachment in operant-learning terms. Paralleling the ethological analyses of that period, Gewirtz's treatment attempted to differentiate the roles of innate unconditioned stimuli (releasers) from stimuli that may cue, shape, and maintain filial responses (discriminative and reinforcing stimuli). In his analysis of the underlying process, Gewirtz detailed the concurrent acquisition of the filial behaviors denoting attachment of infant to parent and of parent to infant, assuming that both parent and infant respond differentially and synchronously to the other's behaviors. With examples from diverse interaction situations, Gewirtz illustrated how the responses of each actor could concurrently influence (condition) the responses of the other. Stimuli provided by the appearance and behavior of the parent could acquire discrimi-native and reinforcing control over diverse infant responses, while stimuli from the appearance and behavior of the infant could acquire discriminative and rein-forcing control over various adult responses. These concurrent control processes denote the acquisition by each of an attachment to the other. This conditioning approach was open to biological preparedness, the operation of unconditioned stimuli (releasers) for species-specific responses, and the like, as identified in animal-behavior research lore of that time.

ATTACHMENT

In approaches to the comparative social behavior of both infrahumans and hu-mans, diverse researchers have dealt, in research and theory, with imprint-ing/attachment phenomena as well as gregariousness and ties that develop between humans and animals of some species (Harlow, 1958, 1966; Hinde, 1974; Scott, 1960, 1967). The work of Bowlby (1958, 1969) has provided the impetus for combining selected psychoanalytic and ethological assumptions with systems-theory conceptions. Bowlby (1958) applied the metaphor "attachment" to label a child's "affectional tie," particularly to its mother-figure. Following Bowlby's lead, others have used the term similarly (e.g., Ainsworth, 1969; Schaffer & Emerson, 1964). In the context of the disruption of early mother-child relationships, Yarrow (1956, 1964, 1967) first used the term "object relationship" and later the term "focused [individualized] relationship" to label what seem to be some of the same behavior systems of the human infant toward its mother-figure. Much of the contemporary flavor of the attachment concept derives from the work of Bowlby (1958, 1969, 1973) and Ainsworth (1972; Ainsworth, Blehar, Waters, & Wall, 1978) and, in the last two decades, particularly through use of the Strange-Situation laboratory procedure for assessing attachment (Ainsworth & Wittig, 1969; Lamb, Thompson, Gardner, Charnov, & Estes, 1984).

In a parallel vein, Harlow and his associates, also employing a systems-theory emphasis (Harlow & Harlow, 1965), proposed the terms "affectional attachment" (Harlow & Zimmerman, 1959) and "affectional system" [which passes through a "comfort and attachment" stage (Harlow & Harlow, 1965, 1966)] to label behavior systems that "bind" the macaque infant first to its mother and then to others in the course of development. In a similar way, Mason (1970) has used the term attachment (apparently synonymously with the term emotional dependence—p. 53) to order the clinging behavior pattern of infrahuman primates. Like Harlow, Scott (1960, 1967), who applied the terms "primary social relationship," "primary bond," or "social attachment" to the patterned behaviors within species of animals with regard to another (or others), assumed this relationship develops in mammals (including humans) dependent on environmental stimulation, requiring "contact" with the mother or others during the species-typical "critical period." In contrast, Cairns (1966) proposed that social attachment in mammals is acquired as a function of association (learning) with an object in a given context, but also of the object's cue weight; and Gewirtz (1961) used the attachment term to summarize the mostly-positive stimulus control (assumed acquired via operant learning) over a variety of the child's orienting and approach responses made in connection with its mother-figure or some other individual.

Bowlby's (1969) synthesis of the literature (and Ainsworth's associated approach—e.g., 1969, 1972; Ainsworth et al., 1978) has greatly influenced the current views of human attachment. Given the dyadic nature of socialization and the species-typical plasticity of *Homo sapiens*, it is useful in this frame to differentiate between proximal approaches to attachment that do not employ conditioning paradigms (e.g., Bowlby, 1958, 1969; Gray, 1958) and proximal approaches that do (e.g., Cairns, 1966; Gewirtz, 1961, 1972b, 1972c; Hoffman

& Ratner, 1973a; Hoffman & DePaulo, 1977). Bowlby's and Gray's conceptualizations stopped short of specifying the role of learning in imprinting, with Bowlby employing instead a goal-direction systems-theory conception. In the context of our focus on proximate acquisition mechanisms, we here emphasize such learning processes in our approach to the phenomena of imprinting/attachment and to socialization in general.

We noted earlier that learning conceptions underlies the classic ethological theories of imprinting, even nativistic theories. Of the latter, Lorenz (1935, 1965) and Hess (1959, 1964, 1973) assumed that imprinting involves biologically-constrained early learning with distinct features. In this frame, it is paradoxical that the theorists of attachment who have relied upon ethological theory and, indeed, have been said to represent the ethological approach to attachment, in particular, Bowlby (1958, 1969), Ainsworth (1969, 1972; Ainsworth et al., 1978) and their associates, have not applied behavioral learning conceptions to the attachment process.

In counterpoint, Gewirtz (1961) presented an early proximal account both to imprinting and attachment employing basic operant-learning paradigms and detailing how the infant's head turns, eye contacts, smiles, protests, and cries, being reinforced and maintained potentially by a mother's systematic responding to them, in that very same context might be reinforcing/maintaining other responses of the mother that the infant's head turns, eye contacts, smiles, cry cessations, and other social behaviors followed routinely (Gewirtz, 1969b, 1972a, 1972b, 1978). These concurrent conditioning processes might occur even without the mother's awareness that her own responses were changing systematically (Gewirtz & Boyd, 1977). The efficacy of the synchrony or mesh among sequential infant and maternal stimuli and behavior might vary for mother-infant pairs, although the modal intrapair acquired-control pattern denoting the attachment of each actor to the other would ordinarily be a synchronous one, converging on the concept of "psychobiological attunement" proposed by Field (1985). A series of paradigmatic experiments on these reciprocal-influence processes was reported (Gewirtz & Boyd, 1977). This theoretical approach to potential conditioning mechanisms underlying infant attachment (e.g., Gewirtz, 1961) and to the influence, via conditioning mechanisms, of infant behavior on maternal responses (Gewirtz & Boyd, 1977), is compatible with diverse avian and mammalian analyses (Hinde, 1974; Hoffman & DePaulo, 1977; Hoffman & Ratner, 1973; Roy, 1980).

Imprinting, Attachment, and the Origins of the Fear Response

Fear reactions to novel stimuli incorporating features that innately evoke filial responses are weak or difficult to identify in ducklings during the first day after hatching. By the time a duckling is a few days old, however, its avoidance of unfamiliar objects may be demonstrated readily (e.g., Hess, 1973; Hoffman & Ratner, 1973b; Hoffman, 1978; Salzen, 1962). This post-hatch age-related development of the fear response to novel stimuli has been assumed typically to have an innate maturational basis (e.g., Hess, 1973; Eibl-Eibesfeldt, 1975). Even so, one-day-old ducklings already imprinted to a particular object have been shown to react positively to a second stimulus object when the first one is withdrawn. A preference test demonstrated those ducklings were able to discriminate the novel stimulus from the one to which they were originally imprinted. Thus, the incongruity between the two objects did not prevent an affirmative response toward the novel one (Hoffman, 1978; Hoffman & Ratner, 1973b). This result is similar to Schaffer's (1966), who found that human infants are capable of discriminating their mother from strangers several months before they manifest stranger fear. According to Schaffer (1966, p. 103), an "age gap" exists during which the stranger is perceived as different but not as frightening. The capacity to distinguish between the familiar and the novel appears to antedate stranger fear, and thus may be a necessary, but not sufficient, condition for evoking stranger fear.

Field and laboratory reports on the imprinting of precocial species have demonstrated that, following imprinting to the object, a fear response is typically exhibited to other potential surrogates ("strangers") by the imprinted young organism (Hess, 1973; Hoffman, 1974; Hoffman & Ratner, 1973a; Hoffman & DePaulo, 1977). As indicated, the parameters of the critical-sensitive period for imprinting and of manifestation of the fear response are debatable (e.g., Bateson, 1979; Gottlieb, 1981; Hess, 1973; Ratner & Hoffman, 1974). Even so, the available reports have contributed to a dominant conceptual mind-set in the psychological-development literature to view the origins of stranger fear in altricial-like species, including the human, as the outcome of a process analogous to the one that restricts social preferences in precocial species under drastically different ecological contingencies.

Recent theory underlying much of the research of human infant fear of strangers in the main has attributed the phenomenon to emergent maturational factors, implying that there is an inherent disposition for very young children to avoid persons perceived as nonparents. No systematic attempts have been made to investigate whether the discriminations between familiar and stranger persons is a necessary or sufficient condition for evoking stranger fear, much less what the contributions are to the stranger-fear outcomes of the functional difference involved or the role of experiential-learning processes. The maturational position holds that stranger fear arises predominantly from the ongoing differentiation in development of the infant's perceptual, cognitive or neurophysiological capacities (e.g., Decarie, 1974; Eibl-Eibesfeldt, 1975, 1979; Emde et al., 1976; Freedman, 1965; Hebb, 1946; Lewis & Brooks, 1974). The representative explanations of a negative reaction to strangers have clustered around an "incongruity-discrepancy hypothesis," which predicts that infant's affective reactions are elicited by strangers as novel events (e.g., Hebb, 1946; Kagan, 1974; Schaffer, 1966), discrepant from a concept of the familiar (that must be based on an experiential-learning process as Hebb, 1946, has noted). However, as Haith and Campos (1977) have observed, the incongruity-discrepancy hypothesis suffers on three counts: (1) the nature of the presumed "incongruity" processes is unclear; (2) no metric is provided for determining the degree and sufficiency of the incongruity; and (3) there is the unresolved issue of whether incongruity-discrepancy (however measured) elicits fear or only prepares an appropriate affective response. Those critics might have added that the discrepancy hypothesis also loses credibility because of the considerable variability of human infant responding to strangers.

Given the developmental and ecological malleability of *Homo sapiens*, diverse effects of procedural, contextual-ecological, control, experiential, and stranger variables on the behavior complex denoting stranger fear/wariness have been demonstrated (e.g., Lewis & Rosenblum, 1974; Sroufe, 1977). These findings appear less puzzling when organized, as we do below, in a constructive analysis under a prepared, constrained process theory of learning that treats the infant's behavior as reflecting a biologically prepared sensitive discrimination and response differentiation in early life.

There have been ample demonstrations of operant learning in early life, involving such responses as cries, eye contacts, head turns, departure and separation protests, smiles and sucks (e.g., Brackbill, 1958; Caron, 1967; Etzel & Gewirtz, 1967; Gewirtz & Pelaez-Nogueras, Chapter 7 this volume, 1987; Paulson, 1983). Further, that human infants appear to have the capacity to make the discriminations that underlie or comprise early learning is supported by evidence that even neonates can discriminate and imitate facial expressions (Field, Woodson, Greenberg, & Cohen, 1982). Other studies have demonstrated that neonates can discriminate their mothers' face (Carpenter, 1974; Field, Cohen, Garcia, & Greenberg, 1983) and voice (DeCasper & Fifer, 1980) in the first days of life from the face and voice of female "strangers." As under alternative paradigms, we conceive learning under the operant paradigm to involve preparedness and constraint (Fitzgerald & Brackbill, 1976; Gewirtz, 1972b, 1972d; Hinde & Stevenson-Hinde, 1973). Even so, the molar learning analysis advanced below may be evaluated on its own terms, without reference to preparedness and constraining processes, and can stimulate research on the stranger-fear process. We here note only that such processes may include the presence or absence of facilitators or inhibitors of endogenous or exogenous origin.

To exemplify how learning can underlie stranger fear, consider the finding that strangers who interfere or prepare to interfere with an infant's ongoing activities produce responses denoting fear in the infant (Schaffer, 1966; Waters, Matas, & Sroufe, 1975). Such responses as pulling away from the stranger and making a cry face may be cued by preparatory movements of the strangers and maintained by the consequence of the stranger's withdrawal. In different circumstances, when an infant is being held and handled by a stranger, its fearful responses may result in its being released by the stranger, and those responses can be maintained by the resulting escape from the stranger's grip (Skarin, 1977). Concurrently, other responses in the infant's repertoire might be maintained by contingent maternal intervention. Consider the finding that the infant picked up by a stranger in the mother's presence exhibits greatest distress crying (Emde, Gaensbaur, & Harmon, 1976). This distress crying may be cued simply by the presence of the mother or by social-reference cues that she provides, and differentiated and maintained when she retrieves her crying infant from the stranger (Gewirtz, 1972a, 1977; Gewirtz & Pelaez-Nogueras, 1987; Schaffer & Emerson, 1964). The finding that strangers in view but distant from the infant, or females, produce less distress crying than nearby strangers, or males, may indicate that the infant discriminates nearby from distant strangers (Skarin, 1977; Sroufe, 1977) and females from males (Greenberg, Hillman, & Grice, 1973; Morgan & Ricciuti, 1969; Skarin, 1977), conceivably due to the differential consequences provided for the discrimination by the behavior of both types of strangers toward the infant.

Because infants infrequently cry or exhibit extreme distress when approached by a stranger, their behavior has been characterized often as only mildly negative or wary (Skarin, 1977; Sroufe, 1977; Waters et al., 1975). Hence, the utility of a specific emotional state or underlying process of fixed endogenous-maturational origin as explanation for these behaviors is in question and alternative hypotheses are required. Kaltenbach, Weinraub, and Fullard (1980) have reported that the mother showed significantly more wariness as the female-stranger's proximity toward her and her infant increased. Their findings suggest that wariness in a stranger-presence context may not be restricted to infants at a particular developmental level, and may reflect as much the parent's and child's history as the contextual and ecological circumstances of the experimental setting. Thus, the Kaltenbach et al. interpretation is that wariness is a socially-adaptive response of both infant and adult to an uninvited and problematic interpersonal interaction.

Similarly, in the present analysis the infant is viewed as an increasingly-sophisticated participant across social situations, discriminating cues provided by its mother, familiar adults, the stranger and the ecological setting. Specifically, by providing a model, cues or consequences for her infant's behavior, an adult's wariness in the presence of a stranger could provide an effective context for fear/wariness learning by the infant in such settings. Likewise, the finding of Clarke-Stewart and colleagues that infants having positive experiences with their mothers respond positively to strangers is to be expected under an operant-learning model, based on the assumption that positive experiences connote maternal cues and reinforcers appropriately provided, that the infant may generalize reinforced responses to strangers in first encounters with them, and that, as did the mother, those strangers will maintain/reinforce those infant responses (Clarke-Stewart, VanderStoep, & Killian, 1979; Clarke-Stewart, Umeh, Snow, & Pederson, 1980).

This account of a developmental fear-of-the-stranger milestone emphasizes experiences organized by a prepared-, constrained-learning paradigm and offers an alternative to the maturational, genetically-programmed account of the process underlying occasional infant behaviors denoting fear of strangers or lack of affiliation with them. The present account assumes that some infants may readily learn the consequences of showing distress or avoidance in the presence of strangers, and not only to those who behave towards them in disagreeable ways. The infants manifest their bio-social preparedness to learn and then learn to respond in ways available to them, by fussing, crying and generating non-affiliative behaviors that remove pre-aversive cues, terminating social contact. Some of these responses are cued and maintained by the stimuli (including consequences) provided by the stranger's behavior, some by the stimuli (including reference cues and positive social consequences) and the modeling provided by the mother's behavior, and some by the contextual factors that are present in the different settings where learning has taken place. It has not been necessary in this analysis to attribute invariant, pre-programmed aversiveness to the stimulus complex provided by the stranger. Rather, it has been noted that unfamiliar persons whose behaviors cue preparations to interfere with the infant's ongoing activities can produce stranger-fear responses in the infant, and that those infant responses can terminate the social encounter. This view is consistent with evidence that unfamiliar persons approaching an infant with toys, or in a noninterfering manner, and soliciting play, can produce affiliative behavior in the infant. In this instance, it may be misleading to conceive that infants respond to "strangers." Instead, infants in specific contexts respond to stimulus complexes provided by the appearance and behavior of particular people with whom they have had limited or no prior contact. Thus, it is proposed that much of what has been termed "stranger fear" is a function of the infant's developmental level and the history involving different stranger initiations to the infant, the presence or absence of cues provided by the mother to the infant about the stranger in the stranger's presence (social referencing), and the mother's reaction to the infant's response (reinforcement or aversion). On this basis, we have presented a parsimonious account for understanding the result pattern that apparently similar stimulus complexes provided by the "stranger" may lead infants to manifest such diverse responses as affiliation, neutrality, escape and avoidance.

IMPRINTING/ATTACHMENT BEHAVIORS INCREASE INCLUSIVE FITNESS IN AN EVOLUTIONARY FRAME

While those researchers of human development who conceive of themselves as operating within an ethological frame have called for filling in the evolutionary gaps in our understanding of imprinting/attachment, there have been few such advances in the last decade. In this section, we begin the necessary analysis. Earlier in this paper and elsewhere (this volume, Chapters 2 and 6), the review of research on a variety of avian and mammalian species has exemplified the role of learning underlying the adaptive process involved in the proximal development of imprinting/attachment behavior. However, an evolutionary-historical perspective for the "ultimate explanation" of the origins of such attachment behavior through biological time requires different considerations from those that are typically employed during life spans by the molar-behavioral scientist in an approach to learning phenomena. The present analysis focuses on the bio-behavioral antecedents and evolutionary processes of *inclusive fitness, kin selection,* and *parental investment* in an attempt to develop an account of the proximate developmental mechanisms operating through the life span in terms of the ultimate processes of evolutionary history.

The term *inclusive fitness* represents a measure of the survival value (i.e., frequency) of genes in the reproductive population, in addition to contributions an individual may have on the reproductive success of others with whom genes are shared. The term *kin selection* refers to behaviors that may lower one individual's reproductive success but enhance the reproductive success of biological relatives. The term *parental investment* refers to any investment by a parent in an offspring that increases the offspring's chances of survival (enhanced reproductive success) at the cost of the parent's ability to invest in others.

In our view, the most plausible contemporary explanation of the evolutionary origins of imprinting and attachment is that the behaviors involved in those processes increase the inclusive fitness of the individuals of species whose mode of reproduction is characterized by intricate patterns of parental investment.

This account departs in important ways from the currently accepted accounts of the evolutionary origins of human attachment (e.g., Bretherton, 1985; Bowlby, 1969/1982; Sroufe & Cooper, 1988; Waters & Dean, 1982). Bowlby (1969/1982) attributed the evolutionary origin of attachment to predatory selection pressure, a view that is widely shared. The response to predation, however, is only one measure of parental investment and, as such, should not deflect our attention from the underlying processes of ultimate causation. Parents invest in gametes, precopulatory behavior, copulation, prenatal and postnatal development, feeding and nurturing of the young, and territorial defense, and they undergo risks from potential predation. It is parental investment in the aggregate that contributes to inclusive fitness of an individual, and that represents an underlying feature of the evolutionary origins of filial behaviors.

The kin selection feature of the proposed theory would lead us to predict that filial behaviors may be found in interactions among organisms in a reproductive population that share a significant number of genes. The concept of psycho-biological attunement, as advanced by Field (1985) and seen earlier (Petrovich & Gewirtz, 1985) to be compatible, at the proximate level of analysis, with the adequacy of the synchrony among sequences of infant and maternal stimuli and behaviors that lead to acquired-control patterns that denote intrapair attachment, would also be compatible with this view. Further, the hypothesis stemming from the kin-selection concept would predict that filial behaviors and attunement on the proximate level may be found among offspring and parents, grandparents, cousins, uncles, aunts, and other members of a social unit. Simply stated, the greater the number of genes shared, the greater the probability for dyadic interactions indicative of affect, attachment, and attunement.

The proposed theoretical approach takes into account both contemporaneous, proximate developmental processes with their controlling variables and distal, ultimate developmental processes of the evolutionary past. Another salient feature of the present approach is that it imbeds social-learning processes underlying imprinting and attachment in a comparative cross-species perspective. In early vertebrates such as fish (McCann, 1980) and reptiles (Froese, 1980), selection has favored the evolution of genetically preset early social-behavior patterns adapted to species-typical "normal" ecological requirements. This generalization should not be misunderstood to imply that contemporaneous experiences in a given context have no effect on the behavior of these vertebrates. For the purpose of the present analysis, however, it is important to emphasize that the current evidence suggests a relatively fixed development of social phenotypes.

In many birds and mammals, the development of filial behavior under the rubrics imprinting and attachment provides an example for the process involving the coaction of biologically inherited predispositions and learning (e.g., Hess, 1973; Hoffman & Ratner, 1973a). At the other end of the spectrum are vertebrates whose life spans are relatively long and start with a period of prolonged infancy, often requiring extensive social interactions among parents, offspring, siblings, or other members of a social unit. Under such *ecological* circumstances, the opportunities for modification of behavioral responses are abundant and the advantages of preset, genetically-fixed, response patterns are reduced. For such vertebrate species, natural selection appears to have favored a shift in a direction of plasticity, learning, and cognition (e.g., Hulse, Fowler, & Honig, 1978; Lorenz, 1969; Petrovich & Hess, 1980). In these vertebrates, learning processes have played a determining role in early social development. Complex forms of social interactions have required individual recognition, thus contributing to selection processes in the direction of environmental-stimulus control and away from genetically-programmed modes of exchange. Once established biologically (via genetic exchange) and culturally (via systematic behavior change), the flexibility and adaptability of these learning processes appear to have paved the way for more remarkable forms of social behavior, including the emergence of culture and tradition (e.g., Campbell, 1975; Lorenz, 1969; Piaget, 1971, 1978).

A corollary feature of the proposed theory predicts that, under ecologically-appropriate conditions, the processes underlying imprinting or attachment and subsequent socialization produce a reliable species-typical behavioral outcome that ultimately may culminate in the production of zygotes and offspring (Petrovich & Hess, 1980). In contrast, the exposure to biologically-inappropriate stimuli during social development may functionally isolate such an individual from a reproductive population. Infanticide and serious infant abuse are likely to be observed under stressful conditions of intensified reproductive pressure, environmental ecological depletion, and/or where the mother's mate is not the infant's biological father (e.g., Dickerman, 1979; Hausfater & Hrdy, 1984; Korbin, 1981; Reite & Caine, 1983). Consider the following examples. In some species, the striking features of distorted imprinting and attachment processes provide a provocative demonstration of sexuality channeled in the direction of the biologically-inappropriate object (e.g., Hess, 1973; Immelmann, 1972). Forced separation from objects of attachment has deleterious effects on avian and mammalian infant behavior (e.g., Hinde, 1974). If separation is prolonged or leads to privation and deprivation (Gewirtz, 1961, 1978), the consequences may be even more severe. In monkeys and chimpanzees, isolation studies have shown that appropriate early social experiences are essential for the normal development of sexual behavior (e.g., Hinde, 1974; Mason, Davenport, & Menzel, 1968; Meier & Dudley-Meier, 1980; Soumi, 1982; Suomi, Collins, & Harlow, 1976; Suomi & Ripp, 1983). In turn, prolonged separation and deprivation may progressively lead to depression and related withdrawal from social interactions (Bowlby, 1973; Gewirtz, 1961; Scott & Senay, 1973). Human data on the development of sexuality and gender identity (e.g., Maccoby & Jacklin, 1974; Money, 1965) suggest also that sexual phenotypes, as genetically programmed at the moment of conception, may be radically modified and altered by various "environmental" stimuli, such as chemical by-products of other genes, hormones, or exposure during development to biologically and psychologically inappropriate stimuli.

REFERENCES

Ainsworth, M. D. S. (1969). Object relations, dependency, and attachment: A theoretical review of the infant-mother relationship. *Child Development, 40,* 969–1025.

Ainsworth, M. D. S. (1972). Attachment and dependency: A comparison. In J. L. Gewirtz (Ed.), *Attachment and dependency* (pp. 97–137). Washington, DC: Winston.

Ainsworth, M. S., Blehar, M. C., Waters, E., & Wall, S. (1978). *Patterns of attachment.* Hillsdale, NJ: Lawrence Erlbaum Associates.

Ainsworth, M. D. S., & Wittig, B. A. (1969). Attachment and the exploratory behavior of one-year-olds in strange situations. In B. M. Foss (Ed.), *Determinants of infant behavior* (Volume 4, pp. 113–136). London: Methuen.

Bateson, P. P. G. (1966). The characteristics and context of imprinting. *Biological Reviews, 41,* 177–220.

Bateson, P. P. G. (1971). Imprinting. In H. Moltz (Ed.), *The ontogeny of vertebrate behavior* (pp. 369–388). New York: Academic Press.

Bateson, P. (1979). How do sensitive periods arise and what are they for? *Animal Behaviour, 27,* 470–486.

Barash, D. P. (1982). *Sociobiology and behavior.* New York: Elsevier.

Bowlby, J. (1958). The nature of the child's tie to his mother. *International Journal of Psychoanalysis, 39,* 350–373.

Bowlby, J. (1969/1982). *Attachment and loss (Vol. 1): Attachment.* New York: Basic Books.
Bowlby, J. (1973). *Attachment and loss (Vol. 2): Separation anxiety and anger.* New York: Basic Books.
Brackbill, Y. (1958). Extinction of the smiling response in infants as a function of reinforcement schedule. *Child Development, 29,* 115–124.
Bretherton, I. (1978). Making friends with one-year-olds: An experimental study of infant-stranger interaction. *Merrill-Palmer Quarterly, 24,* 29–51.
Bretherton, I. (1985). Attachment theory: Retrospect and prospect. In I. Bretherton & E. Waters (Eds.), *Growing points of attachment theory and research: Monographs of the Society for Research in Child Development* (pp. 3–35), *50,* Nos. 1–2, Serial 209.
Bretherton, I., Stolberg, U., & Kreye, M. (1981). Engaging strangers in proximal interaction: infants' social initiative. *Developmental Psychology, 17,* 746–755.
Bronson, G. W. (1978). Aversive reaction to strangers: A dual process interpretation. *Child Development, 49,* 495–499.
Bronson, W. G., & Pankey, W. B. (1977). On the distinction between fear and wariness. *Child Development, 48,* 1167–1183.
Brush, S. G. (1974). Should the history of science be rated X? *Science, 183,* 1164–1172.
Cairns, R. B. (1966). Attachment behavior in mammals. *Psychological Review, 73,* 409–426.
Cairns, R. B. (1972). Attachment and dependency: A psychobiological and social learning synthesis. In J. L. Gewirtz (Ed.), *Attachment and dependency* (pp. 29–80). Washington, DC: Halstead Press.
Campbell, D. T. (1975). On conflicts between biological and social evolution and between psychology and moral tradition. *American Psychologist, 30,* 1103–1126.
Caron, R. F. (1967). Visual reinforcement of head turning in young infants. *Journal of Experimental Child Psychology, 5,* 489–511.
Carpenter, G. C. (1974). Visual regard of moving and stationary faces in early infancy. *Merrill-Palmer Quarterly, 20,* 181–194.
Chagnon, N. (1979). Mate competition, favoring close kin and village fissioning among the Yanomamo Indians. In N. A. Chagnon & W. Irons (Eds.), *Evolutionary biology and human social behavior* (pp. 86–132). North Scituate, MA: Duxbury.
Chagnon, N., & Bugos, P. (1979). Kin selection and conflict: An analysis of a Yanomamo ax fight. In N. A. Chagnon & W. Irons (Eds.), *Evolutionary biology and human social behavior.* North Scituate, MA: Duxbury.
Clarke-Stewart, K. A. (1978). Recasting the lone stranger. In J. Glick & K. A. Clarke-Stewart (Eds.), *The development of social understanding.* New York: Gardner Press.
Clarke-Stewart, K. A., VanderStoep, L., & Killian, G. (1979). Analysis and replication of mother-child relations at two years of age. *Child Development, 50,* 777–793.
Clarke-Stewart, K. A., Umeh, B. J., Snow, M. E., & Pederson, J. A. (1980). Development and prediction of children's sociability from 1 to 2½ years. *Developmental Psychology, 16,* 290–302.
Dawkins, R. (1976). *The selfish gene.* London: Oxford University Press.
Decarie, T. G. (1974). *The infants reaction to strangers.* New York: International Universities Press.
DeCasper, A. J., & Fifer, W. P. (1980). Of human bonding: Newborns prefer mothers' voices. *Science, 208,* 1174–1176.
Durham, W. H. (1976). The adaptive significance of cultural behavior. *Human Ecology, 4,* 89–121.
Eibl-Eibesfeldt, I. (1975). *Ethology: The biology of behavior.* New York: Holt, Rinehart & Winston.
Eibl-Eibesfeldt, I. (1979). Human ethology: Concepts and implications for the sciences of man. *The Behavioral and Brain Sciences, 1,* 1–57.
Eisenberg, J. (1982). *The mammalian radiations: An analysis of trends in evolution, adaptation and behavior.* Chicago: The University of Chicago Press.

Emde, R. N., Gaensbaur, T. J., & Harmon, R. J. (1976). *Emotional expression in infancy: A biobehavioral study.* New York: International Universities Press.

Etzel, B. C., & Gewirtz, J. L. (1967). Experimental modification of caretaker-maintained high rate operant crying in a 6- and a 20-week-old infant (*Infans tyrannotearus*): Extinction of crying with reinforcement of eye contact and smiling. *Journal of Experimental Child Psychology, 5,* 303–317.

Fabricius, E. (1962). *Symposium of Zoological Society of London, 8,* 139–148.

Field, T. (1985). Attachment as psychobiological attunement: Being on the same wavelength. In M. Reite & T. Field (Eds.), *The psychobiology of attachment and separation* (pp. 415–454). New York: Academic Press.

Field, T., Cohen, D., Garcia, R., & Greenberg, R. (1983). Mother-stranger face discrimination by the newborn. *Infant Behavior and Development, 7,* 19–26.

Field, T. M., Woodson, R., Greenberg, R., & Cohen, D. (1982). Discrimination and imitation of facial expressions by neonates. *Science, 218,* 179–181.

Fitzgerald, H., & Brackbill, Y. (1976). Classical conditioning in infancy: Development and constraints. *Psychological Bulletin, 83,* 353–376.

Fraiberg, S. (1975). The development of human attachments in infants blind from birth. *Merrill-Palmer Quarterly, 21,* 315–334.

Froese, A. D. (1980). Reptiles. In M. A. Roy (Ed.), *Species identity and attachment* (pp. 39–68). New York: Garland.

Gaioni, S. J., & Evans, S. C. (1985). *Perception of distress calls by mallard ducklings* (*Anas platyrhynchos*). Animal Behavior Society Meetings, Raleigh.

Gaioni, S. J., Hoffman, S. H., & DePaulo, P. (1978). Imprinting in older ducklings: Some tests of a reinforcement model. *Animal Learning and Behavior, 6,* 19–26.

Gewirtz, J. L. (1961). A learning analysis of the effects of normal stimulation, privation, and deprivation on the acquisition of social motivation and attachment. In B. M. Foss (Ed.), *Determinants of infant behaviour* (pp. 213–229). London: Methuen.

Gewirtz, J. L. (1969). Mechanisms of social learning: Some roles of stimulation and behavior in early human development. In D. A. Goslin (Ed.), *Handbook of socialization theory and research* (pp. 57–212). Chicago: Rand-McNally.

Gewirtz, J. L. (Ed.) (1972a). *Attachment and dependency.* Washington, DC: Winston. New York: Halsted.

Gewirtz, J. L. (1972b). Attachment, dependency, and a distinction in terms of stimulus control. In J. L. Gewirtz (Ed.), *Attachment and dependency* (pp. 139–177). Washington, DC: Winston.

Gewirtz, J. L. (1972c). On the selection and use of attachment and dependence indices. In J. L. Gewirtz (Ed.), *Attachment and dependency* (pp. 179–215). Washington, DC: Winston.

Gewirtz, J. L. (1972d). Some contextual determinants of stimulus potency. In R. D. Parke (Ed.), *Recent trends in social learning theory* (pp. 7–33). New York: Academic Press.

Gewirtz, J. L. (1978). Social learning in early human development. In A. C. Catania & T. A. Brigham (Eds.), *Handbook of applied behavior analysis* (pp. 105–141). New York: Irvington.

Gewirtz, J. L., & Boyd, E. F. (1977). Experiments on mother infant interaction underlying mutual attachment acquisition: The infant conditions the mother. In T. Alloway, P. Pliner & L. Krames (Eds.), *Attachment and behaviour: Advances in the study of communication and affect* (Vol. 3). New York and London: Plenum.

Gewirtz, J. L., & Pelaez-Nogueras, M. (1987). Social-conditioning theory applied to metaphors like "attachment": The conditioning of infant separation protests by mothers. *Revista Mexicana de Analisis de la Conducta/Mexican Journal of Behavior Analysis, 13,* 87–103.

Goldberg, S. (1972). Infant care and growth in urban Zambia. *Human Development, 15,* 77–89.

Gottlieb, G. (1968). Prenatal behavior of birds. *Quarterly Review of Biology, 43,* 148–174.

Gottlieb, G. (1971). *Development of species identification in birds: An inquiry into the prenatal determinants of perception.* Chicago: The University of Chicago Press.

Gottlieb, G. (1973). Neglected developmental variables in the study of species identification in birds. *Psychological Bulletin, 79,* 362–372.

Gottlieb, G. (1980). Development of species identification in ducklings: VI. Specific embryonic experience required to maintain species-typical perception in Peking ducklings. *Journal of Comparative and Physiological Psychology, 94,* 579–587.

Gottlieb, G. (1981). Development of species identification in ducklings: VIII. Embryonic vs. postnatal critical period for the maintenance of species-specific perception. *Journal of Comparative and Physiological Psychology, 95,* 540–547.

Gray, P. H. (1958). Theory and evidence of imprinting in human infants. *Journal of Psychology, 46,* 155–166.

Greenberg, N., Hillman, D., & Grice, D. (1973). Infant and stranger variables related to stranger anxiety in the first year of life. *Developmental Psychology, 9,* 207–212.

Guhl, A. M., & Fischer, G. J. (1969). The behavior of chickens. In E. S. E. Hafez (Ed.), *The behaviour of domestic animals.* 2nd ed. London: Bailliere.

Haith, M. M., & Campos, J. J. (1977). Human infancy. *Annual Review of Psychology, 28,* 251–293.

Hamilton, W. D. (1964). The genetical evolution of social behavior. *Journal of Theoretical Biology, I, II, 7,* 1–52.

Harlow, H. F. (1958). The nature of love. *American Psychologist, 13,* 673–685.

Harlow, H. F. (1966). The primate socialization motives. *Transactions and Studies of the College of Physicians of Philadelphia, 33,* 224–237.

Harlow, H., & Harlow, M. R. (1965). The affectional systems. In A. M. Schrier, H. F. Harlow, & F. Stollnitz (Eds.), *Behavior of nonhuman primates* (pp. 287–334). Vol. II. New York: Academic Press.

Harlow, H. F., & Harlow, M. K. (1966). Learning to love. *American Scientist, 54,* 244–272.

Harlow, H. F., & Zimmermann, R. R. (1959). Affectional responses in the infant monkey. *Science, 130,* 421–432.

Hausfater, G., & Hrdy, S. (1984). *Infanticide: Comparative and evolutionary perspectives.* (Werner-Gren Foundation) New York: Aldine.

Heaton, M. B. (1972). Prenatal auditory discrimination in the wood duck (*Aix sponsa*). *Animal Behaviour, 20,* 421–424.

Hebb, D. O. (1946). On the nature of fear. *Psychological Review, 53,* 259–276.

Hess, E. H. (1959). Imprinting. *Science, 130,* 133–141.

Hess, E. H. (1962). Imprinting and the critical period concept. In E. L. Bliss (Ed.), *Roots of behavior.* New York: Hoeber-Harper.

Hess, E. H. (1964). Imprinting in birds. *Science, 146,* 1128–1139.

Hess, E. H. (1972). "Imprinting" in a natural laboratory. *Scientific American, 227*(8), 24–31.

Hess, E. H. (1973). *Imprinting: Early experience and the developmental psychobiology of attachment.* New York: Van Nostrand.

Hess, E. H., & Petrovich, S. B. (1973). The early development of parent-young interaction in nature. In F. R. Nesselroade & H. W. Reese (Eds.), *Life-span developmental psychology: Methodological issues* (pp. 25–42). New York: Academic Press.

Hess, E. H., & Petrovich, S. B. (Eds.) (1977). *Imprinting: Benchmark papers in animal behavior.* Stroudsburg: Dowden, Hutchinson, & Ross.

Hinde, R. A. (1970). *Animal behavior: A synthesis of ethology and comparative psychology* (2nd ed.). New York: McGraw-Hill.

Hinde, R. A. (1974). *Biological bases of human social behavior.* New York: McGraw-Hill.

Hinde, R. A., & Stevenson-Hinde, J. (Eds.). (1973). *Constraints on learning.* New York: Academic Press.

Hoffman, H. S. (1974). Fear-mediated processes in the context of imprinting. In M. Lewis & L. Rosenblum (Eds.), *The origins of fear.* New York: Wiley.

Hoffman, H. S. (1978). Laboratory investigation of imprinting. In G. M. Burghard & M. Bekoff (Eds.), *The development of behavior: Comparative and evolutionary aspects* (pp. 203–212). New York: Garland.

Hoffman, H. S., Eiserer, L. H., & Singer, D. (1972). Acquisition of behavioral control by a stationary imprinting stimulus. *Psychonomic Science, 26,* 146–148.

Hoffman, H. S., & Ratner, A. M. (1973a). A reinforcement model of imprinting: Implications for socialization in monkeys and man. *Psychological Review, 80,* 527–544.

Hoffman, H. S., & Ratner, A. M. (1973b). Effects of stimulus and environmental familiarity on visual imprinting in newly hatched ducklings. *Journal of Comparative and Physiological Psychology, 85,* 11–19.

Hoffman, H. S., & DePaulo, P. (1977). Behavioral control by an imprinting stimulus. *American Scientist, 65,* 58–66.

Hubel, D. H. (1978). Effects of deprivation on visual cortex of cat and monkey. *Harvey Lectures, 72,* 1–51.

Hulse, S. H., Fowler, H., & Honig, W. K. (Eds.) (1978). *Cognitive processes in animal behavior.* Hillsdale, N.J.: Erlbaum.

Immelmann, K. (1972). Sexual and other long term aspects of imprinting in birds and other species. In D. S. Lehrman, R. A. Hinde, & E. Shaw (Eds.), *Advances in the study of behavior* (Vol. 4) (pp. 147–174). New York: Academic.

Immelman, K. (1975). Ecological significance of imprinting and early learning. *Annual Review of Ecology and Systematics, 6,* 15–37.

James, H. (1959). Flicker: An unconditional stimulus for imprinting. *Canadian Journal of Psychology, 13,* 59–67.

Kagan, J. (1974). Discrepancy, temperament, and infant distress. In M. Lewis & L. A. Rosenblum (Eds.), *The origins of fear* (pp. 229–248). New York: Wiley.

Kaltenbach, K., Weinraub, M., & Fullard, W. (1980). Infant wariness toward strangers reconsidered: Infants' and mothers' reactions to unfamiliar persons. *Child Development, 51,* 1197–1202.

Klaus, M. H., & Kennell, H. J. (1976). *Maternal infant bonding.* St. Louis: Mosby.

Klein, R. P., & Durfee, J. T. (1976). Infants' reactions to unfamiliar adults versus mothers. *Child Development, 47,* 1194–1196.

Klinghammer, E., & Hess, E. H. (1964). Imprinting in an altricial bird: The blond ring dove. *Streptopelia risoria). Science, 146,* 265–266.

Klopfer, P. H. (1967). Stimulus preferences and imprinting. *Science, 156,* 1394–1396.

Konner, M. (1972). Aspects of the developmental ethology of a foraging people. In N. Blurton-Jones (Ed.), *Ethological studies of child behaviour.* Cambridge: Cambridge University Press.

Kuhn, T. S. (1962). *The structure of scientific revolutions.* Chicago: The University of Chicago Press.

Lack, D. (1968). *Ecological adaptation of breeding birds.* London: Methuen.

Lamb, M. G., Thompson, R. A., Gardner, P. W., Charnov, E. L., & Estes, D. (1984). Security of infantile attachment as assessed in the "strange situation": Its study and biological interpretation. *The Behavioral and Brain Sciences, 7,* 127–171.

Lewis, M., & Brooks, J. (1974). Self, other, and fear: Infants' reactions to people. In M. Lewis & L. A. Rosenblum (Eds.), *The origins of fear.* New York: Wiley.

Lewis, M., & Brooks, J. (1975). Infant's social perception: A constructivist view. In L. B. Cohen & P. Salapatek (Eds.), *Infant perception: From sensation to cognition.* New York: Academic Press.

Lewis, M., & Rosenblum, L. A. (Eds.). (1974). *The origins of fear.* New York: Wiley.

Lorenz, K. (1935). Der Kumpan in der Umwelt des Vogels. *Journal fur Ornithologie, 83,* 137–213.

Lorenz, K. (1969). Innate basis of learning. In K. Pribram (Ed.), *On the biology of learning.* New York: Harcourt Brace Jovanovich.

Maccoby, E. E., & Jacklin, C. N. (1974). *The psychology of sex differences.* Stanford, CA: Stanford University Press.

Mason, W. A. (1970). Motivation factors in psychosocial development. In W. J. Arnold & M. M. Page (Eds.), *Nebraska Symposium on Motivation* (pp. 35–67). Lincoln: University of Nebraska Press.

Mason, W. A., Davenport, R. K., Jr., & Menzel, E. W., Jr. (1968). Early experience and the social development of rhesus monkeys and chimpanzees. In G. Newton & S. Levine (Eds.), *Early experience and behavior* (pp. 440–480). Springfield, IL: Thomas.

Mason, W. A., & Lott, F. D. (1976). Ethology and comparative psychology. *Annual Review of Psychology, 27,* 129–154.

Maynard, Smith J. (1964). Group selection and kin selection. *Nature, 201,* 1145–1147.

McCann, L. I. (1980). Species identification in fish. In M. A. Roy (Eds.), *Species identity and attachment* (pp. 23–38). New York: Garland.

McIlwain, T. (1972). Central vision: Visual cortex and superior colliculus. *Annual Review of Physiology, 34,* 291–314.

Meier, G. W., & Dudley-Meier, V. (1980). Old world monkeys: Consequences of atypical rearing experiences. In M. A. Roy (Ed.), *Species identity and attachment* (pp. 181–200). New York: Garland.

Money, J. (1965). *Sex research: New developments.* New York: Holt.

Morgan, G. A., & Ricciuti, H. N. (1969). Infants' responses to strangers during the first year. In B. M. Foss (Ed.), *Determinants of infant behaviour IV.* London: Methuen.

Petrovich, S. B. (1978). Adaptation and evolution of behavior. In G. U. Balis, L. Wurmser, E. McDaniel, & R. G. Grenell (Eds.), *Dimensions of behavior* (pp. 201–225). Boston: Butterworth.

Petrovich, S. B., & Gewirtz, J. L. (1985). The attachment learning process and its relation to cultural and biological evolution: Proximate and ultimate considerations. In M. Reite & T. Field (Eds.), *The psychobiology of attachment and separation* (pp. 259–291). New York: Academic Press.

Petrovich, S. B., & Hess, E. H. (1980). Some issues in prezygotic species-typic identification and isolation: A comparative evaluation. In M. A. Roy (Ed.), *Species identity and attachment* (pp. 371–384). New York: Garland.

Piaget, J. (1971). *Biology and knowledge.* Chicago: University of Chicago Press.

Piaget, J. (1978). *Behavior and evolution.* New York: Pantheon.

Plomin, R., & Rowe, D. (1979). Genetic and environmental etiology of social behavior in infancy. *Developmental Psychology, 15,* 62–72.

Ratner, A. M., & Hoffman, H. S. (1974). Evidence for a critical period for imprinting in Khaki Campbell ducklings (*Anas platyrhynchos domesticus*). *Animal Behaviour, 22,* 249–255.

Reed, G., & Leiderman, P. H. (1981). Age-related changes in attachment behavior in polymatrically-reared infants: The Kenyan Gusii. In T. M. Field, A. M. Sostek, P. Vietze, & P. H. Leiderman (Eds.), *Culture and early interactions* (pp. 215–234). Hillsdale, NJ: Lawrence Erlbaum Associates.

Reite, M., & Field, T. (Eds.). (1985). *The psychobiology of attachment and separation.* New York: Academic Press.

Rheingold, H. L. (1974). General issues in the study of fear. In M. Lewis & L. A. Rosenblum (Eds.), *The origins of fear* (pp. 249–254). New York: Wiley.

Rheingold, H. L., & Eckerman, C. O. (1973). Fear of the stranger: A critical examination. In H. W. Reese (Ed.), *Advances in child development and behavior* Vol. 8 (pp. 185–222). New York: Academic Press.

Ross, H. S., & Goldman, B. D. (1977). Infants' sociability toward strangers. *Child Development, 48,* 638–642.

Roy, M. A. (Ed.). (1980). *Species identity and attachment: A Phylogenetic evaluation.* New York: Garland STPM Press.

Salzen, E. A. (1962). Imprinting and fear. *Symposia Zoological Society of London, 8,* 199–212.

Salzen, E. A. (1967). Imprinting in birds and primates. *Behaviour, 28* (3–4), 232–254.

Schaffer, H. R. (1966). The onset of fear of strangers and the incongruity hypothesis. *Journal of Child Psychology and Psychiatry, 7,* 95–106.

Schaffer, H. R., & Emerson, P. E. (1964). The development of social attachment in infancy. *Monographs of the Society for Research in Child Development, 20* (3, Whole No. 94).

Scott, J. P. (1960). Comparative social psychology. In R. H. Waters, D. A. Rethlingshafer, & W. E. Caldwell (Eds.), *Principles of comparative psychology* (pp. 250–288). New York: McGraw-Hill.

Scott, J. P. (1967). The process of primary socialization in canine and human infants. In J. Hellmuth (Ed.), *Exceptional infant: The normal infant (Vol. 1).* Seattle, WA: Special Child Publications.

Scott, J. P. (1968). *Early experience and the organization of behavior.* Belmont, CA: Brooks/Cole.

Scott, J. P., & Senay, C. C. (Eds.). (1973). *Separation and depression: Clinical and research aspects.* Washington, DC: American Association for the Advancement of Science.

Shapiro, L. J. (1970). Experimental control and automation in a laboratory for imprinting research. *Journal of Comparative and Physiological Psychology, 73,* 421–426.

Shapiro, L. J. (1980). Species identification in birds: A review and synthesis. In M. A. Roy (Ed.), *Species identity and attachment: A phylogenetic evaluation* (pp. 69–112). New York: Garland Press.

Skarin, K. (1977). Cognitive and contextual determinants of stranger fear in six- and eleven-month-old infants. *Child Development, 48,* 537–544.

Sluckin, W. (1962). Perceptual and associative learning. *Symposia Zoological Society of London, 8,* 193–198.

Sluckin, W. (1965). *Imprinting and early learning.* London: Methuen.

Sluckin, W. (1972). *Early learning in man and animal.* Cambridge, MA: Schenkman.

Spalding, D. A. (1873). Instinct: With original observations on young animals. *MacMillan's Magazine, 27,* 282–293. Reprinted in *British Journal of Animal Behaviour,* 1954, *2,* 2–11.

Sroufe, L. A. (1977). Wariness of strangers and the study of infant development. *Child Development, 48,* 731–746.

Sroufe, L. A., & Cooper, R. G. (1988). *Child development: Its nature and course.* New York: Knopf.

Suomi, S. J. (1982). Abnormal behavior and primate models of psychopathology. In J. L. Forbes & J. E. King (Eds.), *Primate behavior* (pp. 171–215). New York: Academic Press.

Suomi, S. J., Collins, M. L., & Harlow, H. F. (1976). Effects of maternal and peer separation on young monkeys. *Journal of Child Psychology and Psychiatry, 17,* 101–112.

Suomi, S. J., & Ripp, C. (1983). A history of motherless mother monkey mothering at the University of Wisconsin Primate Laboratory. In M. Reite & N. Caine (Eds.), *Monographs in primatology* Vol. 1, *Child abuse: The nonhuman primate data* (pp. 49–77). NY: Alan R. Liss.

Tinbergen, N. (1972). *The animal and its world.* London: Allen & Unwin.

Tracy, R. L., Lamb, L. E., & Ainsworth, M. D. S. (1976). Infant approach behavior as related to attachment. *Child Development, 47,* 571–578.

Trivers, R. L. (1972). Parental investment and sexual selection. In B. Campbell (Ed.), *Sexual selection and the descent of man* (pp. 136–179). Chicago: Aldine.

Waters, E., Matas, L., & Sroufe, L. A. (1975). Infants' reaction to an approaching stranger: Description, validation, and functional significance of wariness. *Child Development, 46,* 348–356.

Waters, E., & Dean, (1982). Infant-mother attachment: Theories, models, recent data and some tasks for comparative developmental analysis. In L. W. Hoffman & R. J. Gandelman (Eds.), *Parenting: Its causes and consequences* (pp. 19–54). Hillsdale, NJ: Lawrence Erlbaum Associates.

Watson, J. D. (1968). *The double helix.* New York: Atheneum.

West Eberhardt, M. J. (1975). The evolution of social behavior by kin selection. *Quarterly Review of Biology, 50,* 1–33.

Williams, G. C. (1966). *Adaptation and natural selection.* Princeton: Princeton University Press.

Wilson, E. O. (1975). *Sociobiology: The new synthesis.* Cambridge, MA: Belknap Harvard University Press.

Yarrow, L. J. (1956). The development of object relationships during infancy and the effects of a disruption of early mother-child relationship. *American Psychologist, 11,* 423.

Yarrow, L. J. (1964). Separation from parents during early childhood. In M. L. Hoffman & L. W. Hoffman (Eds.), *Review of child development research.* Vol. 1 (pp. 89–136). New York: Russell Sage Foundation.

Yarrow, L. J. (1967). The development of focused relationship during infancy. In J. Hellmuth (Ed.), *Exceptional infant: The normal infant.* Vol. 1 (pp. 429–442). Seattle, Wash.: Special Child Publications.

III EARLY COMMUNICATION AND ATTACHMENT

6

Preverbal Communication and Attachment: Comparative Views

Hanuš Papoušek
Mechthild Papoušek
Stephen J. Suomi
Charles W. Rahn

ABSTRACT

Preverbal communication has gained relatively little attention in attachment research, although a better understanding of preverbal communication is essential for the interpretation of both the ontogeny and the evolution of attachment processes. Comparative studies have revealed precursors of human speech in the animal world and showed the uniqueness of speech acquisition in a new light.

Microanalytic studies of human mother-infant interactions have detected intuitive tendencies in parental behaviors which seem to have evolved to facilitate speech acquisition as an important means of biological adaptation in humans. Modifications in parental speech addressed to infants represent more than mere affective expressions: they mediate the first categorical messages in parent-infant dialogues and thus contribute to the development of integrative and communicative capacities in infants.

New findings on preverbal communication make us aware of dead-ends in onesided interpretations of attachment and point out the problem of intrinsic motivation as one of the relevant topics for future research.

In this chapter, we consider how relevant the study of preverbal communication may be for the interpretation of parent–infant attachment. To date, two basic approaches have nourished interests in preverbal communication: anthropocentric aspects related to the significance of human preverbal communication for the acquisition of speech during otogeny and zoocentric aspects concerning continuities and differences among species and the evolution of communication. Both kinds of approaches have proved useful for organization and interpretation of a vast amount of descriptive data.

From the bird's eye view of general systems theory, some form of communication is necessary for any ecological coexistence of living organisms. As Raymond (1968, p. 160) indicates, only a single-celled organism might exist for some period of time in the absence of concrete information, if it is provided with food and energy as required for the maintenance of its simplest steady state. In a large organism, communication is carried on through nervous pathways by transmission of pressure through vascular systems and by humoral transmission of hormones and enzymes. In humans too, communication occurs in several modalities, some of which, such as tactile and proprioceptive modalities, are difficult to study without obtrusive techniques. Naturally interacting partners mainly exploit auditory and visual signals, and we pay special attention to these signals.

In biological views, social grouping provides better conditions for survival, reproduction, and longevity than a solitary way of life. However, grouping also requires some effective controls of density, spacing, and coexistence within groups, and such controls largely depend on communication. Human communication is not a mere cultural phenomenon, but it is first and foremost an unusually effective way of biological adaptation. Culture may have evolved together with language, but both have biological roots and lead to biological consequences. Due to culture, man has been able to survive in hostile environments and to overcome biological constraints. This can be seen in locomotion or in resistance against aggressive microorganisms.

We argue that human communication is based on an innate integrative and communicative preadaptedness, including learning, categorization, imitation, and overt expressions of two fundamental regulatory alternatives, the first being interpretable as approach and assimilation, often perceived as pleasure, and the second related to avoidance, rejection, and displeasure. This integrative-communicative preadaptedness supports speech acquisition and then profits from speech as verbal symbolization provides both new dimensions and an open-ended set of topics for processes of thought and communication.

Present research has accumulated enough arguments for the assumptions just mentioned. It is useful to realize that this has been possible due to scientific approaches that have been developmental, comparative, and interdisciplinary. They have also been interactionalistic in two senses of this word, namely, that these approaches have viewed communication as an interactional process and that they have preferred theoretical interactions to divorcing dichotomies between theories.

The uniqueness of human verbal communication in the living universe has been acknowledged many times both in philosophical terms in the general systems theory (for instance, von Bertalanffy, 1968) and in comparative terms (for instance, Lieberman, 1984). Such uniqueness has been seen in the evolution of the vocal tract that enhances vocal differentiation and of the intellectual capacity to exchange conceptual information beyond mere signals standing in a one-to-one relation with objects or events.

According to von Bertalanffy (1968), communication in general is an interactional process that cannot be explained entirely either with Stimulus–Response models or with psychoanalytic models, nor can these processes be fully understood via any utilitarian homeostat or from purely rationalistic positions. Both von Bertalanffy and Lieberman respect the unity of communication and cognitive processes, the unity of biological and cultural determinations in the evolution of human language, and the significance of prosocial tendencies in human evolution.

The capability to use abstract verbal symbols enabled man to create a new symbolic universe separable from the real world. In this symbolic world, man has found possibilities to overcome obstacles present in the real world and to extend exploration beyond the physical limits of his organism. Thus, man had explored the depths of oceans or the surface of the moon in his symbolic world long before technology could allow real visits to those areas.

Moreover, as humans we are capable of metacommunication when, for instance, we communicate about communication in the present chapter. We are able to learn how other species communicate as evidenced in the rich literature on animal communication. Technology has enabled humans to decode communication in modes that humans cannot perceive and to translate it from those modes into the mode of human speech or to intervene in specific modes of other species. In a recent example, a killer whale lost in the Sacramento river was lured back to the Pacific ocean with the help of taped sounds of feeding killer whales. As another example, gypsy moths have been lured into fatal traps with the help of sexual pheromones.

Several aspects of human communication have remained unexplored. One aspect concerns the motivation for the never-ending accumulation of knowledge. Another aspect concerns the beginning of the process of communication. If infants are capable of learning from the beginning of postpartum life but cannot store enough information due to infantile amnesia before speech, what then is the interrelationship between infantile learning and speech development? If adult humans can presently communicate with species as distant from verbal communication as gypsy moths, how did adult humans communicate with young infants in the past? Another interesting aspect is the proportion of agonistic and prosocial behaviors related to speech evolution. Lieberman (1984), for instance, pointed to the difference between chimpanzees, who do not display sufficient social support to sick or handicapped individuals, and humans, for whom there is fossil evidence on prosocial care reaching as far back as 60,000 to 100,000 years ago. Lieberman speculated that altruistic care for older individuals is advantageous for individuals who can communicate their life's experience to the younger members of the community and/or substitute for the natural parents, if they die prematurely. Parental care for infants has been viewed as a typical form of human altruism. However, it remains unclear to what degree this care contributes to the acquisition of as powerful a means of adaptation as speech.

For some reason, preverbal communication in human infants has attracted little attention in research. The reader is often left with the impression that preverbal infants are incompetent as to communicative and cognitive processes, or that certain observable phenomena are denied, only because they have been misinterpreted in one-sided theoretical concepts. In order to avoid misinterpretations, the present authors suggest approaching the study of preverbal communication with open-ended lists of observable items, analyzing them descriptively first, and then testing potential interpretations before accepting them. Modern audiovisual forms of recording make this approach feasible, they help replace speculative interpretations with verifiable ones, and they permit identical observations evaluated by several specialists from various disciplines.

Given the biological relevance of human communication and the theoretical significance of early ontogeny of communication, one can wonder why any theory on interpersonal relations could disregard the role of preverbal communication in general, and why attachment theory in particular would pay only insufficient attention to the role of preverbal communication in mother–infant bonding.

PREVERBAL VOCAL COMMUNICATION
IN COMPARATIVE PERSPECTIVE

Recent conceptual and methodological progress in communication research exemplifies advantages of interdisciplinary, comparative approaches. Increased interests of human researchers in biological precursors or analogies of human communication on the one hand, and the use of psycholinguistic methods in research on animal communication on the other hand, have helped improve the interpretation of preverbal communications in directions relevant to topics of the present chapter. The repertoire of behaviors involved in animal parent–infant interactions that provides potential communicative cues is so rich that it is beyond the scope of this chapter to review it. However, even among primates, the prevailing part of this repertoire concerns nonvocal behaviors (Hinde, 1972; Higley & Suomi, 1986), and even in the most advanced species, vocal communication plays a far less differentiated role in comparison to parent–infant interchanges in humans.

Nevertheless, it becomes increasingly evident that human verbal communication, which has brought about unique forms of adaptation, develops from prerequisites that are not unique in the animal world; they exist in other species and also function in human infants prior to acquisition of speech. Lieberman (1984) considered three main prerequisites of speech: (a) development of the vocal tract including the respiratory system, larynx, and the supralaryngeal parts, which together provide an expeditious production of finely differentiated vocal sounds; (b) development of neural structures that control the functioning of vocal tract and are capable of perceptual processing of complex and rapid strings of vocal sounds; and (c) the gradual formation of automized neural circuits that assign meaning to some of the miriads of potential vocal utterances. Each of these prerequisites exists at least in fundamental forms in species other than *Homo sapiens*. Only the matching coincidence of all of them—and their complexity— are unique to humans. The production of humanlike vocal sounds is known to exist in some tropical birds (Marler, 1975), but it is not utilized for communication with conspecifics. Neural structures providing symbolic representation and communication on environmental objects may be as simple as in the honey-bee, *Apis mellifera,* capable of conveying information on the presence and location of nectar-yielding blossoms to other worker bees in the colony through two types of dance movements (Frisch, 1965). In primates, apes particularly, the complexity of neural structures approaches the complexity of the human brain and allows chimpanzees a detailed differentiation of facial and manual gestures as well as learning to use such gestures as signs for communication with human caretakers (Gardner & Gardner, 1978). However, chimpanzees lack a vocal tract comparable to the human vocal tract, and, hence, they cannot learn speech. Children surpass chimpanzees in the entire communicative capacity at the age of approximately three years and can indeed be viewed as precocious in communication, although in most other respects, human children usually have been considered altricial due to their slow locomotor development relative to other animal species.

Studies of naturalistic primate communication have also outdated the classical dichotomic interpretation according to which only human speech can be semantic, whereas animals and, during preverbal age, human infants can signal only affective states (Premack, 1975). Vervet monkeys effectively categorize and vocally signal their main predators—eagles, snakes, and jaguars—according to Seyfarth, Cheney, and Marler (1980). They also adequately and discriminatively behave when hearing such signals from audiotapes. Seen psycholinguistically, the communication among tamarins includes simple rule systems, comparable to a phonetic syntax in most call sequences and to a lexical syntax at least in two types of chirps (Cleveland & Snowdon, 1982).

Vervet monkeys (and probably most other Old World monkeys and apes) can recognize individuals belonging to their social group (Seyfarth & Cheney, 1982), and this fact alone contradicts a merely affective significance of monkey vocalization (Premack, 1975; Marler, 1977). It seems to be adaptively advantageous to identify individuals by sight and by vocal sounds, and to register the individual's affective state in social groups based on social bonds and hierarchical systems. The semantic, identifying feature, included in affective signals, may, thus, contribute to the establishment of social bonds even on the level of nonverbal sounds. According to Kaplan, Winship-Ball, and Sim (1978) and Symmes and Biben (1985), squirrel monkey mothers discriminate vocalizations of their own infants from vocalizations of other infants. Human infants have recently been reported to discriminate and prefer their mothers' voices shortly after birth (DeCasper & Fifer, 1980). Consequently, the question of mutual recognition between human infants and caregivers should not be disregarded in attachment concepts.

The recent orientation in research on animal communication also signals increased interest in prosocial behaviors that have remained largely uninvestigated compared to approaches stressing the role of aggression in evolution. Thus, next to antagonistic signals, threats, and signals of dominance, more attention is now being paid to signals facilitating coexistence within groups. These include vocal signals on localization of individuals (Brown, Beecher, Moody, & Stebbins, 1979), the regulation of within-group spacing in the wedge-capped capuchin (Robinson, 1982), socially determined vocal patterns in the Japanese monkeys (Green, 1975), and several types of metacommunicative messages (Altmann, 1967; Smith, Newman, & Symmes, 1982).

Recent paleontologic findings of *Australopithecus afarensis* have drawn attention to potential interrelationships between parent–infant bonding and the selection of intellectual capacities during evolution, aspects that were not considered in attachment concepts. Lovejoy (1981) concluded those findings with a suggestion that the evolution of both bipedality and a large neocortex has not been caused by tool use. Bipedality, a disadvantageous, nonsaltatory form of walking, emerged perhaps as a mere variation in genetic reproduction, according to Lovejoy. Instead, bipedality was favored during evolution due to advantages related to the short birth spacing in hominids and the unusual (among primates) necessity to care for two or more dependent offspring simultaneously.

Together with the changing environmental conditions pushing the hominoid males towards intense participation in parenting during the Miocene, reproductive competence led to strong social bonds, monogamy, bifocal groups, a longer period of infant dependency, and complex intellectual and communicative capacities. Monogamy is typical for primates in which the male is clearly and directly involved in the parenting process. Hominids diverged from matrifocal bonding, typical for most monkeys and apes, and developed a bifocal distribution of parenting that, together with a relatively short birth spacing, might have contributed to a successful demographic propagation unparalleled in pongids (Lovejoy, 1981).

The conceptual progress in the interpretation of human evolution adds significance to the studies of early human communication in parent–infant interaction, representing a prototype of prosocial engagement. H. Papoušek and M. Papoušek (1979a, 1982) drew attention to the intuitive forms of parenting that—as we are going to describe in more detail later in the present chapter—represent a well-fitting support for infant communicative development, albeit carried out by parents without much conscious awareness.

Supportive care for communicative development may subserve the acquisition of speech as well as the establishment of firm social bonds. It can hardly be conceptualized without a sufficient knowledge on precursors, without early developmental forms of communicative capacities, and without analogues of these forms in other species. In comparative terms, there are several obvious trends, pointing to the emergence of vocal communication. Vocal signals are only a part of a broad motor repertoire in which all other parts may not only participate in nonvocal communication as well, but are expressed in various other physiological functions.

The phylogenetic scale of motor patterns extends from mere changes in general motility in simple organisms to differentiated facial gestures in mammals, with additional hand gestures and articulatory gestures in primates. Correspondingly, the information mediated within this scale reaches from states of arousal, signifying affective states, up to references on external events, representative symbols, metacommunication, and sophisticated forms of human verbal symbols. During human ontogeny, words are also preceded by changes in general motility and facial expressions, and later by hand gestures and preverbal vocal sounds. The increasing complexity of motor patterns is intimately interrelated with increasingly complex forms of neural regulations that again enable increasing capacities to process communicative signals and to produce them.

Likewise, the genetic determination of response patterns in motor behavior looses its rigidity and is increasingly replaced by newly acquired associations between motor patterns and various purposes to which these patterns may subserve with great plasticity. Thus, for instance, facial expressions of emotions may be displayed deliberately, independently of emotional states, in the form of purposive actions or communicative signals. Chevalier-Skolnikoff (1982) described affective signals, emancipated from the original, biological functions, and ritualized in new, communicative contexts in stump-tailed macaques and in chimpanzees. Fridlund, Ekman, and Oster (1987) discussed similar developmental phenomena in human infants and children. H. Papoušek, M. Papoušek, and Koester (1986) analyzed complex forms of emotionality in human infants and reported developmental, structural changes between 7 and 12 months, indicating transitions from tonic responses with a slow buildup and fading (as in autonomic responses) to phasic responses with a fast buildup and fading (as in communicative signals).

The ontogeny of neural regulation of motor actions in human children was outstandingly conceptualized in Piaget's (1936/1952) theory of cognitive development. All but the last stages of cognitive development have also been found in young chimpanzees by Chevalier-Skolnikoff (1982). Piaget's theory stresses the interrelationships between cognitive, emotional, and communicative aspects of development, and it assigns a particular significance to imitation and play. Similarly, vocal imitation and vocal play have been considered as important to speech learning and to speech evolution (Studdert-Kennedy, 1983; Lieberman, 1984). Vocal play or "babbling" of human infants may be paralleled by a constant stream of highly variable vocalizations in young cotton-top tamarines and marmosets separated from parents (Snowdon, 1982). However, vocal play is otherwise very rare among nonhuman primates, and similarily the vocal imitation has been reported only in a few species of songbirds and marine mammals along with that of humans.

Primate studies have not yet been successful in demonstrating vocal learning, perhaps due to the fact that too few primate species and too few vocalization types have been studied as yet (Newman & Symmes, 1982). The lack of true

FIG. 6.1.
Series A: Humans. A father observes his daughter, while she attends to her environment; as soon as she shows interest in the father, he lifts her closer to his face, achieves eye-to-eye contact, and starts talking to her.
Series B: Gorillas. A mother mostly observes the environment; occasionally she briefly looks at her infant, and some of these looks are followed by grooming. No attempts to reach direct eye-to-eye contact have been observed.
Series C: Pygmy chimpanzees. Similar behavioral tendencies as in the gorilla mother with no attempts to reach direct eye-to-eye contact characterize the pygmy chimpanzee mother.

FIG. 6.1. (*Continued*)

parallelity in the development of vocal communication between humans and nonhuman primates may have been one reason why early communication has gained so little attention in Bowlby's original theory of attachment (Bowlby, 1969, 1980) as compared to the monkey models of separation.

Pointing out not only similarities but also dissimilarities in communicative processes, comparative research has helped reveal the specificity of some behavioral tendencies subserving human communication either in general or in a closer relation to the parental care for infant progeny in particular. One important example was reported by H. Papoušek and M. Papoušek (1979a) in the regulation of eye-to-eye contact between parents and infants. The effect of eye-to-eye contact on the infant's attention has been demonstrated in mirror situations, experimentally modified by the authors (H. Papoušek & M. Papoušek, 1974) so as to distinguish the roles of eye-to-eye contact and contingent movements seen by infants in mirror situations. Eye-to-eye contact also draws the infant's attention to the caregiver's face, where a complex display of muscle activities, particularly in the perioral and periorbital areas, offers finely differentiated examples of the production of both vocal and nonvocal communicative signals, expressions of internal states and emotional feelings, as well as indicators of the course of thought processes (Fridlund et al., 1987). Thus, it seems to be adaptively relevant to the infant to learn to pay sufficient attention to the caregiver's face. Correspondingly, it may be relevant to the parent to support and reinforce this kind of infant learning.

In patterns of intuitive, nonconscious parental behaviors, H. Papoušek and M. Papoušek (1979a) reported a parental support to the direct visual contact with infants in the tendency to maintain a relatively short eye-to-eye average distance of 22.5cm (Schoetzau & H. Papoušek, 1977), a face-to-face position, and to carry out "greeting responses" immediately following the achievement of eye-to-eye contact (H. Papoušek & M. Papoušek, 1979a). However, the tendency to use a direct eye-to-eye gaze for prosocial purposes is most probably unique to humans; in other species, including Old World monkeys and great apes, such a gaze has only been reported in relation to threats and aggressive behaviors. The lack of evidence had not been reinforced by specifically directed search, therefore, H. Papoušek (unpublished data) studied mother–infant interactions in a lowland gorilla (Dolly with her son Schroeder, born 1985, at the Wild Animal Park in San Diego) and in a pygmy chimpanzee (Loretta with her son Lory, born 1985, at the San Diego Zoo). Only infrequent, incidental mutual gaze between mothers and infants—but no behavioral patterns of drawing the infant's visual attention to maternal face—were found in videorecorded samples. The most typical sequences of parental behaviors, observable in humans, gorilla, and pygmy chimpanzee are exemplified in FIG. 6.1.

Direct eye-to-eye gaze has otherwise been reported as a part of sexual behavior in black-capped capuchin monkeys (*Cebus apella*) (Janson, 1984; 1986; Visalberghi & Welker, 1986) and in pygmy chimpanzees (Savage-Rumbaugh & Wilkerson, 1978). Unlike other nonhuman primates, these two species show intriguing variety of body positions and additional behavior exchanges between partners during copulation, including direct eye-to-eye gaze.

THE STRUCTURE AND DYNAMICS OF HUMAN PREVERBAL COMMUNICATION

During human ontogeny, the individual systems necessary for speech acquisition involve both innately determined maturation as well as the gradual learning of automized motor skills and neural devices controlling verbal symbolization under the influence of environment (Lieberman, 1984). No other environmental situations offer such frequent and effective opportunities for learning speech as do dyadic social interactions with stable caregivers (H. Papoušek & M. Papoušek, 1984b).

Modern technology, including objective audiovisual documentation of both vocal sounds and interactional contexts, and spectrographic and computer-aided analyses of sounds, enables the observer of early human communication to fulfill three assumptions necessary for the interpretation of communication: (a) accurate descriptions of the structure of emitted vocal sounds and their sequences; (b) detection of a rule system or grammar formalizing the emission of vocal sequences; and (c) analysis of contexts in which vocal signals are emitted and of meanings assigned to them by recipients.

Human newborns are born with an innate capability of crying, and for the purpose of cry, they can sustain an uninterrupted expirium for several seconds. However, the capacity to produce speech sounds other than the cry lacks the adequate anatomical form of the vocal tract, the proper regulation of breathing, and the neural structures necessary for communicative interactions (Lieberman, 1984; M. Papoušek & H. Papoušek, 1981). Vocal sounds other than crying are rare during the first weeks of life, and fundamental vowel-like voicing, produced occasionally during social interactions, is superimposed on the momentary type of breathing and, thus, sounds like short rhythmical utterances (M. Papoušek & H. Papoušek, 1981). Such utterances lack any communicative adjustment and yet signal the caregiver about changes in the infant's behavioral-emotional state (M. Papoušek, 1989), because changes in state determine the rate and type of breathing.

Rapid changes both in the anatomy of the vocal tract and of brain structures during the first 6 to 8 months lead to the situation in which the infant becomes capable of producing repetitive syllables like "mama," "dada," or "tita." These can be used as protowords representing relevant parts of the infant's immediate environment. To produce them, the infant must control respiration, fraction one voiced expirium with the help of consonants, use reasonably differentiated vowels, and be capable of various integrative processes. In addition to the fundamental forms of instrumental, associative, observational, and imitative learning, processes like pattern detection, rule detection, concept formation, use of abstract symbols, and memory storage are assumed to be involved. The anatomic growth of the skull base, vocal tract, and the chest, which allows an efficient control of expirium with a steady subglottal air pressure and the production of differentiated speech sounds, may show relatively small plasticity in response to environmental factors.

Human newborns appear to be equipped with fundamental neural functions used by adults in speech perception. Interesting recent findings by Eilers (1977), Eimas (1974, 1975a, 1975b), Jusczyk (1977), and Kuhl (1979, 1983, 1985) show that near the beginning of life, infants can process a variety of phonological contrasts such as prevoiced and delayed voice onset time, various positions of stops in articulation, various categories of vowels, liquids and glides, voiced and voiceless fricatives, or various pitch contours. Yet, under naturalistic conditions, the infant obviously perceives categories of similar speech sounds rather than prototypical invariants and depends on categorical perceptual processing. Lieberman (1967) pointed out that vowel categories of different languages represent an almost infinite set of possibilities and that it would be difficult to imagine how a categorical distinction of all possibilities could be fully covered by an innate set of feature detectors in human newborns without further experience with speech in a meaningful context.

The role of practicing is more evident in the infant's production of speech sounds than in their perception. Microanalyses of both infant dialogues with caregivers and infant monologues reveal innumerable episodes readily interpretable as practicing or as vocal play (M. Papoušek & H. Papoušek, 1981). With improving control of subglottal air pressure during the first 8 to 10 weeks of life, the duration of voicing increases, and gliding intonation contours appear in pitch with increasing frequency. Before distinct vowels develop, the fundamental voicing first acquires features of a pleasant, melodic sound approaching the sound of a musical instrument. Melodic intonation contours and voice quality not only add hedonic qualities to these sounds but also allow the caregiver to differentiate various internal states in the infant (M. Papoušek, 1989).

According to the caregiver's comments included in the baby talk, the two main directions of vocal modulations—one standing for expressions of pleasure and the other for displeasure—serve as a particularly important feedback mode signaling the caregiver what the infant likes or dislikes, or how the infant copes with the course of interactions with the environment. Inter-individual variability in the use of melodic contours and voice quality may of course substantially influence the degree to which the caregiver understands the infant. On the whole, between two and three months after birth, modulations in the fundamental vowel-like voicing alone enable an interchange of vocal signals carrying a differential information on internal feelings and thoughts (M. Papoušek, 1989).

Vocal expressions of emotional states may be shaped to simple nonverbal communicative signals (H. Papoušek et al., 1986). Initial expressions of pleasure or displeasure bear a character of tonic responses; however, beyond 7 months, they can also be used as phasic communicative signals characterized by a short duration and sometimes rapid transition from signals of pleasure to signals of displeasure. The interactional context of such phasic signals often clearly indicates volitional communication.

The production of elementary consonant-like sounds between 3 and 6 months of life does not substantially change the role of melodic contours. However, it does influence interactional communication with the caregiver and offers an additional variety of sounds to practice on or play with during infant monologues (M. Papoušek & H. Papoušek, 1989). The frequency of practicing and vocal play, the pleasure in it, and the capacity to imitate models displayed by the caregiver require special attention in comparative research, because they may well belong to species-specific characteristics of human infancy for which there is a potent intrinsic motivation.

This period of development in vocalization is mainly filled up with a differential production of sounds rather than with attention to their future linguistic meaning. In other words, it is the time of procedure-based rather than data-based formation of future potential vocal symbols.

The two types of information involved in preverbal vocal interchanges—the procedure-based and data-based types—should be considered in regard to the questions of infantile amnesia, according to H. Papoušek and M. Papoušek (1985, 1987). Studies of amnesia in human adults have proven that procedure- or rule-based information ("know how") can be retained even in severe cases of Korsakoff amnesia, where data-based information ("know that") has been lost (Cohen & Squire, 1980). H. Papoušek (1967, 1977) demonstrated that repeated exposure to learning tasks accelerates age-dependent increases in the rate of learning in 0- to 6-month-old infants. Thus, it is possible that in spite of infantile amnesia as regards data-based information, human infants benefit from early learning in terms of action-based learning how to learn, how to integrate skills and rules, communicative in particular, and how to process and produce finely differentiated vocal symbols.

During the 1970s and 1980s, research in preverbal communication advanced to such a degree that revision of former concepts and methodological approaches was necessary. The seeming dichotomy between simple, genetically fixed signals of internal, affective states in nonhuman animals or in preverbal human infants, and complex semantic signals based on speech acquisition in adult human beings (Smith, 1965), broke down in the light of recent comparative research. Thus, a concept was revised that dominated much former speculative psychology, traditional ethology (Moynihan, 1970), and consequently the original interpretation of attachment.

The acquisition of speech during ontogeny should be easier to study than the evolution of speech, and yet some of its aspects have remained unclear, such as the question concerning environmental support to speech acquisition. Two arguments are evident: (a) in cases of transcultural adoptions, children acquire the language of adoptive rather than biological parents; and (b) parents and caregivers seem to be unable to convey the rules of grammar and syntax to their progeny prior to their progeny's acquisition of speech.

Some linguists indirectly admitted environmental support insofar as they strongly recommended that parents use only correct forms of language in order to facilitate speech acquisition. In our present study, we find that an increasing proportion of parents in the United States read books to very young infants nowadays in order to facilitate not only speech acquisition but also the present and future learning of foreign languages. Swiss parents are acknowledged breeders of polyglots. However, so far as we know, they have never applied the reading of books to preverbal infants.

Traditions in the care for human infants have been studied rather extensively by various authors. For instance, Fritz Heider (1958) analyzed naive psychology, including parental beliefs on child rearing; Albrecht Peiper (1958) collected rich historical documentation on the care of infants, and Bell and Harper (1977) analyzed child effects on adults in historical perspectives. Nowhere, however, has an evident tradition been reported in relation to the support of speech acquisition in infants during the preverbal age. Thus, at the beginning of our studies, we were left with the impression that infants acquire speech due to maturation of the vocal tract; due to innate capacities of perceptual learning, imitation, abstraction and symbolization; and due to an innate set of rules that allow preverbal infants to grammatically and syntactically arrange the first words into meaningful entities.

However, even if we should have been ready to admit that innate programs *per se* could be sufficient prerequisites for the acquisition of speech during ontogeny, we were still hesitant that innate programs would explain the whole story. Such a story would be very exceptional from a biological perspective, because, in nature, the most significant means of adaptation are not only based on selected genetic programs but also meet ecological counterparts among environmental factors. Supportive environmental factors can often be found in certain surplus that in general simply increases the probability that the biologically significant means of adaptation will function effectively.

The Papoušeks' former interest in the early ontogeny of infant learning and cognitive capacities, and their search for everyday situations in which human infants might practice in those integrative capacities, have drawn attention to those forms of parental behaviors that parents carry out unknowingly and can hardly control consciously—the *intuitive* or *nonconscious* parental behaviors. H. Papoušek and M. Papoušek (1982a) described a set of interesting behaviors that previously escaped the attention of researchers, most probably due to the fact that intuitive behaviors cannot be studied with the help of mere questionnaires or traditional pencil-and-paper type of observational protocols. Intuitive behaviors could only be found when the Papoušeks started using microanalytic techniques in the evaluation of parent–infant interactions in 1968 at Jerome Bruner's Center for Cognitive Studies.

As repeatedly reported since 1977, these intuitive parental behaviors provide young infants with a large amount of episodes—often around 20 per minute during parent–infant interactions—in which parents make themselves contingent, easily predictable, and manipulatable by the infant. From the very beginning, H. Papoušek and M. Papoušek (1977) also pointed out that experimental interventions altering the contingency and predictability of those intuitive parental interventions easily upset the infant and lead to signs of displeasure and frustration in the infant.

A finer analysis of intuitive parental behaviors has revealed that they fulfill criteria of didactic interventions, because parents enhance infant skills and intervene in accordance with the momentary state of infant alertness, attention, affective mood, and limits of tolerance. H. Papoušek and M. Papoušek (1978) suggested that there is a primary, biologically determined model of didactics included in intuitive parental behaviors and that it mainly concerns the means of preverbal communication, namely the preverbal vocal, facial, and gestural patterns of communication. A recent analysis by Bornstein (1985) demonstrated in global parameters how mother and infant jointly contribute to developing cognitive competence in the child.

As M. Papoušek (1984) reported at the International Conference on Infant Studies meeting in New York, the interpretation of parental interventions as didactic interventions is not merely speculative. For instance, a statistical evaluation of the distribution of melodic contours in maternal speech to young infants in relation to various factors in the interactional context showed that the contingency coefficient was lowest for associations with the type of sentences (0.385) and the infant's state (0.391) but increased gradually in relation to infant vocal expressions (0.461) and to the focus of maternal attention (0.630); it reached a maximum in associations with maternal didactic intentions (0.711) that mothers frequently express in the lexical content of their baby talk (Papoušek, Papoušek & Koester, 1986).

In order to understand the significance of intuitive parental interventions, let us first consider some general qualities of intuitive behaviors. Intuitive responses are more flexible than innate reflexes and, thus, allow a fine adjustment to environmental circumstances. They are slower than innate reflexes but still faster than conscious, rational decisions; they are less strenuous than rational responses, and, thus, they occupy less parental attention allowing the parent to stimulate the infant adequately and simultaneously to control other circumstances or ongoing activities.

Intuitive parental interventions may appear finely adjusted to each infant in individual cases; however, the underlying tendencies have been found to be universal across parental sex, age, and across at least some cultures. M. Papoušek, H. Papoušek, and Bornstein (1985), for instance, documented how qualitatively congruent mothers and fathers are in the use of melodic contours in the prosody of baby talk. The use of baby talk is also a good example of the universality of these interventions across age, because children start displaying typical features of baby talk around 2 to 3 years when addressing young infants (Sachs, Brown, & Salerno, 1976; M. Papoušek & H. Papoušek, 1981). Crosscultural comparisons indicate universal tendencies in the use of baby talk, for instance, in pitch modifications (Fernald, Taeschner, Dunn, Papoušek, Boysson-Bardies, & Fukui, 1989) or in forms and functions of prosodic contours (Papoušek, M., & Papoušek, H., 1987, April).

The universality of didactic interventions seems to cause a qualitative homogeneity, necessitated by the constraints of infant learning and cognitive capacities, whereas their quantity seems to be variable across social classes and cultures, and also to depend on the amount of experience in caregiving to infants

(M. Papoušek, H. Papoušek & Bornstein, 1985). For instance, traditionally fathers have been reported to talk less to babies than do mothers (Field, 1978; Pedersen, Anderson & Cain, 1980), and lower-class mothers to talk less than do middle-class mothers in the United States, in England, and in Israel (Field & Pawlby, 1980; Ninio, 1980; Tulkin & Kagan, 1972). Mothers also speak less to babies due to cultural beliefs, for instance, among Guatemalan Indians (Kagan & Klein, 1973) or among African Zambians (Goldberg, 1977).

The infant's visual attention is an important assumption for the acquisition of languages inasmuch as it enables the infant to imitate and learn oral and facial movements involved in the production of speech sounds or nonvocal signs, such as, for instance, in deaf families that use sign languages. Therefore, it is interesting that several intuitive parental interventions support the establishment of visual contact with infants. These interventions again are universal across sex and some cultures, as has been shown in the control of the distance between the parent's eyes and the infant's eyes, in the tendency to achieve a face-to-face position, and in rewarding the achievement of visual contact with a complex greeting response. Recently, the greeting response following the achievement of eye-to-eye contact has been found to function in 3-month-old infants (Haekel, 1985).

ATTACHMENT CONCEPTS
AND EARLY COMMUNICATION

A major reason for the relative neglect of preverbal communication may be seen in the climate of opinion dominating the early 1960s during which the major theories on attachment were constructed. At that time, it was difficult to find theoretical concepts that would view the caregiver–infant dyad as an interactional system, provide techniques for interactional analyses, and encompass both interacting partners. This lack has not yet been satisfactorily overcome. For instance, Bretherton (1985), in a critical analysis of attachment research, concluded that it would be fruitful to integrate into attachment theory recent advances regarding, among others, communication and general representational processes.

Spitz (1965), representing that part of attachment research that primarily tried to analyze the development of attachment as such, integrated communication into the concept of attachment at least in his hypotheses, which he could not verify, however, due to his advanced age. Spitz's interpretation of communication revealed the influence of his former tutor, Karl Buehler. The two fundamental forms that Spitz differentiated in perception and communication—namely the coenesthetic and diacritic forms—roughly correspond to differences between intuitive and rational forms. According to Spitz, mothers activate their capacity for coenesthetic communication during pregnancy and immediately following delivery.

Of those affects involved in coenesthetic communication, Spitz assigned the most important role to two: pleasure as expressed by smile, and displeasure as expressed by crying. He attributed equal significance to both of them in the mental development. Frustration, according to Spitz, is inbuilt in development and is the most potent catalyst of evolution at nature's disposal. In referring to Freud (1953), Spitz (1965) stressed the implementation of thought processes in affects, whenever he commented on the integrative roles of affects in the infant's development. Two developmental periods are important from this point of view. By the eighth week of life, the infant starts manifesting displeasure in increasingly structured and intelligible ways, which the mother views as the beginning of communication. The infant is able to grasp a connection between what he does and the response from the environment. To Spitz, this is the beginning of the ideational category of causality and also of volitional signaling in the form of Buehler's (1934) "appeal." The other important period comes around the age of 8 to 10 months, when the role of pleasure and displeasure becomes intricately implemented in cognitive operations, such as symbol formation, abstraction, logical operations, or what Piaget calls reversibility.

A well-established mother–infant affective communication facilitates speech acquisition and serves as a protection of the dyad against traumatic events, according to Spitz. Recently, Thoman (1981) conceptualized affective communication in preverbal infants as the prelude and context for language learning. She argued, however, that affects and cognitive processes can be separated and that there is both biological and behavioral evidence of the primacy of affect in organization of the infant's earliest communication. Spitz's arguments for the unity of affective and cognitive processes were only hypothetical, and no forms of verification were considered. Ironically, H. Papoušek (1967), who described the regular participation of affective behaviors in infant learning in nonsocial situations, studied early concept formation and problem solving, and he analyzed interrelations between cognitive and affective processes in 4-month-olds (H. Papoušek & Bernstein, 1969; H. Papoušek, 1969) at the same nursery (Infant of Prague Nursery in Denver), in 1966, in which Spitz observed institutionalized infants. Spitz (1965) also considered comparative aspects of mother–infant communication in relation to the face-to-face interactions and to the signaling effect of the eye.

The "mainstream" approach in attachment research has been represented by Bowlby (1951, 1969) and Ainsworth (1962). In constructing his concept, Bowlby tried to avoid both the traditional psychoanalytic and the contemporary behavioristic positions. Instead he attempted to encompass comparative studies regarding maternal deprivation in animals. However, interactional analyses that are more adequate for the study of interindividual relationships and essential for research on communication were not yet sufficiently elaborated at that time. Nor was communication recognized as a phenomenon crucial to social interactions. Moreover, Bowlby has mainly been interested in the ill effects of a disturbed attachment and less in the developmental process of attachment as such.

In addition to the two sources of human motivation—hunger and reproduction—Bowlby postulated a special class of behaviors with its own dynamics, that
is, attachment behaviors attaining and maintaining proximity to some other clearly identified individual who is conceived as better able to cope with the world
(Bowlby, 1982, p. 668). Although attachment behavior is most obvious in early
childhood, it is seen in virtually all human beings at all ages, according to
Bowlby, and it represents an integral part of human nature and one that humans
share with members of other species. Its primary biological function is supposed
to be that of protection.

Unfortunately, observing children only as responders to the absence of attachment objects does not offer adequate ways for studies of the process of attachment that typically grows out of dyadic interactions. The participation of communication may easily be overlooked, if the observer reconstructs the
development of attachment from symptoms caused by loss of the communicative
partner. Probably for this reason, Bowlby did not include either the concept or
the methodological tools of interactional research in his original theory of attachment, and, thus, could not give a timely and proper orientation to experimental
research that has been stimulated by his theory.

Human experimental research in attachment has been mainly stimulated by
Ainsworth (1973). She has offered a standardized test situation—the Strange
Situation—as a base for the assessment of attachment and, thus, enabled a much
broader experimental approach to the problems of attachment than the clinical
study of seriously deprived children. Ainsworth's methodological tool, however,
has not been designed for analyses of finer structures and interactional functions
of behavioral items included in her measures. In fact, the circumstances of the
Strange Situation intentionally reduce specific dyadic interaction and communication between the mother and the infant.

However, Ainsworth (1973) also analyzed the developmental process of attachment as such in longitudinal observations and stimulated research in which
recently an increasing attention has been paid to interactional and communicative
aspects. Grossmann (1985), for instance, analyzed the effects of maternal styles
of conversation on the development of infantile vocalizations and the type of
attachment to the mother. Grossmann differentiated four conversational styles in
mothers (sober, tender, lighthearted, and angry) and showed an increase of
infantile vocalization between ages 6 and 12 months in relation to the sober and
tender styles whereas a decrease was observed in relation to the lighthearted
style. In the Strange Situation at the age of 12 months, infants showed secure
attachment more frequently in relation to the tender style of maternal conversation, and they displayed insecure, avoidant attachment more frequently in relation to the sober and lighthearted styles.

Recently introduced psychobiological approaches help elucidate the role of
vocal communication (M. Papoušek & H. Papoušek, 1981), as discussed previously, and attempt to attack the difficult problem of involvement of emotions,
intrinsic motivators, and thought processes in preverbal communication in strict-

ly scientific terms (Reite & Field, 1985; Marler, 1984; Pribram, 1984). Earlier impressions that cognitive and symbolic processes develop only in humans, following the acquisition of speech, has been corrected by recent findings in preverbal human infants and in animal research. Marler (1984, p. 362) has believed that humans did not invent a new symbolic mode of operation but rather that they enriched and elaborated a system already operating in animals. A similar assumption had led H. Papoušek (1969, 1977) to the successful search for integrative capacities beyond simple forms of learning in preverbal infants; these included concept formation, intentional acts (H. Papoušek, 1967), vocal imitation, (M. Papoušek & H. Papoušek, 1989), and symbolization (H. Papoušek & M. Papoušek, 1984b). H. Papoušek and M. Papoušek (1979b) assigned integrative capacities a fundamental role in the regulation of adaptive behaviors and pointed out that they are very early and regularly connected with changes in facial and vocal expressions independent of the presence of any social partner. Such facial and vocal behaviors may express internal, affective states. However, affective states may have resulted from the course of integrative processes and may indicate the presence of intrinsic motivation for learning and cognition. Within social interactions, the infant's facial and vocal expressions may serve as observational cues informing the social environment of the infant's involvement in a problematic situation or of a successful solution to the problem.

Petrovich and Gewirtz (1985) suggested a comprehensive concept on the evolution of attachment that greatly facilitates the comparison of seemingly diverse data on attachment learning, including avian imprinting as well as mammalian attachment. Attachment in humans is related in this concept to the synchrony or mesh among sequential infantile and maternal behaviors that is based on mutual behavioral shaping in terms of operant learning. The idea of synchrony reminds us of the concepts of "psychobiological attunement" (Field, 1985) or "psychobiological synchrony of rhythms" (Reite & Capitanio, 1985) used in recent interpretations of attachment. H. Papoušek and M. Papoušek (1984a; 1987) also discussed the evolution of attachment in connection with Lovejoy's (1981) revision of human evolution as well as from the view of interactional systems. They point out the function of parent–infant interactions in the selection of integrative capacities and verbal communication.

On the whole, therefore, the original theory of attachment has suffered from lack of attention to preverbal communication rather than contributed to a better understanding of the role of preverbal communication in attachment processes in ontogeny and phylogeny.

CONCLUSIONS

A confrontation of attachment concepts with findings from intersections with attachment evinces vulnerable points in the interpretation of attachment as a developmental process. The crucial issue seems to concern the explanation of motivational factors of bonding. Although even at present we can only speculate on motivational factors, recent research points out interesting possibilities of identifying factors that may be common to emotional and communicative expressions of attachment and may be interrelated with integrative processes. Recent advancement in the studies of endogenous opioids suggests a fruitful approach to the interpretation of integrative-communicative-affective phenomena as they may be involved in social bonding. Although opiates had been mainly known as agents reducing motor activities, perception of pain, and affective expressions, a growing body of evidence indicates that their role is many-sided and differentiated in dependence on dosage and on the brain structures involved. Thus in rats, low doses of morphine increase general motor activities (Ayahan & Randup, 1973), self-stimulating behaviors (Kornetsky, Esposito, McLean & Jacobson, 1979), feeding behavior (Panksepp, Herman, Vilberg, Bishop, & DeEskinazy, 1980), or play behavior (Panksepp, 1979), and facilitate extinction in instrumental learning (DeEskinazy & Panksepp, 1979). In guinea pigs, the distress vocalizations are mediated by neural systems that are confluent with opioid systems and have been shown to be controlled by brain opioids (Panksepp, Najam & Soares, 1979).

The relatedness of opioids, as agents influencing libidinal feelings and overt addiction behaviors, to phenomena interpretable as communicative, integrative, or emotional within social interactions has stimulated a series of studies on the role of opioids in social learning. According to a survey by Panksepp et al. (1980), the results of these studies indicate that morphine reduces the isolation stress and may increase social play and dominance achievement. Although no evidence is yet available that brain opioid systems are crucial for the development of social behaviors, the data support the hypothesis that opioid systems modulate the intensity of emotions arising from social isolation or social interactions, according to Panksepp et al. Such effects may reflect mechanisms by which social bonds are reinforced.

The studies carried out by Panksepp and coworkers have been extended to the early ontogeny of the opioid systems in infant rats by Blass and Kehoe (1987). These authors presented pharmacological and behavioral evidence that behaviorally functional opioid systems are available in 5-day-old rats for learning and reinforcement, both appetitive and aversive (Kehoe & Blass, 1986a), and may also mediate naturally occurring, stress-induced vocalization. The opioid systems appear to be controlled and modulated by some sensory cues of the mother and of the nest, especially olfactory cues. Graded responses to social stimuli related to stress are similar to those in adult rats, as reported by Fanselow (1985). Kehoe and Blass (1986b) also suggested that the opioid systems as mediators of affective responses in rats may in fact serve as a reward mechanism in infant learning related to maternal and environmental events.

Although still present only in rodents and in indicative rather than conclusive forms, the evidence of endogenous opioids as mediators and possibly intrinsic reinforcers of behaviors related to affective, integrative, and communicative aspects of social bonding increase our hope that we shall be able to insert another piece of solid evidence into the mosaic of attachment in the near future. H. Papoušek and M. Papoušek (1979b) speculated on the existence of some intrinsic motivation for the acquisition and sharing of information. Their speculation was based on the experimental evidence that human infants—subjects in whom behavior is much more predictable than in adults—show expressions of pleasant feelings related to successful learning or problem solving in a social vacuum. Detection and mastery of contingency; identification of familiar persons, objects, or events; fulfillment of predictions and expectancies; and successful conceptualization of environmental events have been considered as outcomes of integrative processes, possibly eliciting pleasant internal feelings and sometimes signs of addiction as in the mastery of contingency (Watson, 1972).

Attempts to interpret attachment strictly in terms of social learning without considering intrinsic releasers and reinforcers of integrative processes, emotional expressions and social communication face the risk of dead ends. A bit of introspection can make anyone aware that an environmental stimulation may elicit not only one corresponding response but a whole string of overt and internal responses, including emotional feelings, that depend on the outcomes of the processing of the original stimulation, such as memories of past experience, inspiration to new ideas, and so forth. In an interesting but little known study, Krasnogorskyi (1958) used classical, salivatory conditioning to study such internal releasers in children. For instance, the word "eight" was reinforced with Siberian cranberries to elicit strong salivation. In subsequent experiments, such salivation was triggered by internal calculations, whenever their results equaled "eight." Since then, however, intrinsic releasers of integrative processes have remained underresearched.

Detailed analyses of social interactions between infants and caregivers make evident that learning phenomena coexist with more complex integrative processes from the realm of cognitive psychology (such as detection of regularities in complex situations, concept formation, or organization of adaptive behaviors). These are based not only on trial-and-error, but also on imitation, playful or even creative exploration, and successive automation of best-fitting skills. Before more is known about the nature and regulation of such integrative processes, it seems premature and superfluous to either reduce attention to one particular category of integrative processes or to speculate on the primacy of emotions vs. integrative processes. An infant smile is a particularly salient example of interactional phenomena resisting attempts to categorize it either as a mere social signal or a mere emotional expression. At the same time though, a smile may be elicited by successful internal processes of thought. From this point of view, the study of early communication indicates that a further progress in understanding the process of attachment will be the fruit of crossdisciplinary efforts to which human studies can contribute by delineating universalities and specificities of interactive behaviors, observable in human social bonding.

REFERENCES

Ainsworth, M. D. S. (1962). The effects of maternal deprivation: A review of findings and controversy in the context of research strategy. *Public Health Papers* (No 14). Deprivation of maternal care: A reassessment of its effects. Geneva: World Health Organization.

Ainsworth, M. D. S. (1973). The development of infant-mother attachment. In B. M. Caldwell & H. N. Ricciuti (Eds.), *Review of child development research* (Vol. 3, pp. 1–94). Chicago: The University of Chicago Press.

Altmann, S. A. (1967). The structure of primate communication. In S. A. Altmann (Ed.), *Social communication among primates* (pp. 325–362). Chicago, IL: University of Chicago Press.

Ayahan, I. H., & Randup, A. (1973). Behavioral and pharmacological studies on morphine-induced excitation of rats: Possible relations to brain catecholamines. *Psychopharmacologia, 29,* 317–328.

Bell, R. A., & Harper, L. W. (1977). *Child effects on adults.* Hillsdale, NJ: Lawrence Erlbaum Associates.

von Bertalanffy, L. (1968). General system theory—A critical review. In W. Buckley (Ed.), *Modern systems research for the behavioral scientist* (pp. 11–30). Chicago, IL: Aldine.

Blass, E. M., & Kehoe, P. (1987). Behavioral characteristics of emerging opiate systems in newborn rats. In N. A. Krasnegor, E. M. Blass, M. E. Hofer, & W. P. Smotherman (Eds.), *Perinatal behavioral development: A psychobiological perspective* (pp. 61–82). New York: Academic Press.

Bornstein, M. H. (1985). How infant and mother jointly contribute to developing cognitive competence in the child. *Proceedings of the National Academy of Sciences in the U.S.A., 82,* 7470–7473.

Bowlby, J. (1951). *Maternal care and mental health.* New York: Columbia University Press.

Bowlby, J. (1969). *Attachment and loss.* Volume 1: Attachment. New York: Basic.

Bowlby, J. (1980). *Attachment and loss.* Volume 3: Loss, sadness and depression. New York: Basic.

Bowlby, J. (1982). Attachment and loss: Retrospect and prospect. *American Journal of Orthopsychiatry, 52,* 664–678.

Bretherton, I. (1985). Attachment theory: Retrospect and prospect. In I. Bretherton & E. Watters (Eds.), Growing points of attachment theory and research. *Monographs of the Society for Research in Child Development, 50*(1–2, Serial No. 209, pp. 3–35).

Brown, C. H., Beecher, M. D., Moody, D. B., & Stebbins, W. C. (1979). Locatability of vocal signals in Old World monkeys: Design features for the communication of position. *Journal of Comparative and Physiological Psychology, 93,* 806–819.

Buehler, K. (1934). *Sprachtheorie* [Theory of language]. Jena, Germany: Fischer.

Chevalier-Skolnikoff, S. (1982). A cognitive analysis of facial behavior in Old World monkeys, apes, and human beings. In C. T. Snowdon, C. H. Brown, & M. R. Petersen (Eds.), *Primate communication* (pp. 303–368). Cambridge, UK: Cambridge University Press.

Cleveland, J., & Snowdon, C. T. (1982). The complex vocal repertoire of the adult cotton-top tamarin, *Sanguinus oedipus oedipus. Zeitschrift fuer Tierpsychologie, 58,* 231–270.

Cohen, N. J., & Squire, L. R. (1980). Preserved learning and retention of pattern-analyzing skill in amnesia: Dissociation of knowing how and know that. *Science, 210,* 207–210.

DeCasper, A. J., & Fifer, W. P. (1980). Of human bonding: Newborns prefer their mothers' voices. *Science, 208,* 1174–1176.

DeEskinazy, F., & Panksepp, J. (1979). Opiates lead to persistance of spatial habits with social rewards. *Society for Neurosciences Abstracts, 5,* 315.

Eilers, R. E. (1977). Context sensitive perception of naturally produced stop and fricative consonants by infants. *Journal of the Acoustic Society of America, 61,* 1321–1336.

Eimas, P. D. (1974). Auditory and linguistic processing of cues for place of articulation by infants. *Perception and Psychophysics, 16,* 513–521.

Eimas, P. D. (1975a). Auditory and phonetic coding of the cues for speech: Discrimination of the /r–l/ distinction by young infants. *Perception and Psychophysics, 18,* 341–347.

Eimas, P. D. (1975b). Speech perception in early infancy. In L. B. Cohen & P. Salapatek (Eds.),

118

Infant perception: From sensation to cognition. Volume 2: Perception of space, speech, and sound (pp. 193–231). New York: Academic Press.

Fanselow, M. S. (1985). Odors released by stressed rats produce opioid analgesia in unstressed rats. *Behavioral Neurosciences, 99,* 589–592.

Fernald, A., Taeschner, T., Dunn, J., Papoušek, M., Boysson-Bardies, B., & Fukui, I. (1989). A cross-language study of prosodic modifications in mothers' and fathers' speech to preverbal infants. *Journal of Child Language, 16,* 977–1001.

Field, T. (1978). Interaction behaviors of primary versus secondary caretaker fathers. *Developmental Psychology, 14,* 183–184.

Field, T. (1985). Attachment as psychobiological attunement: Being on the same wavelength. In M. Reite & T. Field (Eds.), *The psychobiology of attachment and separation* (pp. 415–454). New York: Academic Press.

Field, T., & Pawlby, S. (1980). Early face-to-face interactions of British and American working- and middle-class mother–infant dyads. *Child Development, 51,* 250–253.

Freud, S. (1953). Formulation on the two principles of mental functioning. In J. Strachey (Ed. & Trans.), *Standard Edition of the Complete Psychological Work of Sigmund Freud* (Vol. 12). London: Hogarth Press. (Original work published 1911).

Fridlund, A. J., Ekman, P., & Oster, H. (1987). Facial expressions of emotions: Review of literature, 1970–1983. In A. Siegman & S. Feldstein (Eds.), *Nonverbal behavior and communication.* 2nd Ed., pp. 143–224. Hillsdale, NJ: Lawrence Erlbaum Associates.

Frisch, K. v. (1965). *Tanzsprache und Orientierung der Bienen* [Dance language and orientation in honeybees]. Berlin: Springer-Verlag.

Gardner, R. A., & Gardner, B. T. (1978). Comparative psychology and language acquisition. *Annals of the New York Academy of Sciences, 309,* 37–76.

Goldberg, S. (1977). Infant development and mother–infant interaction in urban Zambia. In P. H. Leiderman, S. R. Tulkin, & A. Rosenfeld (Eds.), *Culture and infancy: Variations in the human experience* (pp. 211–243). New York: Academic Press.

Green, S. (1975). Variations of vocal pattern with social situation in the Japanese monkey (Macaca fuscata). In L. A. Rosenblum (Ed.), *Primate behavior: Developments in field and laboratory research* (Vol. 4, pp. 1–102). New York: Academic Press.

Grossmann, K. E. (1985). The development of emotional expression in a social context. In J. T. Spence & C. E. Izard (Eds.), *Motivation, emotion, and personality* (pp. 305–316). XXIIIth International Congress of Psychology. Amsterdam: Elsevier North Holland.

Haekel, M. (1985, July). *Greeting behavior in 3-month-old infants during mother–infant interaction.* Paper presented at the 8th Biennial Meetings of the International Society for the Study of Behavioral Development, Tours, France. (Abstracted in *Cahiers de Psychologie Cognitive, 5,* 275–276).

Heider, F. (1958). *The psychology of interpersonal relations.* New York: Wiley.

Higley, J. D., & Suomi, S. J. (1986). Parental care in nonhuman primates. In W. Sluckin & M. Herbert (Eds.), *Parental behaviour* (pp. 152–207). New York: Basil Blackwell.

Hinde, R. A. (1972). *Non-verbal communication.* Cambridge, UK: Cambridge University Press.

Janson, C. H. (1984). Female choice and mating system of the brown capuchin monkey (*Cebus apella*) (Primates: *Cebidae*). *Zeitschrift für Tierpsychologie, 65,* 177–200.

Janson, C. H. (1986). The mating system as a determinant of social evolution in capuchin monkeys (*Cebus*). In J. G. Else & P. C. Lee (Eds.), *Proceedings of the Xth Congress of the International Primatological Society. Primate Ecology and Conservation* (Vol. 2, pp. 169–179). New York: Cambridge University Press.

Jusczyk, P. W. (1977). Perception of syllable-final stop consonants by two-month-old infants. *Perception and Psychophysics, 21,* 450–454.

Kagan, J. & Klein, R. (1973). Cross-cultural perspectives on early development. *American Psychologist, 28,* 947–961.

Kaplan, J. N., Winship-Ball, A., & Sim, L. (1978). Maternal discrimination of infant vocalizations in Squirrel Monkeys. *Primates, 19,* 187–193.

Kehoe, P., & Blass, E. M. (1986a). Behaviorally functional opioid systems in infant rats: I. Evidence for olfactory and gustatory classical conditioning. *Behavioral Neurosciences, 100*, 359–367.

Kehoe, P., & Blass, E. M. (1986b). Behaviorally functional opioid systems in infant rats: II. Evidence for pharmacological, physiological, and psychological mediation of pain and stress. *Behavioral Neurosciences, 100*, 624–630.

Kornetsky, C., Esposito, R. U., McLean, S., & Jacobson, J. O. (1979). Intracranial self-stimulation thresholds. *Archives of Genetic Psychiatry, 36*, 289–292.

Krasnogorskyi, N. I. (1958). *The higher nervous activity in the child.* (Russian). Leningrad: Medgiz.

Kuhl, P. K. (1979). The perception of speech in early infancy. In N. J. Lass (Ed.), *Speech and language: Advances in basic research and practice* (pp. 1–47). New York: Academic Press.

Kuhl, P. K. (1983). Perception of auditory equivalence classes for speech in early infancy. *Infant Behavior and Development, 6*, 263–285.

Kuhl, P. K. (1985). Categorization of speech by infants, In J. Mehler & R. Fox (Eds.), *Neonate cognition: Beyond the blooming, buzzing confusion* (pp. 231–262). Hillsdale, NJ: Lawrence Erlbaum Associates.

Lieberman, P. (1967). Intonation, perception, and language. *Research Monograph* (No. 38). Cambridge, MA: MIT Press.

Lieberman, P. (1984). *The biology and evolution of language.* Cambridge, MA: Harvard University Press.

Lovejoy, C. O. (1981). The origin of man. *Science, 211*, 341–350.

Marler, P. (1975). On the origin of speech from animal sounds. In J. F. Kavanaugh & J. E. Cutting (Eds.), *The role of speech in language* (pp. 11–37). Cambridge, MA: MIT Press.

Marler, P. (1977). Primate vocalizations: Affective or symbolic? In G. H. Bourne (Ed.), *Progress in ape research* (pp. 85–96). New York: Academic Press.

Marler, P. (1984). Animal communication: Affect or cognition? In K. R. Scherer & P. Ekman (Eds.), *Approaches to emotion* (pp. 345–365). Hillsdale, NJ: Lawrence Erlbaum Associates.

Moynihan, M. (1970). The control, suppression, decay, disappearance and replacement of displays. *Journal of Theoretical Biology, 29*, 85–112.

Newman, J. D., & Symmes, D. (1982). Inheritance and experience in the acquisition of primate acoustic behavior. In C. T. Snowdon, C. H. Brown, & M. R. Peterson (Eds.), *Primate communication* (pp. 259–278). Cambridge, UK: Cambridge University Press.

Ninio, A. (1980). Picture-book reading in mother–infant dyads belonging to two subgroups in Israel. *Child Development, 51*, 587–590.

Panksepp, J. (1979). The regulation of play: Neurochemical controls. *Society for Neurosciences Abstracts, 5*, 172.

Panksepp, J., Najam, N., & Soares, F. (1979). Morphine reduces social cohesion in rats. *Pharmacology, Biochemistry and Behavior, 11*, 131–134.

Panksepp, J., Herman, B. H., Vilberg, T., Bishop, P., & DeEskinazy, F. G. (1980). Endogenous opioids and social behavior. *Neurosciences and Biobehavioral Reviews, 4*, 473–487.

Papoušek, H. (1967). Experimental studies of appetitional behavior in human newborns and infants. In H. W. Stevenson, E. H. Hess, & H. L. Rheingold (Eds.), *Early behavior: Comparative and developmental approaches* (pp. 249–277). New York: Wiley.

Papoušek, H. (1969). Individual variability in learned responses in human infants. In R. J. Robinson (Ed.), *Brain and early behavior* (pp. 251–266). London: Academic Press.

Papoušek, H. (1977). Entwicklung der Lernfaehigkeit im Saeuglingsalter [Development of learning abilities during infancy]. In G. Nissen (Ed.), *Intelligenz, Lernen und Lernstoerungen* [Intelligence, learning, and learning disorders] (pp. 89–107). Berlin/ Heidelberg/ New York: Springer-Verlag.

Papoušek, H., & Bernstein, P. (1969). The functions of conditioning stimulation in human neonates and infants. In A. Ambrose (Ed.), *Stimulation in early infancy* (pp. 229–252). London: Academic Press.

Papoušek, H., & Papoušek, M. (1974). Mirror image and self-recognition in young human infants: I. A new method of experimental analysis. *Developmental Psychobiology, 7,* 149–157.

Papoušek, H., & Papoušek, M. (1977, August). *Biological aspects of early social and cognitive development in man.* Paper presented at the XVth International Ethological Conference in Bielefeld, F. R. Germany.

Papoušek, H., & Papoušek, M. (1978). Interdisciplinary parallels in studies of early human behavior: From physical to cognitive needs, from attachment to dyadic education. *International Journal of Behavioral Development, 1,* 37–49.

Papoušek, H., & Papoušek, M. (1979a). Early ontogeny of human social interaction: Its biological roots and social dimensions. In M. von Cranach, K. Foppa, W. Lepenies, & D. Ploog (Eds.), *Human ethology. Claims and limits of a new discipline* (pp. 456–478). Cambridge, UK: Cambridge University Press.

Papoušek, H., & Papoušek, M. (1979b). The infant's fundamental adaptive response system in social interaction. In E. B. Thoman (Ed.), *Origins of the infant's social responsiveness* (pp. 175–208). Hillsdale, NJ: Lawrence Erlbaum Associates.

Papoušek, H., & Papoušek, M. (1982). Integration into the social world: Survey of research. In P. M. Stratton (Ed.), *Psychobiology of the human newborn* (pp. 367–390). London: Wiley.

Papoušek, H., & Papoušek, M. (1984a). The evolution of parent–infant attachment: New psychobiological perspectives. In J. D. Call, E. Galenson, & R. L. Tyson (Eds.), *Frontiers of infant psychiatry* (Vol. 2, pp. 276–283). New York: Basic Books.

Papoušek, H., & Papoušek, M. (1984b). Learning and cognition in the everyday life of human infants. In J. S. Rosenblatt (Ed.), *Advances in the study of behavior* (Vol. 14, pp. 127–163). New York: Academic Press.

Papoušek, H., & Papoušek, M. (1985). Der Beginn der sozialen Integration nach der Geburt: Krisen oder Kontinuitaeten [The beginning of social integration after the birth: Crises or continuities]? *Monatsschrift der Kinderheilkunde, 133,* 425–429. Berlin: Springer-Verlag.

Papoušek, H., & Papoušek, M. (1987). Intuitive parenting: A dialectic counterpart to the infant's integrative competence. In J. D. Osofsky (Ed.), *Handbook of infant development,* pp. 669–720 (2nd ed). New York: Wiley.

Papoušek, H., Papoušek, M., & Koester, L. S. (1986). Sharing emotionality and sharing knowledge: A microanalytic approach to parent–infant communication. In C. E. Izard & P. Read (Eds.), *Measuring emotions in infants and children* (Vol. 2, pp. 93–123). New York: Cambridge University Press.

Papoušek, M. (1984, April). *Categorical vocal cues in parental communication with presyllabic infants.* Paper presented at the International Conference on Infant Studies in New York. [Abstracted in *Infant Behavior and Development, 7* (Special Issue), 283.]

Papoušek, M. (1989). Determinants of responsiveness to infant vocal expression of emotional state. *Infant Behavior and Development, 12,* 505–522.

Papoušek, M., & Papoušek, H. (1981). Musical elements in the infant's vocalizations: Their significance for communication, cognition, and creativity. In L. P. Lipsitt & C. K. Rovee-Collier (Eds.), *Advances in infancy research* (Vol. 1, pp. 163–224). Norwood, NJ: Ablex.

Papoušek, M., & Papoušek, H. (1987, April). *Models and messages in maternal speech to presyllabic infants in tone and stress languages.* Paper presented at the Sixth Biennial Meetings of the Society for Research in Child Development in Baltimore, U.S.A.

Papoušek, M., & Papoušek, H. (1989). Forms and functions of vocal matching in precanonical mother-infant interactions. *First Language, 9,* 137–158. Special Issue on "Precursors of Speech".

Papoušek, M., Papoušek, H., & Bornstein, M. H. (1985). The naturalistic vocal environment of young infants: On the significance of homogeneity and variability in parental speech. In T. Field & N. Fox (Eds.), *Social perception in infants* (pp. 269–297). Norwood, NJ: Ablex.

Pedersen, F. A., Anderson, B., & Cain, R. (1980). Parent–infant and husband–wife interactions observed at the age of 5 months. In F. A. Pedersen (Ed.), *The father–infant relationship: Observational studies in the family setting* (pp. 71–86). New York: Praeger.

Peiper, A. (1958). *Chronik der Kinderheilkunde* [The chronicle of pediatrics]. Leipzig, D. R. Germany: Thieme.

Petrovich, S. B., & Gewirtz, J. L. (1985). The attachment learning process and its relation to cultural and biological evolution: Proximate and ultimate consideration. In M. Reite & T. Field (Eds.), *The psychobiology of attachment and separation* (pp. 259–291). New York: Academic Press.

Piaget, J. (1952). *The origins of intelligence in children* (M. Cook, Trans.). New York: International Universities Press. (Original work published 1936)

Premack, D. (1975). On the origins of language. In M. S. Gazzaniga & C. B. Blakemore (Eds.), *Handbook of psychobiology*, pp. 591–605. New York: Academic Press.

Pribram, K. H. (1984). Emotion: A neurobehavioral analysis. In K. R. Scherer & P. Ekman (Eds.), *Approaches to emotion* (pp. 13–38). Hillsdale, NJ: Lawrence Erlbaum Associates.

Raymond, R. C. (1968). Communication, entropy, and life. In W. Buckley (Ed.), *Modern systems research for the behavioral scientist* (pp. 157–160). Chicago: Aldine.

Reite, M., & Capitanio, J. P. (1985). On the nature of social separation and social attachment. In M. Reite & T. Field (Eds.), *The psychobiology of attachment and separation* (pp. 223–255). New York: Academic Press.

Reite, M., & Field, T. (Eds.). (1985). *The psychobiology of attachment and separation*. New York: Academic Press.

Robinson, J. G. (1982). Vocal systems regulating within-group spacing. In C. T. Snowdon, C. H. Brown, & M. R. Peterson (Eds.), *Primate communication* (pp. 94–116). Cambridge, UK: Cambridge University Press.

Sachs, J., Brown, R., & Salerno, R. A. (1976). Adults' speech to children. In W. v. Raffler-Engel & Y. Lebrun (Eds.), *Babytalk and infant speech* (pp. 240–245). Lisse, Holland: Swets & Zeitlinger.

Schoetzau, A., & Papoušek, H. (1977). Muetterliches Verhalten bei der Aufnahme von Blickkontakt mit dem Neugeborenen [Maternal behavior related to the establishment of visual contact with the newborn]. *Zeitschrift fuer Entwicklungspsychologie und Paedagogische Psychologie, 9,* 231–239.

Seyfarth, R. M., & Cheney, D. L. (1982). How monkeys see the world: A review of recent research on East African vervet monkeys. In C. T. Snowdon, C. H. Brown, & M. R. Peterson (Eds.), *Primate communication* (pp. 239–252). Cambridge, UK: Cambridge University Press.

Seyfarth, R. M., Cheney, D. L., & Marler, P. (1980). Vervet monkeys alarm calls: Semantic communication in a free-ranging primate. *Animal Behaviour, 28,* 1070–1094.

Smith, H. J., Newman, J. D., & Symmes, D. (1982). Vocal concomitants of affiliative behavior in squirrel monkeys. In C. T. Snowdon, C. H. Brown, & M. R. Peterson (Eds.), *Primate communication* (pp. 30–49). Cambridge, UK: Cambridge University Press.

Smith, W. J. (1965). Message, meaning, and context in ethology. *American Naturalist, 99,* 405–409.

Snowdon, C. T. (1982). Linguistic and psycholinguistic approaches to primate communication. In C. T. Snowdon, C. H. Brown, & M. R. Peterson (Eds.), *Primate communication* (pp. 212–238). Cambridge, UK: Cambridge University Press.

Spitz, R. A. (1965). *The first year of life. A psychoanalytic study of normal and deviant development of object relations*. New York: International Universities Press.

Studdert-Kennedy, M. (1983). On learning to speak. *Human Neurobiology, 2,* 191–195.

Symmes, D., & Biben, M. (1985). Maternal recognition of individual infant squirrel monkeys from isolation call playbacks. *American Journal of Primatology, 9,* 39–46.

Thoman, E. B. (1981). Affective communication as the prelude and context for language learning. In R. L. Schiefelbusch & D. B. Brisker (Eds.), *Early language: Acquisition and intervention* (pp. 181–200). Language Intervention Series (Vol. VI). Baltimore: University Park Press.

Tulkin, S. R., & Kagan, J. (1972). Mother–child interaction in the first year of life. *Child Development, 43,* 323–340.

Visalberghi, E., & Welker, C. (1986). Sexual behavior in *Cebus apella*. *Antropologia Contemporanea, 9,* 164–165.

Watson, J. S. (1972). Smiling, cooing, and the "game." *Merrill-Palmer Quarterly, 15,* 323–340.

7

The Attachment Metaphor and the Conditioning of Infant Separation Protests

Jacob L. Gewirtz
Martha Peláez-Nogueras

ABSTRACT

The "attachment" metaphor has labeled a process, of which infant protests to maternal separations have served as an index in the literature. Yet the potential reinforcing role of maternal behaviors (e.g., her departure delay, vacillation or return, reasoning with and/or reassuring the child) when contingent on cued infant protests (cries, fusses, whimpers, and/or whines) has been overlooked in attachment theory and research. The thesis of the investigation reported here is that, by their contingent responding, mothers (and others) may shape and condition their infant's protests in the very departure or separation settings in which those responses are found. Within the frame of the social-conditioning paradigm, how such infant protests come under the control of *cues* and *contingencies* provided by routine maternal behaviors was examined during her departures and, separately, during the ensuing brief separations. Nine 6- to 9-mo. infants were subjected to a repeated-measures design, in successive daily sessions. Two treatments were implemented: 1) DRO—differential reinforcement of behaviors *other than* protests, in which cued infant protests were *never* followed by contingent maternal responses; and 2) CRF—continuous reinforcement, in which cued infant protests were *always* followed by contingent maternal responses. The cued-protest rates of all infant Ss, both in departures and brief separations, increased from the noncontingent-first (DRO_1) to the contingent-second (CRF_2) treatment and decreased from the contingent-second (CRF_2) to the noncontingent-third (DRO_3) treatment. The reliable result-pattern differences in cued infant responses support the assumption that protests can be conditioned in everyday settings, trained (inadvertently) by the social contingencies provided by caregiver behaviors in the very departure and separation contexts in which the infant protests are found. The relation of cued infant protests to the infant's attachment to mother is considered throughout.

During the early months of life, infant protests during maternal/caregiver depar-

123

tures and separations are not ordinarily observed. Our conception is that those cued responses emerge in the infant's repertory later in the first year due to learning, as a result of inadvertent training by mothers in the very departure and separation settings in which the protests are found. The research reported in this chapter was mounted to ascertain how infant protests can come under the control of cues and contingencies generated by a mother's responses during her departures and after brief separations from her infant. These cued protests have served as an unlearned index of attachment for some theorists (Schaffer & Emerson, 1964) or of the security of attachment (Stayton & Ainsworth, 1973), and as a conditioned index for others (Gewirtz, 1972b, 1978). A demonstration that cued infant protests can be trained by contingent maternal responding would provide evidence for the learned basis of departure and separation protests, and hence for the conditioned basis of the attachment they have indexed. The research being described can incidentally identify procedures that parents might employ to minimize separation difficulties, by precluding their children's protests in these settings.

Approaches based on Skinner's (1938) operant-learning conceptions, such as the social-conditioning behavioral approach (see, for example, Bijou & Baer, 1965; Gewirtz, 1961, 1969, 1972a, 1972b, 1977), operate in the frame of functional analysis with limited a priori expectations. They focus on issues at the level of what is a stimulus for a response, what is a response to a stimulus, and how stimulus control over particular responses is acquired, maintained, changed, and/or reversed. Abstract terms like "learning" and "discrimination" may be invoked occasionally in such work, typically as labels for research activities or as chapter headings, but are the exception not the rule. Yet loose *metaphoric* abstractions are employed by approaches that have set the contemporary tone for theory and work in substantial research areas. It has been noted that "attachment" is such a term, based on the metaphor of "bond" or "tie," that has been employed heavily in nonbehavioral approaches blending ethological with mentalistic cognitive conceptions (Ainsworth, 1972; Ainsworth, Blehar, Waters & Wall, 1978; Bowlby, 1958, 1960, 1969).

Much of the contemporary flavor of the work on infant attachment derives from Bowlby's ethological approach, as extended by Ainsworth and her associates. Under these approaches, the attachment label has been used to account for the process, the process outcome, the antecedent-consequent relations involved, and/or a "bond" that is said to underlie all three. These theorists have emphasized that the system underlying attachment behavior is a part of the equipment of many species. Thus, Ainsworth (1989) has written attachment ". . . is manifested by behavior that has the predictable outcome of keeping the individual in proximity to one or a few significant others . . . attachment behavior is believed to have evolved through a process of natural selection because it yielded a survival advantage . . ." (p.709). We also conceive natural selection and the evolution of the species to be the basis for a portion of human behavior, and a much larger part of the behavior of other species, but our emphasis has been on both the evolutionary and the proximal role of reinforcement contingencies in the acquisition and development of a class of cued responses (i.e., discriminated operants) that comprise, and can index, the phenomena of attachment.

Hess and Petrovich (this Volume) and Hinde (1974, 1983) have provided analyses of the ethological context in which the attachment term was embedded by Bowlby (1958, 1969). In a comparative analysis of the approaches to attachment of ethology and of behavior analyses with operant learning, Gewirtz (1961) attempted to organize both imprinting in precocial species and attachment in human infants as learned outcomes. At the same time, he made the case that the ethology and learning approaches were not incompatible, indeed complementary, in their concern with unlearned behavior, learned behavior, and the environmental conditions under which those behavior types occur, are fostered, maintained, or inhibited. Gewirtz' (1961) case was made notwithstanding the preference of the ethology of that time for hierarchical explanation favoring central nervous system concepts and experiments in natural settings, and the preference of behavior analysis for laboratory experimentation and nonhierarchical, molar, outside-the-skin explanation. Differences in unit size and content and in label preferences were considered incidental to the overlaps and commonalities of the two systems.

Since the early 1960s, the tack taken by ethologists such as Bowlby (1969), Eibl-Eibesfeldt (1979), and Sluckin (1972) in cross-species analyses has involved an increasing emphasis, in an evolutionary context, on the ecological dimensions of behavior with proximal survival contingencies. Since then, also, several ethologists carried out microanalyses of molar behavior (Gottlieb, 1968, 1983; Hess & Petrovich, 1973; Hoffman & DePaulo, 1977), not unlike those of behavior analysis; and Skinner (1966, 1981) emphasized the compatibility, of evolutionary selection with response selection in operant learning by natural consequences, as did Petrovich and Gewirtz (1984, 1985). In this frame, the behavior-analytic approach may be even more compatible with ethology today than it was in the 1960s (Petrovich & Gewirtz, 1985).

Under the attachment metaphor, an extensive literature has evolved on the social relations of infants with the important figures in their lives. From a behavioral vantage, as in behavioral research generally it remains advantageous to carry on work at the level of extrinsic stimulus, response, acquisition of stimulus control, and the like as has been done routinely in the frame of the social-conditioning approach. This tack is illustrated in the present analysis with examples from a program of research on infant protests during maternal separations, as well as on the departure protests that have constituted an index of attachment termed "separation protests" (Schaffer & Emerson, 1964; Stayton & Ainsworth, 1973). The research to be described here highlights the maternal-behavior cues and contingencies that very likely underlie the acquisition and maintenance of infant departure and separation protests in life settings.

The Social-Conditioning Approach

As in the ethological approach, in social conditioning theory the attachment term has served as a convenient label for a process. However, unlike its ethological usage, in the social-conditioning approach attachment involves the acquisition of a close reliance, typically concurrent, of one individual's behavior upon the appearance and behavior stimuli of another, expressed in a variety of cued-response patterns of the former. The attachment metaphor has served to label this influence process that is denoted by the complex of child- response patterns coming to be cued and reinforced/maintained by stimuli provided by the appearance and behavior of an attachment figure/object, in early life primarily the mother, but also others. The child-response pattern might maintain contact proximity, produce attention, comfort, or the like. In this frame, attachment also has labeled concurrent behavioral reflections of the above process, such as differential responding favoring the attachment figure or by exploratory-behavior increases in her presence, as well as behavior disruption due to rejection by, separation from, or the death of, the attached figure, when the behavior can become disorganized and may be accompanied by intense emotional/affective responding (distress).

The cued-response patterns (and their derivatives) denoting attachment are pervasive and may occur in any segment of the life span with diverse, even multiple, interaction partners. These cued responses are *discriminated operants* and are defined by the antecedent stimulus-behavior-reinforcing consequence unit. This three-term contingency is the fundamental unit of analysis in the social-conditioning approach to attachment. Thus, the interaction between an infant and its mother/caregiver must always consider, first, the occasion upon which a response occurs; second, the response itself; and third, the environmental consequences. The interrelations among those three terms are *contingencies of reinforcement* (Skinner, 1969).

The dyadic functional relations between the discriminative (cue) and reinforcing stimuli from an attachment figure/object and the child's responses to that figure (that those stimuli control) that connote attachment, may also involve concurrent influence (i.e., bidirectional) patterns, for instance, child-to-mother and mother-to-child (the same maternal responding that controls infant behavior can come under the close negative-reinforcer control of the infant's stopping its behavior contingent on a maternal behavior). Moreover, initiations could be maintained if only intermittently reciprocated across occasions by an attachment figure. The discriminated operants denoting attachments should not be classified as typologies (such as insecure, avoidant, resistant), nor are they cross-situational traits. By definition, these responses are controlled by particular cue and reinforcing stimuli from the attachment figure, as well as by contextual stimuli (including setting conditions), so their occurrence will vary across situations otherwise defined (cf., Gewirtz, 1961, 1972a, 1972b, 1977, 1978, in press; Gewirtz & Boyd, 1977b; Gewirtz & Peláez-Nogueras, 1989).

Origins of Separation Protests

The research program here being reported has focused, first, on identifying the conditions that encourage the learning of infant departure/separation protests (particularly as such cued protests have served as a prominent index of attachment to the mother) and, second, on developing a procedure parents might use to minimize or preclude behavior problems (including distress) in their infants either during departures, or after brief separations, from them.

In familiar, everyday settings, there are often found patterns of infant separation protests cued by maternal preparations for distancing, departing, and/or separating herself from her infant, by actual departures from the infant's vicinity, and by the ensuing short- or long-term separations. In younger children, these protests may be comprised of cries, screams, fusses, whines, and whimpers; in older children, protests may involve grabbing the parent's body or clothing and pleading, in addition to exhibiting elements of a younger-child's behavior pattern.

These cued protests at departure/separation have served at one time or another as the/an index of attachment for several nonbehavioral theorists and researchers. Thus, in a highly-influential paper, Bowlby (1960, p.14) proposed that the infant's responses to, and particularly protests at, maternal departures/separations was the inverse of the proximity-seeking core of attachment. Based on Piaget's (1954) conception of object conservation/constancy indexed by the object (person) leaving the child's observation field, and on the Bowlby proposal mentioned, a widely cited report by Schaffer and Emerson (1964) of the age course in the first 18 months of life, of the onset and intensity of infants' focused attachments to their mothers, used measures based on what was essentially a single cued-protest response index of attachment derived from maternal reports. Those measures summarized the reported incidence, intensity, and direction of infant protests after seven types of departure/separations from their mothers and others. Schaffer and Emerson plotted summaries of those measures by monthly age, but did not analyze the role of maternal reactions for infant protests.

To date, little attention has been devoted to the *role of the mother* in separation-behavior problems the child manifests in different settings. Understanding the maternal role in separation problems (including infant protests and distress), and procedures to eliminate them, could provide a basis for understanding early child social development and the parent-child interaction process, and for applying these principles/procedures to school and family settings.

As would not be unexpected from use of a theory that was not learning oriented, Schaffer and Emerson (1964, p.51) attended only in passing to, and discounted, the possibility that routine contingent maternal behaviors might foster the operant learning of the cued protest response, on which their attachment index was based, in the very departure and separation settings from which their measures were collected. Yet the pattern of infant protests cued by maternal departures may result simply from operant learning, produced by well-intentioned, contingent maternal reactions to those protests in the departure settings (Gewirtz, 1972b, 1977). In particular, the contingent stimuli provided during a mother's departure by such of her responses as stopping, retracing her steps, hesitating, vacillating, turning immediately to, reasoning with, or returning to hug or pick up her protesting child, could function as reinforcers instrumentally to condition the child's protests to the discriminative cues provided by the mother's preparations to leave, her leaving, and separations from her.

Under this conception, the cued separation protest may well be a prototypic learned behavior during the child's socialization that is, at the same time, representative of the pattern of infant responses cued and reinforced by stimuli provided by the appearance and behavior of the mother (or a significant other). In this frame, in the social-conditioning approach the *separation protest* can serve as one of a number of reasonable indices of infant attachment to the mother as object, insofar as attachment is a metaphoric abstraction for such discriminated operants of the infant under the control of maternal stimuli (Gewirtz, 1972b, 1978).

In the next section, we report results from one of a series of experiments mounted to ascertain if, and how, infant protests can come under the acquired control of stimuli generated by contingent maternal behaviors during departures and after brief separations. A demonstration that infant protests cued by maternal departures and brief separations can be maintained by contingent maternal responding would provide presumptive evidence for the *learned* basis of the departure/separation protests that have served as an attachment index in life settings. This demonstration would also provide some understanding of the case in which the very pattern of maternal responding to her infant's cued protests (that appeals to some conceptions of "loving" mothering) can generate problems of behavior management that prevent the constructive fostering of her infant's developmentally-appropriate behaviors.

THE CONDITIONING OF SEPARATION PROTESTS: A PARADIGMATIC EXPERIMENT

Research Strategy and Tactics

This experiment illustrates in detail how departure and separation conditions separately can acquire stimulus control over the infant's protests by providing discriminable cues that denote (a) a mother's departure including her preparations to leave the infant's vicinity, saying "bye, bye," touching the infant, picking up her purse, walking towards the door, and waving her hand, and (b) a mother's separation including the sight and sound of her opening the door, exiting, and closing the door, and the loss of sight of the mother. The infant protest response manifested in the presence of these discriminative stimuli was shaped differentially by the contingent stimuli. For instance, during departures the frequent responding of a mother immediately contingent on her infant's cued protests or their precursors should shape and condition (i.e., affect more frequent and/or intense) her infant's cued protests; and during separations infant protests should be conditioned by her contingent return to her infant from outside the room. In later research, the independence between departure and separation contexts (cues) for infant protests was empirically demonstrated (see Gewirtz & Peláez-Nogueras, 1989).

Shaping and Differential Reinforcement.   The *shaping* procedure involves systematic provision of the maternal responses contingent upon *successive approximations* of the infant responses to the target response, in this case protesting. For instance, in cases where an infant did not emit a protest when cued, across sessions its vocalizations may be shaped into a protest by the mother responding only to successive increases in their duration, amplitude or some other response feature. In this way, what originally may have started as an incidental vocalization during preseparation events might be shaped gradually into an intense protest. The protest response involved is then routinely followed by contingent maternal responding and is sometimes termed CRF (for *continuous reinforcement*). On the other hand, if a mother were to cue her child that she is departing (e.g., "Bye bye; I'll be right back") and to leave his/her vicinity without vacillation or apparent concern (whether or not the infant were to protest in reaction to the maternal departure cues), the infant's response would not be shaped into a protest and conditioned to the maternal departure cues.

Another procedure (sometimes termed DRO) involves *differential reinforcement of behaviors other than the target,* in which the target protest is ignored and other responses are followed by contingent maternal responding. The differential-reinforcement-of-behaviors-other-than-the-target procedure can be combined with shaping. In this way, for each instance of the protest response, increasingly lengthy pauses are required for the mother to respond, until the nonoccurrence of a protest cues the mother's response to her infant. Then, the mother responds only to alternative infant behaviors (e.g., vocalizations, smiles and/or play). Using this procedure for several training sessions in laboratory settings, a conditioned high protest rate can be reduced, even discontinued, with the child then exhibiting behaviors incompatible with protests.

The research design and experimental procedures employed were focused on maximizing between-treatment differences (effects) while minimizing intrasubject and intersubject differences (i.e., variability). Between-treatment differences were heightened by establishing the two treatments as logical opposites at extremes of the dimension ranging from contingent to noncontingent stimulation. Intrasubject differences were minimized by using a repeated-measures design. Intersubject differences were minimized by using a powerful procedure, including shaping and running each subject under CRF and DRO until a behavioral criterion was attained, so that every infant subject would have received a maximal dose of each treatment, to contribute to overriding unique reinforcement histories, thresholds, capacities, and experiences. In sum, the strategy was to maximize treatment effects and examine the behavior outcomes in a laboratory setting in which relatively-much control was exercised over the proximate conditions thought to be causal, and care taken to limit the operation of potentially confounding and artifactual variables and minimize interindividual and intra-individual differences.

Subjects and Settings. The research procedure involved bringing 9 middle-class infant-mother pairs into the laboratory for successive, typically daily, sessions (ranging from 9 to 11), each lasting about 35 min. The normal middle-class babies included 7 males and 2 females who ranged in age from six to nine months at the start of their participation in the study. Subjects were selected on the basis of their mothers reporting them, or the infants showing themselves, capable of remaining in a playpen in the mother's presence for at least 20 min. without protesting or crying. A daily session was postponed when a mother reported that her child was "out of sorts" or off schedule, or that she had rushed to get him/her to the laboratory on time, or that the infant or infant's sibling was ill.

Each baby was placed in a 1-meter-square playpen, containing several simple toys (e.g., blocks, plastic animals), located in the far corner from the entrance/exit door of a pleasant, yellow, windowless, 15-meter-long by 5-meter-wide room with children's paintings decorating the wall. At the start of a trial, the mother was seated on a small sofa positioned adjacent to the playpen. Two television cameras located in the room concurrently monitored the expressions and behavior of the infant in the playpen and of the mother as she sat initially near the play pen and then walked from her seat to and through the door while cueing and responding either contingently or noncontingently to her infant's protest's, depending on the treatment in force. In an adjacent observation room, the synchronized behavior of infant and mother in interaction was displayed on a video monitor in split-screen format, and recorded on videotape in that mode. From the observation-room video monitor, two experimenters could view the mother-infant interaction in the laboratory, at the same time as one of them was directing the mother's actions via earphone, instructing her on when and how to give the departure cues and when and how to respond to the infant initiations. (For each of the 9 mothers, a natural departure style was noted in a preliminary assessment trial, to be used as the basis of her departure responses in all subsequent sessions.)

Response Definition and Dependent Variable. The outcome measure used in both treatments was the proportion of trials-per-daily session on which the infant made a cued protest. Infant protests during the departure, separation and reunion, and control periods were scored, with the exact time of occurrence noted (for latency computations). A *protest* was defined as a whine, whimper, fuss, or cry sound emitted by the infant in response to the cues provided by a mother's departure or separation. The dependent variable, *proportion of protest trials per session,* was calculated separately for departure and separation settings. (To produce percentage measures, proportions were multiplied by 100.) Proportion of protests was determined by dividing the total number of trials that included a protest by the total number of trials in that session. Pairs of independent observers scored the time and events as they occurred. Five observers were involved in all. One of the observers helped the experimenter in the timing of instructions to the mother, particularly on when the mother should leave/return to the room, and in determining whether or not the subject's response pattern attained the predetermined criterion. Observer-reliability determinations in the scoring of protests, protest latencies, and several other behaviors, were made subsequently from the videotape records. Percentage of agreement on protests was obtained by dividing the total number of agreements between two independent observers by the total number of observations (agreements plus disagreements). Two observers scored independently 573 trails comprising 103 sessions for 13 infants on whether or not at least one protest occurred during a trial under a treatment after the mother cued her departure and, separately, her separation. Overall percentage observer agreement on cued protests was determined to be 94% for maternal departures and 95% for brief separations.

Procedure

An A-B-A (i.e., DRO-CRF-DRO) repeated-measures design was employed. The *departure* condition began when a mother first cued her infant that she was leaving and ended when she closed the room's door after exiting. The *separation* condition began at that point and lasted until the mother opened the door and reentered the room. Before the start of the first session (during a preliminary trial), mothers were instructed to leave the room as naturally as possible, as they would during routine departures in a familiar setting. The pattern of maternal behaviors was noted on this preliminary trial, and subsequently emphasized in experimenter's instructions via earphones to mothers during departure and separation settings across all treatment trial sessions.

There was a 5-min habituation period at the beginning of each daily session. Afterward, the experimenter signaled the mother to leave the room, initiating the first trial. Each trial consisted of a departure period (mean = 28 sec), a period of maternal absence (5 min maximum), a standard reunion period (15 sec) and an intertrial interval (1 min) also termed a control period between trials. Infant protests during maternal departures, when the mother was responding to the infant and in full view, were considered operationally different from the protests occurring during separations when the mother was out of sight and earshot, and were assumed to be independent (uncorrelated). (The independence between the departure and separation contexts as evidenced by maximal differential infant responding under a conditional-discrimination paradigm was demonstrated by Gewirtz & Peláez-Nogueras, 1989.) Each subsequent trial began after 1 min of a control period between trials had elapsed, provided that no observation of an infant protest or potential distress was made. This procedure was useful in precluding carry-over or confounding effects from one trial to the next.

The content and number of maternal cue and contingent stimuli (auditory, visual, tactile) presented to the infant subjects during the departure, separation, and reunion, and the control period between trials, was under the close instructional earphone control of the experimenter. Using her natural departure style (as described earlier), on every trial the mother signaled her departures from the room three times: first, by kissing her child, then by picking up her purse, standing up and waving (e.g., she said "Bye bye, I'll be right back") while turning toward the exit door; second, by starting to walk slowly to the door while giving the child a second verbal cue; and, third, once she had opened the door, by turning to look at her child and once more verbally signaling her departure in her usual style, closing the door and exiting the room. All the maternal behaviors were under the moment-to-moment control of a sequence of instructions from the experimenter given via earphone.

Under the *contingent*-stimulation treatment (CRF), infant protests or precursors of protests to the departure cues were *always* followed immediately (within 2 sec) by maternal auditory and visual stimuli provided by her contingent responses (e.g., turning towards the infant and saying "It's all right, Mommy will be right back" or "What's the matter?"), until the infant's response across sessions was shaped to a protest and/or the criterion met. The criteria for terminating the contingent treatment and initiating the reversal treatment was for a protest to occur in at least 80% of the trials of a session both for departures and separations and, in addition, the protest latency (i.e., the elapsed time between the onset of a maternal cue (S^D) and the onset of a protest) during departures had to be less than 5 sec on each of the last 3 trials of the last session to trigger switching to the noncontingent treatment. When the mother was outside of the room with the door closed during separation under the contingent treatment, the baby's protest brought on contingent maternal responding, the mother's immediate return to the room and approach to her infant while emitting verbal responses (e.g., "Mommy's here!").

Under the "*noncontingent*-stimulation" treatment more properly termed a Variable DRO schedule of reinforcement, wherein *behaviors other than the target response* are followed by maternal contingencies. (In most instances, these other-than-protest behaviors were playing and vocalizing.) Specifically, the maternal response occurred either when the infant was *not* protesting or after at least 10 sec had elapsed from the offset of the most recent protest while the mother was departing.

After the criterion was attained under the contingent treatment in both the departure and separation contexts, the treatment was reversed. The cued infant protest rate was decreased by providing *non*contingent maternal responding relative to protests for several sessions until a reversal criterion ($< 17\%$ of the protest trials) was met. In instances where a protest began during a maternal departure and continued into the ensuing separation, that response was scored as a departure protest. The next protest was scored as occurring during separation only after there had been at least a 10-sec pause after the departure protest and the mother was already outside the room. Under the noncontingent treatment in the separation setting, mothers were instructed initially to return to the infant only after there had been a 10-sec pause without protest and, when feasible, were sent back to their infants on successive trials with systematically increasing nonprotest pauses (30, 60, 90, 120, 150 sec, etc.). Thus, the pause or nonprotest period required for maternal responding (i.e., her return to the infant) was increased gradually from 10 sec up to 5-min. This time lapse without an infant protest served as one criterion for ending the noncontingent-separation treatment sessions. In the rare cases where elicited crying persisted for longer than 45 sec, the session was terminated.

In the event a protest did not occur under the contingent stimulation treatment when the separated mother was outside the experimental room, the maximum time of her absence was 5 min. In such cases of maximum elapsed time without protests, the mother was instructed to return to the room without looking at, or talking to, the infant. A new discrete trial began as usual after a 1-min between-trials *control period* had elapsed without an infant protest. This control period allowed the experimenter to insure that the baby, who was in the playpen, was in good form (not protesting) and not responding emotionally on apparently uncon- ditioned grounds due to hunger, pain, or sleepiness and, as indicated above, precluding potential carryover effects from one trial to the next, thus making the effects of the departure cues (S^Ds) more salient.

The *density* of maternal stimuli refers to the number and content of maternal responses (providing the cues and contingent or noncontingent stimuli either for protests or for alternative behaviors). For all subjects, the density of maternal stimulation provided was comparable in both the contingent and the noncon- tingent treatments, under the departure condition as well as under the separation condition. To equate the pattern and density of discriminative *cues* in these two treatments under experimenter instructions, a mother emitted the same three short *cues* during a *departure* trial (e.g., Bye, bye, mommy will be right back," while looking towards her infant) and the same number of similar responses, either *contingent or non*contingent, depending on the treatment (e.g., "It's all right; Mommy will be back soon;" "What's the matter?" "Don't worry!"). For the *separation* trials, the mother's exiting, closing of the door, and absence were the only cues, and there was only one contingent or noncontingent response possible on each trial (i.e., the mother's return to the child's room while emitting verbal responses). This procedure allowed for controlling the possibility that the different effects of the treatments on the child-behavior pattern could be due to differential elicitation/stimulation/arousal resulting from maternal stimulation preceding the infant responses and not due to the contingent responding (rein- forcement) effects.

Additional criteria for terminating treatments were used in the final noncon- tingent-treatment session for all nine Ss to allow for the reversal decrease or elimination of the rate of cued protests before the infants left the project. Under the noncontingent (reversal) treatment, an infant's protest rate had to be reduced to occur on one-sixth or fewer of the total trials of a session, before the treatment was terminated. Even so, it was necessary occasionally to shift treatments before these criteria were met in cases where the number of daily sessions under one of the treatments reached six. (This restriction made it possible to fail to reach criterion and, hence, to show conditioning under departures, separations, or both. Even so, all nine Ss attained the criterion for each treatment in both settings within those six sessions.

Results

Results are based on 9 individual infant subjects, whose conditioning records are displayed in Fig. 7.1. Analyses were performed within groups on patterns of effects for individual subjects using nonparametric, one-tail, Wilcoxon paired-ranks tests, to evaluate changes from the final session of one treatment phase to the final session of another. The outcome measure used was the percentage of trials-per-daily-session on which the infant made a cued protest. This index seemed sensible in a context where response criterion was used to reverse or terminate a treatment. The logic of using a criterion to terminate/switch a treatment emphasizes the final-session score level (that represents the acquisition-curve asymptote) and deemphasizes such factors as the rate/speed (i.e., the number of trials or sessions per subject) in attaining the criterion level.

Under the ABA design, both for departures and for separations, the 9 individual-response-curve pairs in the aggregate (i.e., their median scores) increase from the "noncontingent" DRO_1 to the contingent CRF_2 condition ($p = .002$, $p = .002$, each test 1 tail) and decreased from the contingent CRF_2 to the "noncontingent" DRO_3 (see Fig. 7.2) ($p = .002$, $p = .002$, each test 1 tail). Moreover, mothers remained outside the room during *separations* for longer periods under the DRO than under the CRF treatment and, in most of the cases, without the infants protesting. Thus, the mothers of every one of the 9 infants showed a marked *decline* in the Median time they remained outside the room during separations from the final "noncontingent" DRO_1 (Mdn. 105 sec) to the final contingent CRF_2 (Mdn. 5 sec) session ($p = .002$, 1 tail) and a marked *increase* in the time they remained outside the room from the final contingent CRF_2 (Mdn. 5 sec) to the final "noncontingent"DRO_3 (Mdn. 124 sec) session ($p = .002$, 1 tail).

The result pattern supports the assumption that the infant protests cued by maternal departures and during brief separations (that have served as an attachment index) can be learned in the very life departure/separation settings in which they appear, *trained* by contingent maternal behaviors. Further, the infant Ss learned to tolerate longer separation-from-mother under the DRO maternal non-

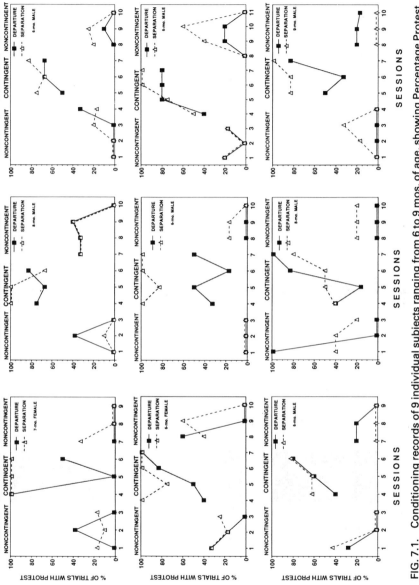

FIG. 7.1.   Conditioning records of 9 individual subjects ranging from 6 to 9 mos. of age, showing Percentage Protest Trials Per Session under successive noncontingent DRO, contingent CRF, and noncontingent DRO stimulation conditions.

135

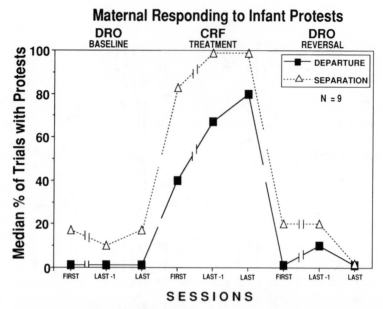

FIG. 7.2.   A composite conditioning curve for the 9 infant Ss, representing Median Percent Protest Trials Per Session, across the First,
Last −1 (i.e., next-to-last), and Last session score under each of the
three successive treatment conditions.

contingent-responding treatment than under the CRF maternal contingent-responding treatment.

DISCUSSION OF THE EXPERIMENT

Learned Protests and Attachment

These early results from our laboratory-research program indicate that 6- to 9-
month-old infants can be trained differentially to protest and not to protest to
maternal departure *or* separation cues by reinforcing contingencies produced by
maternal responding. This learning/training could be occurring on similar bases
in home settings, though due there inadvertently to well-intentioned maternal
responding contingent. on those infant protests in the departure or separation
contexts. These contingencies might involve such maternal behaviors as speak-
ing to, explaining or reasoning with her infant, as well as the mother vacillating,
backtracking, or hesitating during her departure, showing concern, and/or returning to pick up or hug her infant after he/she emits a protest.

A corollary of our finding that protests can be conditioned on an operant basis
is that, by using separation protests to index attachment, Schaffer and Emerson

(1964) and Stayton and Ainsworth (1973) made their conception of attachment hostage to the idiosyncratic factors underlying whether or not, and how, mothers respond to their infants' departure or separation protests. Schaffer and Emerson did not propose that such idiosyncratic maternal factors as maternal responding contingent on the infant protests during separations were at all relevant to their attachment conception.

On the other hand, it was noted for the social-conditioning approach that infant attachment is a metaphor for infant discriminated operants being under maternal-stimulus control. In this context, cued departure or separation protests like those trained in this experiment may be prototypic learned behaviors during socialization that can represent the pattern of infant responses cued and reinforced by stimuli provided by the mother's appearance and behavior. On this learned basis, in the first 18 months of life cued protests can serve well as a representative index of infant attachment to mother (Gewirtz, 1972b, 1978).

The Age Course of Protests

The results of the training reported put into question the assumed-unlearned, diagnostic, "separation-protest" attachment index used by Schaffer and Emerson (1964) to chart the age course of attachment in the first 18 months of life. In the 26 years since its publication, the interview-derived Schaffer and Emerson chart has been emphasized, nearly without exception, to represent the developmental course of attachment in introductory child-developmental psychology textbooks published. For some examples, see Hall, Lamb, and Perlmutter (1986, p. 377), Hetherington and Parke (1986, p. 248), Helms and Turner (1986, p. 199), Liebert and Wicks-Nelson (1981, p. 379), Santrock (1988, p. 219), Santrock and Bartlett (1986, p. 296), Santrock and Yussen (1987, p. 373), and Schaffer (1979, p.153; 1985, p.435; 1988, p.118).

There is also a similar question about the 9-month or so age-of-onset and the temporal course of separation fear/anxiety/distress, as denoted by observed separation protests, summarized for several cultural groups by Kagan, Kearsley, and Zelazo (1978). In the laboratory research we have reported here, high rates of departure protests and of separation protests were conditioned in infants as young as 6 months of age, an age at which infants ordinarily would not protest at separations according to Kagan et al. and to Schaffer and Emerson. Under the contingent-maternal responding treatment, at 6 mos all five of our infant Ss protested their mother's departures/separations, as did our single 7-month-old S, our two 8-month-old Ss, and our single 9-month-old S. In the more natural nontraining circumstances summarized by Kagan et al for four culture groups (their p. 107) and in the home-care and day-care groups (their p. 240) at ages 5 to 10 mos, as well as for the Schaffer and Emerson data, far lower percentages of infants manifested departure/separation protests at our Ss' age points.

With respect to the Schaffer and Emerson (1964) and the Kagan et al. (1978) reports of the age course of protests at separation, our view is that there should be continuity in an infant's protest pattern across age as long as there is continuity across age in the contingent maternal behaviors maintaining that protest pattern. Declines in protests, for instance like that observed by Kagan et al. after 18 mos, may reflect simply a change in the style of maternal responding to infant departure/separation protests, perhaps due to developmental advances in the infant's behavior repertory.

This research has reported that (a) protests during departures were conditioned on an operant basis in every one of the 9 infants and (b) protests during brief separations from the mother were conditioned on the same basis in all 9 infants. The infant subjects of the experiment we report here ranged in age from 6 to 9 months. As with other demographic-type variables (e.g., culture group, social status, sibling position, geographic location), the *age-in-months* (against which the separation-protest scores were plotted by Schaffer and Emerson and by Kagan et al.) is not, in itself, a psychological variable; it must be reduced to the causal variables required by the extant psychological theories to function as proper input variables (Baer, 1970; Gewirtz, 1969). Hence, in a process analysis the infants' age could not be considered to be the causal process variable responsible for the developmental changes observed.

Schaffer and Emerson had reported the onset and rise in separation protests within the 6- to 9-mo. age range, that they took to denote focused attachment. Under our methodology, *no* age differences were found in the conditioning and reversibility of infant protests either to maternal departure or to separation cues. Protests were conditioned in every boy and girl S in the 6- to 9-month range, the age span in which Schaffer and Emerson and Kagan et al detected the onset and rise of such protest patterns. The findings we have reported, showing that separation protests and departure protests can be operant conditioned throughout the 6- to 9-month age range both for girls and boys, is compatible with the logic cited earlier that age, *not* a proximal causal variable, cannot explain the process involved in the learning of such infant outcome patterns. (In the present study, the main proximal variable was contingent vs. noncontingent maternal responding.) This finding suggests that infants can learn to protest, or not to protest, maternal departures or separations, due to differential contingent maternal responding (as reinforcers).

Infant Control of Maternal Responding

The emphasis in the research reported has been on the one-way or unidirectional influence that the mother's behavior-provided cues and contingencies exert over infant protest behaviors. In the laboratory setting employed, the mothers, agents of the experimenters, exhibited invariant behavior under instructional control, while the infant's behavior was free to vary. A one-way influence process was involved. In earlier analyses of free-operant infant *crying* in natural-life settings, it was detailed how a two-way bidirectional influence process is ordinarily involved in mother-infant interaction (Gewirtz, 1977; Gewirtz & Boyd, 1977a). In this bidirectional process, the concurrent conditioning of the behavior of both infant and caregiver takes place, effected by the impact of stimuli provided by the (behavior of) the one on the response of the other. Elicited, and often operant, infant crying is ordinarily aversive to caregivers, due to its shrill, noxious qualities (Bowlby, 1958; Gewirtz, 1961) or because it could reflect a mystery about the cause of the crying, a parent ordinarily being impelled to do what would be required to terminate the crying.

At the same time the infant operant crying is conditioned by the positive-reinforcement contingencies provided by the mother picking up her infant and/or soothing it, those very same maternal responses could come under the negative-reinforcer control of the infant's crying behavior, when infant crying ceases contingent on such parent behavior as picking up and/or soothing the infant. In natural departure and separation settings, it is assumed that a similar two-way influence process operates: At the same time that infant protests cued by departure preparations and brief separations would come under the control of contingent maternal responses, such as reasoning with the child, backtracking, vacillating, picking it up, or returning to the room, those same maternal responses could come under the *negative*-reinforcer control of the contingent termination of infant protests (comprised of fusses, whines, whimpers, and/or cries).

The existence of such two-way influence patterns received some confirmation in this study. Infant high-rate protesting is ordinarily correlated with a high-rate of maternal responsiveness. It is interesting that, under the first or second DRO "noncontingent"-stimulation-on-the-target response treatment, most of the mothers commented spontaneously that they were astounded by the rapid and dramatic decline in the incidence of their babies' protests, that permitted them to remain outside the room for increasing and substantial periods. Before their participation in this experiment, these mothers reported on a questionnaire that, at home, they hesitated to leave their infants' vicinities for fear that the infants would emit intensive, lengthy protests. In other words, the contingent maternal behaviors that were functioning as positive reinforcers for the infant protests were under the negative-reinforcer control of those very protests. Furthermore, before the experiment, at home, nearly all of those same mothers could not readily separate themselves from their infants by closing a door between them, because of a concern that the infant would protest. Hence, those mothers were astonished further by the fact that, under the "noncontingent"-stimulation (DRO) treatment, ultimately their infants could, without protesting, tolerate increasing functional separations, the mothers remaining outside the experimental room, with the door closed, for increasing periods across sessions.

Implications of Misplaced Contingencies

It has long been assumed in the child-care literature that proper caregiving requires that the mother of caregiver respond to alleviate the physical distress underlying various elicited (unconditioned, reflexive, expressive) behaviors, such as intense crying (resulting from identified antecedent causes e.g., hunger, pain). The core aspect of maternal sensitivity as defined by Ainsworth's attachment theory is responsiveness to the infant's signals in communication (Ainsworth & Bell, 1977). Even so, a sensitive caregiver should be able to discriminate between her child's instrumental (manipulative) protests and her child's pained, elicited crying. The problem emphasized in this paper is that, in caregiving situations in life, mothers often provide abundant *misplaced contingencies* to their infants' behaviors, which can encourage developmentally-inappropriate behaviors. A remedy can be provided by maternal *differential responding* to infant behaviors. A sensitive mother responds differentially to her infant's protest, distress cries, or other initiation based on her knowledge of antecedents of the response and the infant's idiosyncrasies (Gustafson & Harris, 1990).

In addition to detailing an important instance of social learning in early life, this study provides some understanding of the case where the very pattern of maternal responding to the infant's cued protests, that appeals to some conceptions of "loving mothering," can generate problems of infant-behavior management that preclude the constructive fostering of developmentally-appropriate infant social and cognitive behaviors. Thus, a paradox is involved in the phenomena being explored in this research analysis. There appears to be a popular belief among educated parents that a child attached to them would necessarily exhibit departure/separation protests, and that an unattached child would not emit protests during separations. Hence, many parents appear to operate under a belief that leads them to encourage (perhaps ambivalently) their children's departure/separation protesting. This paradoxical dilemma is one of the themes underlying this chapter.

Appreciating the maternal role in separation problems and in procedures to eliminate them provides a basis for understanding early child social development and the parent-child interaction process, and for applying these principles/procedures to family, day care, and school settings. It is conceivable that, in such other settings as the home and day-care center, other of the child's instrumental responses emitted during maternal departures and separations could also be trained inadvertently by caregiver reactions like those provided contingent upon infant protests. Understanding the mechanisms involved in the infants' and adults' contingent responses can illuminate the "pathological" as well as the "normal" development of the child.

Naturalistic Observations and Laboratory Experiments

Some comments on the use of laboratory versus natural-life research designs may be useful here. We have reported a research in which observations of infant departure and separation protests in home settings led us directly to mount a laboratory study for efficient validation of the mechanisms abstracted from, and thought to be operating in, the life settings. In this instance, the proximal determinants of cued infant protests were studied employing mothers as experimental agents. Alternatively, a passive-observation study or field experiment (which has many of the same constraints as has the laboratory study) in natural home settings might have been mounted. Nevertheless, a naturalistic description (although useful in the preliminary phases of an investigation) is a deficient research method, insofar as it does not permit the inference of causality (McCall, 1977). This naturalistic tactic was not used as our first alternative because it is routinely found in nature that the magnitude of effect(s) reflecting the phenomena of interest is small relative to the uncontrolled (error) variation there. Hence, passive observation in natural settings with contextual variables uncontrolled ordinarily would give little return relative to investment. And such observation with a preliminary attempt to control, or stratify for, context also was thought less efficient for our purpose than the laboratory study reported here.

In this frame, the researcher must often consider moving between laboratory settings, in which there is relatively much control of the proximate causal dimensions thought to be operating, little independent-variable variation, and few confounding conditions (i.e., high internal validity), *and* life settings in which there may be very limited control and many varying and confounding conditions. This is particularly the case where the researcher intends to make claims about life settings from the laboratory research, as ideally we would like to do here. Ultimately, at least some triangulation will be required between laboratory-generated mechanisms such as those presented here and results obtained from passive observation under the massive inefficiencies prevailing in life settings. This would validate applying the laboratory-generated mechanisms to the life setting. For the moment, our abstraction of the mechanism from extensive observation in home settings, of contingent-maternal responding as the main proximal determinant of infant protests at maternal departures and separations, together with the inherent plausibility of the logic used, will have to stand for the triangulation ultimately required until such time as that proximal mechanism could be validated in the life setting.

EPILOGUE

An experimental analysis of contingent maternal behavior that can train and maintain infant protests cued by maternal departures and separations provides a basis for understanding features of social conditioning in early human life, in particular social discriminated operants that comprise, and can index, the attachment process. The research has illustrated an instance of early infant social learning and some of the maternally-mediated proximal environmental conditions apparently responsible for their acquisition and maintenance. At the same time, the results provide a basis for minimizing or eliminating unconstructive infant behaviors, such as cued departure or separation protests, in this instance by responding differentially, by not providing maternal responding contingent upon such protests. This investigation also illustrated the role a laboratory study can play in providing efficient leverage over questions and solutions for behavioral problems that arise in the real world.

REFERENCES

Ainsworth, M. S. (1972). Attachment and dependency: A comparison. In J. L. Gewirtz (Ed.), *Attachment and dependency* (pp. 92–137). Washington, DC: Winston.

Ainsworth, M. D. S. (1989). Attachment beyond infancy. *American Psychologist, 44,* 709–716.

Ainsworth, M. D. S., & Bell, S. M. (1977). Infant and maternal responsiveness: a rejoinder to Gewirtz and Boyd. *Child Development, 48,* 1208–1216.

Ainsworth, M. S., Blehar, M. C., Waters, E., & Wall. S. (1978). *Patterns of attachment.* Hillsdale, NJ: Lawrence Erlbaum Associates.

Baer, D. M. (1970). An age-irrelevant concept of development. *Merrill-Palmer Quarterly of Behavior and Development, 16,* 238–246.

Bijou, S. W., & Baer, D. M. (1965). *Child development. Vol. 2. Universal stage of infancy.* New York: Appleton-Century-Crofts.

Bowlby, J. (1958). The nature of the child's tie to his mother. *International Journal of Psychoanalysis, 39,* 350–373.

Bowlby, J. (1960). Separation anxiety. *International Journal of Psychoanalysis, 41,* 89–113.

Bowlby, J. (1969). *Attachment and loss. Vol. 1. Attachment.* London: Hogarth (New York: Basic Books).

Eibl-Eibesfeldt, I. (1979). Human ethology: Concepts and implications for the sciences of man. *The Behavioral and Brain Sciences, 1,* 1–57.

Gewirtz, J. L. (1961). A learning analysis of the effects of normal stimulation, privation and deprivation on the acquisition of social motivation and attachment. In B. M. Foss (Ed.), *Determinants of infant behaviour* (pp. 213–299). London: Methuen (New York: Wiley).

Gewirtz, J. L. (1969). Mechanisms of social learning: Some roles of stimulation and behavior in early human development. In D. A. Goslin (Ed.), *Handbook of socialization theory and research* (pp. 57–212). Chicago: Rand-McNally.

Gewirtz, J. L. (1972a). Attachment, dependence, and a distinction in terms of stimulus control. In J. L. Gewirtz (Ed.), *Attachment and dependency* (pp. 179–215). Washington, DC: Winston.

Gewirtz, J. L. (1972b). On the selection and use of attachment and dependence indices. In J. L. Gewirtz (Ed.), *Attachment and dependency* (pp. 179–215). Washington, DC: Winston.

Gewirtz, J. L. (1977). Maternal responding and the conditioning of infant crying: Directions of influence within the attachment-acquisition process. In B. C. Etzel, J. M. LeBlanc, & D. M. Baer (Eds.), *New development in behavioral research: Theories, methods, and applications* (pp. 31–57). Hillsdale, NJ: Lawrence Erlbaum Associates.

Gewirtz, J. L. (1978). Social learning in early human development. In A. C. Catania & T. Brigham (Eds.), *Handbook of applied behavior research: Social and instructional processes* (pp. 105–141). New York: Irvington Press.

Gewirtz, J. L. (1991). Social influence on child and parent via stimulation and operant-learning mechanisms. In M. Lewis & S. Feinman (Eds.), *Social influences and socialization in infancy* (pp. 137–163). New York & London: Plenum Press.

Gewirtz, J. L., & Boyd, E. F. (1977a). Does maternal responding imply reduced infant crying?: A critique of the 1972 Bell and Ainsworth report. *Child Development, 48,* 1200–1207.

Gewirtz, J. L., & Boyd, E. (1977b). Experiments on mother-infant interaction underlying mutual attachment acquisition: The infant conditions the mother. In T. Alloway, P. Pliner, & L. Krames (Eds.) *Attachment behavior* (pp. 109–143). In *Advances in the Study of Communication and Affect* (Vol. 3). New York & London: Plenum Press.

Gewirtz, J. L., & Peláez-Nogueras, M. (1989 April). *Infant protesting to maternal departures and separations: A conditional discrimination process.* Paper delivered at the Biennial Meeting, Society for Research in Child Development, Kansas City, Missouri.

Gottlieb, G. (1968). Prenatal behavior of birds. *Quarterly Review of Biology, 43,* 148–174.

Gottlieb, G. (1983). The psychobiological approach to developmental issues. In P. H. Mussen (Ed.), *Handbook of child psychology* (4th ed.). Vol. 2. *Infancy and developmental psychobiology* (pp. 1–26). New York: Wiley.

Gustafson, G. E., & Harris, K. L. (1990). Woman responses to young infants' cries. *Developmental Psychology, 26,* 144–152.

Hall, E., Lamb, M. E., & Perlmutter, M. (1986). *Child psychology today* (2nd. ed.). New York: Random House. (Fig. 12.1, p.377.)

Helms, D. B., & Turner, J. S. (1986). *Exploring child behavior* (3rd. ed.). Monterey, CA: Brooks/Cole. (Fig. 8.1, p. 199.)

Hess, E. H., & Petrovich, S. B. (1973). The early development of parent-young interaction in nature. In F. R. Nesselroade & H. W. Reese (Eds.), *Life-span developmental psychology: Methodological issues* (pp. 25–42). New York: Academic Press.

Hetherington, E. M., & Parke, R. D. (1986). *Child psychology: A contemporary viewpoint* (3rd. ed.). New York: McGraw-Hill. (Fig. 7-4, p. 248).

Hinde, R. A. (1974). *Biological bases of human social behavior.* New York: McGraw-Hill.

Hinde, R. A. (1983). Ethology and child development. In P. H. Mussen (Ed.), *Handbook of child psychology* (4th ed.), Vol. 2. *Infancy and developmental psychobiology* (pp. 27–93). New York: Wiley.

Hoffman, H. S., & DePaulo, P. (1977). Behavioral control by an imprinting stimulus. *American Scientist, 65,* 58–66.

Kagan, J., Kearsley, R. B., & Zelazo, P. R. (1978). *Infancy: Its place in human development.* Cambridge, MA: Harvard University Press.

Liebert, R. M., & Wicks-Nelson, R. (1981). *Developmental psychology* (3rd. ed.). Englewood Cliffs, NJ: Prentice-Hall. (Fig. 11-8, p.379).

McCall, R. B. (1977). Challenges to a science of developmental psychology. *Child Development, 48,* 333–344.

Petrovich, S. B., & Gewirtz, J. L. (1984). Learning in the context of evolutionary biology: In search of synthesis. *Behavioral and Brain Sciences, 7,* 160–161.

Petrovich, S. B., & Gewirtz, J. L. (1985). The attachment learning process and its relation to cultural and biological evolution: Proximate and ultimate considerations. In M. Reite & T. Field (Eds.), *The psychobiology of attachment and separation* (pp. 257–289). NY: Academic Press.

Piaget, J. (1954). *The construction of reality in the child.* (trans. Margaret Cook.) New York: Basic Books.

Santrock, J. W. (1988). *Children.* Dubuque, IA: W. C. Brown. (Fig. 6.5, p. 219).

Santrock, J. W., & Bartlett, J. C. (1986). *Developmental psychology: A life-cycle perspective.* Dubuque, IA: W. C. Brown. (Fig. 9.2, p. 296.)

Santrock, J. W., & Yussen, S. R. (1987). *Child development: An introduction* (3rd ed.). Dubuque, IA: W. C. Brown. (Fig. 11.3, p. 373.)

Schaffer, H. R., & Emerson, P. E. (1964). The development of social attachments in infancy. *Monographs of the Society for Research in Child Development, 29* (3, Serial No. 94).

Shaffer, D. R. (1979, 1988). *Social and personality development* (1st and 2nd ed.) Monterey, CA: Brooks/Cole.

Shaffer, D. R. (1985). *Developmental psychology: Theory, research, and applications.* Monterey, CA: Brooks/Cole.

Skinner, B. F. (1966). The phylogeny and ontogeny of behavior. *Science, 153,* 1205–1213.

Skinner, B. F. (1969). *Contingencies of reinforcement: A theoretical analysis.* New York: Appleton-Century Crofts.

Skinner, B. F. (1981). Selection by consequences. *Science, 213,* 501–504.

Sluckin, W. (1972). *Early learning in man and animal.* Cambridge, MA: Schenkman.

Stayton, D. J., & Ainsworth, M. S. (1973). Individual differences in infant responses to brief, everyday separations as related to other infant and maternal behaviors. *Developmental Psychology, 9,* No. 2, 226–235.

IV STRESS, TEMPERAMENT, AND ATTACHMENT

Hemispheric Specialization and Attachment Behaviors: Developmental Processes and Individual Differences in Separation Protest

8

Nathan A. Fox
Richard J. Davidson

ABSTRACT

The infant's distress response to brief maternal separation appears during the last quarter of the first year of life and diminishes during the second year. Its significance has been highlighted by a number of theorists working in the area of the attachment relationship between mother and child. Research from our laboratories on cerebral asymmetry and the development of emotion has begun to characterize both the developmental course of separation protest and variations in the intensity of the distress response. Data presented in this chapter indicate that the development of separation protest may be associated with the relative activation of certain regions in the cerebral hemispheres. Ten-month-old infants who exhibited distress at separation displayed greater right frontal activation during separation as compared to infants who did not protest. Differences in relative frontal activation during protest are interpreted as signifying the presence or absence of active inhibition, via the left hemisphere, of right frontal negative affect. In addition, ten-month-old infants who displayed greater relative right frontally-mediated activation during a baseline recording were more likely to exhibit distress at separation than those displaying left frontal activation. Interpretation of these data are consistent with a model emphasizing the role of the two cerebral hemispheres in the expression of both positive and negative emotion and in the display of different affective styles.

The purpose of this chapter is to review research on the possible physiological substrates of the infant's behavior in response to brief separation from mother that occurs during the last half of the first year and into the second year of life. This response pattern has been called separation protest or separation anxiety in the psychological literature (Bowlby, 1958). The infant's distress at separation from its mother has long been viewed as an important indicator of attachment behavior (Bowlby, 1958, 1960, 1969, 1973; Ainsworth, 1973; Mahler & La Perriere, 1965). This behavior has its onset around the last quarter of the first year of life and tends to diminish in the second and third years. Coincident with the modulation of protest at separation is the increase in the infant's representational capabilities, including object permanence, language, and deferred imitation, as well as the child's increasing ability at self-regulation (Kopp, 1982; Vaughn, Kopp, & Krakow, 1984; Weinraub & Smolek).

The hypothesis to be explored in this chapter is that specific patterns of cerebral activation may predict both the occurrence and intensity of distress. Individual differences in cerebral activation and lateralization may underlie both the onset and regulation of protest behavior. This hypothesis has certain implications for classification of infants in the Strange Situation (Ainsworth, Blehar, Waters, & Wall, 1978) as secure or insecure. A number of researchers have noted that infants who display intense separation protest and who are unable to regulate this distress are more likely to be classified as insecurely attached (particularly anxious/resistant C1 or C2) (Kagan, 1984, 1987). Others have claimed that emotional distress in the Strange Situation may reflect individual differences in infant temperament but not directly affect attachment classification (Frodi & Thompson, 1985; Thompson & Lamb, 1984). The data to be presented in this chapter, although not resolving this argument (c.f. Sroufe, 1985), will make the claim that variations in emotional behavior in response to separation may, in part, be the product of individual differences in brain activation.

In the first section of this chapter, a general review of the literature on separation protest will be presented. This will be followed by a review of the data on the neurophysiological substrates of emotional expression, including data on individual differences in electroencephalographic (EEG) activation asymmetries and affective style. In the third section, we will present data from our own program of research on the physiological substrates of emotion expression including data on changes in EEG activation during separation from mother. The final section will present a possible model relating both the ontogeny of left hemispheric specialization and individual differences in cerebral asymmetry to the expression of protest behavior.

SEPARATION PROTEST

During the last quarter of the first year of life, many infants begin to react with distress and crying to the departure of their caregiver. As the infant becomes mobile, many behaviors involved in searching or attempting to retrieve the mother, such as crawling or walking to the door from which mother departed, are elicited during this situation (Ainsworth, 1973; Bowlby, 1969, 1973). The infant's vigourous and often dramatic behavior in response to brief separations seems to wane during the second and third years (Kagan, 1976).

The infant's distress at separation from its caregiver has been studied by developmental researchers for some time. Bowlby (1958, 1960) believed that this initial distress indicated the existence of a bond between caregiver and infant. Distress at separation was the first phase in an infant's response to separation. If the infant was not reunited with the parent, protest and distress diminished, but other behaviors signifying despair and subsequent detachment from the caregiver emerged. Although Bowlby was later to change his position on the importance of separation protest as a marker of the attachment bond (Bowlby, 1973), accepting the view of Ainsworth and colleagues (1973; Ainsworth, et al., 1978) that the infant's behavior at reunion was the more important indicator of the quality of attachment, he continued to view protest at separation as significant, arguing that the promimal cause of protest was the infant's alarm at being left. The intended consequence of the protest was to bring the caregiver back into immediate proximity.

Ainsworth as well initially argued that protest at separation may be a means for assessing the presence of a bond between mother and infant (Ainsworth, 1967). In her early work, separation protest was used as a marker for the existence of an attachment between the infant and mother. Subsequently, Ainsworth argued that distress at separation in and of itself was not sufficient to indicate the presence or absence of an attachment. Rather it was the infant's behavior following separation upon reunion with mother that is most telling of the quality of attachment (Ainsworth, 1973; Ainsworth et al., 1978). Recently Thompson and Lamb (1984) demonstrated that the intensity of protest elicited during brief separation may be temperamental in origin. Infants who display high degrees of protest are more likely to be classified as B3, B4 or C1, C2, whereas infants who show little protest are likely to be classified as A1, A2 or B1, B2. Furthermore, Belsky and Rovine (1987) found that infant attachment classifications to father and mother were more concordant, if samples were split along the A1–B2/B3–C2 axis than if the A, B, C typology were used, but see Fox, Kennedy, and Schafer (in press). Belsky also found using this split that neonatal measures of temperament (the NBAS exam) were better predictors of infant classification than if the A, B, C typology was used. There seems to be some agreement, thus, that display of protest and regulation of distress are temperamental in origin. What remains in question is whether differences within an axis (A1 to B2 or B3 to C2) are the result of sensitive mothering or can also be attributed to temperament.

There has also been a strong body of research that has attempted to explain the phenomenon of separation protest from a learning or operant perspective. Gewirtz (1972a, 1972b; Gewirtz & Peláez-Nogueras, 1987, 1989, & chapter 7, this Volume), for example, has argued that the mother's behaviors immediately prior to separation become salient cues for the infant. The infant's subsequent protest or distress become salient cues for the mother. Thus, mother and infant engage in a chain of behaviors that signal to each other imminent departure and immediate return. As the infant acquires new behaviors in its repertoire, it can make use of them in response to brief separation. In addition, parents may alter their own behavior in response to the distress (Gewirtz, 1976). Thus, the topography of the response may change with newly formed behaviors that are produced in response to the separation.

A number of researchers have attempted to explain the phenomenon of protest in terms of the infant's developing cognitive abilities to appraise and understand her environment. Kagan (1976), for example, argued that protest emerges at a time when the infant develops an ability to recognize discrepancy in certain social situations. However, the infant is unable to resolve these discrepancies and, hence, becomes distressed. At a later age, given subsequent cognitive maturity, the infant is able to resolve the discrepancy and does not protest brief separation. In a series of studies in which context was manipulated, Kagan and others (Littenberg, Tulkin, & Kagan, 1971; Lester, Kotelchuck, Spelke, Sellers, & Klein, 1974) demonstrated that infants were less likely to protest separation, if the situation was familiar. Weinraub and Lewis (1977) presented data that indicated that infants were less likely to protest separation even in an unfamiliar environment, if the mother offered a verbal explanation for her departure rather than leaving with no explanation.

A second major piece of evidence cited by Kagan in support of the cognitive/maturational explanation for the onset and change in response to brief maternal separation involves those studies, which have demonstrated across a variety of cultures, developmental changes in the incidence of protest (Kagan, 1976). Fox (1977), for example, studied separation protest behavior in three age groups of infants raised on the Israeli kibbutz. He found that the incidence of protest increased from 8 to 15 months of age and then decreased thereafter. This age trend was found in response to separation from both mother and the infant's primary caregiver, the metapelet. Lester et al. (1974), studying infants raised in a remote Guatemalan village, found a similar age pattern in the incidence of protest to separation from mother. In addition, Konner (1975) reported a similar age pattern of protest to separation from mother among the !Kung Bushmen. Finally, in two samples, Kagan (Kagan, Kearsely, & Zelazo, 1978) found similar age trends for infants raised either at home or in a day care setting. The increased incidence during the last quarter of the first year, peaking during the second year of life and then diminishing during the third year, appears across four widely different cultures (Israeli kibbutz, Gutemalan village, !Kung bushmen, American family) and across four widely different rearing conditions. These data, Kagan has argued, indicate a strong maturational component to the expression of distress at separation.

In addition to the studies outlined previously, a number of researchers have attempted to relate individual differences in separation protest to variations in certain cognitive abilities. Weinraub and Smolek (1979), for example, studied 55 children ages 15–24 months of age, observing them in a brief separation reunion situation. Children were also assessed with a deferred imitation task and measures of expressive language facility. The authors report that differences in children's language ability were related to behavior at separation. Those children with high language facility were less likely to protest separation, whereas those with low language scores were more likely to exhibit distress at separation. Weinraub and Smolek (1979) argued that as the child develops the capacity to represent conceptually the mother during her absence, he or she is better able to cope with her absence. They cite a study by Passman and colleagues (Passman & Erck, 1978) in which pictures and films of the mother presented to preschool children facilitated play and adaptive behavior in the mother's absence. Unfortunately, Weinraub and Smolek found no relation between children's ability to exhibit deferred imitation and their behavior during separation. Nevertheless, they raise important conceptual issues in understanding developmental changes in the response to separation. The changes in separation behavior reflect the development of a "working model" of the attachment figure and the child's increasing ability to utilize this model to regulate its affective behavior. This notion, raised first by Bowlby (1980) and more recently by Main, Kaplan, & Cassidy (1985) and articulated by Weinraub and Smolek (1979), argues that increasing representational skills during the second and third year enable the child to reduce the distress often accompanying separation. Individual differences in the development of those skills involved in representation (language/deferred imitation) should be related to the child's ability to cope with brief separation.

Although there is some evidence for both a maturational component to the onset and diminution of separation protest and for individual differences in the expression of protest, there is little research with humans attempting to explore the underlying neurophysiological processes associated with the development of protest or individual differences in its expression. The exception is a study by Emde, Gaensbauer, and Harmon (1976), who found changes in sleep EEG that were associated in some infants with onset of stranger fear during the last quarter of the first year of life.

The lack of research in this area is significant given the data on EEG asymmetry and its relation to phasic changes in emotional response and individual differences in patterns of EEG activity related to affective style in adults (e.g., Schaffer, Davidson, & Saron, 1983; Davidson, 1984; Davidson, Schaffer, & Saron, 1985; Davidson & Tomarken, 1989). In addition, there is some work on the development of cerebral lateralization and its relation to language development and possibly the capacity for symbolic representation. There may, thus, be a connection between the cognitive changes mentioned previously and changes in hemispheric specialization, all of which may be related to the child's developing ability to cope with brief maternal separation.

In the next section, we will selectively review studies relating EEG activation to the expression of positive and negative affect as well as studies relating individual differences in EEG and affective style. This will be followed by presentation of our own work with human infants, which has investigated changes in EEG in response to maternal separation as well as individual differences in baseline EEG asymmetry and subsequent response to separation.

EEG ASYMMETRY AND THE EXPRESSION
OF EMOTION

A variety of data have indicated that the left hemisphere plays a more active role in the expression of certain forms of positive affect, whereas the right hemisphere plays a more active role in the expression of certain forms of negative affect. The data are from six different sources: (a) neuropsychological studies of brain damaged subjects, (b) administration of sodium amytal to patients prior to neurosurgery, (c) the study of lateralized signs and the administration of ECT to patients with affective disorders, (d) studies employing lateral eye movements as a measure of asymmetric hemispheric engagement, (e) behavioral studies involving the presentation of lateralized sensory input, and (f) electrophysiological studies of hemispheric activation in response to emotional stimuli. Data from these different areas are reviewed in detail elsewhere (Davidson, 1984; Fox & Davidson, 1984a; Davidson & Tomarken, 1989) and will not be presented here. This literature generally supports the notion that left frontal activation is involved in the experience/expression of positive affect, whereas right frontal activation is observed during the experience/expression of negative affect. However, relatively little information is available that specifies with more precision the functional differences associated with activity in the left and right frontal regions.

A separate body of literature has investigated individual differences in baseline EEG activation asymmetries and behavior. These data, from normal adult subjects, have revealed lawful relations between behavioral performance and baseline EEG activation asymmetries (e.g., Davidson, Taylor, & Saron, 1979; Furst, 1976). Most of the available studies have examined relations between baseline asymmetries in posterior scalp regions and measures of cognitive performance assumed to differentially require the right versus left cerebral hemisphere. These studies have generally supported the notion that for posterior scalp locations, greater left-sided activation at rest is associated with better performance on certain verbal tasks, whereas greater right-sided activation at rest is associated with better performance on certain measures of nonverbal visuospatial processing (e.g., Davidson et al., 1979). Importantly, individual differences in measures of EEG asymmetry have been found to be highly consistent over a 1–3 week period (Ehrlichman & Wiener, 1979; Amochaev & Salamy, 1979, Tomarken, Davidson & Wheeler, 1990). Using behavioral measures of activation biases, similar findings have been obtained (Levy, 1983).

Very few studies have examined relations between individual differences in resting frontal activation asymmetries and affective style. Given that frontal activation asymmetries are related to phasic changes in emotional response, individual differences in these EEG measures of asymmetry should be related to consistent differences in characteristic styles of emotional responding. In a recent study, Schaffer et al. (1983) found that resting asymmetries in the frontal region were related to individual differences in self-reports of depression. Those subjects who had high scores on the Beck Depression Inventory showed less left frontal activation during a resting baseline compared with subjects scoring in the nondepressed direction. Recordings of parietal EEG from the same points in time showed no relation to depressive style, thus, underscoring the specificity of the frontal region for affective processing.

More recently, Davidson and his colleages (Tomarken, Davidson, & Henriquis, in press) found that right frontal activation during rest predicted the intensity of self-reported fear in response to films designed to elicit negative affect in adults. Here it was right frontal activation, not left frontal inhibition that was associated with increased intensity of fear. The findings from the study of depressives suggests that these individuals exhibit deficits in left frontal activation, whereas the subjects in the Tomarken et al. study who reported extreme fear showed right frontal activation. This pattern of data suggests that depression may be associated with underactivation of the cerebral systems mediating approach behavior, whereas extreme fear may be associated with overactivation of the cerebral systems mediating withdrawal (see Davidson & Fox, 1988; Davidson & Tomarken, 1989).

Using positron emission tomography to measure regional cerebral blood flow during rest, it has recently been found (Reiman et al., 1986) that subjects who are prone to panic attacks show significantly more right-sided flow compared with matched controls in an area of the limbic system that has prominent anatomical connections to the frontal cortex (Nauta, 1971; Kelley & Stinus, 1984). In our own work, we have found a relation between baseline frontal EEG asymmetry and infant affective response to maternal separation.

EEG ASYMMETRY AND SEPARATION PROTEST IN INFANTS

For the past five years, we have been investigating the physiological substrates of emotion expression in infants. This work has consisted of recording EEG in awake, alert infants during the presentation of different stimulus conditions. The stimuli were chosen to elicit different patterns of facial, gestural, and vocal behavior.

In our initial research, we established that differences in frontal activation asymmetry associated with positive and negative affect in adults also are found in infants in the first year of life. Davidson and Fox (1982) found greater relative left frontal activation in 10-month-old infants in response to a videotape of an actress portraying happiness and laughter compared with sadness and crying.

Furthermore, Fox and Davidson (1986) found asymmetry differences in the same direction in newborn infants in response to sweet and sour tastes. Interestingly in the latter study, the asymmetry difference between conditions was not restricted to the frontal region but also included the parietal region. These findings may reflect the relative absence of functional specificity early in life, a suggestion consistent with recent findings on maturational changes in cerebral metabolism over the first year of life (Chugani & Phelps, 1986).

In a subsequent study (Fox & Davidson, 1987), we observed 35 ten-month-old infants in a stranger approach/mother approach/maternal separation condition. The experimental design included a 30 second baseline at the beginning of the session, followed by a four-phase approach by the stranger, a four-phase approach by the mother, and maternal separation. Infant facial expression was videotaped during the entire session. EEG was recorded from left and right frontal and parietal scalp regions referred to a common vertex using a lycra stretchable cap. Each of the EEG leads was directed into their separated amplifiers and recorded on separate channels of a Vetter Model D FM Instrumentation recorder for subsequent digitizing and analysis. The videotapes were coded using Izard's Maximally Discriminative Facial Action Coding System (Izard, 1979). In addition, videotapes were coded for presence of a set of discrete behaviors including gaze aversion, vocalization, and motor movement.

The EEG was digitized off-line and then Fourier transformed. Power density in $\mu V^2/Hz$ was computed for all artifact-free EEG in three frequency bands: 3–5 Hz, 6–8 Hz, and 9–11 Hz. The decision to examine power between 3–11 Hz was based on previous data indicating that the majority of power in the EEG of infants of this age is between these frequencies (Mizuno et al., 1970).

From inspection of the videotapes, it was clear that there were two general behavioral patterns that occurred in response to maternal separation. Of the 14 infants for whom there was artifact-free EEG during this condition, 6 cried to maternal separation, whereas the remainder did not cry. The EEG data were examined as a function of the two different patterns of behavioral response during separation. Infant EEG for criers and noncriers in the condition just prior to the separation was compared to EEG during the separation condition. Results of the analyses revealed significant effects in the 3–5 Hz band. The ANOVA on the frontal leads for this band (Condition X Hemisphere X Group) revealed a significant three-way interaction ($F(1,7) = 6.10$, $p = .04$). This same interaction for the parietal leads was not significant. The frontal data are presented in FIG. 8.1. As can be seen from this figure, criers show a complete reversal in their pattern of frontal activation between the mother reach and maternal separation conditions. In response to mother reach, these subjects show left-sided activation, whereas in response to maternal separation, the criers exhibit right frontal activation. The noncriers show no difference in left frontal activation between conditions. Interestingly in response to maternal separation, the noncriers show a pronounced inhibition of right frontal activation (an increase in power). Seven of the nine subjects (three of four criers and four of five noncriers) display these

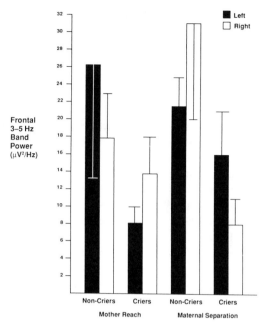

FIG. 8.1.   Mean 3–5 Hz power in the left and right frontal leads for infants who cried and did not cry to maternal separation, recorded during the mother reach and separation conditions. From Fox and Davidson (1987).

changes in frontal asymmetry between the mother reach and maternal separation conditions.

The finding of differences in frontal EEG asymmetry that distinguish between infants who differ in their response to maternal separation is consistent with our model relating changes in frontal EEG to the expression of different positive and negative emotions (Fox & Davidson, 1984b). The infants who cried in response to maternal separation showed an increase in relative right frontal activation in this condition compared with the preceeding condition, whereas those infants who did not cry in response to this stressor showed a decrease in activation of the right frontal region. Coding of infant facial behavior during the separation condition revealed that infants who protested separation exhibited expressions of anger, distress, and sadness, whereas those not crying exhibited expressions of interest. This pattern of emotional expressivity during the separation condition is similar to that reported by Izard (Schiller, Izard, & Hembree, 1986). The decreased activation in the noncriers may reflect an active inhibition of the right frontal region. The degree to which infants exhibited this inhibition may be associated with individual differences in the maturation of certain brain regions associated with the ability to regulate emotional expression.

FACIAL BEHAVIOR INDICATING EMOTION
REGULATION AND EEG ACTIVITY

As mentioned previously, the videotapes of the infant's facial behavior were synchronized to the EEG recordings. This allowed us to investigate the changes in brain activity that were associated with changes in facial expression (Fox & Davidson, 1988). Of interest here is the pattern of smiling behavior that was seen to both mother and stranger during the approach sequences. Darwin (1872/1976) following Duchenne (1856/ in press), noted that smiles that involved only tension in the zygomatic major muscle (cheek) in the absence of tension in orbicularis oculi were not associated with felt happiness (i.e., unfelt smiles). Genuine, or felt smiles, were held to involve tension in both zygomatic and orbicularis oculi muscles. Ekman and Friesen (1982) confirmed these early observations and found that only smiles with both muscle components were correlated with self-reports of happiness in adults.

In response to approach of both stranger and mother, infants displayed comparable amounts of smiling. However, there were significantly more unfelt smiles to the stranger than to the mother during this situation (see Table 8.1). Examination of the pattern of brain electrical activity coincident with the expressions corroborated these differences in smiling. Table 8.2 presents the laterality ratio scores for the felt and unfelt smiling expressions. Positive numbers on this index denote left-sided activation and negative numbers denote right-sided activation. As can be seen from the table, during the expression of felt smiles infants displayed greater relative left frontal activation, whereas during the expression of unfelt smiles, infants displayed greater relative right frontal activation. The significance of the different patterns of smiles may lie in their indicating early attempts by the infant at regulating emotion expression during novel or mildly stressful events such as approach of an unfamiliar person. The child displays a smile, although not a genuine smile, as a possible indication of the ambiguity of the stranger approach situation. Interestingly, each unfelt smile to the stranger was followed by active gaze aversion again indicating the infant's attempt at regulating the emotional situation (see, for example, Gianino & Tronick, 1986, for examples of emotion regulation in infancy). The differential

TABLE 8.1
Number of Infants Displaying Felt and Unfelt Smiles in Response to the Stranger and Mother Approach Conditions

	Felt	Unfelt
Stranger approach	5	15
Mother approach	21	6

Difference in the incidence of two types of smiling between the two conditions is significant ($p = .005$ by Fisher's Exact Test). From Fox and Davidson (1988).

TABLE 8.2
Laterality Ratio Scores (LnR--LnL; 3-12 Hz Power) for the Two Types of Smiles
(N = 10)

	Frontal	Parietal
Felt	.414 (.366)	.623 (.451)
Unfelt	-.259 (.481)	.206 (.109)

pattern of EEG during these events may reflect early signs of active self-regulation. A similar difference in frontal EEG asymmetry between these two smile types in adults has recently been reported by Ekman, Davidson, and Friesen (1990).

INDIVIDUAL DIFFERENCES IN EEG AND AFFECTIVE STYLE

In an attempt to investigate individual differences in resting EEG asymmetry and their possible relation to affective style, we (Davidson & Fox, 1989) examined these indices in a sample of 19 infants (from the study described previously) and explored the relation between baseline, resting activation asymmetries, and subsequent response to maternal separation.

Prior to the experimental situation, a 30 second baseline recording of EEG was obtained. The baseline measures were taken while the mother was in the room with infant. She was instructed not to interact with her infant during this period. During all periods of the experiment, infant behavior was videotaped.

EEG was recorded from the left and right frontal and parietal scalp regions (F3, F4, P3, and P4), referred to a common vertex (Cz), and infant facial expression was videotaped. Behavioral (i.e., from videotape) and physiological data were synchronized by placing event markers coincident with the onset and offset of each event on both the instrumentation recorder and the videotape.

The EEG was digitized and analyzed in the same manner as in the previous study. Power density (in $\mu V^2/Hz$) was computed for each frequency in one Hz bins from 3 to 12 Hz, because the majority of power in the EEG of infants of this age occurs between these frequencies. Inspection of the multivariate ANOVAs revealed that the main effects for the analyses were located in the 6–8 Hz band. A total of 13 infants had usable EEG from the baseline period.

The videotape segments of baseline behavior were coded by two observers blind to the experimental hypotheses. The observers used Izard's MAX facial action coding system (Izard, 1979) and, in addition, noted the presence or absence of crying during the maternal separation condition. Out of the 13 infants with usable EEG, 6 were coded as criers and 7 as noncriers during the maternal separation period. Examination of the facial data revealed no difference in the frequency or duration of discrete emotions or blends during baseline between infants who cried or did not cry at separation. Thus, it is not likely that the infants who subsequently cried in response to separation were simply in a dysphoric mood when they entered the experiment compared with the noncriers.

An ANOVA on the log transformed power at 6–8 Hz was computed with Group (crier/noncrier), Region (frontal/parietal), and Hemisphere (left/right) as factors. The prediction that the criers would show greater right-sided activation (i.e., less power) specifically in the frontal region compared with the noncriers would be supported by a significant Group X Region X Hemisphere interaction. The results of this ANOVA indicated that this interaction was significant as predicted (F(1,11) = 12.85, p = .004). No other main or interaction effects were reliable in this ANOVA.

In order to decompose this significant three-way interaction and to examine whether the group difference in activation asymmetry is restricted to the frontal region, separate ANOVAs with Group and Hemisphere as factors were computed for each of the two regions separately. The ANOVA for the frontal region data revealed a significant Group X Hemisphere interaction (F(1,11) = 8.15, p = .02). No main effects were obtained in this analysis. No significant effects were obtained in the ANOVA for the parietal region data. Figure 8.2 presents the significant interaction. As can be seen from this figure, the differences between groups are pronounced in the frontal region. Noncriers had more left frontal activation (i.e. less 6–8 Hz) power) than did criers (p < .06), and criers had

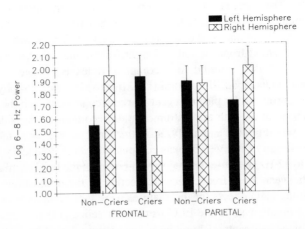

FIG. 8.2.   Mean log 6–8 Hz power for the left and right frontal region for infants who cried during maternal separation. Recording took place during a quiet, alert baseline condition, prior to the separation condition. From Davidson and Fox (1989).

more right frontal activation than did noncriers ($p < .01$). In addition, the noncriers showed significant ($p < .05$) left-sided frontal activation (i.e., less power in the left vs. right lead), whereas the criers showed significant ($p < .01$) right sided frontal activation (i.e., less power in the right vs. left lead).

These findings indicate that infants' affective response to separation can be predicted from baseline frontal activation asymmetry. Those infants who show less left-sided frontal activation during rest are more likely to cry upon maternal separation. Of the 6 infants who cried in this situation, only one did not show absolute right frontal activation during the baseline period (i.e., more 6–8 Hz power in the left versus right frontal lead). It is noteworthy that no main effects for Group were obtained. The lack of Group main effects indicates that the two groups did not differ in overall EEG activation but only in the pattern of activation in the two hemispheres. These results have recently been replicated (Fox, in press; Fox & Aaron, 1990; Fox & Bell, in press). We believe that the individual differences in frontal asymmetry that we have observed in this study may be related to certain features of affective or temperamental style. Whether early cerebral manifestations of these individual differences predict later personality differences or psychopathology is an area that warrants attention in future research (see Davidson, in press).

SPECULATIONS ON A DEVELOPMENTAL NEUROPSYCHOLOGICAL MODEL OF SEPARATION PROTEST

At least two models of hemispheric contributions to affect regulation are compatible with the data presented previously. One model holds that increased left frontal activation by itself is sufficient for the regulation of affective responding to a stressful stimulus. This model would take support from the data on the role of language in the mediation of affective responding and from our own EEG evidence that indicates that infants with left-sided frontal activation are not likely to cry in response to maternal separation. The second and not mutually exclusive model rests on the assumption that activation in the two cerebral hemispheres is in reciprocal balance and that one hemisphere can inhibit the activation in the other (see Denenberg, Hofmann, Rosen, & Yutzey, 1984). According to this model, left frontal activation results in the attenuation of negative affective responding as a function of inhibition of right frontal activation. Partial support for this hypothesis is present in the data on baseline asymmetry differences between criers and noncriers. There we found a reliable interaction of hemisphere with group. Activation of the left frontal region in the noncriers indeed was associated with *decreases* in the activation of the right frontal region as this model would predict. This pattern of data is consistent with the transcallosal inhibition hypothesis (Fox & Davidson, 1984), although only weakly.

To determine whether it is left hemisphere activation directly that mediates these behavioral patterns or left-sided inhibition of right-sided activation will require more finely grained study of relations between activation in each hemisphere over time. The transcallosal inhibition hypothesis would predict that increases in left-sided activation should be associated with decreases in right-sided activation (see Davidson, 1988; Davidson & Tomarken, 1989 for a discussion of the methodological difficulties of testing this hypothesis).

Yet a third possibility would hold that the infants with greater right-sided frontal activation simply have a lower threshold for the triggering of certain negative effects. This lower threshold could arise as a function of differences in appraisal or the relative of coping skills with which to modulate affect, once it is aroused. This view would lead to the prediction that in order to elicit an affective response of a given intensity, subjects with more right frontal activation would require a less intense elicitor, whereas those with less right frontal activation would require a more intense elicitor. In order to disentangle these various possibilities, future research must begin to examine the subcomponents of affect to determine precisely which component is reflected in EEG activation asymmetries. In addition, future work should examine individual differences in the development of language and representational abilities, skills presumably mediated by the left hemisphere, as they are related to changes in separation protest behavior.

These data do, however, argue that the expression of distress to brief separation and its subsequent regulation are not dichotomous events but occur over a broad continuum of underlying physiological activation. The presence of a continuum of physiological activation that may be related to onset and intensity of distress and its regulation argues that differences in these behaviors seen in the Strange Situation may in fact be temperamental in origin. Specifically, differences within an axis (using Belsky & Rovine's model: A1–B2/ or B3–C2) may be the result of individual differences in cerebral activation and lateralization. Within an axis, infants will differ in the intensity of expression of distress and the degree to which they can regulate this distress. These differences will no doubt be the result of their socialization histories to the extent that the likelihood of emotional expression is the result of neurophysiological patterning and maturation.

ACKNOWLEDGMENTS

The research reported in this chapter was supported, in part, by an NIH grant (HD-17899) to Nathan A. Fox and Richard J. Davidson and by NIMH grants (MH-40747 and MH-43454) to Richard J. Davidson. This chapter was completed in 1986. Many of the findings have been replicated and extended since that time by both co-authors. More recent citations have been added in proof stage to provide the reader with sources for current extensions of this research program.

REFERENCES

Ainsworth, M. D. S. (1967). *Infancy in Uganda: Infant care and the growth of love.* Baltimore, MD: Johns Hopkins University Press.

Ainsworth, M. D. S. (1973). The development of mother–infant attachment. In G. Caldwell & H. Riccuiti (Eds.), *Review of Child Development Research* (Vol. 3) Chicago: University Press.

Ainsworth, M. D. S., Blehar, M., Waters, E., & Wall, S. (1978). *Patterns of Attachment: Strange situation behavior of one year olds.* Hillsdale, NJ: Lawrence Erlbaum Associates.

Amochaev, A., & Salamy, A. (1979). Stability of EEG laterality effects. *Psychophysiology, 16,* 242–246.

Belsky, J., & Rovine, M. (1987). Temperament and attachment security in the strange situation: An empirical rapprochment. *Child Development, 58,* 787–797.

Bowlby, J. (1958). The nature of the child's tie to his mother. *International Journal of Psycho-analysis, 39,* 350–373.

Bowlby, J. (1960). Separation anxiety. *International Journal of Psychoanalysis, 41,* 89–113.

Bowlby, J. (1969). *Attachment and Loss. Volume 1: Attachment.* New York: Basic.

Bowlby, J. (1973). *Attachment and Loss. Volume 2: Separation, anxiety and anger.* New York: Basic.

Bowlby, J. (1980). *Attachment and Loss. Volume 3: Sadness and depression.* New York: Basic.

Chugani, H. T., & Phelps, M. E. (1986). Maturational changes in cerebral function in infants determined by 18FDG positron emission tomography. *Science, 231,* 840–843.

Darwin, C. (1976). *The expression of emotions in man and animals.* Chicago: University of Chicago Press. (Original work published 1872).

Davidson, R. J. (1984). Affect, cognition and hemispheric specialization. In C. E. Izard, J. Kagan, & R. Zajonc (Eds.), *Emotion, cognition, and behavior* (pp. 320–365). New York: Cambridge University Press.

Davidson, R. J. (1988). EEG measures of cerebral asymmetry: Conceptual and methodological issues. *International Journal of Neuroscience, 39,* 71–89.

Davidson, R. J. (in press). Cerebral asymmetry and affective disorders: A developmental approach. In D. Cicchetti (Ed.), *Rochester Symposium on Developmental Psychopathology, Vol. 2.* Hillsdale, NJ: Lawrence Erlbaum Associates.

Davidson, R. J., & Fox, N. A. (1982). Asymmetrical brain activity discriminates between positive and negative affective stimuli in human infants. *Science, 218,* 1235–1237.

Davidson, R. J., & Fox, N. A. (1989). Frontal brain asymmetry predicts infants' response to maternal separation. *Journal of Abnormal Psychology, 98,* 127–131.

Davidson, R. J., & Fox, N. A. (1988). Cerebral asymmetry and emotion: Developmental and individual differences. In S. Sesgalowitz & D. Molfese (Eds.), *Developmental implications of brain lateralization.* (pp. 191–206) New York: Guilford Press.

Davidson, R. J., Schaffer, C. E., & Saron, C. (1985). Effects of lateralized stimulus presentations on the self-report of emotion and EEG asymmetry in depressed and nondepressed subjects. *Psychophysiology, 22,* 353–364.

Davidson, R. J., Taylor, N., & Saron, C. (1979). Hemisphericity and styles of information processing: Individual differences in EEG asymmetry and their relationship to cognitive performance. *Psychophysiology, 16,* 197.

Davidson, R. J., & Tomarken, A. J. (1989). Laterality and emotion: An electrophysiological approach. In F. Boller & J. Grafman (Eds.), *Handbook of Neuropsychology* (pp. 419–441). Amsterdam: Elsevier.

Denenberg, V. H., Hofmann, M. J., Rosen, G. D., & Yutzey, D. A. (1984). Cerebral asymmetry and behavioral laterality: Some psychobiological considerations. In N. A. Fox & R. J. Davidson (Eds.), *The psychobiology of affective development.* Hillsdale, NJ: Lawrence Erlbaum Associates.

Ehrlichman, H., & Wiener, M. S. (1979). Consistency of task-related EEG asymmetries. *Psychophysiology, 16*, 247–252.

Ekman, P., Davidson, R. J., & Friesen, W. V. (1990). Duchenne's smile: Emotional expression and brain physiology, II. *Journal of Personality and Social Psychology, 58*, 342–353.

Ekman, P., & Friesen, W. V. (1982). Felt, false, & miserable smiles. *Journal of Non-verbal Behavior, 6*, 238–252.

Emde, R. N., Gaensbauer, T. J., & Harmon, R. J. (1976). *Emotional expression in infancy: A biobehavioral study.* New York: International Universities Press.

Fox, N. A. (1977). The development of attachment on the Israeli kibbutz. *Child Development, 55*, 1237–1260.

Fox, N. A. (in press). Frontal brain asymmetry and vulnerability to stress: Individual difference in infant temperament. In T. Field, P. McCabe, & N. Schneiderman (Eds.), *Stress and Coping*. Hillsdale, NJ: Lawrence Erlbaum Associates.

Fox, N. A., & Bell, M. A. (in press). Electrophysiological indices of frontal lobe development: Relations to cognitive and affective behavior in human infants over the first year of life. In A. Diamond (Ed.), *The development and neural bases of higher cognitive functions.* New York: New York Academy of Sciences.

Fox, N. A., & Aaron, N. (1990). *The relations between frontal brain asymmetry and temperament in 14- and 24-month-old children.* Manuscript submitted for publication.

Fox, N. A., & Davidson, R. J. (Eds.). (1984a). *The psychobiology of affective development.* Hillsdale, NJ: Lawrence Erlbaum Associates.

Fox, N. A., & Davidson, R. J. (1984b). Hemispheric substrates for affect: A developmental model. In N. A. Fox & R. J. Davidson (Eds.), *The psychobiology of affective development* (pp. 353–382). Hillsdale, NJ: Lawrence Erlbaum Associates.

Fox, N. A., & Davidson, R. J. (1986). EEG asymmetry in response to sweet and sour tastes in newborn infants. *Neuropsychologia, 24*, 417–422.

Fox, N. A., & Davidson, R. J. (1987). EEG asymmetry in response to stranger approach and maternal separation in ten month old infants. *Developmental Psychology, 23*, 233–240.

Fox, N. A., & Davidson, R. J. (1988). Patterns of brain electrical activity during facial signs of emotion in ten month old infants. *Developmental Psychology, 24*, 230–236.

Fox, N. A., Kimmerley, N. L., & Schaefer, W. D. (in press). Attachment to mother/attachment to father: A meta-analysis. *Child Development.*

Frodi, A., & Thompson, R. (1985). Infants' affective responses in the Strange Situation: Effects of prematurity and of quality of attachment. *Child Development, 56*, 1280–1291.

Furst, C. J. (1976). EEG asymmetry and visuospatial performance. *Nature, 260*, 254–255.

Gewirtz, J. L. (1972a). Attachment, dependence, and a distinction in terms of stimulus control. In J. L. Gewirtz (Ed.), *Attachment and dependency.* New York: Wiley.

Gewirtz, J. L. (1972b). On the selection and use of attachment and dependence indices. In J. L. Gewirtz (Ed.), *Attachment and dependency,* New York: Wiley.

Gewirtz, J. L. (1976). The attachment acquisition process as evidenced in the maternal conditioning of cued infant responding (particularly crying). *Human Development, 19*, 143–155.

Gewirtz, J. L., & Peláez-Nogueras, M. (1987). Social-conditioning theory applied to metaphors like "attachment": The conditioning of infant separation protests by mothers. *Revista Mexicana de Análisis de la Conducta, 13*, 87–103.

Gewirtz, J. L., & Peláez-Nogueras, M. (1989). *Infant protesting to maternal departures and separations: A conditional discrimination process.* Paper delivered at the Biennial Meeting, Society for Research in Child Development, Kansas City, Missouri, April 27, 1989.

Gianino, A., & Tronick, E. (1986). The infant regulatory model. In T. Field, P. McCabe, & N. Schneiderman (Eds.), *Stress and coping, Volume 1.* Hillsdale, NJ: Lawrence Erlbaum Associates.

Izard, C. E. (1979). *The maximally discriminative facial action coding system.* Newark, Delaware: University of Delaware Press.

Kagan, J. (1976). Emergent themes in human development. *American Scientist, 64,* 186–196.

Kagan, J. (1984). *The nature of the child.* Cambridge, MA: Harvard University Press.

Kagan, J. (1987). Perspectives on infancy. In J. Osofsky (Ed.), *Handbook of infant development* (2nd edition) pp. (1150–1198). New York: Wiley.

Kagan, J., Kearsley, R. B., & Zelazo, P. R. (1978). *Infancy: Its place in human development.* Cambridge, MA: Harvard University Press.

Kelley, A. E., & Stinus, L. (1984). Neuroanatomical and neurochemical substrates of affective behavior. In N. A. Fox & R. J. Davidson (Eds.), *The psychobiology of affective development.* Hillsdale, NJ: Lawrence Erlbaum Associates.

Konner, M. (1975). *Separation protest among the !Kung Bushmen.* Unpublished manuscript, Harvard University.

Kopp, C. B. (1982). Antecedents of self-regulation: A developmental perspective. *Developmental Psychology, 18,* 199–214.

Lester, B. M., Kotelchuck, M., Spelke, E., Sellers, M. J., & Klein, R. E. (1974). Separation protest in Guatemalan Infants: Cross-cultural and cognitive findings. *Developmental Psychology, 10,* 79–85.

Levy, J. (1983). Individual differences in cerebral asymmetry: Theoretical issues and experimental considerations. In J. B. Hellige (Ed.), *Cerebral hemisphere asymmetry: Method, theory, and application.* New York: Praeger.

Littenberg, R., Tulkin, S. R., & Kagan, J. (1971). Cognitive components of separation anxiety. *Developmental Psychology, 4,* 387–388.

Mahler, M. S., & La Perriere, K. (1965, October). Mother–child interaction during separation-individuation. *Psychoanalytic Quarterly,* 483–498.

Main, M., Kaplan, N., & Cassidy, J. (1985). Security in infancy, childhood, and adulthood: A move to the level of representation. In I. Bretherton & E. Waters (Eds.), *Growing points of attachment theory and research.* Monographs of the Society for Research in Child Development, *50,* 209, 66–106.

Mizuno, T., Yamauchi, N., Watanabe, A., Komatsushushiro, M., Takagi, T., Iinuma, K., & Arakawa, T. (1970). Maturation patterns of EEG basic waves of healthy infants under 12 months of age. *Tohoku Journal of Experimental Medicine, 102,* 21–98.

Nauta, W. J. H. (1971). The problem of the frontal lobe: A reinterpretation. *Journal of Psychiatric Research, 8,* 167–187.

Passman, R. H., & Erck, T. W. (1978). Permitting maternal contact through vision alone: Films of mothers for promoting play and locomotion. *Developmental Psychology, 14,* 512–516.

Reiman, E. M., Raichle, M. E., Robins, E., Butler, F. K., Herscovitch, P., Fox, P., & Perlmutter, J. (1986). The application of positron emission tomography to the study of panic disorder. *American Journal of Psychiatry, 143,* 469–477.

Schaffer, C. E., Davidson, R. J., & Saron, C. (1983). Frontal and parietal EEG asymmetries in depressed and non-depressed subjects. *Biological Psychiatry, 18,* 753–762.

Schiller, V. M., Izard, C. E., & Hembree, E. A. (1986). Patterns of emotion expression during separation in the stranger situation. *Developmental Psychology, 22,* 378–383.

Sroufe, L. A. (1985). Attachment classification from the perspective of infant–caregiver relationships and infant temperament. *Child Development, 56,* 1–14.

Thompson, R. A., & Lamb, M. E. (1984). Assessing qualitative dimensions of emotion responsiveness in infants: Separation reactions in the Strange Situation. *Infant Behavior and Development, 7,* 423–445.

Tomarken, A. J., Davidson, R. J., & Henriques, J. B. (in press). Resting frontal brain asymmetry predicts affective responses to films. *Journal of Personality and Social Psychology.*

Tomarken, A. J., Davidson, R. J., & Wheeler, R. E. (1990). *Comparative stability of anterior EEG spectral features across multiple bands.* Manuscript submitted for publication.

Vaughn, B. E., Kopp, C. B., & Krakow, J. B. (1984). The emergence and consolidation of self-control from eighteen to thirty months of age: Normative trends and individual differences. *Child Development, 55,* 990–1004.

Weinraub, M., & Lewis, M. (1977). The determinants of children's responses to separation. *Monographs of the Society for Research in Child Development, 42,* (4 Serial No. 172).

Weinraub, M., & Smolek, L. (1979, March). *Separation distress and representational development.* Paper presented at the meetings of the Society for Research in Child Development, San Francisco.

9 Attachment and Early Separations from Parents and Peers

Tiffany Field

ABSTRACT

Attachment has been studied primarily in the context of early separations. Separation stress in infants, toddlers, and preschool children was studied in four different contexts; separation from the mother during her hospitalization for the birth of another child, repeated separations from the mother during mother's conference trips; separation from peers following graduation to new classes and separations from peers due to transfers to new schools. As compared to baseline behavior, separations from the mother were characterized by agitation (increases in negative affect, activity level, night-wakings and crying) with some of these behaviors returning to baseline and others becoming depressed following the mother's return, suggesting that reunion behavior was affected by changes in the mother–child attachment/relationship. Increases in classroom cooperative play and interactions with other children during the separation period suggest that the children were immersing themselves in peer play as a potential way of coping with their separation stress.

EARLY SEPARATIONS FROM PARENTS AND PEERS

Attachment, or the primary tie between a child and his or her mother, is often studied in the context of early separations. Attachment has been defined by those behaviors that are directed to the person referred to as the "attachement figure" during an impending separation (such behaviors as crying and clinging) and following reunion (proximity seeking and greeting behaviors). Data reviewed by Bowlby (1969) and the Strange Situation studies by Ainsworth (1967) and her colleagues convincingly demonstrate a special attachment to the mother by the infant. However, as we have suggested elsewhere (Field, 1985), the model of attachment derived from these data has some limitations. The attachment figure is too narrowly specified and singular, and the processes are overly confined to a short period early in the lifespan. In addition, the process has been studied in a limited context, the separation situation. A better understanding of the process may require the study of multiple kinds of attachments and may include both overt and physiological behaviors that occur, when attached individuals are both together and apart. To understand attachment would seemingly require observation of how the attached figures interact and what they provide for each other during natural, nonstressful situations in order to know what is then missing during the separation.

The behaviors that operationally define attachment have been limited to those that have been observed during mother–child separations. Other attachments are not necessarily characterized by those behaviors. For example, infants do not necessarily cling to their peers, follow them, or cry during an impending departure nor do they typically run to and cling to them as they return, yet infants are unquestionably attached to peers. Both the data and models presented by Bowlby and Ainsworth are based on the mother being the primary attachment figure. Although both authors have now acknowledged that other attachments may occur, the mother is treated as the primary attachment object, and only thereafter are the father or peers considered potential attachment objects. Other data suggest that multiple, simultaneous attachments may occur to mother, father, siblings, and peers.

For an attachment model to be parsimonious, it must accommodate multiple attachments to a variety of figures. Attachment might instead be viewed as a relationship that develops between two or more organisms as they become attuned to each other, each providing the other some meaningful kinds and amounts of stimulation and modulation of arousal. This "attunement" facilitates an optimal growth state that is threatened by changes in the individuals or their relationship or by separation. The loss of this important source of stimulation and arousal modulation, as in separation, will invariably result in behavioral and physiological disorganization. Thus, attachments may be viewed as psychobiologically adaptive for the organization, equilibrium, and growth of the organism. The organism's behavioral repertoire, physiological makeup, and growth needs are an integrated multivariate complex that changes developmentally, therefore, multiple and different types of attachments are experienced across the lifespan. Data on primates and humans are presented in this chapter to support this attunement model and to suggest paradigms that might be employed.

Early Separations from Parents

The separation paradigm we have used is based on a paradigm of mother–infant separations in infant pigtail and bonnet monkeys by Reite and his colleagues

(Reite, Short, Seiler, & Pauley, 1981; Reite & Snyder, 1982; Reite & Capitanio, 1985). These investigators surgically implanted telemetry in their infant monkeys and monitored both behavior and physiology during a period prior to mother–infant separations, during the separations, and following reunion. Generally a period of behavioral agitation was followed by a period of depression. Shortly after the separation, infants exhibited an agitation reaction with increased motor activity and frequent distressed vocalizations. Depressed behaviors typically emerged shortly thereafter and persisted for the period of separation. The infants moved more slowly than normal, and their play behavior was diminished. Sleep disturbances were characterized by decreases in REM sleep as well as an increase in the number of arousals and time spent awake. The behavioral agitation reaction that occurred immediately after separation was accompanied by increases in both heart rate and body temperature followed by decreases to below baseline. Although most behaviors returned to baseline following reunion for most monkey infants, these behavioral alterations persisted for some infants, suggesting that changes in the mother–infant relationship upon reunion may be as important as the separation per se. Changes in the mother–infant relationship at reunion occurred, for example, when a new infant monkey was introduced to the group by the mother or when the mother was unavailable to the infant upon reunion because of the mother's having come into estrus during the period of separation or because the mother was busily reestablishing herself in the dominance hierarchy.

Using this paradigm, we conducted a study on preschool children's responses to separation from the mother during the birth of another child (Field & Reite, 1984). Agitated behavior and physiology were noted during the period of the mother's hospitalization, and depressed behavior and activity followed the mother's return from the hospital, again suggesting that an altered relationship in addition to the separation may have contributed to the child's depressed behavior. In this study, preschool children's behavioral and physiological responses to separation were monitored before, during, and after the mother's hospitalization for the birth of a new child. During these three periods, play sessions were videotaped simultaneously with activity level and heart rate monitoring. In addition, nighttime sleep was time-lapse videotaped, and the parents were administered questionnaires on changes in their child's behaviors. Increases in negative affect, activity level, heart rate, nightwakings, and crying characterized the hospital period as one of agitation (see Table 9.1). Longer periods of deep sleep at this stage were interpreted as conservation withdrawal.

After the mother's return, decreases were noted in positive affect, activity level, heart rate, and active sleep, suggestive of depression. Changes noted by the parents included clinging and aggressive behaviors, changes in eating and toileting, and sleep disturbances and illnesses. The children were clearly agitated by the mother's separation, although they visited her at the hospital during this period and were cared for by their fathers. Their depression following the mother's return from the hospital may have related to the depressed affect, lesser

TABLE 9.1
Means for Play and Sleep Behaviors of Preschoolers Prior to, During, and Following Their Mothers Hospitalization

Behaviors	Baseline	Separation	Reunion	p Level
Play Behaviors (% time sample unit)				
Smiling	13	2	3	.001
Animation	23	15	16	.05
Aggression	2	8	1	.01
Fussiness	6	10	2	.05
Activity level (actometer)	22	30	10	.01
Heart rate (BPM)	112	128	108	.01
Sleep Behaviors				
Total sleep time (minutes)	543	616	548	.05
Latency to sleep (minutes)	38	26	17	.01
Number of Nightwakings	1	6	2	.005
Crying (minutes)	0	13	5	.05

animation, and exhausted behavior noted in the mother during this period, which together with the arrival of a new sibling seemed to alter the relationship previously experienced by the mother and child. Examples of the child's disturbance regarding this altered relationship were seen in the children's fantasy play, interpreted as active coping on their part. A number of fantasy play themes involved aggression against the mother, as in rushing her to the hospital and having her leg cut off, and against the new sibling, as in teaching the baby to dive off a high bridge.

These behavioral changes may be even more pronounced in infants subjected to a similar separation experience because of their lesser ability to procure adequate stimulation and arousal modulation without the organizing influence of the mother. The infant is closer in age to the new sibling and has greater stimulation and arousal modulation needs than the older child, who in turn has more developed self-regulation skills. In addition, coping behaviors such as fantasy play and other cognitive coping skills are less available to the infant than the preschool child. Thus, it is perhaps not surprising that in a similar study conducted on infants (Field, 1986), separation behavior changes were more dramatic. As can be seen in Table 9.2, the infants, not unlike the preschoolers of the previous study, showed increases in activity level and heart rate, and decreases in smiling and animated behavior, during the separation phase. Also, like the preschoolers, they experienced longer periods of sleep during the separation period. However, unlike the preschoolers, their increased levels of aggression and fussiness during separation remained elevated during reunion, as did the number of night wakings and the amount of crying during sleep. Thus, the infant who is closer in age to the new sibling appears to be more stressed by the actual reunion, probably because the infant has greater stimulation and arousal modulation needs than the older preschool child that are not being adequately met upon the return of the exhausted mother and the new sibling.

The primate infant and the human child may become agitated during separation from the mother because of a loss from an important source of arousal modulation. Young monkeys and children are noted to turn to their mothers for comfort in the face of arousing or stressful situations and return to her as a secure base (Ainsworth, 1967; Bowlby, 1969). Although the children in the Field and

TABLE 9.2
Means for Play and Sleep Behaviors of Infants/Toddlers Prior to, During, and Following Their
Mother's Hospitalization

Behaviors	Baseline	Separation	Reunion	p Level
Play Behaviors (% time sample unit)				
Smiling	9	2	3	.01
Animation	22	15	16	.05
Aggression	2	8	7	.05
Fussiness	15	22	21	.05
Activity level (actometer)	26	35	21	.05
Heart rate (BPM)	117	131	110	.05
Sleep Behaviors				
Total sleep time (minutes)	580	645	575	.05
Latency to sleep (minutes)	28	21	19	.05
Number of Nightwakings	1	5	4	.05
Crying (minutes)	8	15	14	.05

Reite (1984) study had the advantage of both father involvement and mother visits, they were still distressed during the hospitalization. Fathers may not be as effective in modulating arousal of young children because of their lesser experience with the child's arousal modulation needs. Heightened levels of arousal may stimulate the sympathetic adrenergic system resulting in agitated behavior, a behavioral complex that is typically associated with active coping—in this case, active coping to recall the mother. The emergence of depression as the separation continues may relate to a number of factors. Depression may be a homeostatic mechanism offsetting the sympathetic arousal or agitation in the absence of effective arousal modulation, or it may result from inadequate amounts of stimulation. Just as the fathers may be less effective at modulating arousal, they may provide less adequate amounts and types of stimulation by virtue of less familiarity with the child's stimulation needs. The infant monkey and the human child may experience helplessness during the separation because of their failure to recall the mother and during the reunion because of the arrival of the new sibling and the altered relationship. Depression following the reunion was attributed to depressed activity in the mother and an altered relationship between the mother and child as manifested in their play together. Thus, infants and children may continue to experience distress following reunions with their mothers because of temporary disequilibrium in their relationships. Attachment disturbances may appear even in the presence of an attachment object, if the partners to the attachment relationship are not in tune with each other.

Early Separations from Peers

Studies on monkey infant peer separations (Reite, Harbeck, & Hoffman, 1981; Suomi, Collins, & Harlow, 1976) and peer separations in preschool children (Field, 1984) and infants (Field, Vega-Lahr, & Jagadish, 1984) suggest that the disorganizing effects of separation are not limited to mother–infant dyads. In a study by Reite and his colleagues, two pigtail infant monkeys who had been reared together showed behavioral and physiological disorganization following their separation (Reite, Harbeck, & Hoffman, 1981). Just as in the study on infants separated from their mothers, agitated behavior followed separation with increases in activity and vocalizations. Subsequently, both infants showed a decrease in play behavior and an altered cellular immune response. The impaired cellular immune function and agitated behaviors noted in these infant monkeys suggest that significant behavioral and physiological changes accompanied the separations of young primate peers. Despite the frequent reference to strong peer attachments in children, separations between young peers are rarely studied.

A separation that naturally occurs with some frequency during the early preschool years is a transfer of children to new schools. In one study, preschool children who were transferring to new schools after having been classmates for three to four years were observed during a 2-week period prior to separation from their classmates (Field, 1984). The children who were leaving the school showed increases (compared to baseline observations three months earlier) in fantasy play, physical contact, negative statements and affect, fussiness, activity level, tonic heart rate, and illness as well as changes in eating and sleeping patterns (see FIG. 9.1). In addition to the changes in play behaviors and in vegetative functions, the children's drawings of themselves manifested agitation and disorganization (see FIG. 9.2). The drawings included distorted facial and body parts and sad faces. Shortly after the children's departure, this agitated behavior appeared to diminish in the children who were leaving the school.

The anticipatory reactions to separations by these children appeared to mimic the immediate responses to peer separation in young monkeys (Reite, Short, Seiler, & Pauley, 1981). They were also very similar to those behaviors noted in young children immediately following the hospitalization of their mothers for the birth of another child (Field & Reite, 1984). In these studies, the increase in fussiness, negative affect, aggressive behavior, physical activity level, and tonic heart rate are suggestive of agitation. Other similarities across studies include changes in eating, as well as sleep disturbances and more frequent illness. Although changes in eating patterns were variable, with some children eating more and others eating less, as was also noted following the mother–child separations (Field & Reite, 1984), sleep disturbances were uniformly similar across these studies, with more frequent nightwakings, crying, and delayed onsets of sleep. Increased illness, in this study and in the study on mother–child separation, is consistent with reports of changes in the immune system of young primates during mother and peer separations (Reite, Harbeck, & Hoffmann, 1981; Reite & Snyder, 1982).

Although elevated tonic heart rate may be mediated by increases in activity, as in somatic coupling of activity and heart rate (Obrist, 1981), both activity level and heart rate increases as well as sleep disturbances have been attributed to activation of the sympathetic adrenergic system (Breese et al., 1973). These behavior changes have been noted in active coping situations, in contrast to passive coping situations, therefore, the data were interpreted as active coping on the part of the child. That the children leaving the school appeared to experience an anticipatory reaction to the impending separation whereas young primates show these behavioral changes only subsequent to the separation can of course be attributed to the children's cognitive abilities. Their cognitive awareness of the impending separation may have been enhanced by preparatory remarks and discussions by their parents and teachers. Although these data are confounded by the potential anxiety associated with attending a new school, this confound may be instructive. The children who were leaving the school did not appear to experience the biphasic process of agitation followed by depression as had occurred in the mother–child separation study. Of course, there were no reunions and altered relationships to contend with, which seemed to contribute to the children's depression in the mother–child separation study. In addition, the anx-

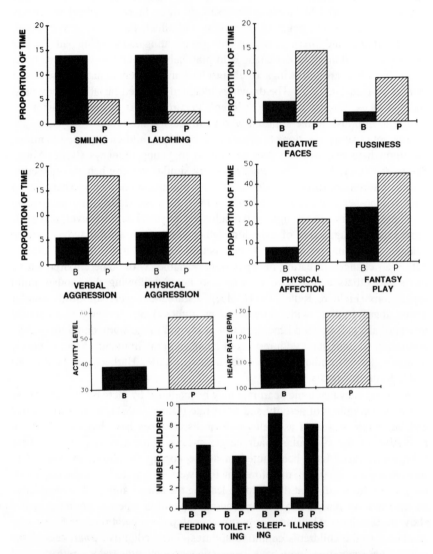

FIG. 9.1. Proportion of preschool play time smiling and laughing, negative faces and fussiness, verbal and physical aggression, physical affection and fantasy play occurred during the baseline (B) and pre-separation (P) periods prior to children's transfers to new schools. Mean activity level and heart rate in beats per minutes (BPM) and number of children experiencing feeding, toileting, sleeping, and illness problems during these periods. Adapted from Field (1986).

FIG. 9.2. Example of self-drawings made prior to the departure of children attending new schools.

iety related to attending a new school and making new friends may have attenuated any expected depression. Anxiety in the preschool children attending these schools may have counteracted the expected decrease in beta-adrenergic activity and associated depression. Perhaps the stressfulness of the situation presented active coping opportunities.

Thus, one can infer from the distressed separation behaviors of these young children that they are already experiencing strong peer attachments. Another illustration of early peer attachment is provided by the observations of children and their play with peers during separations from their mothers (Field, unpublished data). In a study very similar to the Field and Reite (1984) study on mother–child separations, the behaviors of children whose mothers were hospitalized for the birth of another child were observed in their preschool classroom. Observations were conducted prior to the mother's hospitalization, during the hospitalization, and following the mother's return from the hospital. As can be seen in FIG. 9.3, the children showed affective changes during the mother's hospitalization including a decrease in smiling and an increase in fussiness, much like they had in the Field and Reite (1984) study. However, in the classroom, unlike at home, the children showed some positive behavior changes. As can be seen in FIG. 9.3, they engaged in less solitary play, in more constructive play, and in more interactions with the other children during the period of separation from their mothers. Preliminary analysis of data on repeated separations of children from their mothers while they attended national conferences confirms

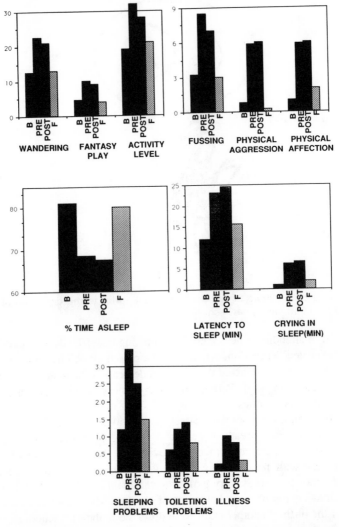

FIG. 9.3. Proportion of preschool play time smiling and fussiness, solitary and constructive play, and interaction with children and adults occurred during baseline (B), separation (S) and reunion (R) periods when children were separated from mothers (hospitalized for the birth of another child) but continued attending preschool.

these data. Increases are noted, for example, in cooperative play and interaction with other children, suggesting that attachments to peers may compensate for the separation distress experience, when the children remain in school during separations from their mothers.

Infants and toddlers as young as 15-months-old also appear to experience distress, when separated from their peers (Field, Vega-Lahr, & Jagadish, 1984).

In this study, 15-month-old infants, following 14 months in an infant nursery, were transferred to a toddler nursery, and 24-month-old infants were graduated from a toddler nursery to a preschool nursery. Both the infants and toddlers demonstrated many of the same behavior changes noted in the previous study on preschool children transferring to new schools. During the week immediately preceding the transfer and the week following the transfer (as opposed to baseline data collected one month prior to the transfer), infants and toddlers showed increases in activity level, wandering about aimlessly, and fantasy play. Increases were also noted in fussiness, physical aggression, and physical affection. Naptime sleep became more irregular, with longer latencies to sleep, more crying during sleep and less time spent sleeping. The parents and teachers noted changes in eating and sleeping patterns as well as a greater incidence of absenteeism (see FIG. 9.4). A comparison between the infants and toddlers suggested that the toddlers experienced greater changes in their behaviors during the period just prior to the transfer to their new nursery, whereas the infants experienced greater behavioral change during the week following the transfer to the new nursery, suggesting that the toddlers were experiencing more anticipatory distress than the infants. This is perhaps not surprising inasmuch as the toddlers had experienced a transfer of this kind nine months earlier, when they were moved from the infant to the toddler nursery, a transfer that they may have remembered.

A comparison was also made between those infants and toddlers who were transferred to the new nurseries without close friends versus those who were transferred with close friends. As can be seen in FIG. 9.5, those infants and toddlers who were transferred with close friends showed less fussiness and less physical aggression but more physical affection during this transitional period. In addition, the children who were transferred with close friends spent more naptime asleep and less naptime crying, suggesting that transferring with a close friend served as a buffer against the stressful effects of separation.

Finally an assessment was made of individual differences in the infants' and toddlers' separation experience based on whether they were externalizers (behaviorally reactive) or internalizers (physiologically reactive) as determined by the Buck externalizer–internalizer rating scale. As can be seen in FIG. 9.6, the externalizers spent more time engaging in fantasy play and showed a higher level of activity as well as a higher level of physical aggression and physical affection, whereas the internalizers showed a greater number of awakenings during naptime as well as deep sleep during naptime, and they also experienced more eating problems and illness than the externalizing children. These individual differences suggest that some children may show their separation distress in overt behavior, whereas others may experience more physiological disorganization.

In summary, the data from this group of studies are a poignant demonstration of the disorganizing effects of separation from mothers or peers on both the behavior and physiology of monkeys and humans. Although these studies have described separation-induced behavior, the data provide indirect evidence for an attachment bond. The process and function of attachment can be inferred from

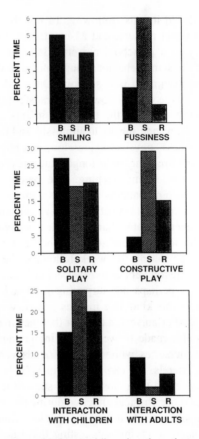

FIG. 9.4. Proportion of infant/toddler play time that wandering and fantasy play occurred, activity level (actometer measure), and proportion of time that fussing, physical aggression, and physical affection occurred during baseline (B), preseparation (PRE), postseparation (POST) and follow-up (F) play observation periods surrounding graduation to new classes. Percentage of naptime spent asleep, latency to sleep (minutes), and crying in sleep during these periods. Adapted from Field (1986).

situations in which it has been disrupted. If the child's normal play and exploratory behavior are disrupted by a separation, and physiological disorganization occurs, one can infer that the relationship between a mother and child or between peers may provide the stimulation necessary to play and exploratory behavior and the modulation of arousal necessary for maintaining physiological equilibrium.

However, separation per se apparently is not the only disrupting factor, inasmuch as both primate and human infants have been noted to remain disorganized following reunion with the attachment object. Rather it would appear that, when there is a change in either partner of the relationship or in the

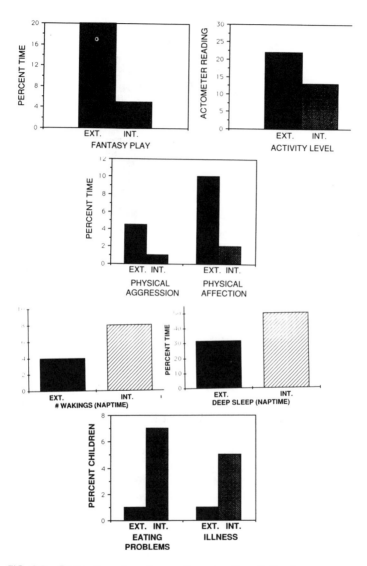

FIG. 9.5. Proportion of postseparation play time (following graduation to new classes) infants and toddlers transferred with close friends
(F) or without close friends (NF) spent fussing and showing physical
aggression and physical affection, crying during naptime, and sleeping during naptime.

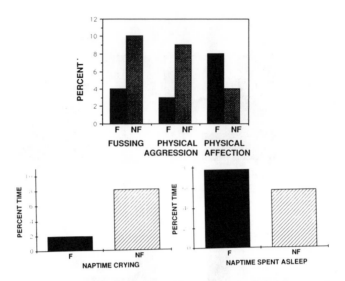

FIG. 9.6.   Proportion of postseparation play time (following graduation to new classes) infants and toddlers who were externalizers (EXT)
or internalizers (INT) spent engaging in fantasy play, mean activity
level (actometer reading), proportion of play time spent engaging in
physical aggression and physical affection, number of wakings, and
deep sleep during naptime, and percentage of infants/toddlers who
experienced eating problems and illness.

relationship itself, whether the dyad is together or apart, behavioral and physiological disorganization may occur. Thus, attachment can be viewed as a relationship that develops between two or more organisms as their behavioral and
physiological systems become attuned to each other. Each partner in the relationship provides for the other a source of stimulation and arousal modulation.
Separation from the partner or a change in the relationship would then under-
standably lead to behavioral and physiological disorganization. Separation may
simply be an extreme example of the attached pair being unable to provide for
each other optimal levels of stimulation and arousal modulation.

ACKNOWLEDGMENTS

This research was supported by an NIMH Research Scientist Development
Award/MH00331. I wish to thank the mothers and children who participated in
this study and my collaborators Martin Reite, Nitza Vega-Lahr, and Shashi
Jagadish.

REFERENCES

Ainsworth, M. D. (1967). *Infancy in Uganda.* Baltimore: Johns Hopkins Press.

Bowlby, J. (1969). *Attachment and loss. Volume 1: Attachment.* New York: Basic.

Breese, G. R., Smith, R. D., Mueller, R. A., Howard, J. L., Prange, A. J., Lipton, M. A., Young, L. D., McKinney, W. T., & Lewis, J. K. (1973). Induction of adrenal catecholamine synthesizing enzymes following mother–infant separation. *Nature, 246,* 94–96.

Field, T. (1984). Separation stress of young children transferring to new schools. *Developmental Psychology, 20,* 786–792.

Field, T. (1985). Attachment as psychobiological attunement: Being on the same wavelength. In T. Field & M. Reite (Ed.), *The psychobiology of attachment and separation* (pp. 415–450). New York: Academic Press.

Field, T. (1986). Affective responses to separation. In T. B. Brazelton & M. W. Yogman (Eds.) *Affective Development in Infancy* (pp. 125–144). Norwood: NJ: Ablex.

Field, T., & Reite, M. (1984). Children's responses to separation from mother during the birth of another child. *Child Development, 55,* 1308–1316.

Field, T., Vega-Lahr, N., & Jagadish, S. (1984). Separation stress of nursery school infants and toddlers graduating to new classes. *Infant Behavior and Development, 7,* 277–284.

Obrist, P. A. (1981). *Cardiovascular psychophysiology.* New York: Plenum.

Reite, M., & Capitanio, J. P. (1985). On the nature of social separation and social attachment. In T. Field & M. Reite (Eds.), *The psychobiology of attachment and separation* (pp. 223–250). New York: Academic Press.

Reite, M., Harbeck, R., & Hoffman, A. (1981). Altered cellular immune response following peer separation. *Life Science, 29,* 1133–1136.

Reite, M., Short, R., Seiler, C., & Pauley, J. D. (1981). Attachment, loss, and depression. *Journal of Child Psychology and Psychiatry, 22,* 141–169.

Reite, M., & Snyder, D. S. (1982). Physiology of maternal separation in a bonnet macaque infant. *American Journal of Primatology, 2,* 115–120.

Suomi, S. J., Collins, M. L., & Harlow, H. F. (1976). Effects of maternal and peer separations on young monkeys. *Journal of Child Psychology and Psychiatry, 17,* 101–112.

V CONCEPTIONS IMPACTING ATTACHMENT

10 Attachment and Close Relationships: A Life-Span Perspective

Mary J. Levitt

ABSTRACT

Intersections of infant attachment theory with models of close relationships and social support in adulthood are proposed within the framework of the social convoy model elaborated by Kahn and Antonucci (1980). Close relationships across the life span are viewed as continuations of early attachment relations, governed by similar processes and serving similar functions. The primary process is hypothesized to be the establishment and maintenance of relationship expectations, forged through familiarity with relationship partners and mutually contingent feedback, and influenced by cultural norms and past relationship experiences. Relationships are thought to be stabilized and given continuity through mutual adaptation to partner expectations, modulation of conflict, and maintenance of behavior within the limits of partner tolerance. Developmental changes in existing relationships and structural changes over the life course in the individual's circle of close relationships are thought to ensue from changes in cognitive ability, individual maturation, and age-related social norms. Changes in the ability to modulate conflict may also play a role in the evolution of relationships. Consistent with an attachment model, personal well-being is hypothesized to be related primarily to close relationships rather than to support networks as a whole, and data are cited to suggest that one such relationship may be sufficient.

For the past several years, researchers have been documenting the importance of social relationships to personal well-being. This research has cut across disciplinary lines and has been focused on populations differing markedly in age, culture, and life circumstances. It includes the work of developmental researchers on infant attachment, a large and growing number of empirical findings on social network relations and social support, and the newer but no less significant work

183

of social psychologists on close relationships in adulthood. A life-span model of relationships must necessarily draw upon these diverse literatures and integrate across age-specific domains. Although such integration is admittedly difficult, it is important to resist the oversimplification that may result from the direct application of models developed exclusively in one domain.

The search for a life-span attachment paradigm began more than a decade ago (Antonucci, 1976). In a continuation of this effort, Kahn and Antonucci (1980) articulated a life-span model linking the concepts of attachment and social support. Support has been viewed traditionally as a function of the network of social relationships within which the individual is embedded. In the Kahn and Antonucci model, the phrase "social support convoy" replaces the more traditional nomenclature, "social support network," to convey the importance of viewing the social network as a dynamic structure that changes with the development of the individual and alterations in the environment.

The convoy model is grounded in theories of attachment and social roles, and dyadic relationships are seen as the basic units of convoy structure and function. The model predicts both continuity and change in convoy relationships. Although some relationships will remain stable, both the composition of the individual's support convoy and the nature of the relationships between the individual and convoy members are expected to change over the life course. This model serves as a point of departure for considering the intersection of the concepts of attachment and close relationships.

The body of this chapter involves first an overview of selected research addressed to the differentiation of attachment relationships from other convoy relationships. Then three specific life-span attachment issues are explored. These include: (a) the issue of continuity and change; (b) the processes accounting for attachment formation, maintenance, and dissolution across the life span; and (c) the link between attachment and personal well-being.

ATTACHMENT RELATIONSHIPS

Attachment relationships can be defined generally as those which, if severed, would precipitate the marked affective and behavioral disruption labeled as grief. An attachment relationship is normatively a source of comfort and assistance to the individual, particularly in times of stress. Such relationships may be said to constitute a specialized subset of the individual's social convoy relationships.

For research purposes, the support convoy has been conceptualized as a series of concentric circles with the individual at the center. The circle diagram used to elicit convoy information is depicted in FIG. 10.1. Respondents are asked to indicate in the inner circle, nearest to the individual, those persons to whom the individual feels "so close that it's hard to imagine life without them." In the middle circle are placed those persons who are "not quite as close but who are

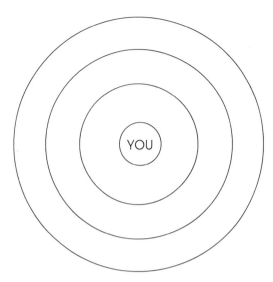

FIG. 10.1. Social convoy diagram.

still very important" to the individual, and in the outer circle are those not included in the first two circles but who are "close enough and important enough" in the individual's life that "they should be placed" in the network. This procedure has been used with samples ranging in age from 18 to 95, with varying degrees of health and socioeconomic status, in English, Spanish, and Japanese language versions, and in both personal interview and mail-in questionnaire formats. Respondents have had no difficulty conceptualizing their relationships in this way (Antonucci, 1986).

Empirically, close relationships can be defined as those between the individual and persons located spatially in the inner circle of the convoy diagram. Defined as relationships without which life would be difficult to imagine, close relationships in adulthood are considered to be functionally equivalent to attachment relationships. This empirical definition of close relationships frees the researcher from arbitrarily designating a relationship as close based on the particular role or category of the relationship partner. Spouses, parents, and children, for example, are generally placed in the individual's inner circle, but they are sometimes found in the outer circles or completely outside the network (Levitt, Weber, & Clark, 1986). Friends are most often relegated to the outer circles but are found occasionally within the inner circle. These findings suggest that important distinctions may be lost, when researchers aggregate relationships along role specific lines, as when friendships are distinguished from family relationships.

Close relationships have common characteristics that differentiate them from other relationships, and these characteristics are shared regardless of specific roles. This premise is supported in research by Sternberg and Grajek (1984).

These authors demonstrated, through an exhaustive analysis of various scales of love and liking, that the factor structures of these scales are identical across such diverse relationships as those between parents and children, lovers, and best friends. Although these relationships may differ in certain characteristics, such as the degree to which partners feel obligated to each other, the content of communications, or the extent of sexual desire or contact, all share as their most important component a common general factor defined by interpersonal communication, shared understanding and affectional exchange, mutual fostering of personal growth, and emotional and instrumental support (Sternberg & Grajek, 1984). Davis and Todd (1982) reported similar results in comparing friendship and love relations.

Data from five samples in which the convoy diagram has been employed are referenced throughout this chapter. The first was a national random sample of elderly respondents interviewed by Kahn and Antonucci (1984). The second was a sample of elderly respondents from the deteriorating South Beach section of Miami Beach (Levitt, Antonucci, Clark, Rotton, & Finley, 1985–1986; Levitt, Clark, Rotton, & Finley, 1987). The third was a sample of mothers of 13-month-old infants (Levitt et al., 1986). The fourth is a recent sample of mothers of high-risk and normal infants interviewed at one month postpartum (Coffman, Levitt, & Deets, 1989). The final sample consists of individuals in three-generation family linkages from both English- and Spanish-speaking families in the South Florida area. Complete data have been collected for a subset of 30 English-speaking young adult women, their mothers, and their maternal grandmothers. Data are also available for a smaller comparison sample of Spanish-speaking women. This three-generation study was designed to explore crosscultural and crossgenerational similarities and differences in relationships as a step toward empirical definition of the evolution of convoy structure and function across the lifespan.

Kahn and Antonucci (1984) included six support functions in their research on the support convoys of elderly respondents. Following completion of their convoy diagrams, respondents were asked to indicate those persons in whom they confide; who reassure them; who would care for them, if they were ill; to whom they can talk about their health; who respect them; and to whom they can talk, when they are upset, nervous, or depressed. In our three-generation study (Levitt & Weber, 1985, 1986; Weber & Levitt, 1986a), respondents have been asked additionally who would help them financially, to whom they turn for advice, and with whom they want to spend "as much time as possible." Factor analytic results suggest that these items can be summed with the six Kahn and Antonucci functions to form a general support scale. A primary focus of each of these studies has been on the relation between social support and personal well-being, and, in each study, a major index of well-being has been the Bradburn (1969) affect balance scale. Assessing both positive and negative affect, the Bradburn scale is sensitive to variations in affect in nonclinical populations.

FIGURE 10.2 depicts, for our sample of English-speaking women in three-generation families, the amount of support provided as a function of the convoy member's placement in the diagram. It is clear from this figure that support is most likely to be provided by those individuals who are considered to be closest to the respondent. Similar results have been obtained across samples, suggesting that social support is largely a function of inner circle relationships. These results, based on widely divergent populations, suggest that one distinguishing feature of close relationships is that they involve relatively high levels of supportive interchange. An associated feature of close relationships emerges from examination of the individual support indices. In all samples interviewed to date, the provision of sick care has been seen primarily as a function of the persons closest to the respondent.

There are two further results from these studies that are significant for a consideration of close relationships. First, the number of individuals placed in the inner circle tends to be limited, with an average of three to five persons across samples and across age and cultural groups within the three-generation samples. These results suggest that close relationships across the life span, like attachment relationships in infancy, tend to involve a few significant figures. Although it is generally assumed that the child develops an increasingly extended set of social contacts into adulthood (Hartup, 1983), our data suggest that the number of close attachment relationships remains relatively constant.

The second finding of significance is that, across age and culture, those placed in the inner circle tend to be close family members and occasionally one or two close friends. Husbands or wives and children, if existent, are typically placed first in the network followed by the individual's parents. In-laws are seldom found in the inside circle. Middle and outer circles typically consist of other family members and friends. This pattern of circle placement is depicted in FIG. 10.3, taken from our study of mothers of infants.

In general, our data reinforce the view that parent–child relationships remain close throughout life (Antonucci, 1985b, 1990; Hagestad, 1982, 1984; Troll, 1980). Only the individual's relationships with spouse and children tend to ex-

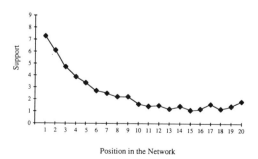

Position in the Network

FIG. 10.2.   Mean amount of support by position in network.

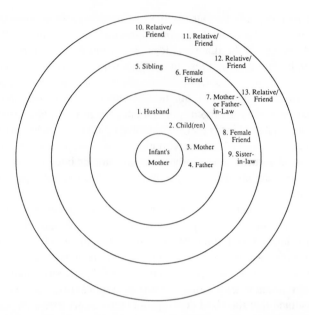

FIG. 10.3. Typical pattern of circle placement by relationship to
mother.

ceed these ties in importance to the individual. Of course, these particular relationships are not always available. Parents die, marriages are dissolved, and
individuals remain single or childless. By focusing on inner circle composition,
we are able to assess what other relationships might occupy this position and
whether these fulfill the same functions for the individual. There are data to
suggest that siblings and other family members may be more important to older
individuals who lack or have lost primary relationships with children, parents,
and spouses (Antonucci, 1985a; Cicerelli, 1982), and that alternative network
linkages may substitute, to some extent, for spousal support for single mothers
(Lopata, 1979; Weinraub & Wolf, 1983). Our own research suggests that friends
in the inner circle provide support equivalent to that provided by close family
members (Weber & Levitt, 1986a). Longitudinal mapping of fluctuations in
convoy composition is needed, and will ultimately provide a means of assessing
structural changes in attachment relationships across the lifespan.

LIFE-SPAN ATTACHMENT ISSUES

The remainder of this discussion is addressed first to the question of life-span
change and continuity in attachment relationships; second to the processes governing the formation, maintenance, and dissolution of close relationships over

the life course; and finally to the relation between attachment and personal well-being.

Issues of Change and Continuity

Issues of change and continuity exist with regard to the evolution of specific relationships over time and to the generalization of early relationship characteristics to new relationships. The following account encompasses both of these considerations.

There are two disparate viewpoints regarding the evolution of close relationships, as articulated by Lewis (1982, 1987; Lewis, Feiring, & Kotsonis, 1984). The first is the psychoanalytically based epigenetic position that the first attachment serves as a prototype for later relationships and, thus, has primacy in determining the quality of the individual's adult linkages. This view is currently expressed by Ainsworth and her colleagues (Ainsworth, 1983, 1989; Bretherton & Waters, 1985; Morris, 1982) in a somewhat modified form. The first relationship is said to effect a homeorrhetic process maintained by an "internal working relationship model," or cognitive representation of the qualities of the relationship, that generalizes across subsequent relationships. Studies demonstrating that infants judged to be insecure in their attachment to the caretaker are less competent in later interactions with adults and peers have been offered as supporting evidence for this position, as have retrospective studies suggesting that poor childhood relationships are carried over to disturbances in parenting behavior (Ainsworth, 1989; Bretherton & Waters, 1985).

In contrast to the epigenetic hypothesis, other researchers have emphasized the adaptability and plasticity of the individual's response to new situations (Cairns, 1977, 1979; Gewirtz, 1972; Lewis, 1982, 1987; Lewis et al., 1984). In the absence of longitudinal data, it is difficult to substantiate either position. Even when longitudinal data are available, they often provide an incomplete picture, because the continuing involvement of parent and child is seldom considered. Most conceptions of early parent–child effects seem to assume a model of sequential family structure. The child develops within one nuclear family unit, becomes independent from that unit, and forms a new family unit. Life-span data suggest that this is only partially true. Mutual parent–child influence may fluctuate in importance at various phases of the life cycle of both parents and children but is likely to remain in effect across the life span (Antonucci, 1990; Hagestad, 1984).

A striking reminder of continued intergenerational involvement was uncovered in our study of women in three-generation families. Comparing across relationships with mothers, fathers, husbands, and children, affective well-being for the middle generation women was related most strongly to their current relationships with their fathers. Continuing involvement across generations is also reflected in the age composition of the convoys of older, middle, and younger generation respondents. The proportion of persons from different age groups represented in the convoy is similar across generations (although younger individuals tend to have more age mates in their convoys). These data are depicted in FIG. 10.4.

The attachment of child to parent is rarely considered beyond the period of infancy and early childhood (Ainsworth, 1989; Maccoby & Martin, 1983). Lewis and Ban (1971) noted some time ago that the behavioral manifestations of attachment undergo change, such that proximal involvement is transformed to distal involvement in early childhood. This trend would seem to continue, as researchers have documented that children spend ever increasing amounts of time with peers and gradually less with parents (Hartup, 1983). It seems likely, however, that parents continue their role as providers of a secure haven for the child, even as the distance between parent and child increases.

Furthermore, there is evidence to suggest that this role continues well into the child's adult life. Adult children continue to derive emotional and instrumental support from parents. We have found that mothers (maternal grandmothers) are second only to spouses in the provision of support to mothers of infants and are increasingly important with the birth of a second child (Levitt et al., 1986). High levels of support are also exchanged between older women and their middle-age daughters (Antonucci, 1990; Hagestad, 1984; Levitt & Weber, 1985; Lopata, 1979; Thompson & Walker, 1984).

Thus, any consideration of life-span attachment must take into account the continuance of the parent–child relationship. Unfortunately there are few data to illuminate the course of parent–child attachment beyond the child's infancy. An intriguing study addressing this issue was conducted by Pipp, Shaver, Jennings, Lamborn, and Fischer (1985). College students were asked to represent schematically with circles their relationships with mothers and fathers from infancy to the present. In representing their relationships with parents, the students typically

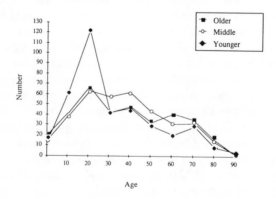

FIG. 10.4.   Number of individuals within age categories by generation.

drew merged self and parent circles in infancy that moved progressively apart, reaching maximal divergence in late adolescence (age 16 to 20). Their current relationships were viewed as somewhat closer but not as close as in early childhood. Affectional changes followed a similar course, with students reporting loving their parents somewhat less during the adolescent period. However, high levels of affection for parents were reported consistently, and respondents generally reported that they loved their parents more than their parents loved them, both during early childhood and at the present time.

These results are consistent with theoretical and empirical accounts of the child's striving toward increased autonomy (Erikson, 1963; Frank, Avery, & Laman, 1988). One might predict additional changes in spatial representations of parent–child relationships across the adult lifespan, with increased distance following the child's marriage, increased closeness following the birth of children, and greater distance again as middle-age children begin to cope with responsibilities for their aging parents. The approach employed by these authors is congruent with our own use of spatial representation to elicit network information and seems to be a promising means of assessing the individual's perception of changes in dyadic relationships over time. Such changes are often difficult to describe verbally.

Under most circumstances, parents are likely to be primary care providers and consequently maintain some exclusivity in relation to the child, at least until the child reaches maturity. At present, however, the evidence does not rule out the possibility that other attachments emerging during infancy or later periods may take on primary significance in explaining relationship outcomes (Lamb, Thompson, Gardner, Charnov, & Estes, 1984; Lewis, 1987). The epigenetic hypothesis is grounded currently in a model of evolution that emphasizes the protective function of the caretaker vis-à-vis the infant (Bowlby, 1969). Given the importance of social relationships to human survival, it does seem likely that attachment formation has ethological underpinnings (Bowlby, 1969; Cairns, 1977, 1979; Gewirtz & Petrovich, 1982; Shaver & Hazan, 1988), to the extent that human evolution has promoted the formation of social bonds. It is plausible, however, that the formation of social bonds may take place without the intermediating link of a singular primary attachment prototype.

Although the exclusivity attributed to the infant's attachment to the primary caregiver in the Ainsworth–Bowlby conceptualization has been tempered somewhat by statements acknowledging the possibility of additional attachments, and, thus, multiple "representational models," these are generally characterized as "secondary" or "surrogate" relationships (Ainsworth, 1989) and little effort has been directed toward the study of multiple attachments. What evidence does exist suggests that infants develop attachments not just to mothers but to fathers, alternate caregivers, and grandparents (Fox, 1977; Lamb, 1981; Myers, Jarvis, & Creasey, 1987). Additional research is needed to ascertain the extent, nature, and interrelations of infant attachments to members of the social network. It might be informative to explore the infant's relationships with those who are in the inner circle of the parents' social convoys.

As Cairns (1977) suggests, it must certainly be the case that earlier relationships mediate later ones, but given that relationship formation is likely to be an overdetermined phenomenon, it may be that long-term adverse relationship outcomes occur only when early relationships are uniformly negative. This view is consistent with reports suggesting that children characterized as "invulnerable" are distinguished from other high-risk children in having at least one relationship with a concerned and caring other, not necessarily a parent (e.g., Bronfenbrenner, 1979). It is also consistent with the well-known report by Freud and Dann of child concentration camp survivors attached to their peers, whom Dann has recently indicated have made successful adjustments to adult relationships (cited in Hartup, 1983). Cairns (1977, 1979) and Lewis (1982, 1987) have offered additional evidence for the robustness of relationships in the absence of "normal" caretaking.

The foregoing discussion provides a basis for the following hypotheses regarding the development of attachment relationships across the life span:

1. The individual exists within a social convoy from the beginning of life (Antonucci, 1976; Cochran & Brassard, 1979; Kahn & Antonucci, 1980; Lewis, 1982, 1987; Weinraub, Brooks, & Lewis, 1977), although the opportunity for direct interaction with others is generally governed by parents in the child's early years (Hartup, 1989; Lewis et al., 1984).

2. The infant develops a limited number of attachment relationships with specific convoy members, according to the processes that govern the formation of close relationships in infancy. These relationships form the initial inner core of the individual's social convoy.

3. Inner circle relationships change as a function of change within the individuals involved or alterations in the external environment. These include both idiosyncratic changes, and normative changes associated with maturation, aging, and the imposition of age-related norms. Parent–child relations, for example, undergo transformations as the child matures and the parent ages. There may be normative transitional points in these relations, initiated by shifts in the child's linguistic and cognitive skills, by the birth of siblings, by the child's leaving home, marrying, and giving birth to grandchildren, the parent's own life-stage changes, and the parent's physical decline in old age.

Other relations, such as those between marital partners, may also undergo transformations over time. Some researchers, for example, have reported longitudinal findings of a negative U-shaped function in marital satisfaction associated with the child-rearing years (Skolnik, 1981). Skolnik (1981) found declines in satisfaction associated not with childrearing but rather with nonnormative events, such as the development of alcoholism or job-related stress in one of the partners. Focusing only on satisfied couples, Reedy, Birren, and Schaie (1981) assessed crosssectional differences in the importance assigned to six components of love relationships for younger, middle-age, and older couples. Consistent with the results reported by Sternberg and Grajek (1984), emotional security was rated as most important to the relationship across generations, followed by respect, communication, help and play behaviors, sexual intimacy, and loyalty. Across age, respondents assigned increased importance to emotional security and loyalty, and decreased importance to communication and sexual intimacy. Although other relationships have received less attention, Cicerelli (1982) cited evidence to suggest that sibling relations also change, with siblings often reporting greater closeness in later life.

4. The boundaries of one's inner circle are permeable, and movement of persons into and out of the inner circle is governed by the processes that govern attachment formation and dissolution in general. In our study of mothers of infants, we were curious as to why one young mother placed her husband outside her inner circle, in sharp contrast to the pattern exhibited by almost all of the other respondents. It came as no surprise that this couple was divorced within the year. Transitions in inner circle composition would be expected to occur normatively in adolescence and youth, as individuals form intimate relationships and enter into marriage. Newborn children would tend to be incorporated into the inner circle, and the death of a close relationship partner would tend to eliminate that person from the circle. However, one of the more intriguing outcomes of our research has been that the boundaries of life and death do not necessarily coincide with inner circle boundaries. Widowed individuals in our elderly samples often included the deceased spouse and a number of mothers did not include their year-old infants in their networks.

5. Once established, there are factors that serve to stabilize and maintain continuity in one's core of close relationships. These include both within-relationship maintenance processes and forces that exist outside of the relationship but serve to stabilize it. External factors might include economic security, community cohesion, and sociocultural norms and sanctions governing relationships, such as prohibitions against child, parent, or spouse abandonment. Within-relationship processes that are thought to govern the maintenance of close relationships are reviewed below, along with those involved in relationship formation and dissolution.

Attachment Processes

Although there are distinct differences in orientation among attachment theorists, most agree that the provision of behavior by the caretaker contingent on the infant's own behavior is fundamental to attachment formation (Ainsworth,

Blehar, Waters, & Wall, 1978; Cairns, 1977; Gewirtz, 1968; Gewirtz & Peláez-Nogueras, 1989; Watson, 1972). Cairns (1972, 1977) has also hypothesized that familiarity provides a basis for attachment. In an analog study testing conditions of familiarization versus contingent feedback, both processes were found to influence infant response to a stranger, but contingent feedback outweighed familiarity in promoting positive behavior toward the stranger (Levitt, 1980).

There is some consistency from the infant to the adult literature on relationships. Familiarity is thought to be a factor in adult relationship formation (Zajonc, 1968), and the importance of contingency is noted in models of adult relationship processes that rely on notions of social exchange (Graziano, 1984). Although there are various forms of exchange theory, the basic assumptions are, first, that adult relationships are governed by processes of reciprocal exchange and, second, that individuals involved in relationships are aware of the equity or inequity of exchange within the relationship. Lack of equity can lead to dissolution of the relationship, particularly if there is an alternative relationship available with greater potential for reward.

Both infant and adult models predict that close relationships are characterized by reciprocity of exchange. Observers of the early interactions of infants with their caretakers have noted the highly reciprocal nature of the interchanges between infant and caretaker (Brazelton, Koslowski, & Main, 1974; Stern, 1974; Tronick, 1989), and these mutually contingent response patterns are thought to underlay attachment formation (Gewirtz, & Boyd, 1976; Cairns, 1977, 1979; Goldberg, 1977). Most authors recognize, however, that the infant's capacity for maintaining reciprocal interchanges is not equivalent to the caretaker's, and it is primarily the caretaker who adapts her behavior to the infant (Ainsworth, 1983; Belsky & Isabella, 1988; Cairns, 1977; Schaffer, 1977).

Thus, the exchanges that take place between infant and adult, between child and parent, are not strictly equitable. In addition, a number of researchers have noted that even relationships with greater potential for equity are not characterized by observable reciprocity of exchange; in fact, expectations of "quid pro quo" or immediate reciprocity are associated with dissatisfaction in close relationships (Clark, 1984; Gottman & Levenson, 1984; Davis & Todd, 1982).

Some theorists have attempted to reconcile these facts by invoking a concept of delayed reciprocation. Parents, for example, accept the imbalance involved in caretaking in exchange for rewards in the future. Thus, parents provide resources to their children in the expectation that children will reciprocate, when the parents are older. Antonucci (1985b) suggested that one builds with one's social convoy members a kind of "support bank," where periodic deposits in the form of support for others may be balanced by support withdrawals at some future point. One's notion of equity or reciprocity, therefore, for close relationships, is based on the balance of reciprocated overtures over an extended time period, rather than on a series of immediately reciprocated interchanges.

The view that exchange processes govern close relationships in adulthood is further complicated by the fact that individual members of a relationship dyad tend to perceive reciprocity in the relationship but seldom agree on the actual level of support exchanged. Antonucci and her colleagues interviewed elderly respondents and at least one of the individuals indicated by the respondents as support providers. Individual members of interviewed dyads perceived high reciprocity in terms of the number and type of support functions exchanged with the other, but these reports were often markedly discrepant. In some cases, persons named by the elderly respondent as sources of support did not even place the elderly person in their networks. Furthermore, the individual's perception of reciprocity was a better predictor of well-being than was the actual match of the respondents' reports (Antonucci & Israel, 1986).

If adult relationships are governed by long-term exchanges that may be more perceived than actual, then how do the reciprocal response patterns that characterize the infant's interchanges with the caretaker become transformed to the delayed exchange processes of adult close relationships? One potential explanation is related to the changing cognitive capacities of the child with respect to the understanding of contingent relations. Infant learning theorists have long noted the necessity for temporal and physical contiguity of response and contingent outcome in the conditioning of young infants (Gewirtz, 1968; Millar, 1972; Rovee-Collier & Gelkowski, 1979; Suomi, 1981; Watson, 1979). Also, Piaget (1954) suggested that the infant does not differentiate between self-produced and other-produced contingencies before the second half of the first year, and continues to improve in causal understanding throughout childhood.

There is reason to suggest that the infant's comprehension of causal relations may underly the formation of specific attachments (Levitt, 1979; Levitt & Clark, 1982). The infant does not understand, for the first several months, that the source of contingent feedback from the environment is located outside the self, therefore it is not until the second half of the first year that the infant can begin to appreciate the role of the caretaker in providing this feedback. At this point, the caregiver takes on a special significance to the infant as a means for the infant to maintain and extend his or her control over the environment. The predictability and control afforded by the caretaker provides the foundation for the secure base phenomenon. Boyce (1985) hypothesized that social support in adulthood functions similarly by providing a stable and predictable environment for the individual and that the roots of this process are in the predictable responses of caretakers in infancy. Ainsworth (1989) also referred recently to the security function of adult attachment relationships.

In the generalized expectancy model proposed by Lewis and Goldberg (1969; Goldberg, 1977), contingent responding on the part of the caretaker is thought to reinforce in the child a generalized expectancy about his or her own efficacy. An expectancy model may apply as well to the maintenance of relationships. Contingent feedback on the part of the caretaker may build in the infant an expectation about the relationship—the expectation that the caretaker will continue to respond to the infant's overtures. Given the limited memory capacity of the infant, however, the contingency experiences must be repeated many times for the infant to retain that expectancy. With development, the increased memory capacity and communicative ability of the infant would continue to increase the allowable distance between reciprocal events, affording the transformation from proximal to distal behaviors. Thus, the child's increased cognitive and linguistic skills reduce the need for immediate reciprocity, and children and parents adjust their behavior accordingly. As Weinraub and Lewis (1977) illustrated, preschool children who are told by their parents that they are leaving, but that they will return within a specified time period, are able to tolerate separation experiences better than those who are not given such information. This kind of information, if followed consistently by the behavior promised, would continue to promote the parent's role as a secure base for the child.

The important point to be made here is that once an older child or an adult has developed expectations regarding a particular relationship, these expectancies may prevail over very long time periods, unchanged unless the partner begins to exhibit behavior that violates those expectations. Given the homeorrhetic nature of close relationships and the tendency for individuals to perceive contingency or reciprocity even in situations where it is objectively absent (Antonucci & Israel, 1986; Crocker, 1981; Weisz, 1986), these violations would need to be either extreme or prolonged to disrupt the relationship.

Consider the example of a close relationship between two boyhood friends that continued well into middle age, until one friend asked the other for badly needed financial assistance. The failure of the friend to comply with this request severed the relationship. Within the proposed model, the friend's failure to assist was a marked violation of the expectation that he would always "come through if needed." This violation was accompanied by strong feelings of disbelief, hurt, and anger. This true to life parable is meant to illustrate that the veridical reciprocity of exchange between two persons may have very little to do with maintaining a relationship over time. It is not the actual support provided but the certainty of one's expectation that support would be provided by the other if needed that binds the relationship. Reciprocity may be evidenced not in the day to day interactions between relationship partners, or even in a long term balance of exchanged support, but rather in the form of shared expectations and mutual commitment. Such expectations can be said to provide the basis for a sense of trust in the relationship (Holmes & Rempel, 1989).

Shared expectations may be built on initial experiences of contingent feedback from the partner in adulthood as well as in childhood. As social psychologists have noted, the initial phases of a relationship involve high levels of responsiveness and self-disclosure (Altman & Taylor, 1973). Note, however, that relationship expectations are derived from external sources as well as from interactions with relationship partners. There are culturally defined expectations regarding the behavior of parents and children, husbands and wives, lovers, and friends, as well as more idiosyncratic expectancies, based on individual personality differences, nonnormative life events, and the interconnected values, attitudes and behaviors of one's social network. It is here too that one's prior relationship history would be influential. To the extent that elements of one's current or potential relationships are similar to those of past relationships, relationship expectations should generalize from past to present.

The fact that partners enter relationships with existing expectations almost guarantees that the construction and maintenance of the relationship will require the communication and mutual accomodation characteristic of the early stages of relationship formation. The need for partners to communicate these expectations and to affirm their commitment through reciprocal exchange should diminish over time. Perhaps the older couples in the study by Reedy et al. (1981) assign less importance to communication, because the need to reaffirm expectations of support continues to decline over the course of a long-term relationship.

As relationships change over time, so may one's expectations about those relationships. Research designed to elicit explicit knowledge about relationship expectancies at different points in development and the sources of these expectancies is needed. One would predict that such factors as cultural norms for age-appropriate behavior, length of time in the relationship, and individual maturation would contribute to normative changes in expectations.

The foregoing discussion is not meant to discount the fact that close relationships are characterized by supportive exchange. Mutual support is an expected aspect of committed relationships but is likely to be delivered on an "as needed" rather than a "quid pro quo" basis. If the needs of one partner outweigh the other's, the relationship may still remain committed, as is the case in parent–child relations.

What is important is that individuals remain within the bounds of the partner's expectations. It is here that the presence of shared expectations is salient. Making a bid for support that exceeds the limitations of the partner is, like failing to respond to the partner's expressed need, a violation of expectancy that may disrupt the relationship. One of the primary attributes of abusive caretakers is that they have unrealistic expectations regarding the response capabilities of their children, and, at the same time, children who are abused tend to be difficult (Maccoby & Martin, 1983; Parke & Collmer, 1975). Even in more normative situations, detrimental effects on maternal affect (Levitt et al., 1986) and on mother–child interaction (Bates, 1980; Campbell, 1979; Weber & Levitt, 1986b; Milliones, 1978) have been found in studies of temperamentally difficult children.

Related research by Gottman with marital partners (Gottman & Levenson, 1984), and by Patterson (1984) with aggressive children and their parents, suggests also that the modulation of conflict may contribute to the maintenance of close relationships. Although conflict is to be anticipated in close relationships (Antonucci, 1985b; Berscheid, 1983; Gottman & Levenson, 1984; Rook, 1984;

Skolnik, 1981), mutual escalation of conflict is risky to a relationship, because it provides an ideal climate for the violation of partner expectations, through the heated use of verbal or sometimes physical abuse that destroys the partner's expectations for security in the relationship. Partners in successful relationships then may act to maintain homeostasis by responding to their partner's expectations to the extent possible, by tempering their own bids for response so as not to exceed the limits of the partner's capability, and by modulating the conflict that arises inevitably within the relationship.

Data from our three-generation study indicate that there may be a trend toward decreased conflict in relationships from the younger to the older generations. Perhaps the ability to modulate conflict increases with age. Of course, there are conflict-habituated partnerships (Berscheid, 1983; Cuber & Haroff, 1966; Skolnik, 1981), as there are close relationships between abused children and their parents (Parke & Collmer, 1975). It would be informative to explore the expectations maintained by individuals in these negative attachment relationships.

In sum, attachment relationships across the life span are hypothesized to be governed by shared expectations, established through familiarity with one's relationship partner, contingent feedback from the partner, cultural norms regarding appropriate relationship behavior, and past relationship experiences. Relationships are maintained by mutual accomodation to partner expectations. Extreme violations of expectations may disrupt the relationship. A schematic representation of this model of close relationship processes is presented in FIG. 10.5.

The final section of this chapter is directed to the role of attachment relationships in the promotion of individual well-being.

Close Relationships and Personal Well-Being

Attachment relationships in infancy are viewed as crucial to the infant's survival (Bowlby, 1969), and the lack of functional caretaking has been linked to negative outcomes, including failure to thrive (Gewirtz, 1968; Ramey, Heiger, & Klisz, 1972). Analogous outcomes have been related theoretically and empirically to lack of social support, particularly for the aged (Antonucci, 1985a, 1990).

In studies of social support, investigators have rarely distinguished between close relationships and other network relationships. However, as indicated previously, most support is provided by persons in the inner circle of the individual's network. Studies that have been addressed to this issue suggest that well-being is related to support from close relationships rather than to support networks in general (Lowenthal & Haven, 1968; Traupmann & Hatfield, 1981; Coffman et al., 1989). In our study of mothers of 13-month-old infants, maternal affect was related primarily to support from the husband and secondarily to support from the maternal grandmother. Similar findings with regard to spousal support have been reported by Crnic and his colleagues (Crnic, Greenberg, Ragozin, Robinson, & Basham, 1983).

The model of close relationships proposed here does not specify that particu-

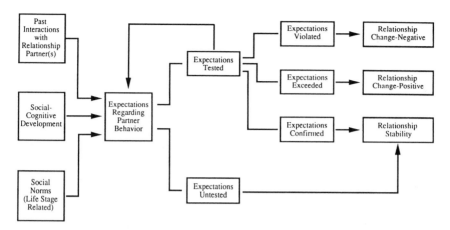

FIG. 10.5. Hypothesized model of processes governing relationship change and continuity across the life-span.

lar categories of relationship are crucial to well-being. Our most recent study of mothers of infants suggests that maternal postpartum affect is related to support from and satisfaction with the person designated by the mother as closest to her, regardless of the individual's role category (Coffman et al., 1989). What is suggested is that personal well-being across the life span, as well as in infancy, is dependent on the presence of at least one close relationship.

This hypothesis is difficult to test empirically, because individuals devoid of close ties are quite rare in the general population. In the national sample obtained by Kahn and Antonucci, only six percent of the respondents lacked an inner circle relationship. In our high-risk sample of South Beach residents, however, fifteen percent were found to have no one in the inner circle, allowing a comparison of individuals lacking close ties with those reporting only one versus those reporting more than one such tie. The affect of those lacking a close relationship was found to be significantly more negative than those with one such relationship, and the latter did not differ from those with more than one close relationship (Levitt et al., 1987). These results suggest that the presence of one close relationship may be sufficient to foster well-being, consistent with Bronfenbrenner's (1979) conclusions about the ameliorative effects of a close relationship for high-risk children.

CONCLUSIONS

A primary thrust of this discussion has been to suggest that close relationships across the life span can be conceptualized as attachment relationships; that they are governed by similar processes and serve similar functions. Related views have been forwarded recently by Ainsworth (1989) and Shaver and Hazan

(1988), but the emphasis of those presentations has been less on processes of attachment and developmental change in attachment relationships, and more on the significance of individual differences in attachment security. The current presentation diverges also in specifying the place of attachment relations within a social network context and in incorporating existing knowledge about social support in the analysis of life-span attachment relations.

Within the proposed model of close relationships, the major underlying process is hypothesized to be the establishment and maintenance of expectations about the relationship, forged through familiarity with one's relationship partner, mutually contingent feedback, and cultural norms regarding appropriate relationship behavior, and colored by one's past relationship experiences. Relationships are stabilized and given continuity through such regulating processes as mutual adaptation, modulation of conflict, and maintenance of behavior within the limits of the partner's tolerance. Stabilizing factors outside the relationship also serve to maintain relationship continuity. Developmental changes in existing relationships and structural changes over the life span in one's close relationship circle are hypothesized to ensue from changes in cognitive ability, individual maturation, age-related norms, and changes in the ability to modulate conflict. Change may also occur as a function of nonnormative events or changes in one or both of the relationship partners.

The presence of at least one close relationship contributes to the individual's well-being. Attachment relationships at any point in the life span serve the function of providing the individual with a secure base from which to encounter the inevitable stresses of life. As with infants, relationships across the life span vary in the extent to which they actually provide this for the individual.

In conclusion, this discussion was intended to facilitate and give substance to a life-span perspective on attachment and close relationships. The proposed intersections of infant attachment theory with models of close relationships and social support in adulthood are in need of empirical verification. In particular, the longitudinal tracking of inner circle relations and the expectations that may govern those relations is required, in addition to further research addressing the distinction between close relationships and other convoy relationships. Research on the contribution of attachment relationships to personal well-being at different life stages is also needed. Whether or not the specific arguments and hypotheses forwarded here will withstand the test of empirical scrutiny, it is hoped that this chapter will provide encouragement for researchers to further pursue the development of attachment relations across the life span.

REFERENCES

Ainsworth, M. D. S. (1983). Patterns of infant–mother attachment as related to maternal care: Their early history and their contribution to continuity. In D. Magnusson & V. L. Allen (Eds.), *Human development: An interactional perspective* (pp. 35–57). New York: Academic Press.
Ainsworth, M. D. S. (1989). Attachments beyond infancy. *American Psychologist, 44,* 709–716.

Ainsworth, M. D. S., Blehar, M., Waters, E., & Wall, S. (1978). *Patterns of attachment*. Hillsdale, NJ: Lawrence Erlbaum Associates.

Altman, I., & Taylor, D. A. (1973). *Social penetration: The development of interpersonal relationships*. New York: Holt, Rinehart & Winston.

Antonucci, T. C. (1976). Attachment: A life span concept. *Human Development, 19*, 135–142.

Antonucci, T. C. (1985a). Personal characteristics, social support, and social behavior. In E. Shanas & R. H. Binstock (Eds.), *Handbook of aging and the social sciences* (pp. 94–129). New York: Van Nostrand Reinhold.

Antonucci, T. C. (1985b). Social support: Theoretical advances, recent findings and pressing issues. In I. G. Sarason & B. R. Sarason (Eds.), *Social support: Theory, research and applications* (pp. 21–37). The Hague: Martinus Nijhof.

Antonucci, T. C. (1986, Summer). Measuring social support networks: Hierarchical mapping technique. *Generations*, 10–12.

Antonucci, T. C. (1990). Social supports and social relationships. In R. H. Binstock, & L. K. George (Eds.), *Handbook of aging and the social sciences* (3rd ed., pp. 205–227). Orlando, FL: Academic Press.

Antonucci, T. C., & Israel, B. (1986). Veridicality of social support: A comparison of principal and network members' responses. *Journal of Consulting and Clinical Psychology, 54*, 432–437.

Bates, J. E. (1980). The concept of difficult temperament. *Merrill-Palmer Quarterly, 26*, 299–319.

Belsky, J., & Isabella, R. A. (1988). Maternal, infant and social-contextual determinants of attachment security. In J. Belsky & T. Nezworski (Eds.), *Clinical implications of attachment* (pp. 41–94). Hillsdale, NJ: Lawrence Erlbaum Associates.

Berscheid, E. (1983). Emotion. In H. H. Kelley, E. Berscheid, A., Christensen, J. H. Harvey, T. L. Huston, G. Levinger, E. McClintock, L. A. Peplau, & D. R. Peterson (Eds.), *Close relationships* (pp. 110–168). New York: Freeman.

Boyce, W. T. (1985). Social support, family relations, and children. In S. Cohen & S. L. Syme (Eds.), *Social support and health* (pp. 151–173). New York: Academic Press.

Bowlby, J. (1969). *Attachment and loss, Volume 1: Attachment*. New York: Basic.

Bradburn, N. (1969). *The structure of psychological well-being*. Chicago: Aldine.

Brazelton, T. B., Koslowski, B., & Main, M. (1974). The origins of reciprocity: The early mother–infant interaction. In M. Lewis & L. A. Rosenblum (Eds.), *The effect of the infant on its caregiver* (pp. 49–76). New York: Wiley.

Bretherton, I., & Waters, E. (1985). Growing points of attachment theory and research. *Monographs of the Society for Research in Child Development, 50*, (1–2, Serial No. 209).

Bronfenbrenner, U. (1979). *The ecology of human development*. Cambridge, MA: Harvard University Press.

Cairns, R. B. (1972). Attachment and dependency: A psychobiological and social-learning synthesis. In J. L. Gewirtz (Ed.), *Attachment and dependency* (pp. 29–80). New York: Wiley.

Cairns, R. B. (1977). Beyond social attachment: The dynamics of interactional development. In T. Alloway, P. Pliner, & L. Krames (Eds.), *Attachment behavior* (pp. 1–24). New York: Plenum.

Cairns, R. B. (1979). *Social development: The origins and plasticity of interchanges*. San Francisco: Freeman.

Campbell, S. (1979). Mother–infant interaction as a function of maternal ratings of temperament. *Child Psychiatry and Human Development, 10*, 67–76.

Cicerelli, V. G. (1982). Sibling influence throughout the lifespan. In M. E. Lamb & B. Sutton-Smith (Eds.), *Sibling relationships: Their nature sand significance across the lifespan* (pp. 267–284). Hillsdale NJ: Lawrence Erlbaum Associates.

Clark, M. S. (1984). A distinction between two types of relationships and its implications for development. In J. C. Masters & K. Yarkin-Levin (Eds.), *Boundary areas in social and developmental psychology* (pp. 241–270). New York: Academic Press.

Cochran, M. M., & Brassard, J. A. (1979). Child development and personal social networks. *Child Development, 50*, 601–616.

Coffman, S., Levitt, M. J., & Deets, C. (1989, April). *Social support and relationship expectations in mothers of sick and well newborns*. Paper presented at the meeting of the Society for Research in Child Development. Kansas City, MO.

Crnic, K. A., Greenberg, M. T., Ragozin, A. S., Robinson, N. M., & Basham, R. B. (1983). Effects of stress and social support on mothers and premature and full term infants. *Child Development, 54*, 209–217.

Crocker, J. (1981). Judgment of covariation by adult perceivers. *Psychological Bulletin, 90*, 272–292.

Cuber, J. F., & Haroff, P. B. (1966). *Sex and the significant Americans*. New York: Appleton-Century-Crofts.

Davis, K. E., & Todd, M. J. (1982). Friendship and love relationships. *Advances in Descriptive Psychology, 2*, 79–122.

Erikson, E. H. (1963). *Childhood and society* (2nd ed.). New York: Norton.

Fox, N. (1977). Attachment of kibbutz infants to mother and metapelet. *Child Development, 48*, 1228–1239.

Frank, S. J., Avery, C. B., & Laman, M. S. (1988). Young adults' perceptions of their relationships with their parents: Individual differences in connectedness, competence, and emotional autonomy. *Developmental Psychology, 24*, 729–737.

Gewirtz, J. L. (1968). The role of stimulation in models for child development. In L. L. Dittman (Ed.), *Early child care: The new perspectives* (pp. 139–168). New York: Atherton Press.

Gewirtz, J. L. (1972). Attachment, dependence, and a distinction in terms of stimulus control. In J. L. Gewirtz (Ed.), *Attachment and dependency* (pp. 139–177). New York: Wiley.

Gewirtz, J. L., & Boyd, E. F. (1976). Mother–infant interaction and its study. In H. W. Reese, & L. P. Lipsitt (Eds.), *Advances in child development and behavior* (Vol. 11, pp. 142–166). New York: Academic Press.

Gewirtz, J. L., & Peláez-Nogueras, M. (1989). Infant protesting to maternal departures and separations: A conditional discrimination process. Paper delivered at the Biennial Meeting, Society for Research in Child Development, Kansas City, Missouri, April 27, 1989.

Gewirtz, J. L., & Petrovich, S. (1982). Early social and attachment learning in the frame of organic and cultural evolution. In T. M. Field, A. Huston, H. C. Quay, L. Troll, & G. E. Finley (Eds.), *Review of human development* (pp. 3–19). New York: Wiley.

Goldberg, S. (1977). Social competence in infancy: A model of parent–infant interaction. *Merrill-Palmer Quarterly, 23*, 163–177.

Gottman, J. M., & Levenson, R. W. (1984). Why marriages fail: Affective and physiological patterns in marital interaction. In J. C. Masters & K. Yarkin-Levin (Eds.), *Boundary areas in social and developmental psychology* (pp. 67–106). New York: Academic Press.

Graziano, W. G. (1984). A developmental approach to social exchange processes. In J. C. Masters & K. Yarkin-Levin (Eds.), *Boundary areas in social and developmental psychology* (pp. 161–194). New York: Academic Press.

Hagestad, G. O. (1982). Parent and child: Generations in the family. In T. M. Field, A. Huston, H. C. Quay, L. Troll, & G. E. Finley (Eds.), *Review of human development* (pp. 485–499). New York: Wiley-Interscience.

Hagestad, G. O. (1984). The continuous bond: A dynamic, multigenerational perspective on parent–child relations between adults. In M. Perlmutter (Ed.), *Minnesota Symposia on Child Psychology: Volume 17. Parent–child interaction and parent–child relations in child development* (pp. 129–158). Hillsdale, NJ: Lawrence Erlbaum Associates.

Hartup, W. W. (1983). Peer relations. In E. M. Hetherington (Ed.), *Handbook of child psychology: Volume 4. Socialization, personality, and social development* (pp. 103–196). New York: Wiley.

Hartup, W. W. (1989). Social relationships and their developmental significance. *American Psychologist, 44*, 120–126.

Holmes, J. G., & Rempel, J. K. (1989). Trust in close relationships. In C. Hendrick (Ed.), *Close relationships* (pp. 187–220). Newbury Park, CA: Sage Publications.

Kahn, R. L., & Antonucci, T. C. (1980). Convoys over the life course: Attachment, roles, and social support. In P. B. Baltes & O. G. Brim (Eds.), *Life span development and behavior* (Vol. 3, pp. 253–286). New York: Academic Press.

Kahn, R. L., & Antonucci, T. C. (1984). Social supports of the elderly: Family/friends/professionals. (Report No. AGO1632). Washington, DC: National Institute on Aging.

Lamb, M. E. (1981). The development of father–infant relationships. In M. E. Lamb (Ed.), *The role of the father in child development* (2nd ed., pp. 459–479). New York: Wiley.

Lamb, M. E., Thompson, R. A., Gardner, W. P., Charnov, E. L., & Estes, D. (1984). Security of infantile attachment as assessed in the "strange situation": Its study and biological interpretation. *The Behavioral and Brain Sciences, 7,* 127–170.

Levitt, M. J. (1979). The effect of response contingent feedback on infants' reactions to a stranger (Doctoral dissertation, Syracuse University). *Dissertation Abstracts International, 39,* 4115B–5156B. (University Microfilms No. 7908568)

Levitt, M. J. (1980). Contingent feedback, familiarization, and infant affect: How a stranger becomes a friend. *Developmental Psychology, 16,* 425–432.

Levitt, M. J., Antonucci, T. C., Clark, M. C., Rotton, J., & Finley, G. E. (1985–1986). Social support and well-being: Preliminary indicators in two samples of the elderly. *International Journal of Aging and Human Development, 21,* 67–77.

Levitt, M. J., & Clark, M. C. (1982, April). *Mother-infant reciprocity, causality, and response to contingent feedback.* Paper presented at the meeting of the International Conference on Infant Studies, Austin, Texas.

Levitt, M. J., Clark, M. C., Rotton, J., & Finley, G. E. (1987). Social support, perceived control, and well-being: A study of an environmentally distressed population. *International Journal of Aging and Human Development, 25,* 247–258.

Levitt, M. J., & Weber, R. A. (1985, November). *Social support and well-being: An exploration of support relationships in three-generation families.* Paper presented at the meeting of the Gerontological Society, New Orleans.

Levitt, M. J., & Weber, R. A. (1986, August). *A cross-cultural exploration of social relationships in three-generation families.* Presented at the meeting of the American Psychological Association, Washington, DC.

Levitt, M. J., Weber, R. A., & Clark, M. C. (1986). Social network characteristics as sources of maternal support and well-being. *Developmental Psychology, 22,* 310–316.

Lewis, M. (1982). The social network systems model: Toward a theory of social development. In T. M. Field, A. Huston, H. C. Quay, L. Troll, & G. E. Finley (Eds.), *Review of human development* (pp. 180–216). New York: Wiley.

Lewis, M. (1987). Social development in infancy and early childhood. In J. D. Osofsky (Ed.), *Handbook of infant development* (2nd ed., pp. 419–493). New York: Wiley.

Lewis, M., & Ban, P. (1971, April). *Stability of attachment behavior: A transformational analysis.* Paper presented at the meeting of the Society for Research in Child Development, Minneapolis.

Lewis, M., Feiring, C., & Kotsonis, M. (1984). The social network of the young child: A developmental perspective. In M. Lewis (Ed.), *Beyond the dyad* (pp. 129–160). New York: Plenum.

Lewis, M., & Goldberg, S. (1969). Perceptual-cognitive development in infancy: A generalized expectancy model as a function of the mother–infant interaction. *Merrill-Palmer Quarterly, 15,* 81–100.

Lopata, H. Z. (1979). *Women as widows: Support systems.* New York: Elsevier North Holland.

Lowenthal, M. F., & Haven, C. (1968). Interaction and adaptation: Intimacy as a critical variable. *American Sociological Review, 33,* 20–30.

Maccoby, E. E., & Martin, J. A. (1983). Socialization in the context of the family: Parent–child interaction. In E. M. Hetherington (Ed.), *Handbook of child psychology: Volume 4. Socialization, personality, and social development* (pp. 1–102). New York: Wiley.

Millar, W. S. (1972). A study of operant conditioning under delayed reinforcement in early infancy. *Monographs of the Society for Research in Child Development, 37*(2, Serial No. 147).

Milliones, J. (1978). Relation between child temperament and maternal behavior. *Child Development, 49,* 1255–1257.

Morris, D. (1982). Attachment and intimacy. In M. Fisher & G. Stricker (Eds.), *Intimacy* (pp. 305–323). New York: Plenum.

Myers, B. J., Jarvis, P. A., & Creasey, G. L. (1987). Infants' behavior with their mothers and grandmothers. *Infant Behavior and Development, 10,* 245–259.

Parke, R. D., & Collmer, C. W. (1975). Child abuse: An interdisciplinary analysis. In E. M. Hetherington (Ed.), *Review of child development research,* (Vol. 5, pp. 509–590). Chicago: University of Chicago Press.

Patterson, G. R. (1984). Microsocial process: A view from the boundary. In J. C. Masters & K. Yarkin-Levin (Eds.), *Boundary areas in social and developmental psychology* (pp. 43–66). New York: Academic Press.

Piaget, J. (1954). *The construction of reality in the child.* New York: Ballantine.

Pipp, S., Shaver, P., Jennings, S., Lamborn, S., & Fischer, K. (1985). Adolescents' theories about the development of their relationships with parents. *Journal of Personality and Social Psychology, 48,* 991–1001.

Ramey, C. T., Heiger, L., & Klisz, D. K. (1972). Synchronous reinforcement of vocal responses in failure-to-thrive infants. *Child Development, 43,* 1449–1455.

Reedy, M. N., Birren, J. E., & Schaie, K. W. (1981). Age and sex differences in satisfying love relationships across the adult life span. *Human Development, 24,* 52–56.

Rook, K. S. (1984). The negative side of social interaction: Impact on psychological well-being. *Journal of Personality and Social Psychology, 46,* 1097–1108.

Rovee-Collier, C. K., & Gekowski, M. J. (1979). The economics of infancy: A review of conjugate reinforcement. In H. W. Reese, & L. P. Lipsitt (Eds.), *Advances in child development and behavior. Volume 13* (pp. 195–258). New York: Academic Press.

Schaffer, H. R. (1977). Early interactive development. In H. R. Schaffer (Ed.), *Studies in mother-infant interaction.* New York: Academic Press.

Shaver, P. R., & Hazan, C. (1988). A biased overview of the study of love. *Journal of Social and Personal Relationships, 5,* 473–502.

Skolnik, A. (1981). Married lives: Longitudinal perspectives on marriage. In D. H. Eichorn, J. A. Clausen, N. Haan, M. P. Honzik, & P. H. Mussen (Eds.), *Present and past in middle life* (pp. 270–300). New York: Academic Press.

Stern, D. N. (1974). Mother and infant at play: The dyadic interaction involving facial, vocal, and gaze behaviors. In M. Lewis, & L. A. Rosenblum (Eds.), *The effect of the infant on its caregiver* (pp. 187–214). New York: Wiley.

Sternberg, R. J., & Grajek, S. (1984). The nature of love. *Journal of Personality and Social Psychology, 47,* 312–329.

Suomi, S. J. (1981). The perception of contingency and social cognition. In M. E. Lamb & L. R. Sherrod (Eds.), *Infant social cognition* (pp. 177–203). Hillsdale, NJ: Lawrence Erlbaum Associates.

Thompson, L., & Walker, A. J. (1984). Mothers and daughters: Aid patterns and attachment. *Journal of Marriage and the Family, 46,* 313–323.

Traupmann, J., & Hatfield, E. (1981). Love and its effect on mental and physical health. In R. W. Fogel, E. Hatfield, S. B. Keisler, & E. Shanas (Eds.), *Aging: Stability and change in the family* (pp. 253–274). New York: Academic Press.

Troll, L. E. (1980). Intergenerational relations in later life: A family system approach. In N. Datan & N. Lohmann (Eds.), *Transitions of aging* (pp. 75–91). New York: Academic Press.

Tronick, E. Z. (1989). Emotions and emotional communication in infants. *American Psychologist, 44,* 112–119.

Watson, J. S. (1972). Smiling, cooing, and "The game." *Merrill-Palmer Quarterly, 19,* 219–228.

Watson, J. S. (1979). Perception of contingency as a determinant of social responsiveness. In E. B.

Thoman (Ed.), *Origins of the infant's social responsiveness* (pp. 33–64). Hillsdale, NJ: Lawrence Erlbaum Associates.

Weber, R. A., & Levitt, M. J. (1986b, March). *Toddler difficulty and maternal responsiveness.* Paper presented at the meeting of the Southeastern Psychological Association, Orlando, FL.

Weber, R. A., & Levitt, M. J. (1986a, November). *Close relationships and social support in three generations of women.* Paper presented at the meeting of the Gerontological Society, Chicago.

Weinraub, M., Brooks, J., & Lewis, M. (1977). The social network: A reconsideration of the concept of attachment. *Human Development, 20,* 31–47.

Weinraub, M., & Lewis, M. (1977). The determinants of children's responses to separation. *Monographs of the Society for Research in Child Development, 42* (4, Serial No. 172).

Weinraub, M., & Wolf, B. M. (1983). Effects of stress and social support on mother–child interactions in single- and two-parent families. *Child Development, 54,* 1297–1311.

Weisz, J. R. (1986). Understanding the developing understanding of control. In Perlmutter, M. (Ed.), *Cognitive perspectives on children's social and behavioral development. Minnesota Symposia on Child Psychology* (Vol. 18, pp. 219–285). Hillsdale, NJ: Lawrence Erlbaum Associates.

Zajonc, R. B. (1968). Attitudinal effects of mere exposure. *Journal of Personality and Social Psychology, 9,* 1–27.

11 Attachment Processes in Adult Political Ideology: Patriotism and Nationalism

Seymour Feshbach

ABSTRACT

This paper is addressed to the proposition that similar mechanisms mediate early attachment to caregivers and later attachment to one's culture and nation. The tendency to equate nations with parental figures is illustrated through quotations selected from literature and the mass media. These quotations suggest that one's nation and government are often viewed in terms of parental imagery and that there is a similarity between affective attachments toward parents and affective attachment toward one's nation. Theoretical reasons for postulating a linkage between early attachment and national "attachment" are also considered.

An exploratory study bearing on the relationship between early attachment and national "attachment" is described. To implement the study, it was first necessary to develop measures distinguishing patriotism from nationalism. A factor analysis of items tapping love of country, belief in the dominance of one's country and attitudes towards other nations yielded several factors, the first two of which were vectors that corresponded to the a-priori conceptions of patriotism and nationalism, respectively. It was postulated that the patriotism factor, in particular, would be positively correlated with early attachments. A questionnaire inventory of attachment feelings and responses in early childhood was developed, and administered to a sample of college undergraduates, along with the patriotism-nationalism scale and measure of current attachment to and conflict with parents. The results reflected a significant relationship between early attachment to the father and patriotic feelings. These and other findings are discussed in terms of their relevance to both the analysis of the intensity of patriotic and nationalistic attitudes and the enhancement of our understanding of early attachments.

Attachment is generally acknowledged to refer to a significant kind of relationship that obtains between a young child and caretaker. However, like many other psychological constructs that refer to significant human phenomena, we recognize its importance but are less clear as to its definition and ramifications. There are some investigators who see attachment as a process that serves to organize the behaviors manifested by the child toward the object of attachment (Ainsworth, Blehar, Waters, & Wall, 1978; Sroufe & Waters, 1977), whereas others see attachment as largely a descriptive term that adds little to our understanding of the relationship beyond the behavior displayed (Cairns, 1972; Gewirtz, 1972; Weinraub, Brooks & Lewis, 1977). In addition to questions concerning the nature of the attachment relationship between child and caregiver, there is greater uncertainty regarding questions concerning the generalizability of the attachment relationship, whether there are many attachments developed by the infant to significant figures in his or her environment that are essentially independent of each other, whether there are one or a few attachment relationships that constitute the basis or prototype for future relationships, and whether there are qualities of attachment that are generic to all attachment relationships.

In this chapter, I may add to the potential diffuseness of the attachment construct by extending it beyond relationships between people to apply to relationships of people to certain symbols, places, and groups. More specifically, I shall explore the proposition that the attachment displayed toward one's nation or culture bears fundamental similarities to the attachment displayed by the young child to his parents, that the behaviors of seeking proximity to the caregiver, of experiencing distress when separated, of displaying positive affective responses when in the caregiver's presence, and of displaying bereavement at the loss of the caregiver have their direct counterparts in the behaviors people manifest toward their nation. I will attempt to provide support for this proposition of a connection between early childhood attachments and national attachment, partly through illustration and analysis and largely through the presentation of empirical findings bearing on this hypothesized connection. In so doing, I hope to enhance our understanding of the phenomenon of attachment to or love of one's country and perhaps our understanding of the attachment process as manifested in the young child.

One of the problems that one encounters in the analysis of attachment is entailed in the term itself. Attachment has a technical meaning, as Bowlby (1969) referred to a particular relationship established between the child and the mother that is not present in a young infant, that is manifested only after the child has had some experience with the caregiver, and that differs from the child's relationship with other kinds of positive reinforcing figures. Attachment also has a more general meaning, connoting preference for, involvement in, and orientation toward an object or person that is related to its more specific technical usage. All attachments have some elements in common, therefore, one is prone to generalize from the phenomena of infant attachment to other kinds of attachment situations. I hope this does not appear to be the case in connection with positing a relationship between early childhood attachments and national attachment. At least, this is not my intention. There is a host of informal observational data as well as theoretical reasons for suggesting that national images function in many ways as parental images and that there is a relationship between affects and needs expressed in these two ostensibly very different contexts.

Poetry and prose are replete with the use of parental metaphors in referring to one's nation. The feelings expressed toward the nation are often reminiscent of the way children feel toward their parents. The following quotations are illustrative of these images and feelings. The minor poet, Samuel Lover, in a poem entitled "FATHER-LAND AND MOTHER-TONGUE" (Carrington, 1894/1970) wrote:

Our Father-land! And wouldst thou know
  Why we should call it Father-land?
It is, that Adam here below
  Was made of earth by Nature's hand;
And he, our father, made of earth,
  Hath peopled earth on every hand;
And we, in memory of his birth,
  Do call our country "Father-land."

At first, Eden's bowers, they say,
  No sound of speech had Adam caught,
But whistled like a bird all day,
  And maybe 'twas for want of thought;
But Nature, with resistless laws,
  Made Adam soon surpass the birds:
She gave him lovely Eve, because,
  If he'd a wife, they must have words.

And so, the native land, I hold
  By male descent, is proudly mine;
The language, as the tale was told,
  Was given in the female line.
And thus, we see, on either hand
  We name our blessings whence they're sprung:
We call our country "Father-land,"
  We call our language "Mother-tongue."

Our nation, in essence, gave birth to us, therefore, it is only natural that we pay it appropriate allegiance. Words of the famous orator Edward Everett Hale (Carrington, 1894/1970) are apropos here:

All our knowledge of facts is worthless unless boys and girls have the life which shall use them well. It is not purchased science which we want. It is passionate love of country and the 137th Psalm, a "Psalm of exile," shows the feeling which compelled Israel to return to Jerusalem, her home. To a people of faith like hers, the love of country is like the love of home and of God. The three indeed are one.

Hale goes on to use such images as "America welcomed them with a mother's arms." As the 137th Psalm to which Hale refers attests, the loss of one's homeland entails the loss of a beloved object. The Psalm (Carrington, 1894/1970) begins:

> By Babylon's still waters we sat down and wept;
> Yeah, we wept as we thought of Zion, our pride.

The anthropomorphizing of one's native country is comnmonplace. One poet (Eichberg, in Carrington, 1894/1970) wrote:

> Upon thy mighty, faithful heart
> We lay our burdens down
> Thou art the only friend who feels
> Their weight without a frown.

Equally germane are the lines of our modern patriot, Rambo, who proclaims "What we want is our country to love us as much we have loved it."

Although I believe these citations are sufficiently illustrative of the proposition that there is a psychological equivalence or connection between love of country and love of parent, I would be derelict, if I did not cite those famous lines by Sir Walter Scott (Carrington, 1894/1970):

> Breathes there the man, with soul so dead,
> Who never to himself hath said,
> "This is my own, my native land!"
> Whose heart has ne'er within him burned,
> As home his footsteps he hath turned
> From wandering on a foreign strand?

Expressions of attachment to one's country, coupled with parental images of one's country, are as ancient as recorded literature—Euripides (1948) wrote in 420 BC: "Their fatherland it seems, is dearest of all to a man" and are as contemporary as the January 10, 1986 issue of *The Los Angeles Times* in which Amal's military leader in Southern Lebanon, Mohammed Abdel Hassan, is quoted as saying "The relationship between us and the Iranian Islamic government is the relationship between a mother and a son". Clearly for many individuals, the equivalence between country and parent is neither unconscious nor remote. I am not suggesting that love of country is a direct function of attachment to one's parents or that early familial attachments are the primary determinants of subsequent national attachments. Attitudes and feelings towards one's nation are complex, perhaps as complex as the constellation of attitudes and feelings that enter into a child's relationship with his parents. However, I am suggesting that individual differences in early familial attachments are related to individual differences in national attachments. I would also hazard the hypothesis that issues in early attachment are *the* primary antecedent of national feelings for some individuals who manifest extreme degrees of nationalism. However, I do not have data that bears on this possibility and will focus on the more general proposition of a linkage between early familial attachments and subsequent feelings towards one's nation.

There are a number of reasons why such a linkage might be obtained. It could be the case that individuals differ in their tendency to form attachments, such that people who manifest strong attachments in one domain will be likely to manifest strong attachments in other domains. Such a mechanism, although important to establish, would not be as interesting as the possibility of dynamic processes mediating linkage. Thus, Winnicott (1965) suggested that as the adolescent matures, attachment relationships and identification begin to extend beyond the immediate family and kinship groups to larger groups, including nations. Dynamically it can be assumed that children who have established strong attachment relationships to caregivers find these relationships highly rewarding; that is, the presence and response of the caregiver is reinforcing, whether the reinforcement is one of reducing distress or providing some kind of positive feedback. These early attachment relationships, although they may influence the child's subsequent relationships with these same caregivers, cannot be maintained in their early form. At the least, the child must physically separate, even if he or she cannot adequately psychologically separate. The nation—terrain, government, customs, with its connotation of father as protector and mother as source of nurturance, offers a socially acceptable context in which early attachment needs can be expressed and analogous reinforcements obtained. In many ways, the nation provides the adult individual with feelings of security and vicarious feelings of approval and related rewards through identification that were directly experienced in the early childhood situation. For these reasons, it is hypothesized that variations in early parental attachments would be positively correlated with variations in national attachment. One can also suggest a contrasting and complicating hypothesis—namely, children who had strong attachment needs that were not gratified by their caregivers would attempt to satisfy these needs through national identification and would express their feelings in the form of strong national attachment. Studies of early attachment indicate that such rejection patterns, while they occur, are relatively infrequent, therefore, it seems likely that studies of the relationship between early familial attachments and national attachments carried out in a normal population would yield a positive rather than inverse correlation.

In order to address these issues and to demonstrate that they were amenable to empirical examination, I carried out an exploratory study, illustrative might be more descriptive. The study that I present here entails a simple, straightforward methodology: namely, the assessment of early attachment, the assessment of nationalistic feelings, and the correlation of these two variables. However, the simplicity of the design obscures the complexity of the questions entailed in attempting to study this relationship. What exactly does one mean by feelings towards one's nation, and how are these measured? Furthermore, I am sure, the meaning of attachment would be the occasion for considerable discussion and differences of opinion, apart from difficulties in attempting to assess in young adults the strengths of their early attachments to caretakers. I will turn first to the nationalism issue.

PATRIOTISM-NATIONALISM

Terms such as nationalism and patriotism have had varied value connotations and meanings for both social scientists and the lay community. These attitudes and sentiments are sometimes positively valued by the larger community and some-times negatively valued, often in a cyclical manner (Klingberg, 1983). One can detect this same ambivalence in scholarly efforts to conceptualize and measure patriotism and nationalism. During World War II and the periods immediately preceding and following that war, there was a great deal of research interest in the study of nationalistic attitudes. Nationalism was perceived in negative terms, with the ideology of Nazi Germany representing the epitome of nationalistic excess. Earlier distinctions that some scholars had made between nationalism and patriotism were essentially disregarded. This distinction appears early in the social psychological literature. In 1927, Floyd Allport, although critical of the role of nationalism in fostering war, stated the following:

> The notion of America as something great and real is rooted in our very nature. It seems to us the source of much that is worthwhile in life. The writer has perhaps not fairly distinguished between nationalism and patriotism. After all, it is not the nationalistic fallacy itself which leads to war, but the way in which it is used. . . . May we not keep our "Nation" but purge it of all sinister motives? (p. 300)

However, as noted, with the onset of the Second World War, this distinction between nationalism and patriotism became obscure. The work, *The Authoritarian Personality* (Adorno, Frenkel-Brunswik, Levinson, & Sanford, 1950), further reinforced this unidimensional view of nationalism, despite the fact that the authors had made a distinction between genuine patriotism ("love of country") and pseudopatriotism, which is what they believed their Ethnocentrism Scale to be assessing. This distinction tended to be lost in later references to the scale, including references by participants in the original investigation (Levinson, 1957).

Later research in this area began to address the relationship of internationalism or "world-mindedness" to nationalism. However, little attention was given to the distinction between patriotism and nationalism although several decades before, in an essay on nationalism, George Herbert Mead (1929) asserted that "we cannot attain international-mindedness until we have attained a higher degree of national-mindedness" (page 406). This distinction would appear to be crucial to the present study for it is patriotism, with its connotation of love of country, that should be most clearly linked to attachment rather than nationalism, with its connotation of national superiority and interest in national dominance. Measures germane to this distinction were fortunately available due to the efforts of a graduate student who had worked with me, Rick Kosterman. To develop measures distinguishing patriotism from nationalism and related attitude areas, Kosterman prepared a set of 120 items written as agree–disagree, 5-point Likert format opinion statements, each with 5 response options ranging from strongly agree to strongly disagree. About half the items were generated specifically for his study, whereas the other half were either borrowed or modified items taken from several existing scales. The items were varied so as to assess patriotic affect, nationalistic attitudes, and international attitudes, and were balanced so as to avoid response acquiescence.

The items were administered to 239 subjects drawn from three different populations. The largest sample consisted of 194 students from the University of California, Los Angeles. Of these, there were 106 females and 88 males, with a great majority being under 21 years of age. A second sample consisted of 24 high school students from a small town (Kennewick) in the state of Washington. These high school students were equally divided as to sex. The third sample involved 21 subjects, 14 males and 7 females, who were involved in an association of building contractors located in the state of Washington. Six members of this group were over 50 years of age, three were in the 41–50 age group, and 11 were in the 31–40 age group, whereas one respondent was under 30 (Kosterman & Feshbach, 1989).

The responses of all three samples were pooled, and an iterated principle factor analysis was carried out yielding six factors. These factors were rotated using the Varimax method, which imposes orthogonality between factors. It may be noted that an oblique rotation yielded a very similar factor structure. The percent of the total variance explained by each factor was 19.2, 6.2, 5.1, 3.2, 2.5, 2.1, respectively. The sixth factor consisted of only three items and accounted for such a small part of the variance, thus, the subsequent analyses will be restricted to the first five factors.

In Tables 11.1 thru 11.5 are presented the items that loaded substantially on one of the five factors. For four of the five factors, all of the positive loadings are .50 or greater, although, in a number of instances, items with lower negative loadings were included in order to achieve better balance for a particular subscale. The items with the strongest loadings on factor 1—"I love my country," "I am proud to be an American," "In a sense, I am emotionally attached to my country and emotionally affected by its actions," clearly indicate this first component to be our patriotism factor. Although those items with high loadings on

TABLE 11.1
Items and Factor Loadings for Factor 1

Items	Factor Loadings		(Varimax Rotation)		
	1	2	3	4	5
10. I love my country.	(.73)	.08	-.09	-.08	.11
25. I am proud to be an American.	(.69)	.03	-.05	.05	-.02
76. In a sense, I am emotionally attached to my country and emotionally affected by its actions.	(.67)	.14	.04	.00	.03
39. Although at times I may not agree with the government, my commitment to the U.S. always remains strong.	(.63)	.05	-.13	.04	-.11
113. I feel a great pride in that land that is our America	(.63)	.31	-.02	.04	-.03
29. It is not that important for me to serve my country.	(-.51)	-.01	.09	.16	.04
23. When I see the American flag flying, I feel great.	(.61)	.22	.05	-.15	-.02
9. The fact that I am am American is an important part of my identity.	(.57)	.08	-.06	-.07	.05
48. It is not constructive for one to develop an emotional attachment to his/her country.	(-.52)				
7. In general, I have very little respect for the American people.	(-.50)	.09	.06	.05	.07
20. It bothers me to see children made to pledge allegiance to the flag or sing the national anthem or otherwise induced to adopt such strong patriotic attitudes.	(-.49)	-.00	.05	.14	.20
50. The U.S. is really just an institution, big and powerful yes, but just an institution.	(-.45)	.06	.08	.09	.26

factor 2—"In view of America's moral and material superiority, it is only right that we should we should have the biggest say in deciding United Nations policy," "The first duty of every young American is to honor the national American history and heritage," "The important thing for the U.S. foreign aid program is to see to it that the U.S. gains a political advantage," "Other countries should try to make their governments as much like ours as possible," denote this component as our nationalism factor. The nine items defining factor 3 apply to world sharing or global welfare, and this subscale can be labeled *Internationalism*. The items loading on factor 4 share the notion that Americans can criticize the country or hold certain unpopular beliefs and still be considered good Americans. This subscale was labeled *Civil Liberties*. Although the items

TABLE 11.2
Items and Factor Loadings for Factor 2

Items	Factor Loadings	(Varimax Rotation)			
	1	2	3	4	5
In view of America's moral and material superiority, it is only right that we should have the biggst say in deciding United Nations policy.	-.00	(.59)	-.08	-.12	-.12
88. The first duty of every young American is to honor the national American history and heritage	.17	(.55)	-.02	-.13	.13
2. The important thing for the U.S. foreign aid program is to see to it that the U.S. gains a political advantage.	-.04	(.54)	-.17	-.13	-.20
85. Other countries should try to make their government as much like ours as possible.	.12	(.54)	.02	-.01	.01
92. Generally, the more influence Americas has on other nations, the better off they are.	.08	(.52)	-.21	-.19	.01
40. Foreign nations have done some very fine things, but it takes America to do things in a big way.	.09	(.52)	.02	-.15	-.11
34. It is important that the U. S. win in international sporting competition like the olympics.	.21	(.50)	.03	-.18	-.10
67. It is really not important that the U.S. be number one in whatever it does.	-.20	(-.37)	.17	.24	.20

on factor 3 refer to a willingness to share our largesse and a concern for the welfare of other national communities, the items on factor 5 pertain to the willingness to support a world government, and that factor was so labeled.

ATTACHMENT MEASURES

We turn now to the assessment of that other domain of interest—namely, early childhood attachments. Unfortunately, the field of adult personality and social behavior does not abound in measures of attachment, much less early attachments. There are some procedures available that utilize projective procedures entailing dream and ink blot interpretation to assess residues of early attachments and object relations and thereby make inferences concerning the nature of these attachments (Blatt & Lerner, 1983, Mayman, 1967). However, these procedures are difficult to implement as well as being in the exploratory stage. Also in the exploratory stage at the time this study was undertaken was the detailed interview developed by George, Kaplan and Main (1985). It was decided then to develop a questionnaire or self-report measure of early attachment to caregivers, recognizing all of the difficulties involved in retrospective reports. It is particularly because of the problems associated with establishing the validity of these retro-

TABLE 11.3
Items and Factor Loadings for Factor 3

Items	Factor Loadings (Varimax Rotation)				
	1	2	3	4	5
44. If necessary, we ought to be willing to lower our standard of living to cooperate with other countries in getting an equal standard for every person in the world.	-.12	-.01	(.68)	-.03	.17
74. The alleviation of poverty in other countries is their problem, not ours.	-.05	.32	(-.66)	-.05	-.05
103. America should be more willing to share its wealth with other suffering nations, even it it doesn't necessarily coincide with our political interests.	-.01	-.15	(.64)	.10	.22
93. We should teach our children to uphold the welfare of all people everywhere, even though it may be against the best interests of our country.	-.07	-.07	.59	.13	.27
32. I would not be willing to decrease my living standard by 10% to increase that of persons in poorer countries of the world.	-.05	.19	(-.57)	.17	.02
110. Children should be educated to be international minded--to support any movement which contributes to the welfare of the world as a whole, regardless of special national interests.	-.08	.07	(.56)	.32	.31
84. The agricultural surpluses of all countries should be shared with the have-nots of the world.	.16	-.08	(.54)	.25	.00
78. The position a U. S. citizen takes on an international issue should depend on how much good it does for how many people in the world, regardless of their nation.	.02	.05	(.51)	.18	.33
116. Countries needing our agricultural surpluses should pay for them instead of getting something for nothing.	-.05	.32	(-.40)	-.06	-.12

spective reports that this study must be considered exploratory in nature. As one step toward determining whether the measure yielded by these reports of early attachments had some distinctive significance associated with early childhood experiences, it was decided to also include in this study a measure of the young adult's current attachment to his or her parents. Although there have been theoretical analyses of adult attachments (Marris, 1982; Weiss, 1982) and of their possible relationship to early attachments, empirical studies with requisite measures are rare. One measure, a self-report instrument, that has some relevance to the question of the attachment of young adults to their parents was developed by Jeffrey Hoffman (1984) in an effort to provide a conceptualization and an assessment of different aspects of adolescent psychological separation from their par-

TABLE 11.4
Items and Factor Loadings for Factor 4

Items	Factor Loadings		(Varimax Rotation)		
	1	2	3	4	5
57. A person who preferred jail to serving in the U. S. Army could still be a good American.	-.08	-.10	.02	(.50)	.24
17. A person who does not believe in God could still be a good American.	.14	-.17	-.12	(.49)	.07
4.A person who believes in socialism could still be a good American.	.02	-.24	.11	(.49)	.22
12. A person who doesn't stand when the Star Spangled Banner is being played could still be a good American.	-.18	-.13	-.00	(.47)	.93
102. It is O. K. to criticize the government.	.11	-.21	.11	(.46)	-.03
109. We should have complete freedom of speech, even for those who criticize the country.	.02	-.11	.12	(.46)	-.01
People who do not want to fight for America should live somewhere else.	.16	.20	-.05	(-.37)	-.26

TABLE 11.5
Items and Factor Loadings for Factor 5

Items	Factor Loadings		(Varimax Rotation)		
	1	2	3	4	5
60. All national governments ought to be abolished and replaced by one central world government.	-.27	-.03	.17	-.08	(.65)
56.I am not willing to surrender my allegiance to my country in order to give it to a world authority represented by all nations.	.15	.16	-.13	-.06	(-.56)
58. We should immediately take steps toward establishing a world government.	-.20	.03	.32	.01	(.55)
100. We should give the United Nations more power.	-.00	-.10	.28	.19	(.53)
55. The U. S. should never give up its military power to a strong world government.	.12	.30	-.10	-.13	(-.52)

ents. The Hoffman measure entails four theoretically derived scales: functional, emotional, conflictual, and attitudinal independence, whose discreteness was subsequently supported by item analysis and confirmatory factor analysis. The emotional independence subscale comes closest to the assessment of the degree of attachment towards the parents. Hoffman (1984) defined emotional independence as "freedom from an excessive need for approval, closeness, togetherness, and emotional support in relation to the mother and father" (p. 171). A high score on this scale is indicative of emotional dependence or excessive attachment. Items such as "I feel longing, if I am away from my mother for too long;" "My mother is the most important person in the world to me;" "I wished that my mother lived nearer so I could visit her more frequently;" "Being away from my mother makes me feel lonely;" are indicative of an attachment relationship, albeit perhaps more appropriate to a young child than to a young adult. In addition, the conflictual independence scale was also of interest. Hoffman (1984) defined conflictual independence as "freedom from excessive guilt, anxiety, mistrust, responsibility, inhibition, resentment, and anger in relation to the mother and father." (p. 171). Examples of items on the conflictual independence scale are: "Sometimes my mother is a burden to me," "I feel like I am constantly at war with my mother," "I blame my mother for many of the problems I have." High scores on this scale are indicative of a conflictual relationship with the parent in question.

The emotional and conflictual independence scales were administered, along with the patriotism–nationalism instrument and a questionnaire measure of early emotional attachment to the mother and to the father to 81 college undergraduates, 42 females and 39 males. The undergraduates were volunteers who could use their participation to satisfy a research participation requirement in Introductory Psychology.

The measures of early attachment were administered as part of an Early Childhood Inventory. The respondent was informed that the questions "refer to your early childhood experiences (as early as you can remember)." One set of items referred to the respondent's interaction with his or her mother, whereas an identical set of items was prepared for the father as the object of attachment. Thirteen items on this scale had specific attachment referents: For example, "Whenever I was upset, I found it easy to go to my mother for comfort;" Often when I needed her, my mother wasn't there;" "I like to be near my mother;" "When I was frightened, it would take a long time before my mother could reassure me;" "There was something about my mother that made me feel safe and secure, when I was with her." A five-point response scale ranging from very uncharacteristic to very characteristic was provided for each item. The total on this set of items constituted the mother attachment score and the father attachment score respectively. There was another set of items that described characteristics of the parent that proved to be highly correlated with the attachment scores. Examples of these latter items are: "My mother was fun to be with;"

"My mother found it difficult to demonstrate affection;" "My mother had a bad temper." These items when combined with the attachment scale yielded a total attachment score. The results were practically identical, whether the attachment or total attachment scores were used in the analyses, as one might anticipate, given that the alpha for the total attachment scale scores were .93 and that the correlation of the early attachment scores with the characteristics of the parent item were above .8. From the item intercorrelations, I think it would be possible to develop a set of reported characteristics of the parent that would be more independent of the reported attachment responses to the parent. However, that effort would entail another study, because it requires a larger pool of items and a larger sample of subjects.

RESEARCH RESULTS

Before turning to the correlations that bear on the relationship between early attachments and patriotism and nationalism, it is of interest to determine whether there are any differences between males and females in reported early attachment, in current attachment to and conflict with parents, and in their political feelings. From Table 11.6, it can be seen that whereas the males in this sample tend to be somewhat more liberal than the females, there are no sex differences on any of the patriotism–nationalism scales. With regard to early attachments, there is a tendency, approaching the .05 level of significance, for males to report greater attachment to their fathers than females. However, this difference does not obtain for current dependency-attachment feelings towards the father. At the same time, females report significantly greater current dependency-attachment feelings towards the mother than do males. This difference in the pattern of sex differences for early and current parent attachments suggests that these young

TABLE 11.6
Mean Differences Between Males and Females On Political and Attachment Scales

	Males	Females	t	p
Mother Attachment	4.1	4.2	1.01	NS
Father Attachment	3.7	3.4	1.86	<.07
Mother Dependency-Attachment	2.2	2.7	3.27	<.01
Father Dependency-Attachment	2.3	2.2	0.90	NS
Mother Conflict	1.9	2.0	.67	NS
Father Conflict	1.8	2.1	2.08	<.05
Patriotism	3.9	3.8	.93	NS
Nationalism	2.8	2.7	1.09	NS
Internationalism	3.6	3.8	1.39	NS
Civil Liberties	3.9	4.1	1.21	NS
World Government	2.7	2.9	0.86	NS
Conservative-Liberal*	3.7	3.4	1.75	<.10

* 1 = very conservative.
   6 = very liberal.

adults are differentiating between their early attachment experiences and their current attachment feelings and behaviors. It is also of interest that females report greater conflict with their fathers than do males. Another perspective on these patterns is provided by the differences in response to mothers versus fathers. As Table 11.7 indicates, both males and females report greater early attachment to their mothers than to their fathers, the difference for females being twice as great as that for males. However, there is no difference for males in the amount of dependency and attachment currently expressed toward mothers in comparison to fathers, whereas females report significantly greater current attachment to mothers than to fathers. Although females also report significantly greater conflict with their fathers than do males, the within group differences between conflict with mothers and conflict with fathers are not significant.

The data of major interest are the correlations between the attachment scales and the patriotism–nationalism scales. It can be seen from Table 11.8 that reports of early attachment to the mother do not correlate with either the patriotism or nationalism subscales. However, high early attachment to the mother is significantly and inversely correlated with prointernationalist and proworld government attitudes. Similar correlations between maternal attachment and the political scales were obtained for males and for females, and also when the sample was separated into liberals and conservatives; that is, the inverse relationship with internationalism and world government appears to be a robust finding. The correlations between the measure of early father attachment and the patriotism–nationalism scales are consistent with expectations. Young adults who report strong early feelings of attachment to their father also tend to have strong patriotic feelings. The correlation with nationalism is weaker and insignificant. Here too, comparable findings were obtained for males and females, although the correlation of .23 for females was not statistically significant. Also, whereas the correlation of early father attachment and patriotism was significant for

TABLE 11.7
Mean Differences Between Mother and Father Early Attachment, Dependence and Conflict
Scores for Males and Females

	Males			Females		
	Mean Differences (Mother-Father)	t	p	Mean Differences (Mother-Father)	t	p
Attachment (Early)	.40	3.21	.01	.83	5.21	<.0001
Dependency/ Attachment (Current)	-.10	1.04	NS	.58	3.43	<.01
Conflict (Current)	.11	1.29	NS	-.05	0.47	NS

TABLE 11.8
Intercorrelations Among Politcal and Attachment Scales

	(Early) F-Att.	M-Dep. Att.	F-Dep. Att.	M-Confl.	F-Confl.	Patriotism	Nationalism	Intern.	Civil Lib.	World Gov.
(Early) M-Att.	.16	.13	.20	-.36**	-.08	.07	.13	-.32**	-.11	-.31**
(Early) F-Att.		-.15	.56***	-.12	-.46***	.28*	.16	-.19	-.13	-.12
M-Dep. Att.			.29**	.15	.23*	.06	.02	.08	-.13	-.01
F-Dep. Att.				.18	-.11	.32**	.19	-.15	-.23*	-.14
M-Conflict					.54	.24*	.05	.08	-.03	-.11
F-Conflict						.01	-.05	.16	-.03	.07
Patriotism							.61***	-.26*	-.47***	-.35**
Nationalism								-.50***	-.64***	-.47***
Internationalism									.34**	.45***
Civil Liberties										.30**

liberals, it was not significant for conservatives. All of the correlations of early attachment to the father and patriotism are in the same direction, and it may be that the failure to achieve significance is due to the small Ns involved rather than to some functional difference between liberals and conservatives or males and females.

It may be noted that the measure of current attachment to the mother, with its strong dependency connotations, does not correlate with any of the political scales, indicating that there is a substantive difference in the construct being assessed by the early maternal attachment scale and the current maternal dependency–attachment measure. The nonsignificant correlation of .2 between these two measures is a more direct indicator that different variables are being assessed. This is not the case for the father dependency–attachment scale, the correlation of this scale with the patriotism–nationalism measures being very similar to those obtained with the early father attachment. In this instance, there is a very substantial correlation (.56) between early and current attachment. However, although these two scales clearly share a substantial amount of common variance, there are also some interesting differences in their correlates. Thus, the measure of current father attachment is unrelated to the amount of conflict reported with the father. However, there is a significant inverse correlation ($-.46$) between the reports of early father attachment and the measure of current father conflict. Interestingly, although a similar pattern of relationships is obtained between mother conflict scores and the measures of current and early attachment to the mother, conflict with the mother, rather than attachment to the mother, is positively correlated with patriotism.

There are also other data indicating that despite the strong correlation between the measures of early and current attachment to the father, the respondents are distinguishing between the nature of their relationship with their fathers in these two time periods. Thus, early father attachment has a nonsignificant negative relationship with current maternal attachment, whereas current father attachment has a small but significant positive relationship to current mother attachment; that is, young adults who feel currently attached to their father also display a tendency to be similarly attached to their mother, a relationship obtained for both males and females. However, there is a striking sex difference in the nature of the relationship found between *early* father attachment and *current* attachment to the mother. This relationship is significantly negative for females ($r = -.40$) and equally significantly positive ($+.41$) for males. Speculations as to the reasons for this intriguing difference would take us beyond the scope of this paper. Suffice it to say that the consequences of early father attachment appear to be different than those of early mother attachment, a theme to which we shall return. Another finding that tempts speculation is the difference between liberals and conservatives in the correlation between current attachment to the mother and current attachment to the father. The correlation between these two measures is .03 for liberals and .65 for those of conservative bent. Whether discrepant degrees of attachment tends to foster a liberal political attitude, or liberals make sharper distinction in their feelings towards their parents than do conservatives, or some third factor is mediating this difference in correlations cannot be ascertained from the present data. Liberals, incidentally, are the only subgroup to manifest a significant correlation between *nationalism* and attachment to the father, the correlation with current attachment to the father being .38 for liberals in comparison to .16 for conservatives. This difference may be a consequence of the greater association between nationalism and patriotism displayed by liberals as compared to conservatives, the respective correlations being .65 and .39.

CONCLUSIONS

To summarize these findings bearing on the relationship between attachment and indices of patriotism, nationalism, and internationalism, reports of both early and current attachment to the father are significantly correlated with patriotic feelings. Although there are some suggestions of a relationship between attachment to the father and nationalism in some populations, a positive relationship between father attachment and patriotism is consistently found. There are many features of the data that indicate that father attachment has different functional consequences than attachment to the mother. Early maternal attachment is unrelated to patriotism but is significantly inversely related to internationalism and proworld government attitudes, young adults reporting greater early maternal attachment tending to manifest more negative attitudes towards internationalism and world government than those reporting weaker early maternal attachment.

What is it about attachment to the father that may foster strong patriotic feelings, whereas attachment to the mother is unrelated to patriotic attitudes? In initiating this study, it was proposed that the reinforcements associated with early attachment to one's parents or caregivers would be replicated or vicariously experienced in subsequent attachment relationships with one's nation. However, this proposition appears to hold only for father attachment, perhaps indirectly holding for mother attachment in the inverse relationship obtained between mother attachment and internationalist and world government attitudes. What might it be about the attachment relationship to the father that makes that relationship uniquely correlated with patriotic impulses? The results of an item analysis in which the early father attachment scale was correlated with each of the items comprising the patriotism and nationalism scales suggests one possible response to this question. The item on the patriotism scale with the highest correlation (.37) reads as follows: "I feel a great pride in that land that is our America." Also correlating relatively highly are the items "I am proud to be an American" and the inversely scored item "It bothers me to see children made to pledge allegiance to the flag or sing the national anthem or otherwise induced to adopt such strong patriotic attitudes." These items all reflect the affect of pride in one's nation. It is of interest that items such as "I love my country" and "In a sense, I am emotionally attached to my country and emotionally effected by its actions" display only weak positive correlations with father attachment. The one item on the nationalism scale that correlated significantly with early father attachment, and incidentally had a loading of .21 on the patriotism scale, was "It is important that the U.S. win in international sporting competition like the Olympics." It seems fair to say that the dominance and power elements that are so characteristic of the other items on the nationalism scale are relatively weak for this item, whereas the pride element remains salient. This admittedly ad hoc analysis leads to the implication that an important feature of the reinforcement associated with early father attachment is the affect of pride. Presumably this is a less important feature of the reinforcement associated with early maternal attachment. That is, the children who felt attached to their father liked to be close to their father and spend time with him, because he made them feel good about themselves, whereas contact with the mother tended to elicit other positive affects. This interpretation would appear to be less applicable to the several distress items on the early attachment scale such as "Whenever I was upset, I found it easy to go to my father for comfort" or "When I hurt myself, my father would try to ease the pain." However, even here it is possible that fathers reassure the child in different ways than mothers, perhaps emphasizing the child's strengths and ability to cope with the distress. In contrast, feelings of warmth and security may be the primary reinforcement that children obtain in their attachment relationship with their mother. Investigations of attachment relationships in the preschool age child could provide evidence that directly bears on these admitted speculations. One could also argue that the warmth and security provided by the early attachment relationship with the mother may foster a reluctance to leave the "motherland" that may be entailed in prointernational, world government attitudes, although, frankly this interpretation appears to me as a little forced. Perhaps it is a linguistic factor such as motherland versus fatherland that mediates the relationship between attachment and patriotic–nationalistic attitudes, although this interpretation also strikes me as not very tenable.

This exploratory investigation has raised many more questions than it has resolved. There are differences suggested between attachment to the mother and attachment to the father that require explanation. It would be helpful to have large enough samples to permit contrasts between those who have strong attachment feelings towards one parent and weak attachment feelings toward the other. It would be helpful to be able to examine the patriotic–nationalistic attitudes of that small sample of individuals who report strong attachment feelings to their father but nevertheless describe his attributes in negative terms. Sex differences and liberal–conservative differences and the correlates of attachment also offer promising research issues to explore, as is the question of the relationship between early childhood and adolescent attachments to parents and the difference in the degree of this relationship that appears to obtain for males as compared to females.

However, the data do permit the overall conclusion that attachment relationships have wide ramifications for the individual's development and are even linked to the way in which the individual feels about his or her nation and other nations. Behavioral scientists know very little about the source of patriotic motivation and individual differences in this motivational area, despite the fact that patriotic motivations are among the most powerful of human motivations, indeed overriding at times the motivation for self-preservation. I would suggest that an important antecedent of differences in patriotic motivation are differences in early attachment. The data that have been reported on here are consistent with this hypothesis.

REFERENCES

Adorno, T. W., Frenkel-Brunswik, E., Levinson, D. J., & Sanford, R. N. (1950). *The authoritarian personality.* New York: Harper & Row.

Ainsworth, M. D. S., Blehar, M. C., Waters, E., & Wall, S. (1978). *Patterns of attachment.* Hillsdale, NJ: Laurence Erlbaum Associates.

Allport, F. H. (1927, August). The psychology of nationalism: The nationalistic fallacy as a cause of war. *Harper's Monthly Magazine,* pp. 291–301.

Blatt, S. J., & Lerner, H. (1983). Investigations in the psychoanalytic theory of object relations and object representations. In Joseph Masling (Ed.), *Empirical studies of psychoanalytic theories.* (Vol. 1, pp. 7–28). Hillsdale, NJ: Analytic Press.

Bowlby, J. (1969). *Attachment and love.* Volume 1. *Attachment.* New York: Basic.

Cairns, R. B. (1972). Attachment and dependency: A psychobiological and social learning synthesis. In J. L. Gewirtz (Ed.), *Attachment and dependency* (pp. 29–80). New York: Winston.

Carrington, H. B. (1970). *Beacon lights of patriotism.* Freedom, NY: Books for Libraries Press. (Original work published 1894).

Euripedes. (1948). Phoenissae 1,358 cited in *The home book of proverbs, maxims and familiar phrases.* New York: Macmillan.

George, C., Kaplan, N., & Main, M. (1985). *The attachment interview for adults.* Unpublished manuscript. University of California, Berkeley.

Gewirtz, J. L. (1972). Attachment, dependence and a distinction in terms of stimulus control. In J. L. Gewirtz (Ed.), *Attachment and dependency* (pp. 139–177) New York: Winston.

Hoffman, J. A. (1984). Psychological separation of late adolescents from their parents. *Journal of Counseling Psychology, 31,*(2), 170–178.

Klingberg, F. L. (1983). *Cyclical trends in American foreign policy moods: The unfolding of America's world role.* Lanham, MD: University Press of America.

Kosterman, R., & Feshbach, S. (1989). Toward a measure of patriotic and nationalistic attitudes. *Political Psychology, 10,* 257–274.

Levinson, D. J. (1957). Authoritarian personality and foreign policy. *Journal of Conflict Resolution, 1,* 37–47.

Mayman, M. (1968). Early memories and character structure. *Journal of Projective Techniques and Personality Assessment, 31,* 17–24.

Mead, G. H. (1929). National-mindedness and international-mindedness. *International Journal of Ethics, 39,* 385–407.

Marris, P. (1982). Attachment and society. In Colin M. Parkes & Joan Stevenson-Hinde (Eds.), *The place of attachment in human behavior* (pp. 185–201). New York: Basic.

Sroufe, L. A., & Waters, E. (1977). Attachment as an organizational construct. *Child Development, 48,* 1184–1199.

Weinraub, M., Brooks, J., & Lewis, M. (1977). The social network: A reconsideration of the concept of attachment. *Human Development, 20,* 31–47.

Weiss, R. S. (1982). Attachment in adult life. In Collin M. Parkes & Joan Stevenson-Hinde (Eds.), *The place of attachment in human behavior* (pp. 171–184). New York: Basic.

Winnicott, D. W. (1965). From dependence toward independence in the development of the individual. In *The maturational process and the facilitating environment* (pp. 83–12). New York: International Universities Press.

VI IDENTIFICATION AND ATTACHMENT

12

A Cognitive-Developmental Approach to Moral Attachment

Lawrence Kohlberg
Rhett Diessner

ABSTRACT

A cognitive-developmental approach to moral attachment is presented, subsuming processes commonly termed attachment and identification, and drawing on both James Mark Baldwin's theory of the imitative "ideal self" and Ausubel's theory of "satellization." Five components of attachment and five components of identification are described to form the moral self. Moral identification arises from (1) natural tendencies to imitate the parent or other model, (2) a desire to conform to the parent's normative expectations, (3) a perception of similarity to the parent (intensified by imitation), (4) a perception of the greater competence or higher status of the parent, and (5) an idealization of the parents' competence or virtue. Moral attachment is comprised of (1) an emotional dependency on parents and empathy with them, (2) vicarious self esteem derived from the parents' competence or status, (3) the ability to derive self esteem from the parent's approval and affection so as to forego other sources of success or competence, with associated security or self esteem, in the absence of direct signs of success, (4) reciprocity and complementarity in this relationship, and (5) a feeling of obligation to persons and relationships characterized by attachment processes. The relationships that characterize the attachment processes are not necessarily limited to the biological parent, but may be to any significant other. The moral attachment process begins in early childhood, usually with a parent as the object, develops with experience, advances in cognition in the 2- to 8-year age span, and later is found aimed toward admired others (e.g., peers, teachers, coaches). This concept of moral attachment attempts to supplement Kohlberg's structural-developmental stage theory of moral-judgment development with a theory of the moral self that Kohlberg deliberately excluded from his earlier work.

For the last 25 years, there have been three prevalent approaches to moral development. The most recent approach is that of situational social learning

229

theory initiated in the mid-1950s by Jack Gewirtz (1956, 1961, 1969, 1976) and others in relation to social dependency and attachment but extended to moral behavior by Burton (1976), Casey and Burton (1986), Gewirtz and Peláez-Nogueras (chapter 7, this volume), Mischel (Mischel & Mischel, 1976), and Bandura (1969, Bandura & MacDonald, 1963). An earlier approach is the structural-developmental approach initiated by Piaget (1932, 1965) and elaborated by Kohlberg (1958, 1984). The third and oldest tradition is the "socialization of character" approach usually based on neopsychoanalytic theory of attachment as integrated with a functional anthropological theory (Levine, 1982). There have been several important studies based on the neopsychoanalytic developmental character-type theories of Horney (Peck & Havighurst, 1960) and Fromm (1947, 1958), as well as the biographical studies by Erikson (1962, 1969) based on his neopsychoanalytic "functional" stage theory (Kohlberg, 1987).

All the above-mentioned approaches took as their point of departure Hartshorne's and May's (1928; Hartshorne, May, & Maller, 1929; Hartshorne, May & Shuttleworth, 1930) classic studies of the organization or consistency of moral behavior with regard to the "virtues" of honesty, service (prosocial behavior), and self-control, and the reactions to them. The results of Hartshorne's and May's monumental study disproved common sense assumptions about character and its basis, as first formulated by Aristotle in his *Ethics* (1962). Aristotle viewed character as a set of cognitively steered habits formed by guided opportunities to practice such virtuous conduct as honesty. Hartshorne and May found no consistent habits or behavioral virtues, and found that behaviors denoting honesty were not influenced by traditional "character education" (i.e., the preaching of virtue along with the opportunity to practice these virtues in public schools, churches, or Boy Scout organizations). They concluded that moral behavior represented situational conformity to classroom or group norms, and to the contingencies of social reinforcement like those elaborated by B. F. Skinner and J. L. Gewirtz. A review of Hartshorne's and May's initial assumptions, findings, and conclusions is presented in Kohlberg (1984, chapter 7; 1987 chapter 7).

As his point of departure, Kohlberg (1958) took several considerations into account. These included Hartshorne's and May's failure to find character and its determinants as initially assumed by them; American concerns in the tradition stemming from Aristotle; the replication of neopsychoanalytic studies done in the 1950s of Hartshorne's and May's findings of the situational specificity of "resistance to temptation" or "prosocial behavior"; and their failure to find consistent correlates between child-rearing practices, protective measures of "superego strength," and moral behavior (Kohlberg, 1963, 1964).

Accordingly in 1958, Kohlberg decided to focus on the development of moral judgment in the stage-structural tradition and to relate it to conduct, first through teacher behavior ratings and comparisons of delinquent with nondelinquent adolescents (Kohlberg, 1958), and later through a variety of other studies (reviewed by Blasi, 1980; Kohlberg, 1984, chapter 7). Following Piaget (1932/1965), this structural-developmental approach to moral judgment has systematically ignored the "self" or "ego" in favor of a rational-epistemic or moral subject. It is from the prescriptive judgments to hypothetical dilemmas of that rational-epistemic subject that a stage progression can be reconstructed rationally (Kohlberg, 1984, chapter 3). Such a hypothetical epistemic subject is the author of the moral judgments offered in response to hypothetical dilemmas (Colby & Kohlberg, 1987), responses philosophers term "deontic" judgments (i.e., of rightness, duty, and justice). In order to link stages of deontic judgment to observations of moral conduct, we have found it necessary to postulate judgments of responsibility in addition to deontic judgments (Kohlberg, 1984, chapter 7). Having such a judgment of rightness or justice, the moral actor must make a further judgment of the self's responsibility to act in accordance with this deontic judgment of justice. Presumably a judgment of responsibility to act morally also implies a judgment of guilt (or shame) at failure to carry out the act for which the actor is responsible.

The idea of a judgment of responsibility points in two directions that go beyond structural deontic judgment. First, responsibility is defined by membership in a social community that has shared or collective norms that the actor is expected to uphold and for which he is the subject of group sanction for failure and of group solidarity for success. This direction, that of neo-Durkheimian anthropological theory, has been applied to our research in school communities and the moral atmosphere and collective norms of the school or community (Higgins, Power, & Kohlberg, 1984; Kohlberg, 1987; Power, Higgins, & Kohlberg, 1989).

The second direction in which our study of moral responsibility and moral action carries us is to the resurrection of the notion of moral character, conceived as the development of the ego or the "moral self." The moral self is the subjective side of the organization or unity of moral behavior postulated by the notion of character. It is the sense of the self's "integrity" or "identity" that becomes at stake in moral action. This is the core of Erikson's (1962) idea of Martin Luther's identity in his statement, "Here I stand, I can do no other" (Blasi, 1984, 1985). In Erikson's terms, prior to moral identity is moral identification, which Erikson interprets in classical Freudian terms of the resolution of the Oedipal conflict through superego function.

A review of a vast body of research on parent–child relations, conscious and unconscious guilt, and moral behavior has failed to confirm the usefulness of classical Freudian superego theory as a general account of moral character (Kohlberg, 1963, 1964). In this paper, we elaborate an alternative theory of the formation of the moral self and the birth of the sense of responsibility based on three sources. The first source is the theories of the moral self of the American symbolic interactionists: J. M. Baldwin (1906), John Dewey (1939), and G. H. Mead (1934). The second source is the neo-psychoanalytic character-typological theories or schools of ego or self-development of Ausubel (Ausubel, Sullivan, & Ives, 1980), Loevinger (1976), and Kohut (1977). The third source is Piaget's

(1932/1965) theory of moral development before he developed a "pure structural approach."

My colleagues and I have written a general introduction to the social-self theories of Baldwin and Mead (Kohlberg, Hart, & Wertsch, 1987). In the present paper, we focus on the child's relations to adults in the years two to eight, the period of the formation of a moral self and a sense of moral responsibility in the theories of Baldwin, Mead, Ausubel, Kohut, and Piaget, as well as the period of superego formation in Freudian theory. Our theory shares with Freudian theory a concern with identification in the formation of the moral self or ego, but construes identification in a very different way than does a Freudian theory of unconscious drives and defenses. It also shares with Freudian theory a concern with love or attachment to parents as related to the development of the moral self, but again in a very different form than the Freudian theory of superego formation.

DEPENDENCY, ATTACHMENT, AND THE MORAL SELF

"Love" or "attachment" or social dependence are seen as arising from what White (1959) called primary competence motivation or motivation for self-esteem as is identification, rather than from primary drives or need gratification (or its frustration) as is held by psychoanalytic theory and in a much weaker sense by ethological theories of attachment like that of Bowlby (1969). The young child's sense of dependence or attachment to the parents and significant others arises, because his self is socially constructed from imitation and idealization of the parent (Baldwin, 1906) and from the social or communicative interaction between self and other in which the self, the "me," is constructed by taking the perspective of the other on the self (Mead, 1934).

Dependency and attachment are not in themselves moral. One can be dependent on a significant other or a group without feeling responsibility to either conform to the expectations of the other or to enhance the other's welfare. In the symbolic interactionist theories of Baldwin (1906), Mead (1934), Dewey (1939), and Royce (1982), in Piaget's theory (1932/1965, 1936/1952), and in Ausubel's (Ausubel et al., 1980) work, however, dependency or attachment typically develop into a sense of moral responsibility to the other that we call moral attachment. Part of moral attachment is what Piaget calls unilateral moral respect (a "sui generis" mixture of fear of superior power and affection"). Another part, however, is attachment and dependence per se, a factor stressed by symbolic interactionists as well as by Gilligan (1982). According to G. H. Mead (1934) morality is the sense of dependence on the society or group to which we belong.

THE ROLE OF IMITATION IN THE MORAL SELF

To understand the concept of a moral self, it will be helpful to explicate what has been termed the Baldwin–Kohlberg view of the developmental self (Broughton

& Freeman-Moir, 1982; Lee, 1982). Baldwin's (1906) view of the creation and development of the self is based on his understanding and elaboration of the role of imitation. It is imitation that allows a child to move from the most primitive stage of selfhood to Baldwin's (1906) second stage, the subjective stage:

> Observation of children shows that the instrument of transition from such a projective to a subjective sense of personality is the child's active bodily self, and the method of it is the *function of imitation* . . . , and of course he imitates persons. (p. 13–14)

In the first of Baldwin's three early stages, the projective, the child discovers its own body (i.e., the reflexes, movement, senses) and differentiates humans from physical objects in the environment. Imitation arises with the growth of "effort" or "volition" and the "subjective" stage is born (cf. Piaget's description of his son's effort to imitate him, stage 3, secondary circular reactions of the sensorimotor period, 1936/1952). Others interest the child, and she makes efforts to capture and copy novel behaviors of others, while simultaneously experiencing the feelings associated with the observed event. The child is aware of herself as an individual and the distinctiveness of her own body. Thus, the child then enters a third stage in which she has noticed that her subjectiveness also exists in others, what Baldwin calls the "ejective" stage. Baldwin (1906) wrote:

> The "ego" and the "alter" are thus born together . . . My sense of myself grows by imitation of you, and my sense of yourself grows in terms of my sense on myself. Both *ego* and *alter* are thus essentially social; each is a *socius* and each is an imitative creation. This give-and-take between the individual and his fellows, looked at generally, we may call the *Dialectic of Personal Growth*. (p. 15)

Regarding this dialectic, Kohlberg (in Kohlberg, Hart, & Wertsch, 1987) stated, "Since the evolution of self-understanding is interdependent with the understanding of the other, the two types of understanding are identical" (p. 232). It is due to this self–other parallelism that imitation leads to identification, and identification allows attachment, which itself allows moral attachment to be coconstructed through child–parent and then child–peer interactions.

MORAL ATTACHMENT RELATED TO MORAL SELF-DEVELOPMENT

Following Piagetian structuralism's focus on "the rational epistemic subject," Kohlberg's approach has ignored: (a) moral content of development as opposed to structure, (b) moral motivation as opposed to moral reasoning, and most fundamentally (c) the existence and function of a moral self. In this paper, we shall elaborate a cognitive-developmental theory of the role of childhood moral attachment to parents in founding the moral self based on the social-self theories of J. M. Baldwin (1906) and D. Ausubel (Ausubel et al., 1980).

The processes that lead to moral development in Kohlberg's structural approach have been defined as involved in any sociomoral interaction, regardless of the special nature of the relationship or the tie to the specific other person. These processes include the basic conditions of moral development: exposure to internal cognitive moral conflict; exposure to disagreement between persons (in the content and structure of their reasons); and more generally in the extent to which the person has role-taking opportunities, conditions for taking the perspective, feelings, and claims of the others on moral issues of conflict. These general processes of role-taking and dialogue have been shown to be effective in naturalistic, experimental, and educational studies in childhood and adolescence (Kohlberg, 1984). In addition to these general processes, there is, however, a process influencing moral learning and development based on a specific relationship to other persons, most typically the parents and later peers and friends. We shall call this process or disposition *moral attachment*. It includes certain features that have sometimes been called identification, although our concept of moral attachment does not involve a Freudian concept of identification but rather emphasizes the processes of basic imitation and of perceived likeness to the parents as part of moral attachment. From the cognitive-developmental point of view, identification is: (a) a generalized tendency to imitate across relatively long periods of time and (b) a very specific other with whom one has a salient relationship and, in that sense, an attachment. This cognitive-developmental notion of identification differs from behavioral social learning theories like that of Gewirtz (1971a, 1971b, and chapter 13 in this volume) in that it leads to the disposition to "internalize," or learn and maintain, without the continuing availability of reinforcement for behavior, the moral values and expectations of the model. Identification in our view rests on a sense of sharing or having recognized a *shared self* (i.e., a perceived likeness between self and other), not of specific behaviors but of a holistic self or constellation of feelings and actions. Attachment in our view also rests on a perception of a shared self, as we shall elaborate. The interrelations of identification and attachment are part of what is involved in the development of moral attachment. Their common source is a sense of a shared self of the child with the parent, who is also seen as more competent or powerful than the child, as is stressed in the social-self theories of J. M. Baldwin (1906) and D. Ausubel (Ausubel et al., 1980).

The concept of moral attachment also has relationship to Gewirtz's (1961, 1969, 1972a, 1972b, 1976; chapters 7 and 13 this volume; Gewirtz & Boyd, 1977) social conditioning theory of attachment as a control process whereby the parent's appearance and behavioral characteristics provide cues and reinforcing stimuli for the child's social behavior. In this connection, we stress that moral attachment is the disposition of the child's behavior to be sensitive to the social reinforcement contingencies, in particular approval and disapproval of the parents. Stressed by our conception, but not by social learning theory, is that the child sees himself as having limited competency or status relative to his parents and, therefore, feels dependent on some more derivative or vicarious source of self-esteem than is provided by his own unaided efforts. Ausubel (Ausubel et al., 1980) called this process of seeking vicarious self-esteem through relation to, and attaining the approval and affection of, the parent "satellization." The term satellization implies that the child has come to feel that his own value is tied into a relationship with someone of greater competence and power. Such vicarious esteem is based not only on the greater competence and power of the parent, a feature they share with other adults, but on the child's perception of a unique relationship to his parents, a relationship of inclusion in the same family and a sense of perceived similarity and sharing among members of the family. We previously discussed imitation and perceived-likeness processes sometimes called identification as one central basis of moral attachment. Here we should note that the perceived-likeness component is also involved in a second, central basis of moral attachment, vicarious self-esteem or sensitivity to parental approval and affection. This sensitivity to parental approval and affection, according to Piaget, begins in the first two years and stems from imitation of the parents, and later from the resulting sense of obligation to the parents. Piaget (1965) wrote:

> There seems to be no doubt that the feelings of authority and respect appear during the first two years, before language, as soon as the little creature has discovered in the big person someone like himself and yet infinitely greater than himself. The feelings compounded of sympathy and fear resulting from this situation explain why the child accepts the examples and, as soon as he has mastered language, the commands coming from his parents, and why, to the simple fact of imitation, there comes so early to be added the feeling of rules and obligation. (p. 378)

When a moral attachment (moral satellization) has been developed, the child's self-esteem does not only derive directly from his/her own performance successes but also from the parent's positive evaluation of the child's performances through expression of either approval or affection. This disposition to define self-esteem in terms of parental approval and affection in turn implies that the child seeks vicarious self-esteem. An additional element of moral attachment implied in the vicarious self-esteem process is that of idealization of the parents. Idealization implies an exaggerated or "bigger than life" notion of the parent's competence, status, and/or virtue. This process of moral attachment is not so much revealed in the development of stages of moral reasoning and judgment as in the formation of a moral self. In part, this sociomoral self is represented by *specific* value content related to the expectations and values of the person to whom the child is morally attached. In part, it is represented in general moral dispositions, as well as in moral reasoning and judgment. The central moral disposition resulting from the formation of a moral self we believe to be a sense of moral responsibility as reflected in the feeling of necessity to act in terms of the self's moral judgments and standards, and the capacity to feel guilt or shame for violation of those standards, and esteem for fulfilling them.

The formation of the moral self, or what may be called "moral internalization," is in part the product of the components we have listed, in particular: (a) imitation, (b) perceived similarity to the parent, (c) sensitivity to parental approval for moral behavior, and (d) idealization of the parent. In addition to these processes forming a moral self, moral attachment involves a disposition toward special obligation or responsibility to the parents' welfare, their expectations, and to the maintenance of the relationship itself. Both children and adults feel general obligation to persons with whom they do not have special relationships. However, the obligations felt toward special relationships are particularly unique and strong. It is the perceived likeness and imitation and its derivatives, shared valuing, sensitivity to approval, vicarious self-esteem, and idealization as processes leading to the formation of a moral self. The feeling of obligation to a special relationship is an additional component of moral attachment and the formation of a moral self. Ausubel (1980) called this moral constellation as follows:

> Motivated interiorization or identification. Identification, therefore, is a motivated form of imitation in which both the *interpersonal relationship* (direct or fantasied) between imitator and imitatee and the imitated act itself are highly significant. . . . Identification implies an underlying motive in one persons' acceptance of another's values. et al, (p. 311)

Following Piaget, we stress that reciprocity is an additional but later occurring cognitive component of moral attachment. Reciprocity has been particularly stressed by Piaget and his followers as a component of friendship and peer relationships. Reciprocity, or "the reciprocity of complement," is also a key element in relation to parents and in moral attachment. The sense that "parents have done a lot for you" and "you should do something for them" is central in this thinking of both parents and children. Prior to this reciprocity that leads to attachment, Piaget (1932/1965) also emphasized the idealization process that comes about due to the bigger-than-life view that the child has regarding the parent: "Such is the prestige of parents in the eyes of the very young child, that even if they lay down nothing in the form of general duties, their wishes act as law" (p. 187). In the parent's very wishes becoming law to the child (i.e., the tendency to conform to parent's normative expectations), we see an element of moral identification.

At a much earlier and more basic level, a moral component of relationship is implied by the child's empathy and affection for the parent, which generates a concern for the welfare of the parent. We should point out that empathy implies perceived likeness between the self and the other, the perception of the parents as another self. Affection as liking as an element added to empathy overlaps with the valuing of the parent already described in terms of vicarious self-esteem as well as representing a form of reciprocity in the seeking of affection. Without gratitude or obligation, there is an early simultaneous reciprocity of gestures of affection between parent and child.

COMPONENTS OF MORAL ATTACHMENT

We have outlined an interrelated double cluster that logically goes together to form the moral self. It includes the following components:

Identification

1. Tendencies to imitate the parent or other model.
2. Tendency to conform to the parent's normative expectations.
3. Perceived similarity to the parent, which is enhanced by imitation.
4. Perception of the greater competence or higher status of the parent.
5. Idealization of the parent and/or of his/her competence and virtue.

Attachment

1. Emotional dependency, affection, and empathy with the parent.
2. Vicarious self-esteem derived from the parent's competence or status.
3. Ability to derive self-esteem from the parent's approval and affection so as to forego other sources of success, prestige or competence, with associated security or self-esteem, in the absence of direct signs of success.
4. Reciprocity or complementarity in relationships.
5. Feeling of obligation to persons and relationships characterized by attachment processes.

It should be noted that the components of this constellation represent an overlapping of two global constructs generally recognized in the literature as identification and attachment–dependency. Although we have dichotomized these ten components, they clearly are interrelated and reciprocally enhance one another.

These components are not in themselves necessarily moral dispositions. As a cluster leading to the development of a moral self and of moral obligation to the parents, they can, however, be called moral attachment.

Different combinations of these components of moral attachment can be found in responses to questions we have asked preadolescent boys and girls about being like their parents and/or about their ideals. One boy, aged 12, when asked about his father, responded: "I'd like to be like my father, because I think of him as nice, and I was brought up by him and learned the things he taught me so I could be a good boy, because he always taught me to be good." This boy expresses the disposition to follow moral expectations of his father: (a) this is part of a more general disposition to be like or imitate his father; (b) this desire to be like or imitate the father in the future is based on perceived present likeness to the father and perceived imitative learning—"I have learned to be good from him, I am good like him;" (c) it is also based on the perceived competence or virtue of the father; and (d) at least a mild idealization of the father's virtue.

Other aspects of moral attachment are demonstrated in response to the same question from the following boy aged 15: "I try to do things for my parents; they've always done things for you. I try to do everything my mother says. . . . Like she wants me to be a doctor, and I want to too." He also expresses his sense of moral obligation or responsibility to his parents: "I try to do things for my parents." He then links this to reciprocity: "They've always done things for you."

When we asked a 15-year-old girl, "Are there any particular people or experiences that have made a strong impact on the kind of person you are?" she responded with a mixture of identification and attachment cluster variables:

"Well, my mother is a single parent, she works. So I look up to her, because she is doing it on her own. She's not looking for nobody to take care of her, and let's say she's going out with someone and she doesn't like what he's doing, she gives him the boot, you know. She's not out for that. She's mature. She's not wanting no hassles. So, I look up to her. She thinks for herself. She doesn't care what other people say about her. As long as its not overboard, you know, or when she gets her attitude. . . . She has her own values, you know, and she tries to pass them on to me, and she raised me good. I think she raised me good, and she's alright . . . one of her values, she likes to think before she does anything. She tells me to think before I act or talk and make sure I'm doing it for the right reason or saying it for the right reason."

Here again is found the tendency to imitate the person that she identifies with and a perception of similarity with the parent. Implied is both an idealization of the parent and the parent's greater competency and status.

Another 15-year-old girl was asked the same question ("Who has had a strong impact on the kind of person you are?"), and she made references to both her father and her mother. Regarding her father, she said, "My father would be the kind where he would like sit you down, talk about 'why did you do it'. . . . I'm like my father in the sense that I like to talk about things;" About her mother, she said, "She lets me talk. If we have an argument, she lets me argue with her, because she's like, 'If you have something to say, then say it.' She tells me how she feels about it, and I'm like her, because I tell people how I feel about certain things." Implied in these quotes is the reciprocity that the attached adolescent seeks with her parents. Also evident is the perceived similarity to the parent, which is enhanced by imitation. This was further highlighted, when she was asked about her ideals of the good person, and she said, "I'd like to be open with my children and let them talk to me and treat them mature so that they can act mature."

This same issue of reciprocity in communication, based on the imitation/identification cluster, is found in a seventeen-year-old boy. When responding to the question about who had a strong impact on him, he said:

"Well, my parents are always a strong influence. . . . My mother, she's very reasonable, and she and I can argue with each other. If I don't agree with her, I can tell her, you know, and she'll listen to what I say, and, you know, I think she's helped me to have patience with other people, to try to reason with them. If they're being unreasonable, just don't say, 'Forget it, its my opinion, that's the way it is.' You have to reason it out, and you have to talk and accept their opinions, even if you disagree."

In these quotations, we see several of the ten components of moral attachment interwoven. Empirical studies (Ausubel et al., 1980; Kohlberg, 1963) suggest correlates among these components that represent a logical cluster. These correlates include liking of parents, perceived similarity to parents, and awarding of authority and competence to the parents; they are all related to acceptance of the conventional moral code or of parental moral expectations, and to self-report measures of adjustment (evidence reviewed in Kohlberg, 1963, 1984).

The development of the constellation we call moral attachment to parents has been thought of by Ausubel et al. (1980) and Baldwin (1906) to first develop between the ages of two and seven, but it seems to be found developing toward mentors in adolescence and adulthood. A familiar case is the moral attachment of a student with a teacher of the same sex. Such relations are based on the competence and interest value of the teacher's behavior generating a desire to be like, or to be in a role like, the teacher, which in turn generates a need to share his normative attitudes and obtain his guidance, approval, and so forth. It generally encompasses a relation of particular moral obligation and of reciprocal concern for the welfare of one another. An example of this type of attachment also comes from a Moral-Self Interview we have been administering in our current research in Just Communities in the Bronx, New York. When we asked a 19-year-old male youth about "whether there are particular people or experiences that have made a strong impact on the kind of person you are," he said:

"My teacher at school. He told me I'm one of his best pupils. I never cut his class; I always got my homework done; I'm never late; I'm always here; I always do what I should in class; I always do my job. So my teacher likes me because of that, I always do what I'm supposed to do."

A somewhat different case of moral attachment in adolescence is discussed at length elsewhere (Kohlberg & Higgins, 1987). This is moral attachment to a group or "moral community," a process postulated by Durkheim (1961) and Lewin (1952) to lead to moral value "internalization," and by J. M. Baldwin (1906) to development of the moral self. This process includes conformity to the group's norms or expectations based on the following components of moral attachment listed: (1) perceived similarity between the self and other members of the group, (2) perception of the competence or status of the group, (3) idealization of the group, (4) vicarious self-esteem derived from the group or for membership in the group, (5) ability to derive self-esteem from the group's approval, (6) reciprocity or complementarity in group relationships. During a Moral Self Interview, a 16-year-old female demonstrated this attachment to the group. She said:

> "In RCS [the Just Community], being a good person is respecting them, in both cases [those you agree with and those you don't]. Be polite, respect people's opinions. Don't pass judgments on other people. You know, and you do what you are supposed to. Let's say they tell you to be quiet or something: you do it, if you are a good person. If you are a good person, you do it in RCS. Also, you pay attention. You follow the rules in both cases. You follow, and you try to be your best that you can."

Of critical importance to the social psychological understanding of attachment to the group is group cohesion, solidarity, or sharing. As stated in social psychology, a social attachment or bond is conceived of as a relation of sharing, communication, and cooperation (or reciprocity) between selves—each recognizing the other selves as alike in general (because all are selves), and as particular or unique (i.e., as having a shared identity distinct from that of other groups or relations). In social psychology, particularly the social psychology of Durkheim, attachment to the group is intrinsically moral. The centrality of a behavior or a norm to group cohesion makes it obligatory or moral. Obviously this view is problematic philosophically in that it is socially relativistic, and the norms central to the cohesion of Nazi Germany were not moral from a philosophic point of view. From a purely social science point of view, however, it is warranted to view such attachment to the group as moral attachment. Obviously the same problem exists with relation to moral attachment to parents, which may not be morally justified from a philosophic point of view.

Given the constellation of components we earlier called moral attachment, which leads to the development of a moral self, a cognitive-developmental psychologist might ask, "Is there any invariant sequence in the development of these components or any centrality to one of them?" In exploring this question, we stand with the social-self theory of James Mark Baldwin (1906). As more recent research supported (Meltzoff & Moore, 1977), Baldwin held that in very early infancy there were "spontaneous" tendencies to imitation, tendencies not dependent on either homeostatic drives/needs or reinforcement contingencies. Piaget accepts this point of view from Baldwin, making imitation a spontaneous functional activity of accommodation and defining stages of imitation in the first two years of life. These Piagetian stages viewed imitation as a progression from the temporary and specific, toward the lasting and more general—close to the process termed identification in much of the literature. Alternatively, our view is that the movement from temporary, specific imitation to more pervasive imitation that we (and Gewirtz, chapter 13 this volume) term identification is a cognitive-developmental stage process. The development of imitation into identification involves more than Piagetian stage movements through levels of the stability and generality of imitation. According to Baldwin, it involves the development of a sense of a shared self.

Baldwin (1906) proposed:

> The growth of the individual's self-thought, upon which his social development depends, is secured all the way through by a twofold exercise of the imitative function. He reaches his subjective understanding of the social copy of imitation, and then he confirms his interpretations by another imitative act by which he ejectively leads his self-thought into the persons of others. (p. 527)

Baldwin's central claim (made also by Mead, 1934) is that the child's self-concept and his concept of other selves necessarily grow in one-to-one correspondence. The child cannot observationally learn the behavior pattern of another without putting it in the manifold of possible ways of acting open to the self. Once it becomes something the self might do, when others do it, they too are ascribed the subjective attitudes connected with the self's performance of the act.

As Baldwin (1906) stated:

> What the person thinks as himself is a pole or terminus at one end of an opposition in the sense of personality generally, and that the other pole or terminus is the thought he has of the other person, the 'alter'. . . . What he calls himself now is in large measure an incorporation of elements that, at an earlier period of his thought of personality he called someone else. . . . For example, last year I thought of my friend W. as a man who had great skill on a bicycle and who wrote readily on the typewriter. . . . But now this year I have learned to do both these things. I have taken the elements formerly recognized in W.'s personality, and by imitative learning taken them over to myself. . . . And further, all the things I hope to learn, to acquire, to become are . . . now, before I acquire them, possible elements of my thought of others. . . . But we should also note that what has been said of the one pole of this dialectical relation, the pole of the self, is equally true of the other also—the pole represented by the other person, the alter. . . . I must construe him, a person, in terms of what I think of myself, the only person whom I know in the

intimate way we call "subjective." I cannot say that my thought of my friend W. is exhausted by the movements of wheel-riding and typewriting; nor by any collection of such acts, considered for themselves. Back of it all there is the attribution of the very fact of subjectivity which I have myself. . . . I constantly enrich the actions which were at first his alone, and then became mine by imitation of him, with the meaning, the rich subjective value, the interpretation in terms of private ownership, which my appropriation of them . . . has enabled me to make. (pp. 15–18)

According to Baldwin, thus, there are two intertwined mechanisms of society, of sharing. The first is imitation of the other, the second is "ejection" (i.e., empathy or "projection" of one's own subjective feelings into the other). Imitation of the other not only leads to a changed self-concept (e.g., a self who rides the bicycles), but it leads to a changed concept of the other, because the activity (bicycle riding) has a new meaning after it is done by the self, and this meaning is read back as part of the other.

We have elaborated Baldwin's view that imitation is early and spontaneous (i.e., not a result of contingencies of reinforcement by the model or social dependency on the model). In his view and ours, it may be elicited by the components of moral attachment: perceived similarity to the parent, competence or status of the parent, and idealization of the parent. This cognitively developing structure of imitation becomes "identification" in the years two to seven. This means that the following exist: (a) a perception of global sharedness or likeness between the self of the child and the parent; and (b) that there is a generally tendency to conform to or imitate the standards of the parent who is thought by the child to know and do what is right, competent, or virtuous.

Once identification has developed, it generates in turn the components of social dependency and sensitivity to social reinforcement and approval that are among the components of moral attachment. Once the parent is established as the authority or guide for imitative behaviors, then approval and affection from the parent have reinforcing value for the child's imitative (and other) behavior.

The sequence we have just proposed, based on Baldwin's thesis, is close to the reverse of that which has been postulated by a number of neopsychoanalytic theories, or integrations of social conditioning, social learning, and psycho-analytic theories reviewed elsewhere (Kohlberg, 1969) (excluding the theories of Gewirtz, 1969; Gewirtz & Stingle, 1968). In these views, the child's attachment and social dependency on the parent is an antecedent or prerequisite of identification with the parent. In the early thinking of Bowlby, appropriate early attachment to parents, especially the mother, was necessary for moral character to develop and to prevent delinquency.

MOTIVATION

We turn finally to what is often treated as the problem of motivation. In one sense, moral attachment sets the stage for what may be seen as a motivation for moral action. This is implied by the notion that moral attachment leads to the formation of a moral self with moral obligations to parents and parental standards. This sense of obligation to the human foci of attachment precedes and induces a sense of responsibility and resulting commitment to moral action regarding those obligations. The sense of responsibility and the commitment to moral action, however, presuppose a more general motivational system that we have termed the *self*. There are, we believe, two components of this system.

The first component is what Robert White (1959) called "competence" or "effectance motivation" and Piaget has called the functional tendencies to assimilation and accommodation. This involves the primary disposition to do things that are interesting, powerful, competent, or causally effective. Such a disposition is involved in early imitation (Kohlberg, 1969). In this sense, the usual notions of motivation are ignored; the organism is active and does not require drives or needs to engage in action. Action is steered cognitively by characteristics of persons, activities, and objects such as being interesting, competent and so forth. The second component of the motivational system we have termed the *self* is a primary tendency to value the self, commonly called a concern for self-esteem. The interest and competence of an activity or person are not only naturally valued, but they are perceived in relation to a self that is of central interest and value to the infant. There is no reason to term such self-valuing narcissism except within a drive theory of motivation. The primacy of such self-valuing is preserved by the notion we developed following Ausubel (Ausubel et al., 1980), that identification and attachment are related to one another and rested on the phenomenon of vicarious self-esteem.

In our stage structure research, we have been able to show that much action involving choice between two norms is predicted and explained by moral reasoning (i.e., by the relative perceived adequacy of the reasons for following one norm over another) (Kohlberg, 1984), what could be termed deontic action. Other moral action, however, involves a conflict between self-interest or valuing the self (and its success prestige and private or egoistic goals), and what we have called the moral self and its integrity or consistency (Blasi, 1984), which may be viewed as a motivational system. This system, as we have held, emanates from moral attachment, a process resting on primary self-valuation or effectance.

CONCLUSIONS

We have discussed a developmental sequence and cluster of imitation leading to identification leading to moral attachment. In the sense in which this attachment cluster leads to a creation of the "contents" and "motivation" of the moral self, it should be considered moral attachment. Those contents that the self comes to value morally is what it has interiorized (Ausubel et al., 1980) through the processes of imitation and identification of those to whom it has become attached: parents, mentors, and groups (i.e., attachment objects/foci—we do not discuss peer attachment; see Youniss & Smollar, 1985). Imitation and identification lead to conformance to parents normative expectations through the perception of similarity to the attachment foci (shared self), a perception of the greater competence of the parent/mentor/group attachment, and consequent idealization of their virtue.

The motivation to act morally comes from the attachment cluster of the following: (a) empathy with the object(s) of attachment, (b) the vicarious self-esteem derived from identification with the idealized moral virtue of the attachment object(s), and (c) feelings of obligation to persons and relationships to whom the self is attached. These features of the motivation to act morally can be considered to be a balance between effectance motivation and self-valuation (self-esteem).

We have argued that the concept of attachment is enhanced by the cognitive-developmental view that stresses that imitation is a cognitive act. Imitation is the first "stage" of attachment and leads the way to identification. Identification is a second stage in which imitation qualitatively changes from an interchange of concrete and specific acts to that of generalized and symbolic interaction. We represented this move as critical for the cognitive internalization of Mead's (1934) "generalized other" or Baldwin's (1906) idealized "socius." The result of identification evolves into moral attachment and a third stage, the creation of a moral self.

REFERENCES

Aristotle (1962). *Nichomachean Ethics* (M. Ostwald, Trans.). Indianapolis: Bobbs-Merrill.

Ausubel, D. P., Sullivan, E. V., & Ives, S. W. (1980). *Theory and problems of child development* (3rd ed, pp. 169–199). New York: Grune & Stratton.

Baldwin, J. M. (1906). *Social and ethical interpretations in mental development.* New York: Macmillan.

Bandura, A. (1969). Social-learning theory of identificatory processes. In D. A. Goslin (Ed.), *Handbook of socialization theory and research* (pp. 213–262). Chicago: Rand McNally.

Bandura, A., & MacDonald, F. (1963). The influence of social reinforcement and the behavior of models in shaping children's moral judgments. *Journal of Abnormal and Social Psychology, 67,* 274–282.

Blasi, A. (1980). Bridging moral cognition and moral action: A critical review of the literature. *Psychological Bulletin, 88,* 1–45.

Blasi, A. (1984). Moral identity: Its role in moral functioning. In W. M. Kurtines & J. L. Gewirtz (Eds.), *Morality, moral behavior, and moral development* (pp. 128–139). New York: Wiley.

Blasi, A. (1985). The moral personality; Reflections for social science and education. In M. W. Berkowitz & F. Oser (Eds.), *Moral education.* Hillsdale NJ: Lawrence Erlbaum Associates.

Bowlby, J. (1969). *Attachment and loss. Volume 1: Attachment.* London: Hogarth (New York: Basic Books).

Broughton, J. M., & Freeman-Moir, D. J. (Eds.). (1982). *The cognitive developmental psychology of James Mark Baldwin.* Norwood, NJ: Ablex.

Burton, R. V. (1976). Honesty and dishonesty. In T. Lickona (Ed.), *Moral development and behavior* (pp. 173–197). New York: Holt, Rinehart & Winston.

Casey, W. M., & Burton, R. V. (1986). The social-learning theory approach. In G. Sapp (Ed.), *Handbook of moral development* (pp. 74–91). Birmingham, AL: Religious Education Press.

Colby, A., & Kohlberg, L. (1987). *The measurement of moral judgment*. New York: Cambridge University Press.

Dewey, J. (1939). *Intelligence in the modern world* (J. Ratner, Ed.). New York: Random House.

Durkheim, E. (1961). *Moral education: A study in the theory and application of the sociology of education.* New York: Free Press.

Erikson, E. (1962). *Young man Luther.* New York: Norton.

Erikson, E. (1969). *Gandhi's truth.* New York: Norton.

Fromm, E. (1947). *Man for himself: An inquiry into the psychology of ethics.* Greenwich, CT: Fawcett.

Fromm, E. (1958). *The sane society.* New York: Rinehart.

Gewirtz, J. L. (1956). A program of research on the dimensions and antecedents of emotional dependence. *Child Development, 27,* 205–221.

Gewirtz, J. L. (1961). A learning analysis of the effects of normal stimulation, privation, and deprivation on the acquisition of social motivation and attachment. In B. M. Foss (Ed.), *Determinants of infant behaviour* (pp. 213–299). London: Methuen.

Gewirtz, J. L. (1969). Mechanisms of social learning: Some roles of stimulation and behavior in early human development. In D. A. Goslin (Ed.), *Handbook of socialization theory and research* (pp. 57–212). Chicago: Rand McNally.

Gewirtz, J. L. (1972a). Attachment, dependence, and a distinction in terms of stimulus control. In J. L. Gewirtz (Ed.), *Attachment and dependency* (pp. 139–177). Washington, DC: Winston.

Gewirtz, J. L. (1976). The attachment acquisition process as evidenced in the maternal conditioning of cued infant responding (particularly crying). *Human Development, 19,* 143–155.

Gewirtz, J. L. (1972b). On the selection and use of attachment and dependence indices. In J. L. Gewirtz (Ed.), *Attachment and dependency* (pp. 179–215). Washington, DC: Winston.

Gewirtz, J. L., & Boyd, E. F. (1977). Experiments on mother-infant interaction underlying mutual attachment acquisition: The infant conditions the mother. In T. Alloway, P. Pliner, & L. Krames (Eds.), *Attachment behavior* (pp. 109–143). In *Advances in the Study of Communication and Affect.* Volume 3. New York: Plenum Press.

Gewirtz, J. L., & Stingle, K. G. (1968). Learning of generalized imitation as the basis for identification. *Psychological Review, 75,* 374–397.

Gilligan, C. (1982). *In a different voice.* Cambridge, MA: Harvard University Press.

Hartshorne, H., & May, M. A. (1928). *Studies in the nature of character. Volume 1: Studies in deceit.* New York: Macmillan.

Hartshorne, H., May, M. A., & Maller, J. B. (1929). *Studies in the nature of character. Volume 2: Studies in self control.* New York: Macmillan.

Hartshorne, H., May, M. A., & Shuttleworth, F. K. (1930). *Studies in the nature of character. Volume 3: Studies in the organization of character.* New York: Macmillan.

Higgins, A., Power, C., & Kohlberg, L. (1984). The relationship of moral atmosphere to judgments of responsibility. In W. M. Kurtines & J. L. Gewirtz (Eds.), *Morality, moral behavior, and development* (pp. 74–106). New York: Wiley.

Kohlberg, L. (1958). *The development of modes of moral thinking and choice in years 10 to 16.* Unpublished doctoral dissertation, University of Chicago.

Kohlberg. L. (1963). Moral development and identification. In H. Stevenson (Ed.), *Child psychology. The 62nd Yearbook of the National Society for the Study of Education* (Part 1, pp. 277–332). Chicago: University of Chicago Press.

Kohlberg, L. (1964). Development of moral character and moral ideology. In M. L. Hoffman and L. W. Hoffman (Eds.), *Review of child developmental research* (Vol. 1, pp. 383–431). New York: Russell Sage.

Kohlberg, L. (1969). Stage and sequence: The cognitive-developmental approach to socialization.

In D. A. Goslin (Ed.), *Handbook of socialization theory an research* (pp. 347–480). Chicago: Rand McNally.

Kohlberg, L. (1984). *The psychology of moral development*. San Francisco: Harper & Row.

Kohlberg, L. (1987). *Child psychology and childhood education: A cognitive-developmental view*. New York: Longman.

Kohlberg, L., Hart, D., & Wertsch, J. (1987). The developmental social self theories of James Mark Baldwin, George Herbert Mead and Lev Seminovich Vygotsky. In L. Kohlberg (Ed.), *Child psychology and childhood education* (pp. 223–258). New York: Longman.

Kohlberg, L., & Higgins, A. (1987). School democracy and social interaction. In W. M. Kurtines & J. L. Gewirtz (Eds.), *Moral development through social interaction* (pp. 102–128). New York: Wiley.

Kohut, H. (1977). *The restoration of self*. New York: International Universities Press.

Lee, B. (1982). Cognitive development and the self. In J. M. Broughton & D. J. Freeman-Moir (Eds.), *The cognitive developmental psychology of James Mark Baldwin: Current research in genetic epistemology* (pp. 169–210). Norwood, NJ: Ablex.

Levine, R. (1982). *Culture, behavior and personality* (2nd ed.). New York: Aldine.

Lewin, K. (1952). *Field theory in social science*. New York: Harper & Row.

Loevinger, J. (1976). *Ego development*. San Francisco: Jossey-Bass.

Mead, G. H. (1934). *Mind, self & society*. Chicago: University of Chicago Press.

Meltzoff, A. N., & Moore, M. K. (1977). Imitation of facial and manual gestures by human neonates. *Science, 198*, 75–78.

Mischel, W., & Mischel, H. (1976). A cognitive-social learning approach to morality and self-regulation. In T. Lickona (Ed.), *Moral development and behavior* (pp. 84–107). New York: Holt, Rinehart & Winston.

Peck, R. F., & Havighurst, R. J. (1960). *The psychology of character development*. New York: Wiley.

Piaget, J. (1965). *The moral judgment of the child* (M. Gabain, Trans.). New York: Free Press. (Original work published 1932)

Piaget, J. (1952). *The origins of intelligence in children* (M. Cook, Trans.). New York: International Universities Press. (Original work published 1936)

Power, F. C., Higgins, A., & Kohlberg, L. (1989).*Lawrence Kohlberg's approach to moral education*. New York: Columbia University Press.

Royce, J. (1982). *The philosophy of Josiah Royce* (J. Roth, Ed.). Indianapolis: Hackett.

White, R. (1959). Motivation reconsidered: The concept of competence. *Psychological Review, 66*, 297–333.

Youniss, J., & Smollar, J. (1985). *Adolescent relations with mothers, fathers and friends*. Chicago: University of Chicago Press.

13

Identification, Attachment, and Their Developmental Sequencing in a Conditioning Frame

Jacob L. Gewirtz

ABSTRACT

Theorists of early social development have long attended to two focal behavior systems, one connoting *attachment* to, and the other *identification* with, the parent-model. The psychoanalytic, cognitive-developmental, and behavior theories have concerned themselves with the sequential appearance of the attachment and identification processes. The social-conditioning approach to attachment and to identification are reviewed, those two processes fleshed out, and their early sequencing considered.

In the social-conditioning approach, *attachment* has served as a metaphor labeling the process wherein a complex of child-response patterns comes to be cued and reinforced/maintained (i.e., controlled) by appearance- and behavior-provided stimuli from an attachment object, in early life the mother among others. The child-response pattern can maintain contact or proximity. *Identification* reduces to pervasive imitation acquired via a conditional-responding process whereby a child acquires the range of behaviors of the repertoire (including behaviors connoting values and standards) of a parent model, usually the parent of the child's gender. Such conditional responses can be emitted after lengthy delays or in the model's absence, and would be acquired/maintained by at least occasional extrinsic reinforcers provided by contingent parent/adult responses. Unreinforced imitations may appear to be instances of "observational learning" to those unaware of the matching-response class' conditioning history.

Freud theorized that the object relationship/attachment typically precedes identification. J. M. Baldwin and later Kohlberg conceived that the identification process precedes attachment. From a behavioral view, the order of appearance of the processes connoting attachment and identification is a pseudo question, as the two processes are conceived to be orthogonal.

Theorists of social learning and development have long attended to two focal behavior systems, one connoting attachment to the parent and the other the "identification" with the parent-model (e.g., Gewirtz, 1969). Moreover, both objectivist social conditioning theories (Gewirtz & Stingle, 1968; Gewirtz, 1969) and constructivist cognitive-developmental theories (J. M. Baldwin, 1895, 1906; Kohlberg, 1963, 1966, 1969; Kohlberg & Diessner, chapter 12 in this volume), not to mention Freud's (1933, 1938) psychoanalytic theory, have concerned themselves not only with attachment and identification but also with the sequential relation in human development of attachment and identification. My task here is to review the background and features of the social conditioning approach to attachment and to identification, to flesh out those two processes in the developmental context, and to relate them to one another sequentially in the course of early human development.

THE ATTACHMENT BACKGROUND

Different terms have been applied in precocial and altricial species to the early influence process wherein, through early systematic exposure/contact, offspring filial responses acquire initially a social-object focus, ordinarily the biological mother. This influence process characteristically has been termed "imprinting" in *precocial* species and "attachment" in *altricial* species (see Hess & Petrovich, chapter 4 and Petrovich & Gewirtz, chapter 5 of this Volume). Precocial species (e.g., the chicken, duck, goose, goat, sheep) are capable of highly adaptive perceptual-motor integration, orientation, and locomotion soon after birth or hatching. Altricial species (e.g., the cat, dog, dove, pigeon, monkey, human) remain helpless for extensive periods after birth or hatching, but can engage in synchronous interaction with parent caregivers and others during those periods. How responses denoting infant imprinting/attachment become focused and restricted to a particular social object in precocial birds and in such altricial-like mammals as infrahuman and human primates have appeared similar and functionally analogous (Petrovich & Gewirtz, 1985). A number of investigators have conceived imprinting to involve a routine learning process, under various paradigms, with the outcomes of that learning being social bonds/relationships (Bateson, 1966, 1971; Cairns, 1966; Gewirtz, 1961; Hoffman & DePaulo, 1977; Hoffman & Ratner, 1973). With Scott (1960, 1968), those investigators emphasized the similarities between the imprinting process in precocial species and the process involved in the formation of primary social bonds in altricial species. Indeed, Gewirtz (1961) proposed that *both* the imprinting and attachment processes are the outcomes of operant learning.

The global concept *attachment* (used synonymously with the terms "affectional bond," "tie," "object relationship") has been used variably and with few constraints typically as a metaphor to label behavior patterns of one individual systematically directed to another individual. Diverse criterion indices have denoted attachments in both precocial and altricial species. The attachment concept and its precursors have been approached in a number of ways over the years. Psychoanalysis and its derivative approaches have considered the phenomena connoting attachment in terms of libidinal cathexis, object formation, and object relations—the "object" being the instrumental person, typically the mother for the child, through whom the "instinctual aim" is satisfied—and suggested etiological determinants of such fundamental relations in like (Freud, 1905, 1936, 1938). At one point, Freud (1936) considered a child's anxiety about separation from his mother to be an indication of an object relation.

In their approaches to human social behavior, diverse others have dealt with this topic in research and theory (see chapter 5 this volume by Petrovich and Gewirtz). The work of Bowlby (1957, 1958, 1960a, 1960b, 1969) provided the impetus for combining selected psychoanalytic assumptions with ethological and, to a degree, cognitive conceptions. Bowlby applied the metaphor attachment to label a child's affectional tie, particularly to its mother-figure, in an ethological frame using mentalistic cognitive conceptions. Thus, early on, Bowlby (1960, p. 14) proposed that the core index of attachment was proximity seeking and that protests cued by maternal departures was the inverse index. Following Bowlby's lead, Schaffer and Emerson (1964) focused on maternal-departure protests as their sole attachment criterion, and Ainsworth (1964, 1967, 1972) proposed more than a dozen indices of attachment. In the context of the disruption of early mother–child relationships, Yarrow (1956, 1964, 1967, 1972) first used the term "object relationship" and later the term "focused [individualized] relationship" to label what seem to be some of the same behavior systems of the human infant toward its mother-figure.

Much of the contemporary flavor of the attachment concept derives from Bowlby's (1957, 1958, 1969, 1973) overall conceptualization and, in that context particularly, from Ainsworth's later emphasis on attachment indices generated by the Strange Situation procedure that she devised (Ainsworth & Wittig, 1969). Ainsworth and her associates crossed the attachment conception with dimensions of security and anxiety, and used Strange Situation-procedure indices to support a fruitful typological theory of attachment security (e.g., Ainsworth, Blehar, Waters, & Wall, 1978).

THE SOCIAL CONDITIONING APPROACH
TO ATTACHMENT

The social conditioning approach is based on operant learning principles (Skinner, 1938, 1953; Catania & Harnad, 1988). In it, *attachment* has served as a convenient metaphoric label for a process involving the acquisition of a close reliance (typically concurrent) of one individual's behavior upon the appearance- and behavior-provided stimuli of another, expressed in a variety of cued-response patterns. Specifically, attachment labels the process wherein a complex of child-response patterns comes to be cued and reinforced/maintained by stimuli provided by the appearance and behavior of an attachment figure/object, in earliest life usually the mother (Gewirtz, 1961, 1972a, 1976, 1977; Gewirtz & Boyd, 1977). The child-response pattern might maintain contact or proximity, produce attention, or the like. The attachment term also has labeled concurrent reflections of the previous process, such as the child's differential responding favoring the maternal attachment figure, distress when separated from her, protest upon preparations for her departures and after brief separations from her (Gewirtz & Peláez-Nogueras, 1987, 1989), or even by increases in child exploration in her presence (Gewirtz, 1972b). The cued-response patterns denoting attachment are pervasive and, upon disruption by separation or rejection, the child's behavior can become highly disorganized or may be accompanied by intense emotional (affective) responding.

In this social conditioning account, the dyadic functional relations between the cue and reinforcing stimuli from the attachment figure/object person and the child's responses they control that connote attachment of the child to the attachment figure may occur in any segment of the life span from infancy onward and with any interaction partners/objects. Further, they may involve several object persons concurrently. Such actor pairs may be involved as mother and child, wife and husband, person and animal, as well as peers or lovers. Thus, several concurrent discriminative-stimulus control patterns denoting attachments, as with mother and father and others, are to be expected routinely. Such diverse discriminative-control patterns also operate for the child in the residential institution, nursery school, or day-care center who is concurrently and/or sequentially in the charge of several persons. It is relevant also in understanding the child's differential behavior to mother and father or of the child reared jointly by several persons in a household (e.g., parent, older sibling, grandparent, and/or maid). In addition, concurrent reciprocal influence patterns may prevail, such as mother-to-child and child-to-mother. Moreover, initiations need not be reciprocated on an occasion by an attachment figure. The discriminated operants denoting attachments are not to be conceived as traits. Those behaviors are controlled by particular cue and reinforcing stimuli, as well as by contextual stimuli, so their occurrence will vary across situations otherwise defined.

IDENTIFICATION LEARNING

Although Freud dealt with *identification* in a scattered way and with many variations through decades of his writing, his work is responsible for much of the contemporary flavor of the identification concept. He employed the term both for a *process* and for the behavior-similarity *outcomes* of that process. Thus, to Freud (1933), identification was a process by which "one ego becomes like another one, which results in the first ego behaving . . . in certain respects in the same way as the second; it imitates it and, as it were, takes it into itself (p. 90)." In one writing, Freud's (1920) index of the outcome of identification was the *imitation* of the model's behaviors. When assumed in Freud's approach to result from complete instrumental dependence on, and an emotional tie (attachment) to the model (typically the parent), identification has been termed "anaclitic." At the same time, it was assumed that "defensive" or "aggressive" identification resulted from fear of punishment (even fear of castration in the boy) from the model figure, with the child avoiding the punishment by becoming like the model.

In a behavior frame, identification as pervasive imitative learning refers to the selective process whereby a child acquires a range of the behavior repertory (including behaviors connoting values and standards) of a parent, usually the parent of the same gender as the child. This pervasive-imitation acquisition process has been termed and denotes "identification" (Gewirtz & Stingle, 1968). In this frame, the phenomena of identification could be reduced parsimoniously to the concept of conditional responding, with the imitation a functional matching-response class comprised of diverse responses matched to a parent-model's behaviors. Such conditional responses could be emitted after lengthy delays or in the model's absence, and would be acquired and maintained by extrinsic reinforcing stimuli usually provided by a parent's or other adult's responding to the child's response (Gewirtz, 1969, 1971a, 1971b; Gewirtz & Stingle, 1968).

Acquisition of the imitative response class is thought to follow operant learning principles (Skinner, 1938, 1953), in particular that diverse responses leading to equivalent consequences are functional members of the same class—in this case a matching-response class—and that the matching-response class can become conditional (i.e., focused) on a particular parent (typically of the same gender) whose presence sets the occasion for extrinsic reinforcement of members of that matching-response class. Moreover, because the matching-response class is ordinarily followed only intermittently by extrinsic reinforcement from the model or from other adults, such matching responses will often occur in the absence of reinforcing contingencies. To those unaware of the conditioning history of the matching-response class in a child, such nonreinforced imitations may appear to be instances of the "observational learning" for which Bandura (1969, 1971) has argued. (An extensive analysis of such considerations has been presented elsewhere—Gewirtz, 1971a).

THE SEQUENTIAL RELATION BETWEEN IDENTIFICATION AND ATTACHMENT

An early framework for focusing on the phenomena characterizing both attachment and identificatory processes and their outcomes was provided by psychoanalytic theory (Freud, 1920, 1933, 1938). Freud early on emphasized: (a) the libidinal object relationship (i.e., attachment) of the child to its mother, (b) the identification of the child with its same-gender parent, and (c) the sequential order of appearance of the two processes/behavior systems in the course of the child's development, with the object relationship/attachment preceding the identification.

It was noted earlier that James Mark Baldwin (1895, 1906), at the turn of the century, and later Kohlberg (1966), following Baldwin's lead, have proposed that the process of pervasive imitation/identification plays a central role in early human social development and that it *precedes* that of attachment in the course of early human development. Hence, their proposal as to the sequencing of the two processes is the reverse of Freud's, for whom the attachment process precedes selective pervasive imitation.

Imitative-identificatory and attachment-dependence phenomena typically have been approached at a gross level of conceptual analysis that obscures the identities and roles of the response classes and of the discriminative, contextual, and maintaining stimuli involved. In that frame, from a behavioral view, the question of the order of appearance in the course of early human development of the processes denoting attachment and pervasive imitation cum identification is considered to be a pseudo issue, as the two processes can be conceived to be orthogonal (Gewirtz, 1969, 1972a; Gewirtz & Stingle, 1968). In life settings, the behavioral processes denoting both attachment and pervasive imitation may be acquired concurrently or sequentially in identical or very similar stimulus contexts, as both behavior classes are emitted in the presence of many of the same parent-provided discriminative stimuli and are maintained by many of the same parent-provided reinforcing stimuli. Even so, one behavior class need not be the basis for the acquisition of the other. The processes involve separate behavior systems that can be represented by distinct paradigms, interdependent only insofar as they involve some of the same stimulus elements in their acquisition and maintenance.

The matching response class in pervasive imitation is ordinarily defined more in terms of similarity to the model's behavior (cue) than in terms of the social stimuli that cue and maintain/reinforce those matched responses. For our behavioral analysis, therefore, the imitative process involves a response class under the same type of stimulus control that is implied in and summarized by the concept of attachment. The matching responses of pervasive imitation and the responses to parents of attachment are in both processes cued and maintained/reinforced by the same classes of parent-provided stimuli. In this sense, the pervasive imitative-learning process that involves numerous matching-to-parent model behaviors cued and maintained by the same parent-provided stimuli may be conceived to constitute a subset of attachment-behavior outcomes under the attachment process.

Although the two processes, pervasive imitation and attachment, are conceived to be independent insofar as they involve distinct paradigms, very different determinants of the two processes may prevail in subsamples of the population. Hence, in some subsamples, pervasive imitation may be fostered earlier and in other subsamples later than attachment. Although such etiological-factor and outcome distribution patterns could be of occasional interest—for instance, in differences between demographically defined population subgroups—they are incidental to the process analysis that is the fundamental objective of a behavioral approach.

REFERENCES

Ainsworth, M. D. (1964). Patterns of attachment behavior shown by the infant in interaction with his mother. *Merrill-Palmer Quarterly, 10*, 51–58.

Ainsworth, M. D. S. (1967). *Infancy in Uganda*. Baltimore: Johns Hopkins Press.

Ainsworth, M. D. S., & Witting, B. A. (1969). Attachment and exploratory behavior of one-year-olds in a strange situation. In B. M. Foss (Ed.), *Determinants of infant behaviour IV*. London: Methuen.

Ainsworth, M. D. S., Blehar, M. C., Waters, E., & Wall, S. (1978). *Patterns of attachment*. Hillsdale, NJ: Lawrence Erlbaum Associates.

Ainsworth, M. S. (1972). Attachment and dependency: A comparison. In J. L. Gewirtz (Ed.), *Attachment and dependency* (pp. 92–137). Washington, DC: Winston.

Baldwin, J. M. (1895). *Mental development of the child and the race: Methods and processes*. New York: Macmillan.

Baldwin, J. M. (1906). *Social and ethical interpretations in mental development*. New York: Macmillan.

Bandura, A. (1969). Social-learning theory of identificatory processes. In D. A. Goslin (Ed.), *Handbook of socialization theory and research* (pp. 213–262). Chicago: Rand McNally.

Bandura, A. (1971). Vicarious and self-reinforcement processes. In R. Glaser (Ed.), *The nature of reinforcement* (pp. 228–278). New York: Academic Press.

Bateson, P. P. G. (1966). The characteristics and context of imprinting. *Biological Review, 41*, 177–220.

Bateson, P. P. G. (1971). Imprinting. In H. Moltz (Ed.), *The ontogeny of vertebrate behavior* (pp. 369–387). New York: Academic Press.

Bowlby, J. (1957). An ethological approach to research in child development. *British Journal of Medical Psychology, 30*, 230–240.

Bowlby, J. (1958). The nature of the child's tie to his mother. *International Journal of Psychoanalysis, 39*, 350–373.

Bowlby, J. (1960a). Ethology and the development of object relations. *International Journal of Psychoanalysis, 41*, 313–317.

Bowlby, J. (1960b). Separation anxiety. *International Journal of Psychoanalysis, 41*, 89–113.

Bowlby, J. (1969). *Attachment and loss. Volume 1: Attachment*. London: Hogarth (New York: Basic Books).

Bowlby, J. (1973). *Attachment and loss. Volume 2: Separation*. New York: Basic Books.

Cairns, R. B. (1966). Attachment behavior in mammals. *Psychological Review, 73*, 409–426.

Catania, A. C., & Harnad, S. (Eds.). (1988). *The selection of behavior: The operant behaviorism of B. F. Skinner—Comments and consequences*. New York: Cambridge University Press.

Freud, S. (1905). Three contributions to the theory of sex. In A. A. Brill (Trans.), *The basic writings of Sigmund Freud* (pp. 553–629). New York: Modern Library.

Freud, S. (1920). (J. Riviere, Trans.). *A general introduction to psychoanalysis*. Garden City, NY: Garden City.

Freud, S. (1933). (W. J. H. Sprott, Trans.). *New introductory lectures on psychoanalysis*. London: Hogarth.

Freud, S. (1936). (A. Strachey, Trans.). *Inhibitions, symptoms, and anxiety*. London: Hogarth.

Freud, S. (1938). (J. Strachey, Trans.). *An outline of psychoanalysis*. London: Hogarth.

Gewirtz, J. L. (1961). A learning analysis of the effects of normal stimulation, privation, and deprivation on the acquisition of social motivation and attachment. In B. M. Foss (Ed.), *Determinants of infant behaviour* (pp. 213–299). London: Methuen (New York: Wiley).

Gewirtz, J. L. (1969). Mechanisms of social learning: Some roles of stimulation and behavior in early human development. In D. A. Goslin (Ed.), *Handbook of socialization theory and research* (pp. 57–212). Chicago: Rand McNally.

Gewirtz, J. L. (1971a). The roles of overt responding and extrinsic reinforcement in "self-" and "vicarious-reinforcement" phenomena and in "observational learning" and imitation. In R. Glaser (Ed.), *The nature of reinforcement* (pp. 279–309). New York: Academic Press.

Gewirtz, J. L. (1971b). Conditional responding as a paradigm for observational, imitative learning and vicarious reinforcement. In H. W. Reese (Ed.), *Advances in child development and behavior* (Vol. 6, pp. 273–304). New York: Academic Press.

Gewirtz, J. L. (1972a). Attachment, dependence, and a distinction in terms of stimulus control. In J. L. Gewirtz (Ed.), *Attachment and dependency* (pp. 139–177). Washington, DC: Winston.

Gewirtz, J. L. (1972b). On the selection and use of attachment and dependence indices. In J. L. Gewirtz (Ed.), *Attachment and dependency* (pp. 179–215). Washington, DC: Winston.

Gewirtz, J. L. (1976). The attachment-acquisition process as evidenced in the maternal conditioning of cued infant responding (particularly crying). *Human Development, 19*, 143–155.

Gewirtz, J. L. (1977). Maternal responding and the conditioning of infant crying: Directions of influence within the attachment-acquisition process. In B. C. Etzel, J. M. LeBlanc, & D. M. Baer (Eds.), *New developments in behavior research: Theories, methods and applications*. Hillsdale, NJ: Lawrence Erlbaum Associates.

Gewirtz, J. L., & Boyd, E. F. (1977). Experiments on mother–infant interaction underlying mutual attachment acquisition: The infant conditions the mother. In T. Alloway, P. Pliner, & L. Krames (Eds.), *Advances in the study of communication and affect: Attachment behavior* (Vol. 3, pp. 109–143). New York: Plenum.

Gewirtz, J. L., & Peláez-Nogueras, M. (1987). Social-conditioning theory applied to metaphors like "attachment": The conditioning of infant separation protests by mothers. *Revista Mexicana de Analisis de la Conducta, 13*, 87–103.

Gewirtz, J. L., & Peláez-Nogueras, M. (1989; April). *Maternal training of infant protests: Infant learning to discriminate between departure and separation settings*. Paper presented at the biennial meeting of the Society for Research in Child Development, Kansas City, MO.

Gewirtz, J. L., & Stingle, K. G. (1968). Learning of generalized imitation as the basis for identification. *Psychological Review, 75*, 374–397.

Hoffman, H. S., & DePaulo, P. (1977). Behavioral control by an imprinting stimulus. *American Scientist, 65*, 58–66.

Hoffman, H. S., & Ratner, A. M. (1973). A reinforcement model of imprinting: Implications for socialization in monkeys and man. *Psychological Review, 80*, 527–544.

Kohlberg, L. (1963). Moral development and identification. In H. Stevenson (Ed.), *Child psychology. The 62nd Yearbook of the National Society for the Study of Education* (Part 1, pp. 277–332). Chicago: University of Chicago Press.

Kohlberg, L. (1966). A cognitive-developmental analysis of children's sex-role concepts and attitudes. In E. E. Maccoby (Ed.), *The development of sex differences* (pp. 82–173). Stanford, CA: Stanford University Press.

Kohlberg, L. (1969). Stage and sequence: The cognitive-developmental approach to socialization. In D. A. Goslin (Ed.), *Handbook of socialization theory and research* (pp. 347–480). Chicago: Rand McNally.

Petrovich, S. B., & Gewirtz, J. L. (1985). The attachment learning process and its relation to cultural and biological evolution: Proximate and ultimate considerations. In M. Reite & T. Field (Eds.), *The psychobiology of attachment and separation* (pp. 257–289). New York: Academic Press.

Schaffer, H. R., & Emerson, P. E. (1964). The development of social attachments in infancy. *Monographs of the Society for Research in Child Development, 29* (3, Whole No. 94).

Scott, J. P. (1960). Comparative social psychology. In R. H. Waters, D. A. Rethlingshafer, & W. E. Caldwell (Eds.), *Principles of comparative psychology.* New York: McGraw-Hill.

Scott, J. P. (1968). *Early experience and the organization of behavior.* Belmont, CA: Brooks/Cole.

Skinner, B. F. (1938). *The behavior of organisms.* New York: Appleton-Century.

Skinner, B. F. (1953). *Science and human behavior.* New York: Macmillan.

Skinner, B. F. (1969). *Contingencies of reinforcement.* New York: Appleton-Century-Crofts.

Yarrow, L. J. (1956). The development of object relations during infancy and the effects of a disruption of early mother-child relationships. *American Psychologist, 11,* 423.

Yarrow, L. J. (1964). Separation from parents during early childhood. In M. Hoffman & L. Hoffman (Eds.), *Review of Child Development Research* (pp. 89–136), Volume 1. New York: Russell Sage Foundation.

Yarrow, L. J. (1967). The development of focused relationships during infancy. In J. Hellmuth (Ed.), *Exceptional infant: The normal infant* (Vol. 1, pp. 429–442). Seattle, WA: Special Child Publications.

Yarrow, L. J. (1972). Attachment and dependency: A developmental perspective. In J. L. Gewirtz (Ed.), *Attachment and dependency* (pp. 81–95). Washington, DC: Winston/Wiley.

14

A Comparison and Synthesis of Kohlberg's Cognitive-Developmental and Gewirtz's Learning-Developmental Attachment Theories

Michael L. Commons

ABSTRACT

Kohlberg's cognitive-developmental and Gewirtz's learning-developmental approaches to attachment are compared and synthesized on the assumption that the sequence of attachment stages and stage-change processes form a supersystem that can unify both approaches to the development of attachment.

Kohlberg's and Gewirtz's theories agree in their basic outline. The apparent differences arise from the emphases that each approach places on issues such as sequence of development and the mechanisms producing change. Whereas Kohlberg concentrates on a macroanalysis, Gewirtz's analysis concentrates on event-by-event analyses of change. Kohlberg posits the self as a source of action. He necessarily finds that people reason at a stage and have free will, because he takes the subjects' reports as representing and reflecting internal processes. Gewirtz does not find traditionally defined stages or free will, because he takes subject's reports as behavior just like any other. He considers attachment an abstraction for a coherent system of responses cued and maintained by the appearance and behavior of an object person and considers the self but an abstraction for that coherent system of responses and other coherent response systems.

Kohlberg's and Gewirtz's attachment theories emphasize that attachment takes place throughout the life span rather than being simply an infant-acquired and -maintained characteristic. This synthesis of their theories suggests that both stage-independent—notions of accommodation and adaptation and their behavioral equivalents in learning theory, such as the necessity of the reinforcement of next-stage behavior for stage change—and stage-dependent conditions produce attachment stage change.

The synthesis also suggests that attachment refers to the nonsubstitutability of reinforcers emanating from different sources. Nonsubstitutable sources are the attachment objects. What the attachment objects can be develops in stages. Simple, generalized, and pervasive imitation are used along with role-taking to construct a shared self and the perspective of the other. The resulting perspective on interaction determines the concept of the attachment object. Behaviorally this equates with the development of increasingly complex interactions.

Kohlberg (1969, Kohlberg & Diessner, chapter 12 this volume) and Gewirtz (1969, chapter 13 this volume, and Gewirtz & Peláez-Nogueras, chapter 7 this volume) in their published and personal discussions over many years, operated on the principle that their apparently different and discrepant theoretical orientations had many features that were coordinate and even transplantable into one another. Before Lawrence Kohlberg's death, he and Jacob Gewirtz encouraged this author to attempt a translation and reconciliation of each theory with the other, and to outline aspects of their general approaches that both address by detailing a core of points at which the approaches correspond and some of the essential points at which they may be discrepant. This was a task they had been planning for years. Kohlberg and Gewirtz present expositions of their own views in the chapters preceding this one. The exposition presented here is based on discussions with Kohlberg (December and January, 1985) and Gewirtz (January, 1985; April, 1987), as well as with the two together at various times. In particular, we discussed the relationship among moral atmosphere and contingencies of reinforcement, as well as of moral attachment and stages of complexity.

    This chapter compares Kohlberg's structural cognitive-developmental approach and Gewirtz's behavioral-analytic social conditioning developmental approach to attachment and attempts to extend them by formulating a synthesis that embodies points of correspondence between them. The theories agree on their basic outline of the development of attachment. The apparent differences arise out of the different emphases that each approach places on issues such as sequence of development and the mechanisms producing change. Catania (1973), Gewirtz (e.g., 1969, in press), and Horowitz (1987), among other, have argued that behavior-analytic and cognitive-developmental approaches are compatible.

    Kohlberg's and Gewirtz's theories can be viewed as overlapping systems belonging to a larger attachment system. To compare each system efficiently, Commons and Richards (1984a) suggested building supersystems that contain each system as a separate subsystem. Building supersystems overcomes many of the problems produced by other ways of comparing systems, insuring that the commonalities are represented and some of the conflicts are resolved. Here I build a supersystem that encompasses and compares Kohlberg's subsystem with Gewirtz's subsystem. The essential properties of each system are methodologically represented by their core and methodological features. The theories not only have systematic cores, but have frameworks or viewpoints that are reflected in their delineation of research questions and methodology. The frameworks are shown in general to be complementary rather than contradictory, as in the case of the light-wave particle duality. There are material disagreements. Conflicting material is shown to be embedded in the framework of each system rather than within the core of each system. If the conflicting material is nonessential to a theoretical model, it is included as a special constraint on the theory.

There are a number of reasons for attempting a synthesis, other than Kohlberg's and Gewirtz's commendable open-mindedness. First, such a synthesis is possible. Their systems fit together well, with some necessary weakening of the assumptions underlying stage theory and detailing of some processes that account for development. Second, both theories differ from the major attachment theories in some similar ways. Third, both theorists would like to address life-span attachment. Fourth, an evolutionary framework seems to imply that both learning and developmental mechanisms are needed to account for life-span attachment. This framework represents neither Kohlberg's nor Gewirtz's approaches but is compatible with and derivative of each. The evolutionary framework suggests why attaching to more developmentally advanced attachment objects may confer evolutionary advantage. These reasons for a synthesis are considered in detail next.

THE SYNTHESIS

It is my claim that these two approaches do not conflict in any major way, but have different emphases. For example, Kohlberg's moral-attachment atmosphere describes relationships the child has to other people in the environment. Changes in attachment pattern produced by the moral-attachment atmosphere can in principle be reduced to changes in the actual contingencies between behavior and surrounding environmental events in that environment—an analysis that Gewirtz's attachment approach emphasizes.

In this synthesis and extension, *attachment* refers to the nonsubstitutability of particular sources of cues and reinforcers. Consequences that increase the likelihood of behavior that they follow are termed reinforcing stimuli or *reinforcers*. *Cues* are events that indicate when particular behaviors will be reinforced. The sources of the cues and consequences are the *attachment objects*. Two events are nonsubstitutable when changing from one to the other alters the strength of control by cues or consequences. For example, a child may be consoled more by being held by the primary caregiver than by others. Caregivers are the sources of cuing and reinforcing stimuli. We assume that infants prefer caregivers who console them more effectively. Preferring the primary caregiver over another means that the events provided by the primary caregiver are chosen over the events provided by others. Making behavioral choices that result in the events delivered by the preferred caregiver becomes more likely. The events provided by caregivers, which may function as stimuli for child behaviors, include those provided by caregiver behavior and by caregiver appearance, and the setting in which the events transpire. Hence, more extensive control by and preference for the primary caregiver over other caregivers means that the child is more *attached* to the primary caregiver than to the other caregivers.

HOW THESE APPROACHES DIFFER
FROM OTHER ACCOUNTS

Both the Kohlberg and Gewirtz approaches differ in some similar ways from other attachment approaches:

Process versus Trait

Both Kohlberg and Gewirtz see attachment as a set of processes, not as traits or typlogies such as "being securely attached." Instead of asking whether a child is securely attached (Ainsworth, 1972) and what the consequences of being securely attached are, the *process* of the development of attachment is the focus of interest. Kohlberg and Gewirtz concentrate on stage-change and conditioning processes.

Attachment is More Than Seeking Proximity

Both Kohlberg and Gewirtz hold different notions of attachment from those of Ainsworth (1972) or Bowlby (1969). They share the notion that the attachment process involves more behaviors than just seeking to be physically close to an attachment object. Kohlberg and Gewirtz focus on the person doing the attaching as having more than a personal need to be close to the other. The children do more than cling to the people to whom they are attached or show distress in those people's absence. In this paper, people who have formed an attachment to some object will be referred to as "the attached." Both Kohlberg (1969) and Gewirtz (1969, 1972b) conceive of a vast number of potential attachment behaviors.

Life-span Attachment

In common with many researchers (Gewirtz, 1976; Greenberg, Siegel, & Leitch, 1983; Kahn & Antonucci, 1980; Kalish & Knudtson, 1976; Lerner & Lerner, 1983; Lerner, Palermo, Spiro, & Nesselroade, 1982; Levitt, chapter 9 this volume; Main, (in press); Troll & Smith, 1976; Weiss, 1982), Kohlberg and Gewirtz see attachment processes operating throughout the life span. Two of the possible views of life-span attachment differ in one fundamental regard. The first sees most aspects of attachment remaining constant over the life span (e.g., traditional learning theory), whereas the second sees fundamental changes taking place (e.g., developmental-self theory of Kegan, 1982). The synthesis provided here suggests a possible solution—that while the learning processes may remain constant across the life span, what is to be learned may not. Thus, the objects of attachment may change. Although stage theory provides a rationale for the order of development of what may serve as attachment objects, stage theory requires locally operating learning mechanisms to account for development. Thus, the processes of how the attachment objects of change remain constant.

To account for changes in life-span attachment, this chapter considers how the attachment processes may change (learning) and how they may change in a sequential fashion (stages). The fundamental assumption in this paper is that the attachment processes are transformed by three factors. They are described as following: (a) the development of the proficiency of the attached to solve per-spective-taking tasks (Commons & Rodriguez, 1990; Selman, 1980), (b) the interactions of the attached with the environment, and (c) the conditioning histo-ries underlying the behavior of the attached. At all points, the process of moral development of attachment will be impacted by such physical changes such as endocrine secretions.

Attachment and Stage

From an empirical perspective, the attachment process is examined by observing that attachment behaviors develop in a sequence; that is, the acquisition of later behaviors depends on earlier behavior having been established (Campbell & Richie, 1983, Gewirtz, 1961). In contradistinction to social conditioning devel-opmental approaches, investigations of cognitive development have generally addressed the problem of finding the order in which behavior develops. The order is represented by sequential level or stages for many developmentalists. There has been no generally apparent explanation for why behavior might devel-op in a given sequence, thus, cognitive-developmental researchers typically as-sumed that reasoning and other psychological processes determined behavior.

Some variant of stages might be useful to account for developmental changes in attachment. As Kohlberg and Armon (1984) noted, notions of stage, level, and period vary widely. Stage may be separated into two parts: an empirical and an analytic portion. For Kohlberg, functional developmental levels (*"soft stages"*) represent the empirical order in which behaviors develop. The empirical portion, referred to here as levels, accounts for the development of performance on such tasks. When performances develop in an orderly fashion, Kohlberg referred to the points along the way as functional levels or soft stages. This writer infers that Kohlberg (Kohlberg & Diessner, chapter 12, this volume; Kohlberg & Armon, 1984; Kohlberg, Hart, & Wertsch, 1987) has considered his approach to attach-ment to be a soft-stage or functional approach, because he drew his notions of the moral self from function theorists such as Ausubel, Sullivan, & Ives (1980), Erikson (1962, 1969) and Mead (1934). Kohlberg (Kohlberg & Armon, 1984) characterized functional theories as soft-stage theories. In this volume, Kohlberg sees psychological faculties such as the self developed in functional levels. The notion of *"hard stages"* requires a logic that constrains and organizes the developmental sequences of behavior into a hierarchy. Kohlberg's moral reasoning stages and Piaget's logical, mathematical, physical reasoning stages are hard stages.

To synthesize Kohlberg's and Gewirtz's approaches, some assumptions of Kohlberg's notion of hard stages must be weakened slightly. The philosophic underpinnings are set aside, and notions of the underlying process of development are altered somewhat. These proposals weaken stages much less than Kohlberg's (Kohlberg & Diessner, chapter 12, this volume) proposals, because soft stages of attachment are not produced. In my weakening, the logic of hard stages (e.g., Inhelder & Piaget, 1958; Kohlberg, 1984) is applied to the development of attachment so as to yield hard stages. Kohlberg (1984, Kohlberg & Diessner, chapter 12 this volume) has already made the empirical case for the sequence of levels being supported by his research on the moral self (Snary, Kohlberg, & Noam, 1987) and will not be reviewed here.

Such a separation among the analytic and the empirical and philosophical bases for moral development seems to be consistent with both Kohlberg's and Gewirtz's approach to behavioral sequences. From Gewirtz's perspective, such a separation may eliminate the problem with traditionally conceived of stages of requiring a multitude of nontestable assumptions. Kohlberg nowhere accepted the separation. The simplifications of stage theory used here might strengthen Kohlberg's argument that moral stages could even be argued on purely logical grounds. He encouraged their development in both moral and self domains. Kohlberg (e.g., 1984) has always asserted that the hierarchical arrangement of the stages has a purely logical, rather than a psychological or philosophical basis. The hierarchical arrangement of stages can be viewed as depending solely on the logical relationships that order the implicit task demands at different stages. In this frame, Kohlberg viewed the application of stage to attachment as controversial, an endeavor in its infancy.

Listing a minimum number of constraints under which stages would be generated, Commons and Richards (1984a, 1984b) have proposed The General Stage Model, a theory of hierarchical complexity, of a task. The hierarchical rankings of tasks so generated meet all of Kohlberg's and Armon's (1984) logical requirements for a hard-stage theory. The psychological aspects may require a weakening of the structure-of-the-whole assumption. Commons and Richards asserted that the rankings of the hierarchical complexity of a task are universal, whereas when proficiency develops in dealing with those tasks might vary depending on nonstage factors. Their hierarchical task-complexity theory shows that certain sets of task-required actions form a hierarchy, although other sets do not.

In this task-complexity theory, each new task-required action in the hierarchy is one stage more complex than the lower-stage, task-required actions out of which it is built. For a task to be more *hierarchically complex* than those from another set of tasks, the more hierarchically complex task requires actions that are *defined* in terms of lower-stage actions and *organize* the less complex actions in a *nonarbitrary* fashion. Similarly, the lower-complexity actions are also defined in terms of even lower-complexity actions. The number of times that a less complex actions must be applied to an even less complex task in order to define the hierarchical sequence gives the ordinal stage number of the task.

In behavioral terms, Commons and Rodriguez (1990) defined stage of performance as the hierarchical complexity of a task that is successfully performed—they make required discriminative responses. What is required at a particular attachment stage is to discriminate among social stimuli with that stage's hierarchical complexity and respond to the members of that stimulus class that have provided reinforcing consequences for such behaviors. Individuals' respond in a manner that increases the overall rate of reinforcement.

INTRAGENERATIONAL AND INTERGENERATIONAL EVOLUTIONARY ACCOUNTS OF ATTACHMENT

An evolutionary framework for synthesizing Kohlberg's and Gewirtz's approaches is presented here. Learning may be viewed as evolution of behavior within a generation or life span (*intragenerational*) and of genetic changes as evolution between generations (*intergenerational* Cavalli-Sforza, 1981, 1982). As modified here, Kohlberg's stage theory represents the hierarchical ordering of cultural as well as biological tasks. Gewirtz's social conditioning theory addresses biologically based mechanisms of adaptation and the role of the cultural content embodied in the applications of learning mechanisms. One might guess that a synthesis could not make a cultural- and mind-oriented theory fit with a more biologically oriented approach. The trick is to see that evolution might be indifferent to the form of information that is passed.

Both Kohlberg's and Gewirtz's approaches are proximal *intragenerational* accounts of attachment. Cognitive development (Kohlberg & Diessner, chapter 12 this volume) examines the overall patterns of development of attachment. Cognitive development sees human attachment differing from attachment in other organisms in what may serve as an object of attachment. Other organism may attach to their young, parents, mates, groups, and possibly territories or inanimate objects. People, however, in addition, attach to friends and abstract objects including companies, towns, countries, and so forth. (See this volume, Feshbach, chapter 11 on this point.) Attachment to these more complex and abstract objects may confer evolutionary success. For example, people who attached to abstract entities such as villages were more able to repel the incursions of marauders than individual families living in isolation. Villagers formed into tribes were more successful than isolated villagers. Nations formed of tribes were more successful yet. In each successive case, the complexity of the attachment object increases. The more immediate causes of behavior are discussed in terms of moral or attachment atmosphere of the social situations in which role-taking takes place.

Behavior analysis (Gewirtz, chapter 13 and Gewirtz & Peláez-Nogueras, chapter 7 this volume) examines the proximal causes and maintenance of the development of attachment in detail. The cognitive-developmental and the behavior-analytic social conditioning approaches both support the long-term evaluation of developmental patterns and the effects of various long-term interventions.

The intragenerational attachment activities affect the intergenerational outcomes. Attachment patterns and processes affect the transmission of information between generations. Attachment patterns reflect the moral-attachment atmosphere (Power, Higgins, & Kohlberg, 1989) in which a child is raised, on the one hand, and the actual contingencies between behavior and surrounding environmental events that occur in those situations, on the other. From a behavioral-evolutionary perspective, if there is little biological or cultural knowledge, or if such knowledge is easy to pass on, there will be little investment in passing such information to the next generation. If the distribution of information is uniform across individuals, having a large number of offspring passes on the biological information. If differential investments in passing on cultural information affect the survival of the information, more effort will be put into that than into having large numbers of children. If the number of people that have the information affects whether it is passed on, there will be more emphasis on producing a large number of children. Likewise, if passing on genes depends on cultural survival, then passing on culture will be followed by more investment in the cultural enterprise. Attachment will play a more prominent role in such processes.

The phenotypic manifestations of the biological-evolutionary information are unconditioned and releasing stimuli, unconditioned reflexes and reinforcers. The biological carriers are DNA, mitochondria, and the like. The carriers of the cultural-evolutionary forces are reinforcers and conditioned stimuli and the behavior patterns of individuals. Carriers can be mixtures, because the proximate causes of behavior are stimuli for both cases. The nature of the stimuli might vary as to which force they carry.

Attachment behaviors that get caretakers to nurture their young likely have a biological base. Attachment behaviors that get organizations and societies to nurture individuals likely have both a biological and cultural basis. The orderliness in the development of attachment suggested here supports Kohlberg's stage notions, whereas the universal nature of the processes that promote development supports Gewirtz's learning notions. Culturally universal and relative normative expectations and the social interactions that lead to their being met support cultural transmission.

Gewirtz (personal communication, December 3, 1988) said commonality of parental and infant action in each culture is due to implicit agreement on what is to be reinforced and by whom. The customs and norms indicate which behaviors children and adults are to exhibit and those they are not. Community members reinforce parental behaviors that meet norms for child-rearing practices, especially when the child's behavior concurrently meets the societal norms. These cultural practices with respect to child rearing are acquired and maintained through reinforced immediate and delayed imitation. Parents and others reinforce children's behaviors that meets cultural norms. Hence, customs and bi-directional interaction control both which behaviors of attachment objects are reinforced and which behaviors are involved in the attachment, object-attached dyad.

THE DEVELOPMENT OF ATTACHMENT

Cognitive-Developmental and Social Conditioning Approaches Compared

To compare the approaches of Kohlberg and Gewirtz, their approaches are synthesized into a theory of stages of attachment. The language used to express the positions of Kohlberg's view and of Gewirtz's view of stages comes from the General Stage Model (Commons & Richards, 1984a, 1984b) and does not necessarily conform to the language either Kohlberg or Gewirtz would use. Thus, two contrasting views of what changes during the development of attachment will be presented. For Kohlberg, a structuralist, the internalized actions and mental structure that organize them changes. For Gewirtz, the behavior analyst, the complexity of stimuli that are discriminated changes. In the behavior-analytic approach, the stimuli to be discriminated are the relationship between outcomes of other people's behavior as consequences of one's own behavior. Such relational stimuli are reinforcement contingencies.

Stage of Attachment

Kohlberg and Gewirtz give sequential levels different roles. For both, each successively higher level differs in the complexity needed for task-required sets of actions characteristic of that level. Kohlberg and Armon (1984) partially based their notion of hard stages on the hierarchical organization of internalized actions. Kohlberg (1984) thought that *thoughts* or *internalized actions* controlled the overt task-required actions. Internal actions are acts carried out within the organisms's brain that were first performed externally. Stages consist of internalized actions that share a common logic, thus, the overt responses at a stage form a structured whole within a domain. That means that the complexity of the perceptions, of reasoning, and of associated actions are all independent of the particular moral task. The logic of a later stage is qualitatively more complex than the logic shared by internal actions at earlier stages, therefore, the resulting stages form an invariant sequence. Each higher stage increasingly differentiates from and integrates the required actions of previous stages.

Gewirtz (1969, 1977; personal communication, September 24, 1989) and most social conditioning and continuity theorists are sympathetic with approaches that order behavior according to its complexity. It would not be difficult for Gewirtz to organize actions into levels and name those levels. On the other hand, Gewirtz does not define stage in his terms nor employ the traditional notion of stage. Stages are not causes but labels for the hierarchical complexity or level of the required actions maintained by attachment-object provided contingencies. Labels should describe where in a developmental sequence action of a given complexity would occur. The danger is that such labels might limit a search for causal determinants of those actions. Social conditioning and continuity approaches are process theories, thus, the search for causes of behavior is what is essential.

Gewirtz sees sequential life levels or phases characterizing the complexity of actions persons emit and the parallel complexity of the discriminative stimuli that cue those behaviors. The order of acquisition of behaviors is fixed by their complexity but not their use. Actions characteristic of a lower stage are continuously available in contrast to their decreased availability under Kohlberg's or Piaget's emergentist notion. In some behavior realms, increasingly complex behaviors are reinforced by the environment. In other behavior realms, the simple behaviors are maintained by the environmental consequences, that is they are reinforced. Higher-stage actions only lose their availability on a permanent basis, if there is injury to person, or if the environment only reinforced lower-stage behavior.

The stage notion used here has the hierarchical ordering actions like Kohlberg's and many of behavior-analytic restrictions like Gewirtz's. Commons and Richards (1984a, 1984b) defined a general stage sequence as hierarchical linearly ordered sets of task-required actions. A stage theory of attachment requires descriptions and ordering of the attachment tasks that a person must perform. As in the social conditioning developmental perspective, there is no reference necessary to cognitive processes that may be used to solve such tasks other than those comprising operant learning paradigms. In the behavior-analytic terms of social conditioning developmental theory, actions with the order of hierarchical complexity of a given stage may produce stimuli for the actions of the next stage. That is, higher-stage actions act on products of the lower-stage actions; the required higher stage actions appear later in a chain of actions. The ordering of the actions in the chain cannot be changed, because the order is not in any sense arbitrary. Chains of same-stage actions can, however, be arbitrarily reordered.

The Attachment Object.

Attachment objects have two properties. First, as discussed previously, they are not substitutable for other sources of cues, behavior, and consequences without loss of value. For example, people prefer cues, behavior, and outcomes that come from the attachment object rather than others. Second, the interconnective aspect of attachment arises in a three-actor social interaction. Attachment is shown in a situation with a subject, an attachment object, and an outside party, in which the subject's actions modify a third party's response to the attachment object's behavior. Of course, this attachment is not only directed at other people (Csikszentmihalyi & Rochberg-Halton, 1981). Consider a homecoming game in which nonparticipants successfully cheer their team on: When the team wins and is given a trophy by the referees, the cheering is reinforced. Hooting the other team (negative attachment object) is similarly reinforced.

The attached come to prefer the reinforcing value of their own responses that help the attachment object to obtain reinforcing consequences for the attachment object's behavior. The degree to which people's own behavior is influenced—how likely they are to cheer at the next game—indicates the degree of attachment to the team. When attachment is reciprocated between people, they can feel in difficult situations that they are "in it together." In addition, because the hierarchical complexity of the cues and contingencies among actors or entities may change as the subject's reasoning develops in stage, the hierarchical complexity of the attachment to an object also changes.

How Stage Change in Attachment is Examined

Five aspects of attachment are thought to change with stage: attachment processes, interactions between self and objects that can be discriminated, attachment objects, events that reinforce attachment behaviors, and attachment behaviors. Attachment processes will be discussed first.

Attachment processes. Kohlberg (1984, Kohlberg & Diessner, chapter 12, this volume) applied Baldwin's (1906) and Piaget's notions of *accommodation* and *assimilation* as the two key processes for intellective development. Kohlberg suggested that the development of the self, although depending on other processes as well, requires intellectual development as a prerequisite. Otherwise, moral attachment would occur in infants. From Commons's understanding of Gewirtz's position and his own perspective (Commons, 1985; Gewirtz, 1961, 1969, 1972a, 1972b, 1976, 1977, Gewirtz & Boyd, 1977; Gewirtz & Peláez-Nogueras, 1987, 1989, & chapter 7, this volume; Grotzer, Commons, & Davidson, 1986), attachment to objects irrespective of their level (assimilation) and attachment to more hierarchically complex objects that stand in some specific part of the chain (accommodation) both follow behavior-analytic laws of acquisition. These include the necessity of immediate, contingent reinforcement by the attachment object of the attached's interactional behavior. A necessary but not always sufficient part of the attachment process is as follows. An attachment object becomes a nonsubstitutable cue for reinforcement. The activities that bring one in contact with the attachment object institute a reinforcement schedule. This is a *chain schedule* (Ferster & Skinner, 1957) in which behavior to get or be close or maintain closeness (link 1) leads to interactions with the attachment object from which reinforcement is obtained (link 2). The matching law shows that the more reinforcement that is obtained from an interaction, the more interaction there will be with that source of reinforcement. Hence, there will be increased behavior to maintain closeness to the object of attachment.

The cognitive-developmental and social conditioning developmental approaches to the development of attachment use different time scales and different units of analysis. Whereas Kohlberg's cognitive-developmental approach concentrates on a macro analysis of change, Gewirtz's behavioral-analytic approach focuses on more immediate changes by using learning paradigms. Macroanalysis examines changes over long time segments (e.g., months and years), whereas Gewirtz's analysis examine changes over intermediate time segments such as behavior aggregated into sessions or parts of sessions, and moment-to-moment, event-by-event changes (see Gewirtz & Peláez-Nogueras, chapter 7, this volume).

As to the units of analysis, the cognitive-developmental approach tends to use stage as measured on standard instruments such as moral dilemmas or Piagetian tasks. That approach examines an individual's stage mixtures at different points in time, usually spanning months or years. The data so generated help clarify what is the sequence of behaviors that develop. The cognitive-developmental approach may be contrasted with the social conditioning study of how a situation's moral and attachment atmosphere affects the development of behavior at the next level or stage. Changes over long periods are likely to appear as jumps (Commons & Calnek, 1984). The conditions of change are not observed, leading structural-developmentalists such as Kohlberg and Piaget to see developmental change as an emergent property of the person.

The social conditioning developmental approach tends to use rate or probability of cued or elicited behaviors denoting attachment in a situation as the basic unit of analysis. It examines changes in the probability or rate of responding an individual during a session or over several sessions. Change measured over very short periods can appear continuous (Commons & Calnek, 1984). When change is measured over short periods, the conditions that promote change can be identified under an assumption of continuity across time. Notions that development is an emergent property of organisms are rejected. Thus, the effects on behavior of schedule of reinforcement or schedule of pairings of stimuli is of major interest.

Role accorded the subject.   One important area of disagreement between the cognitive-developmental and the behavior-analytic-developmental approaches is in the role of the subject. The cognitive-developmental approach regards the subject as an independent, internally guided actor with a phenomenal self concept. Behavior analysts see the subject as actively manifesting behavior inextricably bound up with immediate units of the environment with which the subject is in interaction. The subject's behavioral history with environmental events, current behavior, and environment all form a network of interaction, each determining the other (Gewirtz, 1969). Small changes in behavior or in the environment can produce very different outcomes in the course of a person's life.

Kohlberg's work reflects a great interest in what situations support stage change (Kohlberg, 1984; Power et al., 1989) work. Like Piaget, he posits that individuals construct a new reality based on a process of resolving inconsistencies in their previous internal constructions of external reality rather than simply by adapting to external reality imposed by the environment. In the same vein, summarizing Piaget and Inhelder's position on stage, Gallagher and Reid (1981) state that the actor constructs reality that is independent to a degree from the interventions provided by feedback and reward. They reason that the subject constructs the meaning of the feedback and reward as well as of the situation, and claim that reinforcers and instruction can train specific behaviors but not alter the active construction of reality by the subject. In other words, learning is not a "passive" process (Siegel & Hodkin, 1982).

The old idea of the passive organism (Langer, 1969), however, is not consistent with behavior analysis. First, as people mature, stages of attachment change, because people actively interact with the changing environment. First, behavior theorists generally believe that behavior is probabilistic and, hence, to that extent indeterminate. Only by looking at aggregate measures do influences of behavior appear orderly. In this frame, Hull actually posited indeterminacy independently of Bridgman. The action at any moment in time cannot be attributed with certainty to particular events in the environment.

Second, Hull and Spence (Hull, 1943, 1952; Spence, 1956) posited an organism whose responses are elicited/cued and reinforced. They assumed that the overall probability of the response to the stimulus changed—the subject acquired a S–R association. Whether one used the rate of obtained and programmed reinforcement was not an issue as it now is in behavior analysis. Obtained reinforcement is jointly under the control of the organism and the environment whereas programmed reinforcement is totally under the control of the environment. The Hull–Spence and behavior-analytic approaches note, however, that before the rate of probability of a behavior can be modified, behavior must occur (Gewirtz, 1969; Skinner, 1938). What is modified is the mix of behaviors that occur and in what situations. Both approaches require that new behaviors be assembled. The mix of behaviors is determined by what is effectively reinforced. Whereas an experimenter reinforces behaviors, which are operationally defined, whatever the organism is doing that produces the reinforcer is what actually increases in likelihood. Commons and Armstrong-Roche (1984) assert that response-reinforcer relations are usually acquired before stimulus–response relations (also see Pear & Eldridge, 1984; Rescorla 1988). The generality of behavioral control depends on how varied the conditions were under which the behaviors were reinforced.

Verbal explanation, implicit rule following, and action.   A difference between Kohlberg's cognitive-developmental and Gewirtz's social conditioning perspective is that, for Kohlberg, persons' explanations represent how behavior is controlled. On the other hand, rules that describe how people behave are verbalizable. From a social conditioning developmental perspective, what people verbalize about their behavior is also behavior. As such, what they verbalize may be controlled by the same reinforcement contingencies that control their nonverbal behavior. In addition, people can appear to be following rules when their behavior is being controlled by reinforcement contingencies. Or they may behave as they do, because their behavior is actually rule-governed, which rule governance may be established by reinforcement, contingency-based rule learning (Skinner, 1957, 1969). At the most rudimentary level, explicit rules are descriptions of the relationship between situations and behavior. Thus, rules may describe which acts obtain certain outcomes under a given set of conditions. Responses that satisfy a complex set of contingencies and, thus, solve a problem, can come about in two ways. For contingency-controlled behavior, responses are directly shaped by contingencies. Reinforced behavior occurs more often in the presence of the stimuli that cue it. For rule-governed behavior, responses may be evoked by contingency-related stimuli constructed either by the problem-solvers themselves or by others.

A sequence suggested by Piaget (1976) that Kohlberg and Gewirtz might agree on would be that contingency-controlled behavior develops first (*action*), then it is followed by descriptions of the behavior (description), which in turn leads to the possibility of explaining what has been described (*explanation*). When the resulting behavior is reinforced, the explanations become the rules that then control behavior in the future (Kohlberg & Candee, 1984; Gewirtz & Peláez-Nogueras, in press; Skinner, 1969). Descriptions and explanations of behavior develop after the behavior itself develops (Commons, Stein, & Richards, 1988; Stein & Commons, 1987).

Commons, et al. (1988) and Schrader (1988) suggested three levels of explaining what has been described: pragmatic, normative, and epistemic. Tappan (1990) suggested these levels are actually separate dimensions. He referred to the descriptive level as metacognitive. Reports about the acts and rules one uses to solve problems and make judgments are metacognitive. Commons, Stein, and Richards found pragmatic rules that control behavior (*pragmatic*). The pragmatic rules are justified in what Kohlberg has stated as a normative manner (*normative*). The norms are used to answer the question why one should take a certain course of action. The norms have a philosophical and logical rather than a cultural and social basis. Finally there are rules about the truth or value of the system of such rules (*epistemic*). Such reflection upon systems of rules may yield principals. Kohlberg and Gewirtz seem to agree on the role rules play in attachment, but they use different language to discuss those roles.

Stage-Independent Conditions for Producing Stage Change

How discrepant should environmental features be? Cognitive-developmental and social conditioning approaches both posit that there has to be an "optimal" mismatch between what the person now does and what behavior is required for the delivery of a reinforcer by the attachment object to whom the person's behavior denotes attachment. In the optimal case, the mismatch would be maximized between how a person now discriminates (understands) and what discriminations that person can immediately acquire (Commons & Richards, 1984a; Kohlberg, 1984). With respect to attachment, the mismatch most often occurs in role and perspective taking. The child's version of the role behavior only very loosely approximates matching the adult's. Outside of play situations, the mismatch leads to fewer reinforcers than would be available with a more developed pervasive-imitative performance (Gewirtz, 1969; Gewirtz & Stingle, 1968).

Processes that describe the stage change of attachment. Kohlberg's and Gewirtz's approaches have similar notions of how development is influenced, although they seem different at first glance. The cognitive-developmental notion is one of equilibration between accommodation and assimilation. From a behavioral-analytic perspective, *accommodation* corresponds to the notion of acquisition and *assimilation* to the notion of transfer of training. The behavior-analytic formulation is more precise and event-focused. For quantitative versions of such laws, see Herrnstein's (1970) reinforcement-matching law describing the allocation of behavior and Herrnstein's (1982; Herrnstein & Vaughan, 1980) melioration law or the Commons, as (Commons, Bing, Griffy, & Trudeau, 1991; Commons & Hallinan, 1989; Commons, Woodford, & Ducheny, 1982) models describing acquisition. Both cognitive-developmental and behavior-analytic approaches see different aspects of development happening concurrently and assume that the forces that affect development have many loci and operate throughout the life span (Commons, Grotzer, & Davidson, submitted; Gewirtz, 1969, 1978, chapter 13, this volume; Kohlberg, 1964, 1978; chapter 12 this volume).

Feedback underlies the changing relationship between self and other. Accommodation and assimilation or the earlier-described behavioral counterpart can account for the stage-change process. Cognitive-developmental and social conditioning approaches agree on the function of feedback. They differ on why that feedback works. From either the cognitive-developmental or the social conditioning learning-developmental perspective, one aspect of attachment is the individual's behavioral sensitivity to social reinforcement, usually in the form of feedback or approval from a specific significant other—parent, teacher, or peer.

Insofar as there is moral attachment, the self's status or sense of being good is related to feedback from the specific other. A social conditioning approach would say that people might discriminate whether or not their behavior is seen by others as good.

Kohlberg and Gewirtz differ most on the role of the self. A cognitive-developmental approach posits the self as the source of action. Although the self is not a term most behavior-analysis oriented researchers such as Gewirtz use, Skinner (1953, 1957) considered the self a device for representing a functionally unified system of responses. Apart from the possibility of such usage, a social conditioning approach does not require the notion of the self as an explanation of action or has it focused on a higher-order reflection of action and reasoning that would support a conception of self.

The reason for the different roles of the self arises from how each approach selects and interprets data. Most research in the cognitive-developmental tradition mixes the actual behaviors, or as Piaget (1976) refers to them *pris de conscience,* with persons' descriptions and explanations of those behaviors. Subjects describe their actions while performing them or afterward. Subjects give justifications for what a person should, could, or might do. Cognitive-developmental researchers take the subjects' reports as representing and reflecting internal processes.

Behavior analysis is generally concerned with behavior itself rather than with *tacts,* which are communications about events including behaviors (Skinner, 1957). Descriptions of behavior are tacts, and justifications of such reflective descriptions are tacts of tacts. Notions such as the *self* can represent such second-order reflections. Skinner (1957) saw such tacts as responses that are reinforced socially. One might deduce that Kohlberg finds personal stage, personal traits, and the will, because he uses as his data higher-order reflections of actions and verbalized thoughts. Gewirtz focuses on behavior, thus, he does not find personal stage, traits, and the will to be useful conceptions.

FIVE ASPECTS OF ATTACHMENT THAT CHANGE
WITH STAGE

Five changes will be described: (a) what the attachment processes are (processes), (b) what chain of responses of others interacting with those of oneself are discriminable (perspective taking), (c) from what unique entities do reinforcers emanate (attachment objects), (d) what events will serve as reinforcers (outcome valuing), and (e) what discriminatively controlled behaviors are in the repertoire of the individual (response patterns). Further, developmentally oriented behavior-analytic approaches (Commons & Richards, 1984a, 1984b; Fischer, 1980; Fischer, Hand, & Russell, 1984) can be used to describe how some of these aspects of attachment change. Some changes in task-required actions can be organized into stages. In these developmentally oriented behavior-analytic approaches, the hierarchical organization of task requirements gives rise to the observed order of acquisition of behaviors. Contrast this to Kohlberg and Piaget's notions of stages, which posits that changes in behavior result from to the development of internal schemes. Behaviorally the hierarchy reflects actual increases in complexity. The person acquires more complex discriminative-response patterns required by the tasks at each new stage (Commons et al., in preparation; Fischer, 1980).

From either a behavioral or cognitive perspective, one needs to show that successful performance of one stage's tasks precede and are prerequisites for successful performance of tasks at the next stage. For instance, certain relational stimuli are only discriminable after simpler relational stimuli have been discriminated. The sequence of attachment-stage transitions may be like the cognitive-stage sequence shown by Piaget and may also show many-stage regularities suggested by Kegan's (1982) and Perry's (1968) notion of the spiral (also see Fischer, et al., 1984). What constitutes the attachment situation, however, changes with stage of attachment.

WHAT ARE THE ATTACHMENT PROCESSES

The processes by which people become attached to objects change. The nature of the change has not been fully described. Some portion depends on the zone of proximal influence, including the type of contingencies to which a person is exposed. Garbarino and Bronfenbrenner (1976) reported that concentration camp children did not identify with adults until they had a one-to-one relationship with them. Attachment to a collectivity occurs much earlier in Soviet children and kibbutz children than in children in the United States. Some portion of the development of attachment processes depends on the development of perspective taking and imitation.

Kohlberg (1969) suggested that identification precedes moral attachment. Gewirtz (1969; chapter 13 this volume; Gewirtz & Stingle, 1968) saw imitation as a major process in identification and conceived of the attachment and identification processes as being orthogonal. He, therefore, posited that there is no fixed sequential order of occurrence involving attachment and identification. Kohlberg (1969) and Kuhn (1973) argued that processes like imitation develop without a reinforcement history. Gewirtz (1969, 1971b) argued for the necessity of reinforcement to institute imitation. He saw organisms as more likely to acquire certain behaviors at certain periods in their development and thought the empirical analysis has to be carried out in each case. Like other behavior-analytic theorists, Gewirtz also thought that understanding what events serve as reinforcers for particular behaviors requires an empirical analysis. The fundamental processes that produce attachment are described next.

Familiarity and Habituation

People appear more attached to familiar objects. Familiarization is similar to habituation. *Habituation* is the repeated presentation of an event, the responses to which are not followed by any specific environmental event. Responses to such events, such as "fear," are systematically reduced by the repeated exposure to the environmental events. Response habituation occurs in the youngest infants (sensory & motor actions stage, as in Table 14.1). It may partly account for preference for specific caregivers, especially if odor stimuli are included.

Simple, Generalized, and Pervasive Imitation

As Gewirtz (1969, 1971a, 1971b) pointed out, his view of imitation learning is compatible with cognitive-developmental analyses based on observation in life settings. As in Piaget (1951), there can be stages of imitation. Not only does the generality increase, but the organization of the imitative responses also appears to increases. The earliest forms of imitation may be elicited, such as smiles to smiles (Meltzoff & Moore, 1977, 1983a, 1983b). Yet these *reflexive-imitation* responses soon appear to drop out (Uzgiris, 1981). *Operant imitation* occurs during the second stage, termed here as *circular sensory-motor actions* as shown in Table 14.1. *Generalized imitation* begins in the *nominal* (very early preoperational) stage and continues well into *primary operations* (early concrete operations). *Pervasive imitation* begins in preoperations and continues throughout life. It includes delayed imitation or observational learning. The imitated action may be portrayed in written and other reproduced means. Imitation comes in two forms (a) others imitating one's actions and (b) one imitating other's actions.

Form One of Imitation. Having others imitating one's actions means that one's own behavior controls the behavior of others. The outcomes produced by controlling other people's behavior may reinforce one's own acts that are imitated. This type of reinforcement has no drive reduction associated with it. Power and status in both the pecking and social order are likely explanations for why controlling other's behavior by serving as a model can reinforce one's behavior. Given that the behavior being imitated has no particular value in itself, this explanation may be correct. If the value of the behavior is negative, people might not prefer to have that behavior imitated. Babies might not prefer to hear crying, when they are crying. Many people's behavior is reinforced by producing followers, and imitators. Controlling other people's behavior is partially the basis of cultural transmission. Being imitated can reinforce one's own behavior after circular sensorimotor actions are attained and before sensorimotor actions are attained.

Form Two of Imitation. Imitating the behavior of others (Gewirtz, 1969) is the second form of imitation. Imitating another is reinforced by behavior of that

TABLE 14.1
Stages of Attachment

Stage 0a (Kohlbergian -1) Sensory-motor Actions: (simple discrimination)

Infants are dependent on their caregivers. Habituation, and positive and negative reinforcement are the main attachment contingencies. Both positive and negative reinforcement increase or maintain the frequency of behavior that they follow. Positive reinforcement adds an event after a behavior. Negative reinforcement subtracts an event after a behavior. Infants can discriminate their primary caregivers from others. There is a small preference for that primary caregiver, which seems to be partially based on familiarity. The familiar caregiver is more effective at pacification than others. Decreasing distress serves as a negative reinforcer. Much of infants behavior maintains a simple positive feeling and seeks comfort from distress. Infants fail to maintain that feeling by discriminating that the attachment object is not available during some distress episodes and others cannot alleviate it as well. Some activities and games are preferred. There seems to be little preference for place. Toys preferred on the basis of function and form. Babies are recognized as objects to be manipulated midway. Imitation is mostly reflexive, such as smiling to smiles.

Stage 0b (Kohlbergian -1/0) Circular Sensory-motor Actions (conditional and other complex discriminations)

Infants imitate on an operant basis. They follow hidden objects. They discriminate separation from attachment figures. They develop a clear preference for one or at most two attachment objects. These three facts results in there being degree of separation protest. Gewirtz finds that the separation protest can be conditioned further. The appearance of and, imitations by, smiles and laughs from the primary caregiver are more reinforcing of behavior then when they emanate from others. Infants can recognize familiar people in mirrors, looking first at person and then the image. They do not recognize themselves. They have favorite toys. Operant laughing and crying clearly appear. Reaching towards the main caregiver develops as one of the attachment behaviors.

Stage 1a (Kohlbergian 0) Sensory-motor Actions: (concepts)

There is generalized imitation and beginning identification with increased matching to similar category objects. Infants recognize self (in a mirror for instance) without explicit training, indicating a further separation of self from others. Because they can name themselves and others, there is categorical separation. Gender labels are attached to the sex categories. Infants become mobile and can act independently in a broader arena leading to some independence from the primary attachment object.

Stage 1b (Kohlbergian 0/1) Nominal Actions. (named concepts)

Pervasive imitation and identification develops. Children use objects that the attachment objects use. They discriminate the effects of acts on others. They act like an executive and manipulates others without discriminating what the others' goals are. They give verbal opposition, quite often saying "no." (terrible 2s). They fail to control caretakers and are unable to obtain their planned objects on their own. They see peers as individuals to be manipulated but are attached to them (Field, this volume). There are clear favorite toys. Children clearly associate peer relations and routines with place (Field, this volume). The place is discriminative for the activities. The child who remains misses the one that moves and not visa versa. Hence there is really only partial attachment to friends and it is conditional on the environment. Routine is important. If a mother leaves the area for a trip, the child is less upset when routine is maintained. Words have a literal meaning and quite often even a name like orange juice can be taken as an instruction to drink the orange juice. Mands are followed. There is no independent rule-governed behavior. Words take on social-reinforcing value. Perceptions of monsters are real.

Stage 2a (Kohlbergian 1) Sentential Actions. (described concepts)

Instructions in sentence form are followed. There are simple rules. The child can state a rule as well as follow them. Rules have the form of role of description, explanation and moral imperative. Children select children who are somewhat similar as playmates. Children verbalize about what they like and want. Often they do not understand the difference between their own orders and those given by adults. The superiority of rules of adults is only partially understood. Only bits and pieces of adult behavior can be imitated. Being someone and

(continued)

TABLE 14.1 (Continued)

their opposite comes into play. One may be the bad person as well as the good one. Possible selves are explored thorough imitation. Monsters can be fought and subdued.

Stage 2b (Kohlbergian 1/2) Preoperational Actions. (paragraphs length concepts)

Paragraph length sequences of instructions can be followed. By the end of this period, a child in this culture has formed a group identity, they have a sex-role preference (Kohlberg, 1966; Miller & Commons, 1973). There is strong pervasive imitation of same sex parents and figures. A child begins to follow an older person. The pervasive imitation of the older is identification. It is seen in role playing. There is no distinction between a personal interpretation of another's action and what the true perspective. There is no sense of a shared self yet there is some empathy. Abstractions of superiority of the adult caretaker is now partially but not consistently discriminated. There is still complete dependence. Pervasive imitation can be reinforced by producing similar appearing outcomes. The observed appearance of similarity to the adult model may make those outcomes reinforcing.

Stage 3a (Kohlbergian 2) Primary Operations, Moral Attachment Stage (reality-verified objects)

There is actual rule governed behavior in addition to pervasive imitation. The verbal behavior of attachment objects is vocalized as rules. The children follow rules accurately across time. Children can coordinate their actions with attachment objects. Children recognize their own dependence on the parent. They can discriminate the greater power and competence of the attachment object. If children are asked who is better, they reply that the attachment object is better. Also authority in general is seen as better, more competent, more virtuous. Children compare themselves to the attachment object--this social comparison requiring primary operations.

Children see parental perspective in the form of stated parental rules. Insofar as there is moral attachment, feedback from the attachment object affects not only specific behaviors but mood as well. The discriminated value of the self changes with such evaluation. Producing pervasively matched behavior is reinforced not only by the usual outcomes produced by such behaviors but by the appearance of similarity, which is valued in itself. Outcomes delivered to the parents may reinforce behavior of the child, because of the shared self.

Stage 3b. (Kohlbergian 2/3) Concrete Operations. (concrete others)

Two new sources of attachment objects appear. The attachment objects increasingly can be peers. While with peers, people ignore the basic attachment figure to some degree. Immediate social reinforcement from peers is sometimes more effective than more general rules in controlling behavior. Hence, parental authority is sometimes ignored. While in the preoperational and primary stages, children will act out what they see in the adult world or hear, during concrete operations the shared-self may extend to models that appear in written or spoken stories. These are models that appear quite real as opposed to the mythical figures from the earlier two stages.

Shared activity with some degree of compatibility is the basis of peer attachment. People change the way they behave with different friends. The perspective of the other is discriminated by considering how one's own behavior will effect another's behavior, the other person's behavior possibly reinforcing ones own. Such perspective taking makes it possible to have for attachment objects named peer groups, such as cub scouts, brownies, camp fire girls. The school has a name and so do the teachers. Authority figures in general are good. There is a strong sense of shared self, the objects now being extended to informal local organizations. Rules are good and to be followed.

Stage 4a. (Kohlbergian 3) Abstract Operations. (abstract others)

Actors can take the perspective of another abstract rather than actual-concrete person (viewing the actor). Rules are so well discriminated and followed that in implicit rules of groups become important. People select attachment figures other than caregivers. Group identification develops along with serious attachment to groups (imitation of group behavior). People see themselves as belonging to one of the acceptable groups or an out group. People, who do not attach to groups appear distinct to themselves and others. One sees nationalism and parochialism. The group's displayed view of themselves can serve as reinforcers and punishers. When caught breaking rules by new attachment figures there is rage and shame. There is opposition to parental figures with the rules of peers used as challenges. Formal groups are important. Following the rules makes one good. There are multiple sources for the rules.

(continued)

276

TABLE 14.1 (*Continued*)

Stage 4b. (Kohlbergian 3/4) Formal Operations. (subsystems of others)

The perspective is that each sector of the world consists of a number of relationships, the rules that guide them have to be discovered or learned by the person. Hence, with respect to social perspective taking, how abstract others will behave can be experimentally and logically examined. The causal information is fragmented and not built into a system. The sectors of the world seems to be fixed. Subgroup are to be affiliated with. Usually the subgroup of which one is a member is superior to all others as well as its rules and definitions. The costs of belonging to an outside group are high. There is opposition to norms of basic attachment objects, rebellion, weakening of interdependence. People can figure out what to do to influence other people. The rules about influence are abstract, and in some sense are like general principle, they just have not been applied widely. The truth of the rules is independent of one's position in the social hierarchy. There is increasing opposition to parents but conformity to age-appropriate groups, not in just superficial ways as in the abstract stage but in terms of the effectiveness of the group to use rule governed behavior to subtly define the relationship between the person and the hierarchy. The person is seen as subordinate to the hierarchy.

Stage 5a. (Kohlbergian 4, early 4/5) Systematic Operations. (ordered subsystems of others)

People take the perspective that may affiliate with any possible system. At the later levels of this stage, although these systems have relative validity the person must choose among them (Perry, 1976). People can see inter-relationships between the actions of one person in the social hierarchy and another and how that interaction affects the system at different levels in the hierarchy. The rules that govern identity are arbitrary and may be reconstructed by the group. There is independence but with conformity to group norms. People may view themselves as independent individuals. A change in a system most often appears as a new ordering individual and subgroup status. The new order is the one a person has to live with and care about. The attachment to the system makes it likely that people, whether liked or not, will be afforded the procedures of the system. In the later part of this stage, tolerance of others who are different from oneself develops as one of the main positive attachment behaviors. Cynicism towards the system develops as one of the main negative attachment behaviors.

Stage 5b. (Kohlbergian 5, and 6) Metasystematic Operations. (system of universal others)

People attain autonomy (Armon, 1989). They respect others and value them as human beings irrespective of agreeing them. The opposition of the previous stage that may have required some hostility towards controlling objects, has dissipated. The perspective taking ability allows the person to see the other in more similar terms to the other. They can not only stand in their shoes, view the relationship from a third person perspective, and see how that relationship fits into the system, but they can assume the perspective of the other to the extent that they are informed. They also discriminate the inability to do so fully. Dependency is acknowledged.

Stage 6a. (Kohlbergian new stage 6) Paradigmatic Operations. (differentiated universal others).

Perspective-taking now not only includes an integrated self and other but self and nature (Commons & Sonnert, 1987; Sonnert & Commons, in preparation). People see there are no possible social perspectives that are both logically consistent and powerful enough to solve all problems. People see themselves as part of nature, not in opposition to it. They see that there is no way to transcend nature or impose themselves on it. There is recognition that human endeavors have limited complexity in the face of the possibly infinite complexity of the universe. The mappings between self and other, self and society, self and nature formed at stage 5b are transformed so to solve problems among people, a perspective has to be co-constructed that remains consistent but incomplete. The attachment objects include universal entities, such as everyone and all of nature. There is unconditional respect for everything in nature including ones place in it.

other. Kohlberg and Gewirtz have somewhat different views of what can serve as a reinforcer for such imitation and why. Kohlberg (1969) attacked the obsolete Hullian (1952) position that reinforcers have to have drive-reduction properties. In the contemporary behavior-analytic frame, Gewirtz identified events subsequent to responses as reinforcers, when they alter the probability of future responding across situations or are necessary to maintain future responding. If changing any behavioral consequence contingent on the imitative behavior alters its rate, then reinforcement is involved. Although his cognitive-developmental approach does not contain terms like "reinforcement," it is remarkable that Kohlberg found that concept useful. However, he found the operational definition of the reinforcing stimulus theoretically unsatisfying, because of his interest in *why* some environmental events are reinforcing. On the other hand, Gewirtz (see Petrovich & Gewirtz, 1985) conceived that events that function to reinforce the behavior upon which they are contingent, if they have not attained their power via the conditioning history, may have attained that power via the evolutionary history of the species. Both of these origins, conditioned or unconditioned, can explain the bases of reinforcer power.

Praise is only one type reinforcement for behavior. The reinforcing value of praise for behavior can be independent of social dependency. The outcome of observing that one is behaving like an attachment object can reinforce ones behavior. Kohlberg has suggested such observations will reinforce behavior, when the attachment object is perceived as competent and valuable. What reinforces such imitative acts still requires more research. What people imitate depends on what they detect in other's behavior and what aspects of stimuli control reinforced behavior at different stages. If reinforcers for acts such as imitation could be better identified, Kohlberg would have been more sympathetic to Gewirtz' behavior-analytic notion of reinforcement. Their views on the adequacy of imitation to generate moral attachment would be even closer, as will be shown.

Pervasive imitation is used to construct the self.   Kohlberg (1969; Kohlberg & Diessner, chapter 12 this volume) posited that moral attachment follows identification. During the preoperational stage, when identification develops, children form a *bipolar self*. With a bipolar self, children vacillate between action governed by self and action governed by imitation of others. That is, whereas they behave according to selfish needs and desires, they also imitate and internalize adult rules.

From Gewirtz's perspective, attachment situations quite often provide an opportunity for identification. Identification consists of pervasive imitation and observational learning (Gewirtz, 1971, chapter 13 this volume). Pervasive imitation or identification describes how a person becomes like another. Pervasive imitation begins in the nominal stage but becomes most prominent during the primary stage. For Kohlberg, the transformation of identification into moral attachment requires a shared self.

A *shared self* develops after a bipolar self. Kohlberg's notion of a shared self is that parts of another are incorporated into one's self. With the transition to a shared self, the child moves from following rules of the authority of the parent to following the parents' rules, because they have become the child's own. The child feels that everything learned from the adult is shared with the adult. Both are subject to the same outside contingencies. As a result, whereas the bipolar self serves only to regulate behavior within the parent–child dyad, the shared self regulates behavior within a larger context. It is only at this point that moral attachment is possible. The shift to rule-following behavior helps transform a bipolar self into a shared self.

The shared-self notion is illustrated in a retelling of Kohlberg's quotation of the Baldwin's example of the boy on the bike. The boy observed another's bike riding last year. This year, he is like the other and can also ride a bike. He discriminates which activities are possible by observing the other boy's activities. He plans to imitate and thereby acquire the other's behavior. The imitation is delayed. The behavior is engaged in only when the child has a similar opportunity to act successfully as the other boy had.

For Gewirtz, pervasively imitating adult behavior could be a basis for behavior systems connoting the "normative self" or "shared conscience," the behavior mechanisms involved benefiting from further study. For Gewirtz, the development of shared rules passes one generation's cultural information to the next. For Kohlberg, moral attachment plays a role in insuring that transmission. For Gewirtz, sharing contingencies programmed by the environment (Petrovich & Gewirtz, 1985) make us nurturant, social-affiliative on one hand, and competitive and status-seeking on the other. These contingencies have their roots in cultural and biological evolution. The local contingencies that influence people to adopt shared sets of rules need studying.

This writer's behavioral-developmental perspective synthesizes the Kohlberg and Gewirtz notions of the development of the shared self. From a meta-systematic perspective, the shared self arises from the transformation of the preoperational perspective-taking form of imitation into the primary operational perspective-taking form. In preoperations, the child becomes different and independent from the other (Damon, 1983). There is no way of coordinating discriminative properties of the self with those of the other person. This coordination develops with primary operations, as illustrated by being able to coordinate the sequences of number names with the numerosity of objects. Lining up one person's characteristics with another's also requires primary operations.

For Kohlberg, to have a shared self, one has to have a perspective on the power and virtue of the others and their standards, and to coordinate what one might imitate in others as potentially being a discriminative characteristic of one's self. For Gewirtz, children may discriminate that a behavior might be acquired but also discriminates that their present imitations are inadequate. To discriminate potentially imitated behavior as a characteristic of one's self requires primary operational perspective-taking as discussed following.

Role taking.   Kohlberg (Kohlberg, 1985; Kohlberg & Candee, 1984) reviewed the variety of role-taking conditions (in homes and schools) that seem to stimulate moral reasoning and attachment. Gewirtz has recognized that such global conditions exist, but he would like to identify the actual contingencies that underlie the conditions that produce attachment to higher-stage objects. A behavioral approach will show that reinforcement contingencies underlie the effectiveness of Kohlberg's procedures. The role-taking conditions have at least two effects for the behavioral approach. First, the role-taking contingencies support the acquisition of discrimination of higher-stage objects. Second, contingencies for role taking include the attachment processes that produce attachment behaviors as discussed by Gewirtz.

Role taking versus identification.   Unlike psychoanalytic theory, Kohlberg and Gewirtz have stressed that moral attachment or identification do not provide the central, or even necessary core, of moral development. From both of their perspectives, moral stage development occurs through more generalized processes of role taking, or taking the perspective of others. From the cognitive-developmental perspective, role taking occurs in a variety of types of social relationships with peers and adults. Role taking is the action that promotes perspective taking. Both involve the attribution of thoughts and feelings to others, and an engagement in communication and cooperation with others. The attribution might be verbal behavior from the behavior-analytic perspective. People might state to themselves or others that the other person will have certain thoughts and feelings, if they, the actors, behave in a given manner.

Play.   Infants recognize other infants and play with adults and toys. Even newborns a few days after birth will touch a toy that produces a reinforcing effect. Later on, play involves infants in relationships with peers. Field (chapter 9 this volume) has shown that preschoolers miss departed playmates, therefore, the play they engage in is sufficient to form some type of attachment. (See Table 14.1 for examples.)

Assumption of roles.   The assumption of new roles is to some extent programmed on the basis of stage. Children become students, when "they are ready." Assuming the role, which is what happens during preschool, seems to make it more likely that children are ready for elementary school.
Next, how stimulus functions change with development and how those changes account for some of the changes in attachment are discussed.

Stimulus Functions

Elicitors and Evokers.   Some behaviors of the object to which the person is attached act as distress-reducing stimuli for the subject from early infancy on. Consoling stimuli may evoke subject responses that compete with distress.

Reinforcers. The sources of reinforcement changes. For example, sexual activity shows a marked change in the extent to which events are reinforcing of behavior. This has a clear biological component. The persons and entities who may effectively reinforce behavior change. Sexual partners become sources of reinforcement for behavior in adolescence.

WHAT INTERACTIONS CAN BE DISCRIMINATED: PERSPECTIVE TAKING

The perspective-taking aspect of attachment meets the stage criteria (Fischer et al., 1984; Kohlberg, 1980; Rodriguez & Commons, in preparation; Selman, 1980). The four criteria of Kohlberg and Armon (1984) as discussed previous are met as well as the axioms of Commons and colleagues (Commons and Richards 1984a, 1984b; Commons, Stein, & Richards, 1987, submitted). In behavior-analytic terms, perspective taking is the discrimination of relationships among events. The events usually constitute a causal chain consisting of a situation (stimulus), the behavior of one individual (behavior), and its effects (outcome). A contingency between the behavior of one person and its advantage to another is an example of a relational event. The verbal diagrams of Skinner (1948) formalize such interactions:

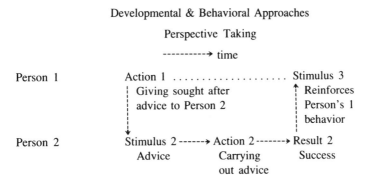

Developmental & Behavioral Approaches

Perspective Taking

- - - - - - - - - → time

Person 1   Action 1 . . . . Stimulus 3
                  Giving sought after   Reinforces
                  advice to Person 2   Person's 1
                                       behavior
Person 2   Stimulus 2 - - - - - → Action 2 - - - - - - → Result 2
                  Advice   Carrying   Success
                               out advice

In this interaction, the behavior of each person serves as a stimulus for the others behavior, including verbal behavior. The success of someone else's behavior (Person 2), such as carrying out advice, may reinforce one's own behavior, such as giving sought after advice (Person 1). Commons and Rodriguez (1990; Rodriguez & Commons, in preparation) described the explicit logic of perspective-taking stages used here. They included the higher-order stages and the diagrams of interactions (also see Cook-Grueter, 1990). For the longer chains of interactions to become verbalized and turned into rules, they have to be discriminated. Hence, social perspective taking from a behavioral-analytic perspective would depend on being able to discriminate the effects of increasingly longer chains of interaction.

WHAT ARE THE ATTACHMENT OBJECTS?

Kohlberg (1984), Rodriguez and Commons (in preparation), and Selman (1976) pointed out that perspective taking becomes more complex with increases in stage, which must of course be the case by definition. As perspective taking increases in stage, Kohlberg's and Selman's researches show that the sources of social reinforcement change. Behavior-analytically attachment refers to the non-substitutability of reinforcers emanating from different sources. Mommy's hug is worth more to an infant than another caregiver's hug. Later, a girlfriend's or boyfriend's hug may be more reinforcing for behavior than the mother's. Such changes represent changes in attachment objects. Listed in order of increasing interactional complexity, the entities could be caretakers, things, places, pets, peers, groups, organizations, the culture at large, and the universal community. The degree of substitutability can be measured in a number of ways, as Gewirtz (1972b, 1972c) pointed out. These can include the equivalent power of care-givers' behavior to pacify or console a person's cries as well as equivalent power of caregivers' behavior to cue, reinforce, or punish a person's behavior. If some person's behavior will pacify or disturb, or reinforce or punish the subject's behavior more effectively than another person's or entities's exact same behavior, then the subject is attached differentially to the first person or entity. Mothers versus other caregivers often meet this definition. Moral attachment rather than infantile attachment requires more than simple nonsubstitutability. Specifically it requires a shared self in which there are shared outcomes.

Interaction Perspectives Determine Concept of Object. What perspective people take in viewing interactions determines their concept of an object. One such object is the self. As Kohlberg (1984) pointed out, schemes of the self and schemes of others have to be at the same stage. The self is defined in terms of interaction. People have convoys (Levitt, chapter 10 this volume) that go with them, wherever they are. Convoys consist of all attachment objects and can be ranked in descending value to self. Attachment stage and affiliative experience determine what is in the convoy. The attachment atmosphere in which the convoys are acquired consists of a number of proximate contingencies. Two main sets exist: first, pervasive- and simple-imitative acts; and second, cooperative and dependent acts and their shared outcomes.

The Development of the Shared Self and How it Affects Reinforcing Value

As discussed previous, for social consequences from a specific other to reinforce behavior, or in Kohlberg's language, to be supportive of self-esteem, the standard used by the unique other must be felt to be shared with the self. In economic terms, social consequence delivered by some non-unique other have less value than consequences delivered by the unique other. The degree of nonsubstitutability is one measure of attachment.

Stated in somewhat different terms, there must be sense of a shared social self. In behavior-analytic terms, a shared social self would mean more than cooperation, dependency, or instrumental imitation (matching behavior reinforced by getting something from another for imitating) in that delivery of reinforcers contingent on one person's behavior would also serve as a reinforcer for behavior of the person who attaches (Commons & Barnett, 1984). From this perspective, how this comes about is an empirical question that needs more study.

WHAT EVENTS CAN SERVE AS REINFORCERS?

The identity of events can serve as reinforcers for behavior depends on the attachment objects that can be formed with the subject's perspective-taking stage. Events that reinforce or punish attachment-object behavior may reinforce subject behavior depending on attachment stage. Such events can be reinforcers or punishers, only if the objects are attachment objects. For instance, people who show little empathy for a person and are below the systems-attachment stage may not find gratitude in return for giving help reinforcing for their behavior. In a broad behavior-analytic sense, thus, attachment refers to the nonsubstitutability of reinforcers emanating from different entities, such changes represent changes in attachment objects.

THE ATTACHMENT STAGES

The attachment stages shown in Table 14.1 were derived from three sets of sources by considering what objects of actions can be discriminated at each stage. Then attachment behaviors associated with those attachment objects were enumerated. The objects of actions in Kohlberg's hard-stage account of moral development (Colby & Kohlberg, 1987a, 1987b) and soft-stage account of moral attachment and of the self (Armon, 1984, 1988, 1989; Kohlberg & Diessner, chapter 11 this volume, 1969; Snary, et al., 1987) were the primary sources.

These attachment stages were then checked by using the General Stage Model (Commons & Richards, 1984a, 1984b) to examine the stages of the objects of actions and finally by making sure the stages were consistent with the social perspective-taking stages (Commons & Rodriguez, 1990; Rodriguez and Commons (in preparation). Gewirtz might approve of the General Stage Model being behavioral in its cast, especially because the discrimination of a given stage's objects and contingencies have generally been shown to be a necessary precursor for the discrimination of the next stage's objects and contingencies (e.g. Case, 1985). The social perspective-taking stages were derived in part from Selman's stages using the General Stage Model (Commons & Richards, 1984a, 1984b). Social perspective-taking theory assumes that the development of the self as an object parallels the development of the other. Due to the parallelism and that fact that the other is what may serve as an attachment object, stages of development of the self were useful in determining what attachment objects and behaviors would exist at each attachment stage.

To construct a stage of attachment from the stage associated with objects of action in Kohlberg's hard and soft stages, one assumes that the stage sequence is the same in every domain (Kegan, 1982). Only the system of numbering stages can differ in various stage theories. In a theorem on the uniqueness of the stage sequence, Commons et al. (1987, submitted) used axioms of the General Stage Model to logically demonstrate that hierarchical complexity of tasks forms only one order. The ordering of task-required actions by their hierarchical complexity yields the same stage sequence irrespective of domain. Using that theorem, Commons and Grotzer (1990) showed how to number Kohlberg's Moral Stages (the Kohlbergian numbering in Table 14.1) using the General Stage Model. Table 14.2 shows how the numbering of the stages of attachment parallels Kohlberg's numbering of moral stages. His half stages (0/1, 1/2, 2/3, 3/4) were shown to be stages with the exception of 4/5. In addition to adding the sentential stage before the preoperational stage, his stages had to be extended downward, yielding negative numbers. Kohlberg (1990) was interested in whether meeting the conditions of the General Stage Model was sufficient to produce his hard stages, but he was not fully convinced. In sum, the attachment stages consist of the attachment objects that can be constructed at a given social perspective-taking stage and the behaviors that require those objects.

TABLE 14.2
Relationships Among Stage Models

General Model	Kohlberg (modified)	Approximate Age
0a sensory & motor actions	-1	0 - .5
0b circular sensorimotor actions	-1/0	.5 - .8
1a sensorimotor actions	0	.8 - 1.4
1b nominal actions	0/1	1.4 - 2.5
2a sentential actions	1	2.5 - 4
2b preoperational actions	1/2	4 - 6
3a primary operations	2	6 - 8
3b concrete operations	2/3	8 - 10
4a abstract operations	3	10 - 12
4b formal operations	3/4	12 - 17+
5a systematic operations	4	18 +
5b metasystematic	4/5-6	20 +
6a paradigmatic	New 6	?
6b cross-paradigmatic	New 7	?

What are the Discriminatively Controlled Attachment Behaviors

Many of these attachment behaviors are identified in Table 14.1. Only the ones related to language are discussed next.

Language and Rule-Governed Behavior. The role of language is that it forms the basis of rule-governed behavior. Language development controls the rule's form. Syntax dictates the form of the interactions that can be represented by language and, therefore, made into rules. For instance, abstract-stage propositional rules are necessary before the self can be discriminated from the formal-operational roles "required" by systems. Language for supporting universal forms such as every time, and so forth, are necessary for the development of such propositional rules. In turn, such rules are necessary to develop independence of the systematic stage as discussed in Table 14.1.

Stageness of the language means that its function in controlling behavior of self and others is a developmental process. Almost all the tenses are necessary for rule-governed behavior. Only variable names (abstract stage) and the subjunctive, especially the "if" forms and the future subjunctive (formal operations) develop later. The major forms are used in inner speech (Skinner, 1957; Kohlberg, Yaeger, & Hjetholm, 1968; Berk & Garvin, 1984) to guide action and probably the "internalization" of imitative acts. Concrete and lower-stage planning is limited by having to linguistically represent past task solutions. Abstract and formal-stage speech allow one to check the consequences of various possible actions implied by a sequence of propositions.

CONCLUSIONS

The construction of a behavior-developmental metasystem containing both the cognitive-developmental and social conditioning views of the development of attachment represents one way of fitting these views together. Both Kohlberg and Gewirtz would have to modify their position on some matters. Kohlberg would have to adopt a behavior-analytic view of reinforcement. Gewirtz would have to adopt the notion of an epistemologically sequenced set of task requirements associated with the development and transformation of attachment. A number of specific points were taken from other studies and used in the integration suggested here. The suggested stage sequence of perspective taking, attachment, attachment objects, and reinforcers emanating from those objects all need to be studied over the life span.

ACKNOWLEDGMENT

Patrice M. Miller's, Jacob L. Gewirtz's, and Lawrence Kohlberg's work on attachment formed the foundation out of which this chapter grew. My mother, Natalie Consuelo Lamport Commons, did her B.A. thesis at Vassar College on friendship. Her interest in what binds people together and maintains their relationships precedes my own interest in the question. In addition to the editors who spent endless hours trying to clarify the chapter, I thank Maria A. Broderick, Tina A. Grotzer, Sharon A. Stein, and Rebecca M. Young for their editorial comments, suggestions, and stimulation.

REFERENCES

Ainsworth, M. D. S. (1972). Attachment and dependency: A comparison. In J. L. Gewirtz (Ed.), *Attachment and dependency.* (pp. 123–143). Washington, DC: Winston.

Armon, C. (1984). Ideals of the good life and moral judgment: Ethical reasoning across the life span. In M. L. Commons, F. A. Richards, & C. Armon (Eds.), *Beyond formal operations: Volume 1. Late adolescent and adult cognitive development* (pp. 357–380). New York: Praeger.

Armon, C. (1988). The place of the Good in a justice reasoning approach to moral education. *Journal of Moral Education, 17*(3), 220–229.

Armon, C. (1989). Autonomy. *Adult Development, Comparisons and Applications of Adolescent and Adult Developmental Models. 1,*

Ausubel, D. P., Sullivan, E. V., & Ives, S. W. (1980). *Theory and problems of child development* (3d ed., pp. 169–199). New York: Grune & Stratton.

Baldwin, J. M. (1906). *Thoughts and things or genetic logic* (Volumes 1–3). New York: Macmillian.

Berk, L. D., & Garvin, R. (1984). Development of private speech among low-income Appalachian children. *Developmental Psychology, 20,* 271–286.

Bowlby, J. (1969). *Attachment and loss. Volume 1: Attachment.* New York: Basic.

Campbell, R. L., & Richie, D. M. (1983). Problems in the theory of developmental sequences: Prerequisites and precursors. *Human Development, 26,* 156–172.

Case, R. (1985). *Intellectual development: Birth to adulthood.* Orlando Florida: Academic Press.

Catania, A. C. (1973). The psychologies of structure, function and development. *American Psychologist, 28,* 434–443.

Cavalli-Sforza, L. L., & Feldman, M. W. (1981). *Cultural transmission and evolution: A quantitative approach.* Princeton, NJ: Princeton University Press.

Cavalli-Sforza, L. L., Feldman, M. W., Chen, Kuang-Ho, & Dornbusch, S. M. (1982). Theory and observation in cultural transmission. *Science, 218,* 19–27.

Colby, A., & Kohlberg, L. (1987a). *The measurement of moral judgment: Vol. 1. Theoretical foundations and research validation.* New York: Cambridge University Press.

Colby, A., & Kohlberg, L. (Eds.). (1987b). *The measurement of moral judgment: Standard form scoring manuals.* New York: Cambridge University Press.

Commons, M. L. (1985, April). *How novelty produces continuity in cognitive development within a domain and accounts for unequal rates of development across domains.* Paper presented at the meeting of the Society for Research on Child Development, Toronto.

Commons, M. L., & Armstrong-Roche, M. (1985, March). *When and why the free will illusion occurs.* Paper presented at the annual meeting of the Eastern Psychological Association at Boston. (Available from the Dare Institute, 234 Huron Ave., Cambridge, MA.)

Commons, M. L., & Barnett, M. A. (1984). Action as a function of stage, bonding, and affiliative experience. *The Genetic Epistemologist, 14*, 17–23.

Commons, M. L., Bing, E. W., Griffy, C. C., & Trudeau, E. J. (1991). Models of acquisition and preference. In M. L. Commons, S. Grossberg, & E. G. Staddon (Eds.), *Neural network models of conditioning and action: Quantitative analyses of behavior, 13.*

Commons, M. L., & Calnek, A. D. (1984). On the empirical undecidability between the hypotheses that stage change is or is not a discrete, discontinuous, stepwise process. *The Genetic Epistemologist, 9*(2). (pp. 11–16).

Commons, M. L., & Grotzer, T. A. (1990). The relationship between Piagetian and Kohlbergian stage: An examination of the "necessary but not sufficient relationship." *Adult Development, Models and Methods in the Study of Adolescent and Adult Thought, 2.*

Commons, M. L., Grotzer, T. A., & Davidson, M. N. (in preparation). The necessity of reinforcing problem solutions for transition to formal operations: An examination of Piaget's equilibration theory of stage change.

Commons, M. L., Hallinan, P. W., Fong, W., & McCarthy, K. (1989). Intelligent pattern recognition: Hierarchical organization of concepts and hierarchies. In M. L. Commons, R. J. Herrnstein, S. M. Kosslyn, & D. B. Mumford (Eds.), *Models of behavior, Computational and clinical approaches to pattern recognition and concept formation, 9.*

Commons, M. L., & Richards, F. A. (1984a). A general model of stage theory. In M. L. Commons, F. A. Richards, & C. Armon (Eds.), *Beyond formal operations: Volume 1. Late adolescent and adult cognitive development* (pp. 120–140). New York: Praeger.

Commons, M. L., & Richards, F. A. (1984b). Applying the general stage model. In M. L. Commons, F. A. Richards, & C. Armon (Eds.), *Beyond formal operations: Volume 1. Late adolescent and adult cognitive development* (pp. 141–157). New York: Praeger.

Commons, M. L., & Rodriguez, J. A. (1990). "Equal access" without "establishing" religion: The necessity for assessing social perspective-taking skills and institutional atmosphere. *Developmental Review.*

Commons, M. L., & Sonnert, J. G. (1987, June). *In search of Stage 6: Methods, forms, norms and institutions.* Paper presented at the Third Beyond Formal Operations Symposium: Positive Development During Adolescence and Adulthood, Harvard University, Cambridge.

Commons, M. L., Stein, S. A., & Richards, F. A. (1987, April). *A general model of stage theory: Stage of a task.* Paper presented at the Society for Research on Child Development, Baltimore.

Commons, M. L., Stein, S. A., & Richards, F. A. (1988, June). *Implicit and explicit rule governed behavior, hierarchical task complexity, and reflectivity.* Presented at The Eleventh Symposium on Quantitative Analyses of Behavior Held at Harvard: Implicit and Explicit Rules in People, Animals and Machines, Cambridge, MA.

Commons, M. L., Stein, S. A., & Richards, F. A. (submitted). *On the existence of developmental stages: An analytic model.*

Commons, M. L., Woodford, M., & Ducheny, J. R. (1982). How reinforcers are aggregated in reinforcement-density discrimination and preference experiments. *Quantitative Analyses of Behavior, 2: Matching and Maximizing Accounts,* 25–78.

Cook-Greuter, S. R. (1990). Maps for living: Ego-development theory from symbiosis to conscious universal embeddedness. *Adult Development, Models and Methods in the Study of Adolescent and Adult Thought, 2.*

Csikszentmihalyi, M., & Rochberg-Halton, E. (1981). *The meaning of things: Domestic symbols and the self.* New York: Cambridge University Press.

Damon, W. (1983). *Social and personality development.* New York: Norton.

Erikson, E. (1962). *Young man Luther.* New York: Norton.

Erikson, E. (1969). *Gandhi's truth.* New York: Norton.

Ferster, C. B., & Skinner, B. F. (1957). *Schedules of reinforcement.* New York: Appleton-Century-Crofts.

Fischer, K. W. (1980). A theory of cognitive development: The control and construction of hierarchies of skills. *Psychological Review, 87,* 477–531.

Fischer, K. W., Hand, H. H., & Russell, S. (1984). The development of abstractions in adolescents and adulthood. In M. L. Commons, F. A. Richards, & C. Armon (Eds.), *Beyond formal operations: Volume 1. Late adolescent and adult cognitive development* (pp. 43–73). New York: Praeger.

Fischer, K. W., Hand, H. H., Watson, M. W., Van Parys, M. M., & Tucker, J. L. (1984). Putting the child into socialization: The development of social categories in preschool children. In L. G. Katz, P. J. Wagemaker, & K. Steiner (Eds.), *Current topics in early childhood education. Volume 5.* (pp. 27–72). Norwood, NJ: Ablex.

Gallagher, J., & Reid, D. K. (1981). *The learning theory of Piaget and Inhelder.* Montery, CA: Brooks-Cole.

Garbarino, J., & Bronfenbrenner, U. (1976). The socialization of moral judgment and behavior in cross-cultural perspective. In T. Lickona (Ed.), *Moral development and behavior* (pp. 70–83). New York: Holt, Rinehart & Winston.

Gewirtz, J. L. (1961). A learning analysis of the effects of normal stimulation, privation, and deprivation on the acquisition of social motivation and attachment. In B. M. Foss (Ed.), *Determinants of infant behaviour* (pp. 213–229), London: Methuen.

Gewirtz, J. L. (1969). Mechanisms of social learning: Some roles of stimulation and behavior in early human development. In D. A. Goslin (Ed.), *Handbook of socialization theory and research* (pp. 57–212). Chicago: Rand McNally.

Gewirtz, J. L. (1971). The roles of overt responding and extrinsic reinforcement in "self" and "vicarious-reinforcement" phenomena and in "observational learning and imitation." In R. Glaser (Ed.), *The nature of reinforcement* (pp. 279–309). New York: Academic Press.

Gewirtz, J. L. (1972a). *Attachment and dependency.* Washington, DC: Winston.

Gewirtz, J. L. (1972b). Attachment, dependency, and a distinction in terms of stimulus control. In J. L. Gewirtz (Ed.), *Attachment and dependency.* (pp. 139–177). Washington, DC: Winston.

Gewirtz, J. L. (1972c). On the selection and use of attachment and dependence indices. In J. L. Gewirtz (Ed.), *Attachment and dependency* (pp. 179–215), Washington, DC: Winston.

Gewirtz, J. L. (1976). The attachment acquisition process as evidenced in the maternal conditioning of cued infant responding (particularly crying). *Human Development, 19,* 143–155.

Gewirtz, J. L. (1977). Maternal responding and the conditioning of infant crying: Directions of influence within the attachment-acquisition process. In B. C. Etzel, J. M. LeBlanc, & D. M. Baer (Eds.), *New developments in behavioral research: Theories, method and application* (pp. 31–57). Hillsdale, NJ: Lawrence Erlbaum Associates.

Gewirtz, J. L. (1978). Social learning in early human development. In A. C. Catania & T. A. Brigham (Eds.), *Handbook of applied behaviour analysis.* (pp. 105–141). New York: Irvington.

Gewirtz, J. L., & Peláez-Nogueras, M. (in press). The development of rules that control moral action. In M. L. Commons, M. A. Broderick, J. L. Gewirtz, & L. Kohlberg, (Eds.), *From moral action to judgment and back: The relationships between action and stage.*

Gewirtz, J. L., & Boyd, E. F. (1976). Mother–infant interaction and its study. In H. W. Reese (Ed.), *Advances in Child Development and Behavior, 11,* 141–163.

Gewirtz, J. L., & Boyd, E. F. (1977). Experiments on mother–infant interaction underlying mutual attachment acquisition: The infant conditions the mother. In T. Alloway, P. Pliner, & L. Krames (Eds.), *Advances in the study of communication and affect: Volume 3. Attachment behaviour* (pp. 109–143). New York and London: Plenum.

Gewirtz, J. L., & Peláez-Nogueras, M. (1987). Social-conditioning theory applied to metaphors like "attachment": The conditioning of infant separation protests by mothers. *Revista Mexicana de Análisis de la Conducta, 13,* 87–103.

Gewirtz, J. L., & Peláez-Nogueras, M. (1989, April). *Infant protesting to maternal departures and separations: A conditional discrimination process.* Paper delivered at the Biennial Meeting, Society for Research in Child Development, Kansas City, Missouri, April 27, 1989.

Gewirtz, J. L., & Peláez-Nogueras, M. (in press). Rules that govern moral behavior. In M. Commons, M. A. Broderick, J. L. Gewirtz, & L. Kohlberg (Eds.), *From moral action to judgement and back: The relationship between action and stage.*

Gewirtz, J. L., & Stingle, K. G. (1968). The learning of generalized imitation as the basis for identification. *Psychological Review, 75,* 374–397.

Greenberg, M. T., Siegel, J. M., & Leitch, C. J. (1983). The nature and importance of attachment relationships to parents and peers during adolescence, *Journal of Youth and Adolescence, 12* (5), 373–386.

Grotzer, T. A., Commons, M. L., & Davidson, M. N. (1986, May). *The role of motivation in the mechanism of stage change: A consideration of equilibration theory and cultural values.* Paper presented at the meeting of the Jean Piaget Society, Philadelphia.

Herrnstein, R. J. (1970). On the law of effect. *Journal of the Experimental Analysis of Behavior, 13,* 243–266.

Herrnstein, R. J. (1982). Melioration as behavioral dynamism. In M. L. Commons, R. J. Herrnstein, & H. Rachlin (Eds.), *Quantitative analyses of behavior: Vol. 2. Matching and maximizing accounts* (pp. 433–458). Cambridge, MA: Ballinger.

Herrnstein, R. J., & Vaughan, W., Jr. (1980). Melioration and behavioral allocation. In J. E. R. Staddon (Ed.), *Limits to action: The allocation of individual behavior* (pp. 143–176). New York: Academic Press.

Horowitz, F. D. (1987). *Exploring developmental theories: Toward a structural behavioral model of development.* Hillsdale, NJ: Lawrence Erlbaum Associates.

Hull, C. L. (1943). *Principles of behavior.* New York: Appleton-Century-Crofts.

Hull, C. L. (1952). *A behavior system: An introduction to behavior theory concerning the individual organism.* New Haven, CT: Yale University Press.

Inhelder, B., & Piaget, J. (1958). *The growth of logical thinking from childhood to adolescence: An essay on the development of formal operational structures.* (A. Parsons & S. Seagrim, Trans.). New York: Basic. (Original work published 1955)

Kahn, R. L., & Antonucci, T. C. (1980). Convoys over the life course: Attachment, roles, and social support. In P. Baltes, & O. Brim (Eds.), *Life-span development and behavior* (pp. 253–286). New York: Academic Press.

Kalish, R. A., & Knudtson, F. W. (1976). Attachment versus disengagement: A life-span conceptualization. *Human Development, 19,* 171–181.

Kegan, R. (1982). *The evolving self.* Cambridge, MA: Harvard University Press.

Kegan, R., Noam, G., & Rogers, L. (1982). The psychologic of emotion: A new-Piagetian view. In D. Cicchetti & P. Hesse (Eds.), *New directions for child development: Volume 16. Emotional development.* (pp. 105–128). San Francisco: Jossey-Bass.

Kohlberg, L. (1964). The development of moral character and ideology. In M. L. Hoffman & L. W. Hoffman (Eds.), *Review of child developmental research* (Vol. 1.). New York: Russell Sage.

Kohlberg, L. (1966). A cognitive-developmental analysis of children's sex-role attitudes. In E. Maccoby (Ed.), *The development of sex differences.* (pp. 1–30). Stanford, CA: Stanford University Press.

Kohlberg, L. (1969). Stage and sequence: The cognitive-developmental approach to socialization. In D. A. Goslin (Ed.), *Handbook of socialization theory and research* (pp. 347–480). Chicago: Rand McNally.

Kohlberg, L. (1978). Preface. In P. Scharf, (Ed.), *Readings in moral education.* Minneapolis: Winston Press.

Kohlberg, L. (1980). High school democracy and educating for a just society. In R. Mosher, (Ed.), *Moral education: A first generation of research and development.* New York: Praeger.

Kohlberg, L. (1984). *The psychology of moral development: Essays on moral development*. San Francisco: Harper & Row.

Kohlberg, L. (1985). A just community approach to moral education in theory and practice. In M. Berkowitz & F. Ozer (Eds.), *Moral education: Theory and practice*. Hillsdale, NJ: Lawrence Erlbaum Associates.

Kohlberg, L. (1990). Which postformal levels are stages? *Adult Development. Models and methods in the study of adolescent and adult thought. 2.*

Kohlberg, L., & Armon, C. (1984). Three types of stage models used in the study of adult development. In M. L. Commons, F. A. Richards, & C. Armon (Eds.). *Beyond formal operations: Volume 1. Late adolescent and adult cognitive development* (pp. 383–394). New York: Praeger.

Kohlberg, L., & Candee, D. (1984). The relation of moral judgement to moral action. In W. Kurtines & J. L. Gewirtz (Eds.). *Morality, moral behavior and moral development: Basic issues in theory and research.* (pp. 52–73). New York: Wiley.

Kohlberg, L., Hart, D., & Wertsch, J. (1987). The developmental social self theories of James Mark Baldwin, George Herbert Mead and Lev Seminovich Vygotsky. In L. Kohlberg (Ed.), *Child psychology and childhood education* (pp. 223–258). New York: Longman.

Kohlberg, L., Yaeger, J., & Hjetholm (1968). Private speech: Four studies and a review of theories. *Child Development, 39*(3), 691–786.

Kuhn, D. (1973). Imitation theory and research from a cognitive perspective. *Human Development, 16*, 157–180.

Lerner, J. V., & Lerner, R. M. (1983). Temperament and adaptation across life: Theoretical and empirical issues. In P. B. Baltes & O. G. Brim (Eds.), *Life-span development and behavior, Vol. 5*. New York: Academic.

Lerner, R. M., Palermo, M., Spiro, A., & Nesselroade, J. R. (1982). Assessing the dimensions of temperamental individuality across the life span: The Dimensions of Temperament Survey (DOTS). *Child Development, 53*, 149–159.

Main, M., Goldwin, R. (in press). Interview based adult attachment classification, related to infant mother infant father attachment. *Developmental Psychology.*

Meltzoff, A. N., & Moore, M. K. (1977). Imitation of facial and manual gestures by human neonates. *Science, 198*, 75–78.

Meltzoff, A. N., & Moore, M. K. (1983a). Newborn infants imitate adult facial gestures. *Child Development, 54*, 702–709.

Meltzoff, A. N., & Moore, M. K. (1983b). The origins of imitation in infancy: Paradigm, phenomena, and theories. In L. P. Lipsitt & C. Rovee-Collier (Eds.), *Advances in infancy research: Volume 2*. Norwood, NJ: Ablex.

Miller, P. M., & Commons, M. L. (1973, April). *The development of toy preferences as determined by external sex labels*. Paper presented at the meeting of the Society for Research in Child Development, Denver.

Pear, J. J., & Eldridge, G. D. (1984). The operant-respondent distinction: Future directions. *Journal of the Experimental Analysis of Behavior, 42*, 453–467.

Perry, W. G. (1968, 1970). *Forms of intellectual and ethical development in the college years: A scheme*. New York: Holt, Rinehart and Winston.

Petrovich, S. B., & Gewirtz, J. L. (1985). The attachment learning process and its relation to cultural and biological evolution: Proximate and ultimate considerations. In M. Reite & T. Field (Eds.), *The psychobiology of attachment and separation* (pp. 259–291). New York: Academic Press.

Piaget, J. (1951). *Play, dreams, and imitation in childhood*. New York: W. W. Norton.

Piaget, J. (1976). *The grasp of consciousness: Action and concept in the young child*. Cambridge, MA: Harvard University Press.

Power, F. C., Higgins, A., & Kohlberg, L. (1989). *Lawrence Kohlberg's approach to moral education: A study of three democratic high schools*. New York: Columbia University Press.

Rescorla, R. A. (1988). Pavlovian conditioning: It's not what you think it is. *American Psychologist, 43*(3), 151–160.

Rodriguez, J. A., & Commons, M. L. (in preparation). Life-span stages of social perspective taking. In M. L. Commons, A. Cheryl, & F. A. Richards (Eds.), *Adult cognitive and social development.*

Schrader, D. E. (1988). *Moral metacognition and its relation to moral judgment: A description and analysis.* Unpublished doctoral dissertation, Harvard University.

Selman, R. L. (1976). Social-cognitive understanding: A guide to educational and clinical practice. In T. Lickona (Ed.), *Moral development and behavior* (pp. 299–316). New York: Holt, Rinehart & Winston.

Selman, R. L. (1980). *The growth of interpersonal understanding.* New York: Academic Press.

Siegel, L., & Hodkin, B. (1982). In S. Modgil, & C. Modgil (Eds.), *Jean Piaget: Consensus and controversy* (pp. 95–96). New York: Praeger.

Skinner, B. F. (1938). *The behavior of organisms: An experimental analysis.* New York: Appleton.

Skinner, B. F. (1953). *Science and human behavior.* New York: Macmillan.

Skinner, B. F. (1957). *Verbal behavior.* New York: Appleton-Century-Crofts.

Skinner, B. F. (1969). *Contingencies of reinforcement.* New York: Appleton-Century-Crofts.

Skinner, B. F. (1974). *About behaviorism.* New York: Knopf.

Snary, J. K., Kohlberg, L., & Noam, G. (1987). Ego development and education: A structural perspective. In L. Kohlberg (Ed.), *Child psychology and childhood education* (pp. 329–391). New York: Longman.

Sonnert, J. G., & Commons, M. L. (in preparation). A definition of Moral Stage 6.

Spence, K. W. (1956). *Behavior theory and conditioning.* New Haven, CT: Yale University Press.

Stein, S. A., & Commons, M. L. (1987, May). *Verbal description and explanation appear lower in stage than nonverbal performance on a formal operational task.* Paper presented at the meeting of the Jean Piaget Society, Philadelphia.

Tappan, M. B. (1990). The development of socio-moral cognition during young adulthood: A three-dimensional model. *Adult development, Models and methods in the study of adolescent and adult thought, 2.*

Troll, L. E., & Smith, J. (1976). Attachment through the life span: Some questions about dyadic bonds among adults. *Human Development, 19,* 156–170.

Uzgiris, I. C. (1981). Two functions of imitation during infancy. *International Journal of Behavioral Development, 4,* 1–12.

Weiss, R. S. (1982). Attachment in adult life. In C. Parkes & J. Stevenson-Hinde (Eds.), *The place of attachment in human behavior* (pp. 171–184). New York: Basic.

VII PATHOLOGY AND ATTACHMENT

15 Attachment, Separation, and Phobias

Donald K. Routh
Jean E. Bernholtz

ABSTRACT

Evidence is reviewed linking attachment and separation in infants and preschool children to separation anxiety disorder, agoraphobia, and panic attacks in later life. The first hypothesis reviewed concerns possible functional similarities underlying some of the diverse phenomena of attachment, separation, and phobias. Several biological findings relate separation anxiety disorder/school phobia in children to depression, agoraphobia, and panic disorders. For example, research reports abnormal results of the dexamethasone suppression test in children with separation anxiety disorder as well as in depressed children. Imipramine, an antidepressant, also relieves the symptoms of school phobia and agoraphobia. Haloperidol and pimozide can produce a drug-induced separation anxiety disorder. Agoraphobia has been spoken of as adult separation anxiety, and behaviorally agoraphobics prefer the presence of a particular person or in some cases a nonhuman attachment object that is similar to behavior found in toddlers separated from their mothers. Another hypothesis reviewed concerns the continuity of individual and family differences in attachment behavior. Early attachment behavior predicts later social and cognitive behavior, with insecure attachment leading to an increased risk for psychopathology. Childhood separation anxiety has been linked with agoraphobia in adulthood. The evidence reviewed in this chapter is, for the most part, suggestive rather than conclusive.

This chapter addresses one intersection between attachment and psychopathology. It sets up the scaffold for a building that can be only partially constructed at present, because the current data base is so small. It explores the connections between the phenomena of attachment and separation as seen in infants, young children, and in adults, and the most prevalent and severe phobias and related conditions seen in older children and adults, namely separation

295

anxiety disorder, agoraphobia, and panic attacks. Our main thesis is that attachment, separation, and these types of related psychopathology may be issues for people throughout life and not merely in early childhood. This idea is not particularly controversial as a clinical working hypothesis, but scientific evidence for it is still sparse.

There are of course other areas of psychopathology that may have intersections with attachment, notably childhood autism, depression, and the so-called reactive attachment disorder of infancy. The present chapter will not explore these. Although autistic children are extremely deviant in their human relationships, including those with their parents, there has been remarkably little systematic study of attachment behavior in autistic children. Although attachment behaviors, particularly separation protest, appear to be highly similar to some of the phenomena of depression, research on this in children is problematic, because the existence of a clinical syndrome of depression in childhood is still a matter of debate (e.g., Lefkowitz & Burton, 1978). Furthermore, the relationship of reactive attachment disorder in infancy to attachment is still clouded by the lack of control of nutritional variables in relevant research on nonorganic failure to thrive in infants (e.g., Drotar, 1988). Thus, we have chosen to focus on the relationship of attachment to separation anxiety disorder, agoraphobia, and related phenomena in this chapter.

The first hypothesis to be considered concerns possible functional similarities underlying some of the diverse phenomena of attachment, separation, and phobias. This hypothesis might lead one to expect some type of behavioral similarity (i.e., the proximity seeking, separation protest, and reunion behaviors seen in toddlers could in some ways resemble the behaviors of children with separation anxiety disorder, postdivorce individuals attached to their exspouse, or agoraphobic adults). At a physiological level, it might be possible to find resemblances in the pattern of tachycardia, palmar sweating, and stress hormone release in separation protest, acute reactions of phobic children on school mornings, or the panic states experienced by many agoraphobics. Possibly some of the drugs that ameliorate or precipitate phobic reactions have similar effects on postdivorce attachment difficulties or on separation protest in toddlers. In looking for areas of functional similarity, a broad search should be conducted. Perhaps the multimodal assessment schema introduced by Lazarus (1975, 1976), a therapist well known for his interest in treating phobias, can suggest the variety of possible areas. The acronym used by Lazarus, BASIC ID, stands for behavior, affect, sensation, imagery, cognition, interpersonal relations, and drugs, and it serves as a reminder to assess functioning in each of the seven areas to assure broad coverage. Thus, diverse problems can be addressed in an integrated, comprehensive manner, facilitating understanding between these various disorders.

A second hypothesis that is explored concerns the continuity of individual and family differences in attachment behavior. A continuity hypothesis might lead one to expect that toddlers who are insecurely attached to their caregivers (e.g., as measured in the Ainsworth Strange Situation) might be more vulnerable than others to develop separation anxiety disorder as defined in the Diagnostic and Statistical Manual of Mental Disorders, (DSM–III; American Psychiatric Association, 1980). They might later have more difficulty than others adjusting to divorce because of the persistence of attachment after the relationship had been legally dissolved. Similarly, children with separation anxiety disorder or persons with postdivorce attachment problems might be expected to be more vulnerable than others to develop agoraphobia. Also, parents who themselves were more insecurely attached as toddlers, had separation anxiety disorder as children, were distressed by continuing postdivorce attachment, or were agoraphobic as adults might be expected to have offspring with similar problems. We will examine the data that pertain to continuity of attachment behavior over the lifespan.

Let us now briefly discuss the key term attachment and then examine some of the existing evidence for the hypotheses just stated. We define attachment in what we take to be a conventional way, following Bowlby (1973) and Ainsworth (1964). Attachment is a property of a dyad rather than of a single person. It has to do with the formation of lasting affective bonds to particular others. It refers to behavior that serves to increase or maintain proximity of the individual and some specific object of attachment such as the parent, spouse, or other preferred familiar person, including surrogates for persons such as pets, teddy bears, blankets, and so forth. At least in young children, the behaviors include physically following the attachment object and other actions that would have the effect of maintaining proximity, such as separation protest, differential vocalization, and many others that have been catalogued and studied extensively by researchers (e.g., Belkin & Routh, 1975; Routh, Walton, & Padan-Belkin, 1978; Shaw & Routh, 1982).

ATTACHMENT AND SUBSEQUENT SOCIAL AND EMOTIONAL ADJUSTMENT

According to Ainsworth, securely attached infants can use the mother as a base from which to explore the environment and, thus, develop competent coping abilities. The insecurely attached infant could be expected to be at some risk for developing future psychopathology. The basic question to be asked here concerns the continuity of attachment behavior—Does the infant's early attachment behavior predict his or her later behavior? Yes, according to recent research findings. Compared to infants who were insecurely attached at 12 months, infants who were securely attached were more likely to obey their mothers and to cooperate with a female stranger at 21 months (Londerville & Main, 1981). Secure attachment in an infant at 18 months predicted a two-year-old who was more curious, more sociable with peers, and enjoyed solving problems more than the previously insecurely attached infants (Matas, Arend, & Sroufe, 1978; Pastor, 1981).

The relationship of early attachment to social and cognitive behavior in the preschool years has also been studied. Waters, Wippman, and Sroufe (1979) measured the quality of infants' attachments at 15 months of age and then observed them in a preschool setting at 3.5 years of age. Children who had been securely attached at 15 months were described as social leaders in their classroom who attracted the attention of others, often initiated play activities, were sensitive to the needs of other children, and were very popular with their classmates.

Arend, Gove, and Sroufe (1979), using this same sample at 4.5 years of age, found further coherence in individual development. Children earlier classified as securely attached were more able to respond flexibly, persistently, and resourcefully, and they were more curious than insecurely attached infants. These characteristics were described as competent or adaptive behavior that within a stable environment could be expected to be relatively constant from infancy through the preschool years.

At least naively, we might suppose that infants who are very closely attached to their mothers might grow into excessively dependent children. Research by Sroufe, Fox and Pançake (1983) points to the opposite conclusion, however. Four-year-old children who were securely attached as infants showed less emotional dependence on their nursery school teachers than those who had been insecurely attached. Both groups who had been insecurely attached (resistant and avoidant) were overly dependent on their nursery school teachers, interfering with their ability to form friendships with other children and to engage in age-appropriate behavior.

The finding that the security of attachment reflects the current status of the mother–infant interaction (Thompson, Lamb, & Estes, 1982) led to a search for an interaction of variables thought to predict later psychopathology. Lewis, Feiring, McGuffog, and Jaskir (1984) assessed social-emotional competence and psychopathology in a large sample of children observed over the first 6 years of life. Environmental risk factors were also assessed. The data partially supported the hypothesis that the early attachment relationship predicts later social and emotional competence. Boys who were securely attached at age one exhibited fewer behavior problems than boys who were insecurely attached. Deviant behavior in girls was not predicted by attachment group. The fact that 40% of the insecurely attached males showed later signs of psychopathology and conversely that only 6% of the securely attached boys showed signs of psychopathology at age 6 suggests some connection between early attachment relationships and later behavior problems. In particular, a secure attachment strongly predicted a later healthy adjustment, but whether this was due to an enduring trait within the child or a stable environment could not be ascertained. Two environmental factors, birth order (i.e., being second born) and planning (i.e., unplanned birth) affected the risk for subsequent psychopathology in insecurely attached males. This finding supports an interactive model of developmental psychopathology for insecurely attached males. More research is needed to uncover how the relationship of intervening risk factors in conjunction with early attachment behavior produces later social-emotional psychopathology.

Research on infants' attachment to persons other than the primary caregiver suggests that attachment is due to more than infant trait characteristics, because studies of infants' attachment to both parents have found very little consistency (Lamb, 1978) or no consistency (Main & Weston, 1981) between the attachment patterns to mothers and fathers. This differential attachment behavior argues against the view that individual temperamental differences in infants are the main contributor to attachment behavior and points again to the interactional nature of the attachment relationship.

Investigating the larger social context within which family interactions occur, Crockenberg (1981) found infant temperament and maternal characteristics, as well as social variables, contributed to infant attachment at one year. Social support was determined at three months and included support from the father and other relatives as well as extra-familial support. Infant irritability measured during the first ten days of life was associated with insecure attachment only for those in the low support group.

Changes in attachment behavior have also been linked to changes in parenting and social support. Vaughn, Egeland, and Sroufe (1979) and Egeland and Farber (1984) found that shifts in attachment were related to changes in life stresses, social supports, and maternal competence. In addition to parental competence and individual infant temperament, research suggests that life stresses and available social supports contribute to infant attachment.

The finding that insecure attachments are related to later interactions outside the family may be particularly relevant to understanding the later development of child and/or adult psychopathology. Unpopularity with peers and age-inappropriate play have been linked to anxiety and emotional disturbance in children (Hartup, 1983). Children's peer interactions provide opportunities for the child to develop social and emotional competence. In addition, play with peers can provide an important arena for working through social and emotional problems, whatever their origin.

ATTACHMENT AND SEPARATION
ANXIETY/SCHOOL PHOBIA

The current DSM–III (American Psychiatric Association, 1980) defines separation anxiety disorder in the following way:

A. Excessive anxiety concerning separation from those to whom the child is attached, as manifested by at least three of the following:

1. Unrealistic worry about possible harm befalling major attachment figures or fear that they will leave and not return.

2. Unrealistic worry that an untoward calamitous event will separate the child from a major attachment figure, e.g., the child will be lost, kidnapped, killed, or be the victim of an accident.

3. Persistent reluctance or refusal to go to school in order to stay with major attachment figures or at home.

4. Persistent reluctance or refusal to go to sleep without being next to a major attachment figure or to go to sleep away from home.

5. Persistent avoidance of being alone in the home and emotional upset if unable to follow the major attachment figure around the home.

6. Repeated nightmares involving theme of separation.

7. Complaints of physical symptoms on school days, e.g., stomachaches, headaches, nausea, vomiting.

8. Signs of excessive distress upon separation, or when anticipating separation, from major attachment figures, e.g., temper tantrums or crying, pleading with parents not to leave (for children below the age of six, the distress must be of panic proportions).

9. Social withdrawal, apathy, sadness, or difficulty concentrating on work or play when not with a major attachment figure.

B. Duration of disturbance of at least two weeks.

C. Not due to Pervasive Developmental Disorder, Schizophrenia, or any other psychotic disorder.

D. If 18 or older, does not meet the criteria for Agoraphobia. (p. 53)

Among the first writers to use the term "school phobia," Johnson, Falstein, Szurek, and Svendsen (1941) described this type of phobia as a symptom of the child's anxiety over separation from the mother. School phobic children were often clinically observed to be concerned about the health of their mothers. From the perspective of the psychoanalytic theory of phobia so prevalent in that era, the child's anxiety was interpreted as being possibly related to the child's unconscious aggression against the mother and guilt over this feeling toward her.

Kennedy's (1965) paper on the rapid treatment of 50 cases of school phobia listed criteria for distinguishing between so-called Type I ("neurotic crisis") and Type II ("way of life") phobias. Both types were said to be characterized among other things by a symbiotic relationship with the mother and fear of separation. In addition, among differential criteria for a Type I phobia were also two that seem relevant to separation anxiety: the child's concerns about death and about the mother's physical health. This classification was to some extent validated by its ability to predict response to treatment, with the "neurotic crisis" group recovering faster and the "way of life" group (as the words suggest) continuing to have difficulty. However, it may be possible to predict the prognosis just as well from knowing the child's age as from the symptom list (Miller, Barrett, Hampe, & Noble, 1972).

Waldron, Shrier, Stone, and Tobin (1975) found that twice as many school phobic children as those with other neurotic problems showed excessive separation anxiety, dependency, and depression. Seventy-five percent of children with school phobia had more than minimum separation anxiety versus only 32% of children with other neuroses, a statistically significant difference. There is evidence that the child with school phobia has an overly involved parent and manifests overly dependent behavior (Coolidge, Brodie, & Feeney, 1964; Waldron et al., 1975). Overprotection may be shown in different ways: encouragement of dependency, invasion of the child's privacy, excessive control of the child's behavior, and the exclusion of outside influences. Waldron et al. (1975) found evidence also for parental hostility accompanying the pathological dependency shown by a greater resentment of the child's demands and a greater scapegoating of the school phobic child. Closely related to the mother's difficulty in separating from the child was the finding of imbalance in the families of school phobic children. Thirty-eight percent of the mothers of school phobic children indicated that their children were more important to them than their husbands were. These authors pointed out, however, that some school phobias were of a different type, involving fear of real situations at school threatening failure, bodily harm, and so on rather than fear of separation from the mother. The present paper concerns only the separation anxiety disorder variety.

Recent biological findings relating to separation anxiety disorder in children also provide interesting possibilities for future comparisons with other clinical conditions, including depression, agoraphobia, and panic disorders. One of these is the finding of abnormal results of the dexamethasone suppression test (DST) in 3 out of 5 children with separation anxiety disorder as well as in depressed children (Livingston, Reis, & Ringdahl, 1984). The DST is usually considered a marker for severe depressive disorders but is turning out to be somewhat nonspecific to these (separation anxiety is not the only condition besides depression to which it appears to be sensitive).

A related biological finding concerns imipramine. This drug, generally described as an antidepressant, was found in placebo-controlled research to significantly relieve the symptoms of school phobia (Gittelman-Klein & Klein, 1971, 1973). Other relationships of separation anxiety disorder and depressive syndromes, thus, need to be further explored.

A third biological finding is the discovery of a drug-induced separation anxiety disorder. Fifteen child and adult psychiatric patients treated with the drug haloperidol (because of Tourette's syndrome, i.e., multiple tics) developed, as a side effect, school and work avoidance syndromes resembling separation anxiety, according to Mikkelsen, Detlor, and Cohen (1981). One of these patients who developed a drug-induced phobia, a 12-year-old boy, was reluctant to leave home in the morning and at school repeatedly insisted on telephoning his mother. Another patient, a 20-year-old college student, for the first time in his life began to fear leaving home on weekends to return to school. He would say to his parents, "Mom and Dad, I don't want to leave you" (Mikkelsen et al., p. 1573). Interestingly, these phobic syndromes disappeared completely with the discontinuation of the drug in each case. Recently a similar phenomenon of a neuroleptic-induced school phobia/separation anxiety syndrome was also reported by Linet (1985). The drug in this case was pimozide (rather than haloperidol). The symptoms induced by each of three separate trials of pimozide were said to be indistinguishable from DSM–III separation anxiety disorder. Incidentally, this child had a family history of agoraphobia.

ATTACHMENT AND ADJUSTMENT TO DIVORCE

The view that the concept of attachment encompasses adults' relationship with a spouse as well as children's relationships with parents has been elaborated by the sociologist Weiss (1975). He maintained that most men and women going through a divorce continue to feel attached to their spouses and that this attachment is the primary cause of distress in both separating spouses regardless of who initiated the separation. He has found this idea useful in counseling persons going through a divorce. An adult may remain attached to the former spouse, even when severe conflict has ended other aspects of the relationship, and activities aimed at combating this attachment may be an important part of adjusting to a divorce. A number of psychometric scales have now been developed by various investigators to try to measure such adult attachment. Kitson (1982), for example, developed a scale of attachment to the spouse in divorce and found that 86% of a sample of divorcing individuals indicated some signs of attachment to their exspouse. Evidence was found in this study that attachment might be an important cause of subjective distress among the divorced.

ATTACHMENT AND AGORAPHOBIA

The DSM–III (1980) criteria for agoraphobia are as follows:

A. The individual has marked fear of and thus avoids being alone or in public places from which escape might be difficult or help not available in case of sudden incapacitation, e.g., crowds, tunnels, bridges, public transportation.
B. There is increasing constriction of normal activities until the fears or avoidance behavior dominate the individual's life.
C. Not due to a major depressive episode, Obsessive Compulsive Disorder, Paranoid Personality Disorder, or Schizophrenia. (p. 227)

Although agoraphobia was originally defined by Westphal (1871–1872) as a fear of open spaces (the Greek word *agora* means place of assembly or marketplace), agoraphobia is not a specific fear of streets and crowds as external stimuli. Westphal himself recognized the influence that human companionship or even inanimate objects have in agoraphobia. Marks (1970) observed that 95% of agoraphobics are markedly more fearful when they are alone. Many of them totally avoid being alone, and others require the presence of a companion at least when attempting to venture beyond their "safety zones." According to Chambless (1982), such agoraphobics prefer the presence of one particular family member—most commonly the spouse, but in certain cases even a nonhuman attachment object such as a pet may be of help). Such a companion significantly expands the boundaries of their safety zone. The similarity of this to Ainsworth's (1964) description of the young child's use of an attachment object as a secure base for exploration is certainly striking. Behavioral avoidance tests of agoraphobia do not ask the patient to approach crowds or open places; they ask him or her to walk away from "safety" (safe places or safe persons) (Thorpe & Burns, 1983).

Allen (1982) drew an explicit parallel between agoraphobia, attachment, and separation. He spoke of agoraphobia as "adult separation anxiety," and stated that the adult "experiences the panicky feelings of a two-year-old separated from his or her mother in the supermarket" (p. xviii). Thorpe and Burns (1983) also stated explicitly that Bowlby's (1973) concept of separation anxiety fits the clinical observations of agoraphobia.

Klein and Fink (1962) reported that imipramine was an effective treatment of agoraphobia. Subsequent research has confirmed their original observations. Klein believed that agoraphobia has three components, namely panic attacks, anticipatory anxiety, and avoidance behavior. Imipramine seems to abolish the panic attacks but has little effect on either of the other components. In contrast to its effects on agoraphobia and on panic disorder, imipramine has no effect on simple phobias. The implication is that the physiological mechanisms of these different disorders are different. What makes these facts interesting here is that, as already noted, Gittelman-Klein and Klein (1971, 1973) also found that imipramine relieved the symptoms of school phobia.

The DSM–III (1980) definition of panic disorder is worth stating here because of the findings just discussed. It is as follows:

A. At least three panic attacks within a three-week period in circumstances other than during marked physical exertion or in a life-threatening situation. The attacks are not precipitated only by exposure to a circumscribed phobic stimulus.
B. Panic attacks are manifested by discrete periods of apprehension or fear, and at least four of the following symptoms appear during each attach:

1. dyspnea
2. palpitations
3. chest pain or discomfort

4. choking or smothering sensations
5. dizziness, vertigo, or unsteady feelings
6. feelings of unreality
7. paresthesias (tingling in hands or feet)
8. hot and cold flashes
9. sweating
10. faintness
11. trembling or shaking
12. fear of dying, going crazy, or doing something uncontrolled during an attack

C. Not due to a physical disorder or another mental disorder, such as Major Depression, or Schizophrenia
D. The disorder is not associated with Agoraphobia. (p. 231)

There is also a separate DSM–III category for agoraphobia with panic attacks.

CONTINUITY OF EARLY ATTACHMENT BEHAVIORS AND SEPARATION ANXIETY DISORDER

The continuity of separation anxiety disorder with early attachment behaviors as well as the modification of attachment behavior by the child's developing cognitive competence is suggested by the following instructive case history taken from the monograph by Weinraub and Lewis (1977) on the determinants of children's response to separation:

> A 5-year-old child was terribly frightened of being left at school by her mother. A week of school failed to reduce the anxiety. The parents could not understand why the child was so upset. She had been in nursery school at a different location for 2 years before she entered kindergarten. Inquiry finally determined that she was terrified because she did not know how to get home from school. Literally, she had no cognitive map, so that once she left home she knew that she could not get back again. Understanding this, the child was taught how to travel back and forth to school. Her fear disappeared, and a total adjustment to school and being left resulted. (p. 65)

The general findings of the Weinraub and Lewis study were that, among two-year-olds, the more information the mother gave the child upon her departure, and the brighter the child, the less separation distress there was. What was important was, therefore, not that the mother be physically present but that the child know how to reach her should the need arise. The continuity hypothesis under consideration in the present paper would suggest that this point has relevance for the understanding of more severe separation anxiety disorder and agoraphobia as well.

One logical way to study the continuity of early attachment behaviors and separation anxiety disorder would be to observe infants at 10–18 months of age in some variant of the Ainsworth Strange Situation (Ainsworth & Wittig, 1969) and then follow them up in elementary school to observe the relative prevalence of separation anxiety disorder school phobia in securely attached versus insecurely attached children. The closest thing to this research design study among existing published studies is the work of Lewis et al., (1984), who assessed the quality of early attachment in one-year-olds and later, when the children were six-years-old, obtained the mothers' ratings on the Achenbach and Edelbrock Child Behavior Profile (Achenbach, 1978). Indeed, for males, those who were insecurely attached at one year were significantly more likely to manifest psychopathology at age six. Unfortunately, however, a specific measure of separation anxiety disorder was not included in the study.

At an even nonspecific level, the study of Kagan, Reznick, Clarke, Snidman, and Garcia-Coll (1984) is somewhat relevant to the continuity issue under discussion. These investigators observed children at 21 months of age and then again at age 4 years. They found that indices of behavioral inhibition to the unfamiliar were moderately stable over this time. Also, there have been a number of follow-up studies of child psychopathology, of which the recent one by Fischer, Rolf, Hasazi, and Cummings (1984) is representative. The generalization that can be made from these studies is that "externalizing" or antisocial behaviors tend to be relatively stable, whereas "internalizing" ones are more transient. The hypothesis of the present paper is that although this may very well be true in general, the case of attachment–separation anxiety disorder and agoraphobia may be an exception. More research needs to be done with this focus.

CONTINUITY OF SEPARATION ANXIETY AND AGORAPHOBIA

There are enough formal similarities in childhood separation anxiety or school phobia on the one hand and agoraphobia on the other that one might expect to find a link between them in the same individuals. However, a well-designed earlier study by Berg, Marks, McGuire, and Lipsedge (1974) surprisingly failed to find evidence for any such specific association. A British sample of nearly 800 agoraphobic women were interviewed, as were a control group of 57 neurotic outpatients. In each of these groups, about 22% reported a history of school phobia. This suggested that although school phobia might be a precursor of adult neurosis, it did not seem to be specifically predictive of agoraphobia. Pittman, Langsley, and Deyoung (1968) previously found that of a series of 11 adults with work phobias, 9 had a history of school phobia, suggesting some continuity of the two conditions. They did not have a control group, however.

A recent study by Gittelman and Klein (1984) contains results more consistent with a continuity hypothesis. They found that 50% of a group of 58 agoraphobics had a history of childhood separation anxiety, as compared to only 27% of a control group of 59 individuals with simple phobia, a significant difference at the $p < .01$ level. Further analysis showed that the association was found in females but not in males. These investigators pointed out that the Berg et al. (1974) study did not include information on whether any of the neurotic control group had panic attacks; if so, this could have made for a fuzzy comparison, in that panic attacks are thought to be linked to agoraphobia.

In Thorpe and Burns' (1983) National Survey of Agoraphobics in Britain, approximately 32% reported that they had had fears of going to school. There was, however, no comparison sample in this study.

Future research needs to follow prospectively a sample of children meeting explicit criteria for separation anxiety disorder into adulthood and to do the same with various comparison groups to observe the relative prevalence of agoraphobia. The work of Miller et al., (1972) already mentioned suggests that continuity might be more likely to be found, if the original sample was over 11 years of age. They found that the prognosis of children's phobias in those 10 years and younger was markedly better than that for their older group.

CONTINUITY OF DIVORCE ADJUSTMENT AND AGORAPHOBIA

Several investigators have pointed out that the disruption of a relationship is a common antecedent to agoraphobia (Chambless & Goldstein, 1981; Shafar, 1976). In fact, this was regarded as an important precipitant in 50% of Shafar's (1976) 90 cases. Goldstein and Chambless (1978) observed that a frequent pattern in the development of agoraphobia was that an individual with low levels of self-sufficiency experienced conflict concerning separation from parents in late adolescence or the desire to escape from an unsatisfactory marriage. Agoraphobia indeed usually does not begin before the mid or late twenties, almost never occurring before 18 or after 35, according to Goodwin (1983). Fry (1962) described a pattern of "compulsory marriage" in which agoraphobic symptoms serve to maintain a marriage that may be otherwise unsatisfactory. The agoraphobic spouse cannot be alone or travel anywhere unless accompanied by the husband or wife; therefore, neither one can escape the relationship.

PARENT–OFFSPRING CORRELATIONS

Solyom, Silberfeld, and Solyom (1976) tested the mothers of agoraphobic adults. Using an objective inventory, they found that these mothers were higher on overprotection than even the overprotective mothers in a normative sample. They were higher specifically on scales tapping maternal control and maternal concern. The mothers' own anxiety scores were correlated with their degree of overprotectiveness and with the prevalence of fears in the agoraphobic offspring. One problem with this study is that the information was collected retrospectively, after the offspring's agoraphobia developed, and thus, might, be subject to selective bias on the part of the respondents.

Gittelman and Klein (cited by Shader, 1984) found that a history of separation anxiety was significantly more common among parents of school phobic children (16 of 83, or 19%) then among parents of hyperkinetic children (2 of 84, or 2%).

CONCLUSIONS

Are attachment and separation as studied in infants and preschool children linked to separation anxiety disorder, agoraphobia, panic attacks, and difficulties in adjusting to divorce in later life? The evidence just reviewed is intriguing, suggestive, but at this point hardly conclusive. This is in fact one of the most tentative sounding papers we have ever had to write. What is most interesting about this exercise is that it does, as stated at the outset, provide the scaffolding for what could turn out to be a very interesting and useful theoretical building. Now we need to go out and collect the necessary evidence and to put in the energy needed to construct it. Of course, that leaves the possibility that it will not be so imposing a structure as it now appears to be, in prospect, or that it could have a significantly different shape than we now foresee.

REFERENCES

Achenbach, T. M. (1978). The Child Behavior Profile. I: Boys aged 6–11. *Journal of Consulting and Clinical Psychology, 46,* 478–488.

Ainsworth, M. D. (1964). Patterns of attachment behavior shown by the infant in interaction with his mother. *Merrill-Palmer Quarterly, 10,* 51–58.

Ainsworth, M. D. S., & Wittig, B. A. (1969). Attachment and exploratory behavior of one-year-olds in a strange situation. In B. M. Foss (Ed.), *Determinants of infant behavior* (Vol. 4). London: Methuen.

Allen, R. G. (1982). Introduction. In R. L. DuPont (Ed.), *Phobia: A comprehensive summary of modern treatments.* New York: Brunner/Mazel.

American Psychiatric Association. (1980). *DSM–III: Diagnostic and statistical manual of mental disorders* (3rd ed.). Washington, DC: APA.

Arend, R., Gove, F. L., & Sroufe, L. A. (1979). Continuity of individual adaptation from infancy to kindergarten. *Child Development, 50,* 950–959.

Belkin, E. P., & Routh, D. K. (1975). Effects of presence of mother versus stranger on behavior of three-year-old children in a novel situation. *Developmental Psychology, 11,* 400.

Berg, I., Marks, I., McGuire, R., & Lipsedge, M. (1974). School phobia and agoraphobia. *Psychological Medicine, 4,* 428–434.

Bowlby, J. (1973). *Separation: Anxiety and anger.* New York: Basic.

Chambless, D. L. (1982). Characteristics of agoraphobics. In D. L. Chambless & A. J. Goldstein (Eds.), *Agoraphobia: Multiple perspectives on theory and treatment.* New York: Wiley.

Chambless, D. L., & Goldstein, A. J. (1981). Clinical treatment of agoraphobia. In M. Mavissakalian & D. Barlow (Ed.), *Phobia: Psychological and pharmacological treatment.* New York: Guilford.

Coolidge, J. C., Brodie, R. D., & Feeney, B. (1964). A ten-year follow-up of sixty-six school-phobic children. *American Journal of Orthopsychiatry, 34,* 675–684.

Crockenberg, S. B. (1981). Infant irritability, mother responsiveness, and social support influences on the security of infant–mother attachment. *Child Development, 52,* 857–865.

Drotar, D. (1988). Failure to thrive. In D. K. Routh (Ed.), *Handbook of pediatric psychology.* (pp. 71–107). New York: Guilford.

Egeland, B., & Farber, E. A. (1984). Infant–mother attachment: Factors related to its development and changes over time. *Child Development, 55,* 753–771.

Fischer, M., Rolf, J. E., Hasazi, J. E., & Cummings, L. (1984). Follow-up of a preschool epidemiological sample: Cross-age continuities and predictions of later adjustment with internalizing and externalizing dimensions of behavior. *Child Development, 55,* 137–150.

Fry, W. (1962). The marital context of an anxiety syndrome. *Family Process, 1,* 245–252.

Gittelman, R., & Klein, D. F. (1984). Relationship between separation anxiety and panic in agoraphobic disorders. *Psychopathology, 17,* 56–65.

Gittelman-Klein, R., & Klein, D. F. (1971). Controlled imipramine treatment of school phobia. *Archives of General Psychiatry, 25,* 204–207.

Gittelman-Klein, R., & Klein, D. F. (1973). School phobia: Diagnostic considerations in the light of imipramine effects. *Journal of Nervous and Mental Disease, 156,* 199–215.

Goldstein, A. J., & Chambless, D. L. (1978). A reanalysis of agoraphobia. *Behavior Therapy, 9,* 47–59.

Goodwin, D. W. (1983). *Phobia: The facts.* Oxford: Oxford University Press.

Hartup, W. W. (1983). Peer relations. In P. H. Mussen (Ed.), *Handbook of child psychology* (Vol. 4). New York: Wiley.

Johnson, A. M., Falstein, E. J., Szurek, S. A., & Svendsen, M. (1941). School phobia. *American Journal of Orthopsychiatry, 11,* 702–711.

Kagan, J., Reznick, J. S., Clarke, C., Snidman, N., & Garcia-Coll, C. (1984). Behavioral inhibition to the unfamiliar. *Child Development, 55,* 2212–2225.

Kennedy, W. A. (1965). School phobia: Rapid treatment of fifty cases. *Journal of Abnormal Psychology, 70,* 285–2891.

Kitson, G. C. (1982). Attachment to the spouse in divorce: A scale and its application. *Journal of Marriage and the Family, 44,* 379–393.

Klein, D. F., & Fink, M. (1962). Psychiatric reaction patterns to imipramine. *American Journal of Psychiatry, 119,* 432–438.

Lamb, M. E. (1978). Interactions between eighteen-month-olds and their preschool-aged siblings. *Child Development, 49,* 51–59.

Lazarus, A. A. (1975). Group therapy and the "BASIC ID." In C. M. Franks & G. T. Wilson (Ed.), *Annual review of behavior therapy: Theory and practice* (Vol. 3; pp. 721–732). New York: Brunner Mazel.

Lazarus, A. A. (1976). *Multimodal behavior therapy.* New York: Springer.

Lefkowitz, M. M., & Burton, N. (1978). Childhood depression: A critique of the concept. *Psychological Bulletin, 85,* 716–726.

Lewis, M., Feiring, C., McGuffog, C., & Jaskir, J. (1984). Predicting psychopathology in six-year-olds from early social relations. *Child Development, 55,* 123–136.

Linet, L. S. (1985). Tourette syndrome, pimozide, and school phobia: The neuroleptic separation anxiety syndrome. *American Journal of Psychiatry, 142,* 613–615.

Livingston, R., Reis, C. J., & Ringdahl, I. C. (1984). Abnormal dexamethasone suppression test results in depressed and nondepressed children. *American Journal of Psychiatry, 141,* 106–108.

Londerville, S., & Main, M. (1981). Security of attachment, compliance, and maternal training methods in the second year of life. *Developmental Psychology, 17,* 289–299.

Main, M., & Weston, D. R. (1981). The quality of the toddler's relationship to mother and to father: Related to conflict behavior and the readiness to establish new relationships. *Child Development, 52,* 932–940.

Marks, I. M. (1970). Agoraphobic syndrome (phobic anxiety state). *Archives of General Psychiatry, 23,* 538–553.

Matas, L., Arend, R. A., & Sroufe, L. A. (1978). Continuity of adaptation in the second year: The relationship between quality of attachment and later competence. *Child Development, 49,* 547–556.

Mikkelsen, E. J., Detlor, J., & Cohen, D. J. (1981). School avoidance and social phobia triggered by haloperidol inpatients with Tourette's disorder. *American Journal of Psychiatry, 12,* 1572–1576.

Miller, L. C., Barrett, C. L., Hampe, E., & Noble, H. (1972). Comparison of reciprocal inhibition, psychotherapy, and waiting list control for phobic children. *Journal of Abnormal Psychology, 79,* 269–279.

Pastor, D. L. (1981). The quality of mother–infant attachment and its relationship to toddlers' initial sociability with peers. *Developmental Psychology, 17,* 326–335.

Pittman, F. S., Langsley, D. G., & Deyoung, C. D. (1968). Work and school phobia: A family approach to treatment. *American Journal of Psychiatry, 124,* 1535–1541.

Routh, D. K., Walton, M. D., & Padan-Belkin, E. (1978). Development of activity level in children revisited: Effects of mother presence. *Developmental Psychology, 14,* 571–581.

Shader, R. I. (1984). Epidemiologic and family studies. *Psychosomatics, 25,* 10–15.

Shafar, S. (1976). Aspects of phobic illness: A study of 90 personal cases. *British Journal of Medical Psychology, 49,* 221–236.

Shaw, E. G., & Routh, D. K. (1982). Effect of mother presence on children's reaction to aversive procedures. *Journal of Pediatric Psychology, 7,* 33–42.

Solyom, L., Silberfeld, M., & Solyom, C. (1976). Maternal overprotection in the etiology of agoraphobia. *Canadian Psychiatric Association Journal, 21,* 109–113.

Sroufe, L. A., Fox, N. E., & Pancake, V. R. (1983). Attachment and dependency in developmental perspective. *Child Development, 54,* 1615–1627.

Thompson, R., Lamb, M., & Estes, D. (1982). Stability of infant–mother attachment and its relationship to changing life circumstances in an unselected middle-class sample. *Child Development, 53,* 144–148.

Thorpe, G. L., & Burns, L. E. (1983). *The agoraphobic syndrome: Behavioural approaches to evaluation and treatment.* Chichester, UK: Wiley.

Vaughan, B. E., Egeland, B. R., & Sroufe, L. A. (1979). Individual differences in infant–mother attachment at twelve and eighteen months. *Child Development, 50,* 971–975.

Waldron, S., Jr., Shrier, D. K., Stone, B., & Tobin, F. (1975). School phobia and other childhood neuroses: A systematic study of the children and their families. *American Journal of Psychiatry, 132,* 802–808.

Waters, E., Wippman, J., & Sroufe, L. A. (1979). Attachment, positive affect, and competence in the peer group: Two studies in construct validation. *Child Development, 50,* 820–829.

Weinraub, M., & Lewis, M. (1977). The determinants of children's responses to separation. *Monographs of the Society for Research in Child Development, 42* (No. 4, Serial No. 172).

Weiss, R. S. (1975). *Marital separation.* New York: Basic.

Westphal, K. (1871–1872). Die agoraphobie: Eine neuropathische erscheinung. [Agoraphobia: A neuropathic interpretation.] *Archiv fur Psychiatrie und Nerverkrankheiten, 3,* 138–171, 219–221.

Author Index

Subject Index